PRAISE FOR

REBIRT

"A remarkable book. . . . As J   one of
the best of his (and my) gene   is difficult but necessary for us to reinsert ourse   the lost present that has become our
past. Lears can do this better than most because of the depth and breadth
of his reading. His strengths, as writer, interpreter, and synthesizer, are
grounded in a voracious appetite for source material. . . . A startling new
synthesis."   —David Nasaw, *The American Prospect*

"Good historians do not want to be agreed with; they want to change the
terms of the argument. Jackson Lears has written a wonderful history
that has done just that. Lears has grasped with *Rebirth of a Nation* an
opportunity for reinterpreting a period that seems almost a doppelgän-
ger of our own. . . . Lears is a cultural historian, one of the founders of
the mordern field and in many ways its most illustrious American practitioner. . . . Wherever the history of this period goes from here, it will have
to go through Jackson Lears."   —Richard White, *The Nation*

"Jackson Lears is one of the few preeminent historians of our time. As we
dream for a rebirth of America in the age of Obama, this magnificent and
magisterial book on the making of modern America could not be more
timely. Don't miss it!"   —Cornel West, author of *Race Matters*

"Fascinating. . . . Lears vividly recounts the rise of populism and its more
sophisticated relative, progressivism. . . . Peppered with lively language,
Rebirth of a Nation warrants close reading around this observance of the
Declaration of Independence."   —*Pittsburgh Post-Gazette*

"*Rebirth of a Nation* is without doubt the finest contribution to U.S. history that I have encountered in recent memory. It may well be the best
book on the subject I have ever read. . . . Jackson Lears cuts through the
cant and humbug to offer his readers truths that are as essential as they
are disturbing. But don't take my word for it. Read this remarkable book
yourself."   —Andrew J. Bacevich, *Commonweal*

REBIRTH OF A NATION

HARPER PERENNIAL

NEW YORK • LONDON • TORONTO • SYDNEY • NEW DELHI • AUCKLAND

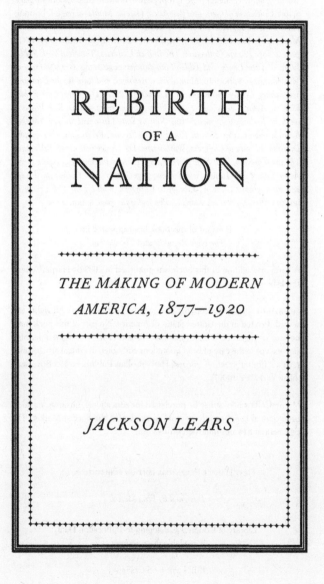

REBIRTH

OF A

NATION

THE MAKING OF MODERN
AMERICA, 1877–1920

JACKSON LEARS

Grateful acknowledgment for permission to reproduce illustrations is made to the following: *Prints and Photographs Division, Library of Congress, Washington, D.C.*: insert page 1, top; page 4, bottom; page 5, bottom; page 8, top. *Collection of Gene and Bev Allen, Helena, Montana*: page 1, bottom; page 2, bottom. *Harry Peters "Pictures in Stone" Collection, National Museum of American History, Smithsonian Institution, Washington, D.C.*: page 2, top. *Picture Collection, The Branch Libraries, The New York Public Library, Astor, Lenox and Tilden Foundations*: page 3, top. *Chicago History Museum*: page 3, bottom. *Manuscripts, Archives, and Rare Books Division, Schomburg Center for Research in Black Culture, The New York Public Library, Astor, Lenox and Tilden Foundations*: page 4, top. *Rob Powers, www.builtstlouis.net*: page 5, top. *Kansas State Historical Society, Topeka, Kansas*: page 6, top. *Kermit Roosevelt Collection, Prints and Photographs Division, Library of Congress, Washington, D.C.*: page 6, bottom. *Billy Rose Theatre Division, The New York Public Library for the Performing Arts, Astor, Lenox and Tilden Foundations*: page 7, top. *Bain Collection, Prints and Photographs Division, Library of Congress, Washington, D.C.*: page 7, bottom. *Brown Brothers, Sterling, Pennsylvania*: page 8, bottom.

Portions of this book have appeared in
The New Republic and *The Nation*.

A hardcover edition of this book was published in 2009 by HarperCollins Publishers.

HarperCollins books may be purchased for educational, business, or sales promotional use. For information, please e-mail the Special Markets Department at SPsales@harpercollins.com.

FIRST HARPER PERENNIAL EDITION PUBLISHED 2010.

Designed by Fritz Metsch

Library of Congress Cataloging-in-Publication Data
is available upon request.

ISBN 978-0-06-074750-3

HB 06.21.2021

For Rachel and Adin
Radical Hope

Shadows present, foreshadowing deeper shadows to come.

— HERMAN MELVILLE, "Benito Cereno"

CONTENTS

REBIRTH OF A NATION

INTRODUCTION
Dreaming of Rebirth

◆

All history is the history of longing. The details of policy; the migration of peoples; the abstractions that nations kill and die for, including the abstraction of "the nation" itself—all can be ultimately traced to the viscera of human desire. Human beings have wanted innumerable, often contradictory things—security and dignity, power and domination, sheer excitement and mere survival, unconditional love and eternal salvation—and those desires have animated public life. The political has always been personal.

Yet circumstances alter cases. At crucial historical moments, personal longings become peculiarly influential in political life; private emotions and public policies resonate with special force, creating seismic change. This was what happened in the United States between the Civil War and World War I. During those decades, a widespread yearning for regeneration—for rebirth that was variously spiritual, moral, and physical—penetrated public life, inspiring movements and policies that formed the foundation for American society in the twentieth century. As daily life became more subject to the systematic demands of the modern corporation, the quest for revitalization became a search for release from the predictable rhythms of the everyday. Few figures embodied this yearning more vigorously than Harry Houdini, the modern magician who was famous for one big trick: escape. Limitation coexisted—at least vicariously—with liberation. Dreams of rebirth kept boredom at bay.

Still, the dreamers had always wanted more than mere relief from routine. Longings for rebirth had a rich and complex history: rooted in Protestant patterns of conversion, they also resonated with the American mythology of starting over, of reinventing the self. After the Civil War, the entire country was faced with the task of starting over. The idea that the Union had reaffirmed its very being through blood sacrifice promoted a postwar dream of national renewal through righteous war. This militarist

fantasy animated key developments in post–Civil War politics, beginning
with the reunion between the white North and the white South. After Reconstruction, political leaders in both sections redefined the war as an epic
expression of Anglo-Saxon martial virtue. Racism, often with scientific
legitimacy, reinforced militarism. Dreams of rebirth involved renewal of
white power, especially in the former Confederacy. Elite white Southerners who called themselves "Redeemers" recaptured state governments, and
their successors solidified white rule—purifying electoral politics by disenfranchising blacks (and many poor whites), recasting social life by codifying
racial segregation, and revitalizing white identity through the occasional
blood sacrifice of lynching.

Rituals of racial superiority fueled imperial ambition. "The color line,"
said W. E. B. DuBois in 1906, "belts the world." The triumph of white supremacy at home accompanied the conquest of dark peoples abroad. The
mythologies of race and empire were intertwined; both reinforced the worship of force. Americans, no less than Europeans, were afflicted by that faux
religion. U.S. leaders' favorite dreams of regeneration involved military violence. Militarist fantasy runs like a red thread from the Civil War to World
War I, surfacing in postwar desires to re-create conditions for heroic struggle, coalescing in the imperialist crusades of 1898, overreaching itself in the
Great War and subsiding (temporarily) thereafter. The core of this fantasy
might well be described by the phrase the economist Joseph Schumpeter
used to characterize capitalism: "creative destruction"—the notion that a
dynamic future best emerges from devastation.

The high tide of regenerative militarism came at the turn of the century.
In 1900, after a quarter century of class strife had ended in the acquisition
of an overseas empire, Indiana senator Albert Beveridge announced that
God had "marked us as His Chosen People, henceforth to lead in the regeneration of the world." Progress and Providence converged in the rhetoric of empire, whether it was inflected with the schoolboyish bellicosity of
Theodore Roosevelt or the schoolmasterish moralism of Woodrow Wilson.
Militarism was flagrant in Roosevelt, who never abandoned his adolescent
faith in the tonic effects of combat; it was less apparent but still present in
Wilson, who finally decided that only American entry into the Great War
could usher in the "Peace Without Victory" he craved. The very intensity of
longings for rebirth opened up intoxicating possibilities to men with power,
and left them peering into an abyss of grandiosity. Roosevelt promoted U.S.

hegemony in the name of stability throughout the Western hemisphere and parts of the Far East. Wilson declared a war to end war, aimed at nothing less than "the regeneration of the world." No wonder they both stirred up so much trouble.

But violence was not the only instrument of revitalization. Other voices spoke in other idioms, evoking other visions. Progressive reformers targeted corruption in all its forms, hoping to cleanse individual and society alike. The melding of political and personal animated Raoul Walsh's film of 1915, *Regeneration*. It told the story of Owen Conway, an Irish street kid turned gangster, who is redeemed by Marie Deering, a socialite turned settlement-house worker. The film is sentimental and formulaic but powerful in its evocation of the urban working-class world in the early twentieth century. It is a world of people just scraping by, staying a step ahead of the eviction notice or the arrest for vagrancy, of tenements teetering toward collapse and alleyways littered with garbage, of undernourished babies crying for milk and unsupervised urchins swarming in the streets. Mothers are always fretting about the next month's rent; fathers are often swilling beer in buckets from the local saloon. Wives and children get periodic beatings. Owen learns to survive in this world through swaggering toughness but soon reveals a larger heroism when he rescues a boatload of children from fire and drowning.

Marie and her colleagues at the settlement house have opened up a new and more humane set of possibilities for Owen—literacy, civic engagement, and the chance to look out for other people beyond himself. Touched by Marie's expectations, Owen quits drinking, and it is not long before he is cradling babies and learning to read in the settlement-house schoolroom. The idyll is interrupted when Marie is fatally wounded by Owen's old pal Skinny, who has been trapped into a shootout by the police. Marie dies quoting Scripture to Owen—"Vengeance is mine, saith the Lord"—and Owen renounces any reprisal against Skinny, vowing to continue Marie's work.

Though *Regeneration* elevated nurturance over vengeance, it would be a mistake to see the film as merely a feminine counterpoint to conventional manliness. To be sure, many settlement-house workers were affluent young women like Marie Deering, seeking a moral purpose amid a life of aimless ease. (Jane Addams, the founder of the pioneer settlement Hull House, was one.) But many young men were equally distressed by poverty, and equally determined to do something about it. Most Progressives, male and female, were motivated by their own vision of Christianity—Social Christianity, as they called it. They redefined rebirth as unselfish devotion to the commonweal. In popular melodrama, social reform (like military heroism) might require blood sacrifice, as it did for Marie. Yet more commonly the reformers practiced a different sort of heroism, what one might call the heroism of everyday life.

The idea of commonweal linked public and private morality, inspiring the broad and diverse Progressive movement. The Progressives' dream of a cooperative commonwealth provided a powerful alternative to the dream of regeneration through military intervention abroad. Yet the two visions were not mutually exclusive. They competed but also coexisted, sometimes within the same minds—as in Beveridge's, Roosevelt's, and Wilson's.

Longings for rebirth did not always lead to politics; indeed they swept up seekers with a variety of personal or political aims (or both)—everyone from Populist farmers to avant-garde artists and writers. Some pursued purification, others reconstruction; others simply alluded to reconnection with "more life." Some wanted to restore a sense of wholeness to fragmented selves, others to reinvigorate an entire society. But all were engaged in regenerative enterprises, which linked private with public aims and reached into the White House itself.

The half-century between the Civil War and World War I was an age of regeneration. Seldom if ever in our history have longings for rebirth played a more prominent role in politics. By tracing the interplay between private desires and public policies, I offer a new lens through which to view a period of critical transformation. It is only one lens among many. Other scholars have provided other powerful perspectives, but my approach seeks fresh insight—first by stressing the lingering impact of the Civil War on Americans' inner lives, as memories and fantasies of heroism encouraged faith in regeneration through war; and second, by focusing on the convergence between the specific circumstances of the late nineteenth century and the deep-rooted traditions of American Protestantism. Few historians would deny the importance of Protestant Christianity in the shaping of American culture between the Civil War and World War I; but nearly all have focused on the role of Protestant morality in promoting Prohibition, Progressive reform, and missionary imperialism. Much of this book rests on that scholarship, but I have tried to press the interpretation further—to explore spirituality as well as morality, inchoate yearnings as well as systematic prescriptions. To understand the public transformations of this period, we need to return to their origins in private feeling. The impulse to conduct a world crusade began in the recesses of the Protestant soul.

THE PROTESTANT REFORMATION was an epochal event in the history of longing. The desire to be spiritually reborn, to experience a sense of personal regeneration through fusion with the deity, is universal and timeless, but early Protestants recast it in a powerful new mold: the conversion experience. This was the rebirth into more abundant life, the profound personal transformation that became (in many traditions) the key to salvation. In the English Puritan tradition, the unsaved were known as "unregenerate." And the English Puritan influence was nowhere more far-reaching than in the colonies that became the United States.

Regeneration was the molten core of American Protestantism—the fluid desire for immersion in divine grace. And grace was ineffable, nothing less than the feeling of the indwelling presence of God. For some seekers, this experience was immediate, intense, and independent of existing norms and hierarchies. It unleashed the unpredictable potential of the saved soul. The desire for unmediated grace put mystics like Anne Hutchinson in direct conflict with Puritan authorities in Massachusetts Bay, who sought to contain her challenge to ministerial authority. The molten core of conversion needed to be encased in a solid sheath of prohibitions, rules, agendas for self-control—the precisionist morality that we know as the Protestant ethic. An ethos of disciplined achievement counterbalanced what the sociologist Colin Campbell calls an other Protestant ethic, one that sought ecstasy and celebrated free-flowing sentiment, sending frequent revivals across the early American religious landscape. The two ethics converged in a cultural program that was nothing if not capacious: it encompassed spontaneity and discipline, release and control. Indeed, the rigorous practice of piety was supposed to reveal the indwelling of the spirit, the actuality of true conversion.

Yet the balance remained unstable, posing challenges to established authority in Virginia as well as Massachusetts. The tension between core and sheath, between grace abounding and moral bookkeeping, arose from the Protestant conviction that true religion was not merely a matter of adherence to outward forms, but was rooted in spontaneous inner feeling. Evangelical Protestants in particular (the descendants of Calvinists and Pietists) were haunted by the specter of faith congealed into cold formalism and religion gone "dead." Fears of spiritual decline were exacerbated by millennialist hope, the anxious expectation that Christ's Second Coming might not be far off. This cauldron of emotions created an atmosphere of recurrent crisis, constant self-surveillance (and surveillance of others) to discover evidence of decline from righteousness and need for moral revival. The jeremiad—a sermon lamenting lost virtue and recalling the community to its commitments—became a characteristic mode of Protestant public speech, beginning in New England pulpits during the mid-1600s but spreading a century later into revolutionary politics.

Of course not all public speech was Protestant. Indeed, James Madison, Benjamin Franklin, and other framers of the U.S. Constitution had done their best to create a secular document—"a machine that would go of itself"—which repudiated the establishment of religion and resisted tyranny by depending on internal checks and balances rather than moral exhortation. Still, the framers' emphasis on restraint remained a minority tradition in U.S. political culture. At crucial moments, the constitutional tradition proved critically important for restricting the concentration of power or protecting minority rights. But the framers' skeptical sensibility was seldom at the center of popular debate.

What was more often at the center was an apocalyptic fervor, a feeling that the moral fate of the nation was hanging in the balance of whatever controversy was raging at the time. This emotional charge emerged out of the Protestant consensus that dominated American politics from the Revolutionary Era into the twentieth century.

Much of American history is the story of how tensions that originated in religious conflict—between spontaneity and authority, release and control—were translated at various times into secular, public terms. The earliest example was the way that republican moral tradition hastened the coming of the Revolutionary War. By promising the cleansing of British corruption from American shores, republican ideologues recast a set of static rational principles ("the rights of Englishmen") into a regenerative creed. Through the mid-nineteenth century, longings for moral transformation periodically set fire to political life, as antebellum reform movements—

temperance, peace, antislavery—promised salvation of the individual and ultimately of the nation. Defenders of the status quo sought to restrain the release of moral energy and redirect it toward the maintenance of existing institutions.

Similar patterns of tension characterized economic life. The laissez-faire culture of market exchange played on ancient carnival traditions but detached them from constraints of time, place, and local authority. In an expanding capitalist economy, the representatives of the market were mobile and marginal. Often they were itinerant peddlers of exotic goods—perfumes, jewelry, magic elixirs. Patent medicines in particular became the focus for fantasies of regeneration through purchase. The promise of magical self-transformation through market exchange animated the endless renewal of consumer desire. Other institutions and idioms of control arose to stabilize the sorcery of the marketplace, to contain its carnival spirit. Horatio Alger and other success ideologues celebrated self-made men, whose sincerity and rationality were supposed to counteract the creative destruction unleashed by the market.

By the late nineteenth century, dreams of rebirth were acquiring new meanings. Republican moralists going back to Jefferson's time had long fretted about "overcivilization," but the word took on sharper meaning among the middle and upper classes in the later decades of the nineteenth century. During the postwar decades, "overcivilization" became not merely a social but an individual condition, with a psychiatric diagnosis. In *American Nervousness* (1880), the neurologist George Miller Beard identified "neurasthenia," or "lack of nerve force," as the disease of the age. Neurasthenia encompassed a bewildering variety of symptoms (dyspepsia, insomnia, nocturnal emissions, tooth decay, "fear of responsibility, of open places or closed places, fear of society, fear of being alone, fear of fears, fear of contamination, fear of everything, deficient mental control, lack of decision in trifling matters, hopelessness"), but they all pointed to a single overriding effect: a paralysis of the will.

The malady identified by Beard was an extreme version of a broader cultural malaise—a growing sense that the Protestant ethic of disciplined achievement had reached the end of its tether, had become entangled in the structures of an increasingly organized capitalist society. Ralph Waldo Emerson unwittingly predicted the fin de siècle situation. "Every spirit makes its house," he wrote in "Fate" (1851), "but afterwards the house confines the spirit." The statement presciently summarized the history of nineteenth-century industrial capitalism, on both sides of the Atlantic.

By 1904, the German sociologist Max Weber could put Emerson's proposition more precisely. The Protestant ethic of disciplined work for godly ends had created an "iron cage" of organizations dedicated to the mass production and distribution of worldly goods, Weber argued. The individual striver was caught in a trap of his own making. The movement from farm to factory and office, and from physical labor outdoors to sedentary work indoors, meant that more Europeans and North Americans were insulated from primary processes of making and growing. They were also caught up in subtle cultural changes—the softening of Protestantism into platitudes; the growing suspicion that familiar moral prescriptions had become mere desiccated, arbitrary social conventions. With the decline of Christianity, the German philosopher Friedrich Nietzsche wrote, "it will seem for a time as though all things had become weightless."

Alarmists saw these tendencies as symptoms of moral degeneration. But a more common reaction was a diffuse but powerful feeling among the middle and upper classes—a sense that they had somehow lost contact with the palpitating actuality of "real life." The phrase acquired unprecedented emotional freight during the years around the turn of the century, when reality became something to be pursued rather than simply experienced. This was another key moment in the history of longing, a swerve toward the secular. Longings for this-worldly regeneration intensified when people with Protestant habits of mind (if not Protestant beliefs) confronted a novel cultural situation: a sense that their way of life was being stifled by its own success.

On both sides of the Atlantic, the drive to recapture "real life" took myriad cultural forms. It animated popular psychotherapy and municipal reform as well as avant-garde art and literature, but its chief institutional expression was regeneration through military force. As J. A. Hobson observed in *Imperialism* (1902), the vicarious identification with war energized jingoism and militarism. By the early twentieth century, in many minds, war (or the fantasy of it) had become the way to keep men morally and physically fit. The rise of total war between the Civil War and World War I was rooted in longings for release from bourgeois normality into a realm of heroic struggle. This was the desperate anxiety, the yearning for rebirth, that lay behind official ideologies of romantic nationalism, imperial progress, and civilizing mission—and that led to the trenches of the Western Front.

Americans were immersed in this turmoil in peculiarly American ways. As the historian Richard Slotkin has brilliantly shown, since the early colonial era a faith in regeneration through violence underlay the mythos of the American frontier. With the closing of the frontier (announced by the U.S. census in 1890), violence turned outward, toward empire. But there was more going on than the refashioning of frontier mythology. American longings for renewal continued to be shaped by persistent evangelical traditions, and overshadowed by the shattering experience of the Civil War. American seekers merged Protestant dreams of spiritual rebirth with secular projects of purification—cleansing the body politic of secessionist treason during the war and political corruption afterward, reasserting elite power against restive farmers and workers, taming capital in the name of the public good, reviving individual and national vitality by banning the use of alcohol, granting women the right to vote, disenfranchising African-Americans, restricting the flow of immigrants, and acquiring an overseas empire.

Of course not all these goals were compatible. Advocates of various versions of rebirth—bodybuilders and Prohibitionists, Populists and Progressives, Social Christians and Imperialists—all laid claims to legitimacy. Their crusades met various ends, but overall they relieved the dis-ease of the fin de siècle by injecting some visceral vitality into a modern culture that had seemed brittle and about to collapse. Yearning for intense experience, many seekers celebrated Force and Energy as ends in themselves. Such celebrations could reinforce militarist fantasies but could also lead in more interesting directions—toward new pathways in literature and the arts and sciences. Knowledge could be revitalized, too. William James, as well as Houdini and Roosevelt, was a symbol of the age.

The most popular forms of regeneration had a moral dimension. Prohibitionists believed that a ban on alcohol consumption, far from imposing another "thou shalt not" on a hapless population, would in fact liberate the inebriate from bondage, body and soul. The word "bondage" itself shifted in meaning, losing the political connotations it had during the struggle to end slavery, and acquiring associations with struggles for self-mastery, against enslavement to drink or drugs. But personal reform meant social reform as well. Many feminists and pacifists made this connection, as did Progressive reformers of various stripes who believed that reborn individuals could renew an entire society. If society could be conceived as an organic whole that, like the individual human being, melded physical and moral components, then it was easy to link the political and the personal.

That is what many Americans did during the decades after the Civil War. Following the lead of the Prohibitionists, moral reformers began to support government intrusion into areas that previously had been deemed beyond public scrutiny—such as the human body, and what the individual chose to put in it. The rhetoric of revitalization animated drives for national purity, but this was not the whole story. There were other, more capacious definitions of revivifying force, such as the utopian home imagined by domestic feminists, or the Christian love that Social Gospel Progressives believed could lead to legislation ending the war between labor and capital, or even the alternative universe of possibility created by the "sporting crowd," who surfaced everywhere—mixing classes and races, redefining regeneration as reckless generosity.

The language of rebirth remained largely Protestant. Catholics and Jews might well view it with skepticism, correctly suspecting the assimilationist agenda that lay behind longings for national purification. And many Protestants as well as nonbelievers preferred to remain on the fringes of the righteous community. Numerous Progressive reformers were more inspired by German social democracy and civic pride than by homegrown visions of moral reformation. Yet the pervasiveness of evangelical Protestantism in Gilded Age America made it the dominant, indeed the inescapable discourse of American public life. Small wonder, then, that Populist farmers, labor-union agitators, even Socialists like Eugene Debs all spoke an evangelical idiom of corruption and regeneration. It was the coin of the political realm, adaptable to an endless variety of circumstances. Insurgents like Debs and the Populists used it to help create the beginnings of a Progressive synthesis, based on a more expansive and humane version of the liberal state—a welfare state.*

Still, there were darker dimensions to this story. The age of regeneration coincided with the apogee of scientific racism, which legitimated white su-

---

* Throughout this book, I have capitalized the terms *Populist, Socialist, Democrat,* and *Republican* when they are used to refer to political parties and their members, and lowercased those terms when they are used to refer to the political traditions in question. The term *Progressive* is capitalized in references to reformers who characterized themselves with that term and lowercased in references to a general belief in progress.

premacy at home and empire abroad. For decades following the end of Reconstruction, racial terrorism and Jim Crow legislation combined to ensure that the rebirth of a nation would be designed for whites only. By 1920, the reborn nation was a racially purified polity where segregation was official public policy and "American" meant "Caucasian." Yet even as white supremacy triumphed, other dark meanings of regeneration became discredited. The militarist faith in the morally transformative power of American intervention abroad was a casualty of the Great War. Amid piles of corpses, Roosevelt's bluster seemed worse than idle rant. Wilson's more benign vision fell victim to the inertia of Old World politics, as well as to the skepticism of nationalists and constitutionalists at home. His grandiose dreams of global redemption went unfulfilled. Fantasies of revitalization through force perished—for a time—on the Western Front.

The failure of Wilson's crusade brought an end to the age of regeneration. From the ashes of war emerged a few benign consequences. The gross violations of civil liberties on the home front provoked a strengthening of liberal jurisprudence, a new concern for civil liberties and minority rights that ultimately would extend to racial minorities as well as political dissenters. And the exposure of the war to end war as a delusion led to a necessary chastening of humanitarian hubris. The idea of regenerative war fell into well-deserved disgrace for several decades, even through World War II, which most Americans viewed as a dirty necessity rather than a moral crusade.

But the Cold War and the "war on terrorism" revived all the old, destructive fantasies—the belief in America's capacity to save the world; the faith in the revitalizing powers of combat; the cult of manly toughness in foreign policy. And those fantasies have fostered disastrous policy decisions: the willingness to put the world under the shadow of nuclear war (as John Kennedy did in the Cuban Missile Crisis) rather than risk the appearance of weakness; the determination to demonstrate "national resolve" at the cost of thousands of lives (as Lyndon Johnson and Richard Nixon did in Vietnam) rather than acknowledge error; the fixation on countering terrorism with torture, covert violence, and preemptive military strikes (as George W. Bush did following the attacks of September 11, 2001) rather than through strategies involving multilateral diplomacy and international law. Militarism, often wrapped in humanitarian intentions, still proves alluring to policymakers and intellectuals. The age of regeneration is over, but its spirit stalks our lives like an uninvited ghost.

CHAPTER ONE

The Long Shadow of Appomattox

✦

Wars have a way of staying in the mind. Scenes of unimaginable carnage cannot be casually shrugged off; visceral fears and rages cannot be easily forgotten. So it was in the United States after the Civil War ended at Appomattox Court House, Virginia, in 1865. For the victors as well as the vanquished, the fight left many wounds festering. Sectional bitterness flourished for years after grass covered the corpses. Widespread popular weariness failed to dry up the wells of resentment, in the North as in the South.

There were good reasons for this. The Civil War was not only the most destructive war in U.S. history but the most morally and emotionally charged, as well—a total war in every sense. As hostilities intensified, both armies soon abandoned the West Point Code, which was rooted in just war tradition. The code's key principle was proportionality: commanders were expected to keep their own and their enemy's casualties to a minimum consistent with limited battlefield objectives, and to avoid inflicting any damage on the civilian population.

The principle of proportionality was an early casualty of the war. Within a year after the firing on Fort Sumter, both sides had targeted civilians and sustained losses in the field that would previously have been unimaginable. Yet popular opinion, North and South, submitted to the slaughter. Both armies were cheered on by ideologues who were convinced of the sanctity of their cause and the impossibility of compromise. Only a handful of observers—most prominently, Abraham Lincoln, in his second inaugural address—saw the tragic complexity of the conflict. Most commentators preferred the simplicities of nationalist melodrama. Romantic notions of nationhood flourished in pulpits and the press. Preachers and editors invoked visions of blood sacrifice, endowing mass death with an aura of the sacred. For many Christians, the wartime atmosphere became charged with millennial expectancy, with the hope that the creation of a righteous nation would somehow coincide with the coming of Christ's Kingdom. Such extravagant visions sustained strategies of total war. Gradually it became apparent that the North was far better equipped than the South to pile up corpses without counting the cost, and to reduce an entire region to a wasteland.

Northern nationalism triumphed, and with it the dream of a messianic destiny for America, a nation bound to play a redemptive role in the sacred drama of world history. Southerners, having drunk deeply of millennial nationalism themselves, eventually embraced the Northern version as their own. But this would happen only after Radical Republicans had failed to implement their sweeping version of Reconstruction, after Northern politicians had decisively abandoned the freed slaves, and the meaning of the war—at least for white people—had been transformed from Emancipation to Reunion. The key to that transformation was a revived ethic of martial valor, an ethic rooted in Civil War memories and entangled with a developing discourse of Anglo-Saxon supremacy. By the 1890s, Anglo-Saxon militarism would solidify the reconnection of the white North and the white South, to the exclusion of black Americans. This could not happen overnight. The memory of the war—not as moral crusade or lost cause but as actual experience—was too fresh. Farmers in Virginia were still turning up skulls in their cornfields.

AS EARLY AS April 1862, Americans had a sense of what happened when massive assaults provoked massive counterassaults. Near Shiloh Church in Tennessee, Generals Beauregard and Grant threw armies at each other for thirty-six hours. As reports of the battle filtered back to the home front, the staggering losses mounted, eventually up to 24,500 killed, wounded, or missing on both sides. The numbers were numbing; in any case there was little popular protest, North or South. A few Democratic newspaper editors in the North, never too keen on the war in the first place, deplored the losses and demanded Grant's scalp. No one knew that they had seen the future. Shiloh was only the first of many bloodbaths—the first of many indications that the most successful Union commanders would be the ones most willing to sacrifice unprecedented numbers of men. The West Point Code was on the way out.

Neither side sought to avoid bloodbaths; both seemed addicted to frontal assaults (preferably uphill) on entrenched fortifications. The casualties were fearful, in the mass and in detail. The failed assault on Fort Wagner in

July 1863 by the Massachusetts Fifty-fourth, the black regiment under the command of Colonel Robert Gould Shaw, left an eyewitness aghast: "The ditch was literally choked up with dead bodies and it was possible to walk upon them for fifty yards without touching ground." Those who survived often faced their own protracted horrors, as Walt Whitman reported from a Washington hospital: a Union soldier shot through the bladder, marinating in his own piss; a Confederate soldier the top of whose head had been blown off and whose brains were suppurating in the sun, surviving for three days while he dug a hole in the ground with his heel. These scenes were repeated by the hundreds of thousands. And there were many witnesses.

Looking back on the war in *Specimen Days*, Whitman strained to capture the enormity of the evil unleashed by raw rage. After describing John Mosby's Confederate guerrillas gunning down the Union wounded they had captured near Upperville, Virginia, Whitman then recalled the Union cavalry's counterattack, capture, and summary execution of seventeen guerrillas in the Upperville town square, where they left the bodies to rot. "Multiply [this scene] by scores, aye hundreds," Whitman wrote, "light it with every lurid passion, the wolf's, the lion's lapping thirst for blood—the passionate volcanoes of human revenge for comrades, brothers slain—with the light of burning farms, and heaps of smutting, smouldering black embers—and in the human heart everywhere black, worse embers—and you have an inkling of this war."

Whitman's recollection of "the light of burning farms" underlined the other major feature of total war: the treatment of civilians as belligerents. Early in the war, Confederates fantasized about bombarding Northern cities, and Stonewall Jackson was always champing at the bit to bring the war to the Northern people. But despite Jackson's murderous ferocity, the Confederates did not have the resources to sustain an aggressive war. Apart from the two abortive invasions that ended at Antietam and Gettysburg, the main damage done by the Confederate Army to the Yankee population was the tactically pointless burning of Chambersburg, Pennsylvania, in 1864. The chief Southern war on civilians was conducted in Missouri, by guerrillas and other irregulars who resisted the Union army of occupation and terrorized its civilian sympathizers, torching their property and gunning them down at random. William Quantrell and his guerrilla band in Missouri, along with John Mosby and his raiders in Virginia, led what might today be characterized as the terrorist wing of the Confederate insurgency.

While Confederate guerrillas practiced insurgent terrorism, the Union Army gradually embraced a policy that can accurately be characterized as state terrorism. By 1865, fifty thousand Southern civilians had been killed as a direct result of Northern combat operations. The policy was embodied in Lincoln's General Order #100, authored by Francis Lieber, a German émigré, romantic nationalist, and erstwhile professor at the University of South Carolina. The first part of the order aimed to restrict "savage" behavior, such as the bombardment of civilian areas in cities or the pillage of farms; the second part eviscerated those restrictions by stating that any of them could be ignored in the event of "military necessity." In a counterinsurgency campaign, the phrase justified shelling cities and torching farms. Like other insurgencies, the secessionist movement depended for its support on the local population. The recognition of that fact was behind Grant's famous order to Philip Sheridan: "turn the Shenandoah into a barren waste so that crows flying over it for the balance of the season will have to carry their own provender." Other rationales for treating civilians as belligerents foreshadowed contemporary excuses for "collateral damage." Sherman bombarded Atlanta neighborhoods, he said, because the Confederates were using civilians as human shields. The mass of the Southern population was neither armed nor dangerous. But they were in the war, whether they wanted to be or not. Total war swept all before it.

Conventional accounts of Appomattox and its aftermath have everyone rolling up his sleeves and getting ready to pitch into an expansive economy. But given the ravages of total war, North and South, one could just as easily describe a postwar landscape littered with lost souls. Consider, for example, how the war shaped the lives of two James boys: Garth Wilkinson James and Jesse James.

Wilky James was the younger brother of William and Henry James, one of the two less favored sons in a talented, ambitious family. Plump, good-natured, and fervently antislavery, Wilky enlisted in the Forty-fourth Massachusetts regiment in September 1862. Both his older brothers managed to avoid the army, with their father's approval and connivance. Henry James Sr. showed no such solicitude for his younger boys. But war would be Wilky's one chance to step out of his brothers' shadow. Transferred to Shaw's Fifty-fourth, Wilky became one of the white officers who led the black regiment's doomed charge on Fort Wagner. He was seriously wounded, hit by a shell in the side and a canister ball in the foot. After months of convalescence he returned to the Fifty-fourth, but he never really recovered from his wounds. He survived for eighteen years after Appomattox, in nearly constant pain from rheumatism in his wounded foot. He bumped from one bad business venture to another, beginning with the failure of his idealistic plan to provide recently freed black families an economic foothold by employing them on his farm in Florida. Having run through many thousands of his father's dollars, he was finally disinherited and died in poverty in Milwaukee, where he and his family had been scraping by after several failed business ventures. For Wilky the war brought not regeneration but ruin. He was one of many men whose physical and emotional wounds never healed.

Jesse James, in contrast, was not physically wounded but psychologically brutalized by the war. Coming of age amid the white-hot hatreds of wartime Missouri, he grew up in a world where casual murder was a manly sport and a rite of passage, the only conclusive proof that you had become (and remained) a man. He proved himself many times during the war, when he rode with Quantrell's raiders. After Appomattox new opportunities presented themselves. In Missouri, ten years of blood feuds had bred widespread longings for retribution. Many returning veterans could not give up the habit of violence and helped to swell a postwar crime wave. Gunslinging became a way of life.

Much of the violence was rooted in Reconstruction politics. Bushwhackers wanted revenge against Radical Republicans and money from the companies the Republicans financed. That was enough, among embittered Confederates, to make the James gang seem more than mere bandits and killers. But that is what they were. For fifteen years, they took money at gunpoint from banks and later from express companies, whose monies were being transported on the expanding network of railroads. They also killed a lot of innocent people. Throughout his short life, Jesse remained irresistibly attracted to arbitrary violence.

Garth Wilkinson James and Jesse James were both permanently scarred by the war, though in profoundly different ways. Wilky limped through the postwar period, failing at everything he tried, knowing that nothing he did would ever match the heroism of storming Fort Wagner. Jesse was filled with partisan rage and vicious notions of manhood that transformed him into a driven killer. The war ravaged lives in unpredictable ways and left a wounded nation.

Lincoln grappled with the magnitude of the destruction in his second inaugural address. He believed the war was not a melodrama but a tragedy, not a struggle of good versus evil but a bloody expiation visited on North and South alike for the national sin of slavery. And as the historian C. Vann Woodward once argued, Southerners like Robert E. Lee also derived a tragic sense of life from the experience of defeat. But what is remarkable is how unusual Lee and Lincoln were, how thoroughly their contemporaries on both sides evaded the tragic significance of the war. Public moralists, North and South, wanted to turn it into a melodrama—and they succeeded.

THE CHATTERING CLASS played a crucial role in charging the conflict with moral and religious fervor. As casualties mounted, Americans felt an increasingly desperate need for a coherent narrative to justify the horror. Preachers, politicians, and journalists on both sides deployed narratives of triumphant nationhood to meet that need. Still, nationalism by itself was an abstraction; what mattered was how it entered the viscera of the people, how it became part of a narrative that made sense of mass killing.

The Confederates' nationalism was more ambivalent than the Yankees'. As the war dragged on, Southern Honor and eventually the Lost Cause itself acquired the numinous quality at first ascribed to the Confederate nation—the capacity to command blood sacrifice. In the early years, editors still entertained hopes of a successful revolution. The *Richmond Enquirer* predicted that the Confederates, like the French revolutionaries, would "pass to the promised land through a sea of red blood." Soldiers and civilians alike attributed redemptive powers to the conflict. Especially civilians. Virginia governor Henry Wise (who hanged John Brown) was not atypical. "I rejoice in this war," Wise said soon after it began. "It is a war of purification. You want war, fire, blood, to purify you; and the Lord of hosts has demanded that you shall walk through fire and blood—You are called to the fiery baptism and I call you to come up to the altar. . . . Take a lesson from John Brown." Many Southerners were willing to take that lesson, but they lacked sufficient resources to implement a successful war of purification.

The success of the Northern strategy depended on redemptive purpose combined with superior force. Narratives of personal and national regeneration intertwined with the determination to realize them on the battlefield. Individual and collective identities merged in a mass ritual of blood sacrifice.

The Unionist narrative became the core of the civil religion that justified the emerging American empire in the decades following the Civil War. Unionist ideology dissolved republican and democratic ingredients in a romantic nationalist stew that was in many ways neither republican nor democratic. The sheer scale of this creed's grandiosity was breathtaking. "A National Fast Day Hymn," which appeared in an evangelical newspaper in 1861, revealed a vision with imperial implications. After praying to God the Father to "smite the rebel bands, until / Of traitors there are none," the hymn then asked to be led by His Son "o'er earth's bloodless fields / Till all the world is won." This was the absolutist habit of mind that bred doctrines of unconditional surrender and dreams of exterminating traitors. And if the nation was to be universal, it was also to be eternal. On Thanksgiving Day, 1864, the Rev. Alexander Vinton spoke what he called "both a prayer and a prophecy": "My country, be thou as perpetual as the ages." Since many millennial nationalists were Protestant preachers, with a penchant for Old Testament texts, the language of righteous vengeance came easily to their lips. The devastation of Atlanta and the Shenandoah Valley were fiery retribution for rebellion, said the Rev. O. T. Lanphear of New Haven, Connecticut: "Let it be shown that when a state insults the law of the land, by deliberate secession, it is like a withered branch cast forth from the national tree, to be gathered, cast into the fire, and burned."

The organic imagery embodied in "the national tree" reflected a new strain of romantic nationalism, which melded the individual with the collective by likening the nation to a natural organism. According to Edward Everett Hale's popular didactic tale, *The Man Without a Country* (1863), one's personal identity—indeed one's very life—was dependent on immersion in a larger national identity. While Lincoln used the language of "the people" to elevate democracy as well as nationhood, more typical orators deployed the same idiom in the service of organic nationalism, wrapping the government and the citizenry in the sacred garment of the nation.

The sanctity of the nation justified its demands for blood. Redefining unspeakable losses as religious sacrifice, Northerners forged a powerful link between war and regeneration. In some formulations, personal rebirth seemed to arise simply from the decision to risk combat—to plunge into action as an end in itself, heedless of the consequences. (This would be the version that Oliver Wendell Holmes Jr. would eventually celebrate, as he recalled his own war experience, and that Theodore Roosevelt would unwittingly parody.) More commonly, the revitalization was explicitly moral. For generations, republican moralists had been haunted by visions of a citizenry grown soft through indulgence in luxury and other vices of commerce. The many forms of sacrifice demanded by the war provided a perfect opportunity for Americans to redeem themselves from commercial corruption, to transcend private gain in pursuit of a larger public good. So moralists said.

Sacrifice was most appealing when imagined from a distance. As usual in such cases, the loudest yelps for blood often came from those farthest from the battlefield. Charles Eliot Norton, a well-connected young Brahmin intellectual, waxed eloquent over "the Advantages of Defeat" after the Union Army was routed at the first battle of Manassas. The humiliation might have the salutary effect of sobering us, soldiers and civilians—of reminding us that this "religious war" would require a mass blood sacrifice. "But there must be no shrinking from the prospect of the death of our soldiers," the young man warned. "Better than that we should fail that a million men should die on the battlefield." Victory would eventually come; and meanwhile Northern character—so long sunk in selfishness and softness—would be purified by protracted struggle. Years later, Norton would repudiate these youthful fatuities and become an outspoken anti-imperialist. But during the Civil War, his breathtaking arrogance was commonplace. Men routinely praised the cleansing power of war from a comfortable distance.

Some turned in therapeutic directions. The *Albany Argus* predicted that "A vigorous war would tone up the public mind, and impart to it qualities that would last after the calamities of war had passed." And the historian Benson Lossing wrote to Sue Wallace (the wife of General Lew Wallace) in 1862: "I have felt profoundly impressed with the conviction that out of all this tribulation would come health, and strength, and purification for the nation." From the perspective of the people who actually fought it, or were swept up in it, one could attribute few more bizarre effects to the war than "health, strength, and purification." Here as elsewhere, one can glimpse the connections between millennial dreams of collective rebirth and the sort of organic nationalism that could eventually mutate into fascism.

The political meaning of regeneration remained contested long after the guns fell silent. Certainly the freed slaves embraced a version of regeneration far more rooted in lived experience than the vaporous version of press and pulpit. For them, emancipation was a genuine rebirth. Free blacks in the North, too, had reason to exult. The black abolitionist Frederick Douglass, who had escaped from bondage himself, remembered the crowds of ecstatic black people celebrating the news in Boston. "My old friend Rue, a colored preacher, a man of wonderful vocal power, expressed the heartfelt emotion of the hour," Douglass later wrote, "when he led all voices in the anthem, 'Sound the loud timbrel o'er Egypt's dark sea, Jehovah hath triumphed, his people are free.'" The black vision of freedom was the most powerfully justified version of rebirth to come out of the war—and the most cruelly disappointed.

The freed people and their Radical allies hoped that if the fruits of emancipation could be secured, then the regenerative possibilities of the war might actually be realized. Longings for racial equality animated the ambitious agenda of Radical Reconstruction, which included a thorough redistribution of property and power in the former Confederate states. Yet despite the decisive transformation wrought by ending slavery, the political meaning of Northern victory came to focus exclusively on reunion; the importance of emancipation slipped to the margins and eventually disappeared from public discourse altogether.

This change culminated a complex reshuffling of military and political strategies. Before the war, the Republican Party was determined to put slavery on the road to extinction by restricting it to the areas where it already existed, though most Republicans were more concerned with protecting free labor from competition with slave labor than with alleviating the plight of the slaves themselves. After the attack on Fort Sumter, the restriction of slavery was subsumed in what most white Northerners thought was the more urgent task—saving the Union—even while Republicans remained committed to the eventual end of slavery. But military victory was a prerequisite for that end, and except to abolitionists and slaves, the Emancipation Proclamation was primarily a military strategy. Still, emancipation had a life of its own. The sight of freed slaves scattering northward from the collapsing Confederacy, many joining the Union Army, revived Republican antislavery sentiments and radicalized Northern war aims. Victory, some Republicans dared to hope, might actually mean a social revolution in the South. And indeed for a decade after the war, freed blacks and their white allies pursued an ambitious approach to racial politics, seeking to secure the fruits of emancipation in a reconstructed South. But by the mid-1870s that effort had stalled.

As Reconstruction faltered, the politics of regeneration became restricted to whites only. Gradually white Southerners made common cause with Northern whites—taking advantage of the racism that pervaded both sections. As Republican policy-makers shifted focus from emancipation to economics, Yankees and Confederates made peace on the backs of blacks. The ideology of reunion was millennial nationalism, celebrating blood sacrifice but adding a racial component of Anglo-Saxon supremacy. Religion and race combined to legitimate the drive toward overseas empire. Providence offered religious sanctions for imperial adventure; race supplied scientific sanctions. For the Congregational minister Josiah Strong, the establishment of an American empire converged with the creation of Christ's kingdom on earth. Those who believed there might be some conflict between the two realms had nothing to worry about, Strong wrote, because modern science had revealed "that races develop in the course of centuries as individuals do in years, and that an undeveloped race, which is incapable of self-government, is no more a reflection on the Almighty than is an undeveloped child who is incapable of self-government." Paternalist racism underwrote the merger of Christianity and empire. Among believing American Protestants, millennial expectations combined with missionary commitments to expand the vision of regeneration from the individual and the nation to the entire world. This religiously charged hubris would fitfully animate American foreign policy for much of the century to come.

Despite its grand abstractions, imperial rhetoric was rooted in an appeal to individual experience. Imperial ideologues increasingly defined revitalization in bodily terms, merging manliness and militarism, the personal and the political. The notion of manliness deserves some explanation to contemporary readers. In the twenty-first century, the word itself jars. We have become used to associating it with Arnold Schwarzenegger and James Bond—with testosterone-induced displays of hypermasculinity, detached from any larger meaning. In contrast, nineteenth-century manliness was embedded in a republican moral tradition that emphasized honest labor and economic independence as well as devotion to family, community, and commonweal. This conception of manliness survived the Civil War, though by the 1880s it had begun to change in subtle ways. Manliness became less a condition to be cultivated than a goal to be pursued. It acquired a therapeutic dimension, reshaping the desire for revitalization into a lifelong project, sending men in search of new sites for self-testing, new frontiers. Here was a worldview suitable for an age of empire.

It would not be the only game in town. Idiosyncratic thinkers sustained different definitions of heroism—or antiheroism, in the case of Mark Twain. Jane Addams disrupted the public equation of heroism and manhood, offering women the opportunity for courage and sacrifice in the slums of Chicago. William James rejected the very idea of American empire and sought a moral equivalent of war. Yet even such dissenters remained preoccupied with preserving opportunities for heroism; even they believed that life *"feels like a real fight"*—in James's phrase—and that if it did not, it would not be worth living. Sometimes the shadow of Appomattox fell with a special force on those who did not actually fight in the war.

Still the definition of heroism that would prove the most politically powerful would be the one most suited to elite Anglo-Saxon males. The idea of personal and national regeneration through the exercise of military force would provide a new basis for their hegemony in an age of empire. Before that could happen, though, the political meaning of Union triumph had to be divested of any lingering associations with racial equality.

TWELVE YEARS AFTER Appomattox, the formal end of Reconstruction marked the beginning of sectional reconciliation—but only the beginning. Recently freed slaves and their Radical Republican allies had been determined to implement revolutionary change in the Southern social order; white Southerners, especially among the propertied classes, had been equally determined to resist it. Reconstruction politics was the arena where the social meanings of the war were fought out. By the spring of 1877, in most parts of the conquered Confederacy, the issue was no longer in doubt: the Northern army of occupation was withdrawn from Southern soil; the recently freed slaves were left, largely if not entirely, to the mercy of their former masters. In public discourse, the primary meaning of the war became Reunion, not Emancipation.

The Compromise of 1877 sealed the deal. The negotiations that led to it epitomized the back-room horse trading of post–Civil War Washington. What was at stake was the election of 1876. The Democratic candidate, Samuel J. Tilden of New York, had defeated the Republican, Rutherford B. Hayes of Ohio, in the popular vote. But the count was so hotly disputed in Louisiana, South Carolina, and Florida that these states' electoral votes remained in doubt. Congress was charged with deciding the matter. To put Hayes over the top, Republicans needed to peel off some Southern Democrats, prominent white men like Wade Hampton of South Carolina and L. Q. C. Lamar of Mississippi, who had just clawed their way back into power and were eager to dispel the last vestiges of federal rule from the South.

But the Southerners wanted more than "home rule" and the restoration of white supremacy—a President Tilden could have given them that. They also wanted federal subsidies: to clear canals and harbors from Norfolk to New Orleans, to remove mud bars from the Mississippi, and lay down railroad tracks from somewhere, anywhere, in the South to the Pacific Coast. In short, they wanted an infrastructure that would allow them to join the commercial-industrial revolution convulsing the rest of the country. Northern capitalists saw the logic of this; they recognized that the South could be a junior partner in many a joint venture, not to mention a source of cheap labor and raw materials—the classic colonial economy. A few fortunate businessmen had more particular investments in the South. Among them was Thomas Scott, head of the Pennsylvania Railroad, whose plans for the Texas and Pacific Railway dovetailed nicely with Southern Democrats' dreams of coast-to-coast economic development along the nation's lower rim.

For a time, Southern dreams blended with the drift of Republican politics. Since the late 1860s, the Republican Party had been haltingly shifting its focus from black rights to business interests. With many postwar Southern Democrats, they had in common a prewar Whig vision of industrial development through government-business cooperation. The Northern Democrats who clustered around Tilden did not share this vision. They were suspicious of federal spending and determined to pay off public debts. Southern devotees of government-sponsored economic growth could expect no encouragement from them. So the Southern Democrats cut a deal with the Republicans and for a little while received everything they wanted in the way of patronage and subsidies. But within a few months the bloom was off this bipartisan rose. Northern Republicans began to complain of the alliance's expense; Southern Democrats began to consort openly again with their Northern counterparts, minimal-government men who were willing to leave capital to its own devices.

By 1880, the Compromise of 1877 was a dead letter—except for its one lasting proviso, the withdrawal of federal troops from the South and the end of any sustained federal effort to protect black rights. Yet the restoration of white supremacy was by no means complete. African-Americans still held public office and exercised political power in scores of Southern places. A fluid racial situation existed in many parts of the South through the 1880s and even into the 1890s; black disenfranchisement and racial segregation were only gradually implemented. In fact it would be another twenty years before the full effects of the Compromise of 1877 were felt—before the betrayal of the freed slaves was fully accomplished. By the spring of 1877, the political framework of white supremacy was in place at the national level. But the regime of race-based power had not yet reshaped the texture of everyday life. The triumph of Jim Crow would require not only the local deployment of terrorist tactics but also the cultural convergence of the white South and the white North. The remarriage of these warring sections—so recently resentful foes—was proposed in the Compromise of 1877 and consummated gradually over the next two decades.

As black Americans' hopes faded, one can only imagine the bitterness they felt, even the most privileged among them. Frederick Douglass, for example, was far more fortunate than most former slaves. For a man with the initial bad luck of being born into slavery, Douglass had what could be called a charmed life. At crucial moments, sometimes unwittingly, white people with power encouraged his ambition—beginning with his master's wife, Sophie Auld, who began teaching him to read when he was six years old. As Douglass transformed himself from a caulker (and a slave) in a Baltimore shipyard to one of the leading political orators of his time, he struggled to free himself from the expectations of white people, whether abolitionists or slaveholders. He yearned to develop a more capacious self.

Even as a boy, he dreamed of a personal regeneration achieved through the sublime experience of freedom. "What a moment this was to me!" he recalled of his first morning as a free man, stepping off the ferry onto lower Broadway in New York. "A whole year was pressed into a single day. A new world pressed upon my agitated vision." The "sensations," he later wrote, were "too intense and too rapid for words." Douglass devoted his life to spreading that regenerative experience among African-Americans.

His quest melded personal and political aims. After the Civil War, his main task was to preserve the emancipatory meaning of Northern victory. The best way to do that, he thought, was by securing black people the vote. The passage of the Fifteenth Amendment seemed the fulfillment of his hope, yet it soon became apparent that constitutional guarantees of black suffrage were insufficient, as Southern whites reclaimed power and began a systematic campaign of racial disenfranchisement. Douglass became an increasingly marginal figure in post-Reconstruction Washington. Visions of sublimity were hard to sustain as black leaders sought to maintain a foothold in a government that had abandoned them. Under Hayes and Garfield, Douglass held obscure bureaucratic positions that allowed him to keep some access to power and patronage. (Federal appointments created the basis for a black middle class in the District of Columbia.) In 1889, President Benjamin Harrison appointed Douglass minister to Haiti, but he soon found himself at odds with the imperialists in the American press, who wanted the harbor of Mole St. Nicholas as a coaling station for the American fleet. Accused of insufficient bellicosity, he resigned in 1891. There was no place for him in the emerging politics of empire.

Still, he had his powers of eloquence. In August 1893, he addressed the World's Columbian Exposition in Chicago. It was Colored People's Day, an event imagined by the fair organizers to be little more than a joke. Watermelon vendors positioned themselves throughout the grounds, and many black leaders stayed home. Douglass did not. He spoke on "The Race Problem in America" to an amphitheater full of mostly black faces. Interrupted by white hecklers, he put aside his notes and shouted directly to the crowd: "Men talk of the Negro problem. There is no Negro problem. The problem is whether the American people have loyalty enough, honor enough, to live up to their own Constitution." The hecklers fell silent; Douglass went on forcefully for an hour. "We Negroes love our country. We fought for it. We ask only that we be treated as well as those who fought against it." The crowd roared its approval. The seventy-five-year-old orator had returned to top form. It was like old times.

But as Douglass no doubt suspected, his plea was futile. The American political landscape had decisively altered in the thirty years since the Emancipation Proclamation. Yankees and Confederates had reached a new plateau of reconciliation. It involved more than Northern politicians trading freed people's rights for money and votes, or Southern politicians manipulating racist rivalries and fears. For the North-South merger to take place, there had to be an alchemical change in the meaning of the Civil War itself, a change that would promote reunion between whites by transforming wartime longings for regeneration into an Anglo-Saxon quest. Emancipation dissolved in the discourse of reunion. Black soldiers, despite their ubiquity and courage, disappeared from the proliferating narratives of battlefield heroics. Rather than a struggle to end slavery, the war became a testing ground for personal heroism—a theater of the sublime where white men, North and South, had repeatedly demonstrated their valor in ways that made mere politics seem venal and corrupt.

The recoil from sectional partisanship was rooted in an understandable sympathy for the sufferings of the common soldier. Pain, fear, and death transcended sectional boundaries and policy debates, evoking the common lot of humanity in extremis. Atrocity and counter-atrocity merged in a flood of appalling scenes that made political ideals, however noble and necessary, seem pale by comparison. Certain images and memories could not easily be put to partisan use. Whitman's *Specimen Days* (1882) collected his war notes into an eloquent case for sectional reconciliation as a form of healing—and forgetting. Apolitical mourning was a wholly understandable response to memories of mass slaughter. Yet the public memory that emerged from this mourning, however apolitical it seemed, proved to have profoundly political consequences.

IN THROWING A common mantle of chivalric virtue over the mounds of corpses at Shiloh and Cold Harbor, postwar rhetoricians refashioned the regenerative nationalist creed, placing it in the service of white supremacy at home and Anglo-Saxon empire abroad. Despite the protests of Douglass and other African-American leaders, Memorial Day orations became occasions for remembering the equal heroism of blue and gray and forgetting the black struggle for freedom. In New York on May 30, 1877, the retired Union general John Cochrane, who had been John C. Frémont's vice-presidential candidate in 1864, celebrated the withdrawal of federal troops from the South as the "birth of constitutional liberty," while across the East River that same day the former Confederate officer Roger Pryor lectured an audience at the Brooklyn Academy of Music on the innocence of the South and the irrelevance of slavery to the meaning of the war. During the next two decades, such sentiments became the commonplaces of commemoration, as generic soldiers appeared atop monuments from the White Mountains to the Mississippi Delta, and veterans appraised their former enemies with grudging but genuine respect. Bitterness dissolved in festivals of fraternity. The visceral experience of the war vanished from the official memories of it. So did the experience of black soldiers and rebellious slaves, as the celebration of white soldiers' valor melded with emerging ideologies of race. By 1891, the journalist John Robes could look back at "the War as we see it now" and declare it "an exhibition of the Anglo-Saxon race on trial," one that served "to bring out the resolute and unyielding traits belonging to our race," above all its "unconquerable determination." The politics of the war disappeared in a fog of racist platitudes, a celebration of Anglo-Saxon will.

By the 1880s, even critics who were dismayed by the praises of war were struck by their popularity. Some believed there was a racial explanation. "Whether just or unjust, wise or unwise, an aggressive policy [toward anything] will be popular . . . in harmony with the traditions, the practice and the ambition of the Anglo-Saxon," wrote General M. M. Trumbull in *Open Court* magazine. Given the "resistless march" of Anglo-Saxons, "it may be that their fighting habit has become an instinct that must be gratified." Racialist thinking and biological determinism reinforced notions of inevitable war. The phrase "survival of the fittest" had been coined by Herbert Spencer, a pacifist who believed that humankind was evolving toward universal harmony. Darwin put Spencer's phrase in later editions of his *Origin of Species*, and his popularizers used it to justify human aggression. This Social Darwinism found less favor among businessmen seeking to justify laissez-faire than it did among social scientists and other intellectuals who became increasingly fascinated by force for its own sake, by energy as an end in itself. For intellectuals on both sides of the Atlantic, no force seemed more compelling than the organized violence of war. But Trumbull thought that popular militarism was especially strong in America, embodied in sentiments rather than institutions. While Europe is an armed camp, he wrote, "martial *feeling* there is not so strong as here." There one found unwilling conscripts; here, "volunteers chafing in war harness without war." The "military passion" in the United States was being fed by the constant stimulation of Civil War memories, through countless reunions of veterans, "sham battles," and much "flattery of warriors from pulpit, press, and stump." As military schools and battle stories created military models of heroism for youth to emulate, a "fiery eruption must make an outlet for the patriotic valor and the pent-up phrensy of our sons." For Trumbull, writing in 1889, the psychological basis for a new war was already in place.

But for many other observers, too many American youths—especially among the upper classes—had succumbed to the vices of commerce: the

worship of Mammon, the love of ease. Since the Founding Fathers' generation, republican ideologues had fretted about the corrupting effects of commercial life. Norton and other moralists, North and South, had imagined
war would provide an antidote. During the Gilded Age those fears acquired
a peculiarly palpable intensity. The specter of "overcivilization"—invoked
by republican orators since Jefferson's time—developed a sharper focus:
the figure of the overcivilized businessman became a stock figure in social
criticism. Flabby, ineffectual, anxious, possibly even neurasthenic, he embodied bourgeois vulnerability to the new challenges posed by restive, angry workers and waves of strange new immigrants. "Is American Stamina
Declining?" asked William Blaikie, a former Harvard athlete and author of
How to Get Strong and Stay So, in *Harper's* in 1889. Among white-collar
"brain-workers," legions of worried observers were asking similar questions. Throughout the country, metropolitan life for the comfortable classes
was becoming a staid indoor affair. Blaikie caught the larger contours of the
change:

> A hundred years ago, there was more done to make our men and
> women hale and vigorous than there is to-day. Over eighty per cent
> of all our men then were farming, hunting, or fishing, rising early, out
> all day in the pure, bracing air, giving many muscles very active work,
> eating wholesome food, retiring early, and so laying in a good stock of
> vitality and health. But now hardly forty per cent are farmers, and nearly
> all the rest are at callings—mercantile, mechanical, or professional—
> which do almost nothing to make one sturdy and enduring.

This was the sort of anxiety that set men (and more than a few women)
to pedaling about on bicycles, lifting weights, and in general pursuing fitness
with unprecedented zeal. But for most Americans, fitness was not merely a
matter of physical strength. What was equally essential was character, which
they defined as adherence to Protestant morality. Body and soul would be
saved together.

This was not a gender-neutral project. Since the antebellum era, purveyors of conventional wisdom had assigned respectable women a certain
fragility. So the emerging sense of physical vulnerability was especially novel
and threatening to men. Manliness, always an issue in Victorian culture, had
by the 1880s become an obsession. Older elements of moral character con-

tinued to define the manly man, but a new emphasis on physical vitality began to assert itself as well. Concern about the over-soft socialization of the young promoted the popularity of college athletics. During the 1880s, waves of muscular Christianity began to wash over campuses.

It was only a short step from manliness to militarism. A bland but significant example was the dedication of a strip of land adjacent to Harvard as "Soldiers Field," where young men could be reminded of the heroes who marched before them, even while they cavorted at character-building games. Henry Lee Higginson, the wealthy Bostonian who donated the land in 1890, made clear that its new name was meant to identify sport as training for sacrifice and duty. Higginson hoped to create a public-spirited antidote to the crass pursuit of money, to encourage the kind of commitment that might send a young man on soldierly service in distant lands. In the absence of such opportunity, longings for personal testing might send a young man on an Arctic exploration, such as the one led by Adolphus Greely in 1884, but it remained an open question just how regenerative such an experience might be (especially since Greely's men ended up cannibalizing one another). For those eager to harmonize manliness and morality, there was no melody so pleasing as the threnody of military heroism.

Still the fascination with force spilled over the boundaries of bourgeois convention. The martial ethic remained unstable, unpredictable, and by no means reducible to an ideological cover for ruling-class interests; its popularity embodied more diffuse yearnings. Affluent Americans were becoming impatient with the inherent limitations of a society given over to material comfort, as well as with the anemic gentility of late-Victorian religion and culture. The sheer banality of a utilitarian standard of values made a chivalric stance seem all the more attractive. Military heroism repudiated calculating gain and affirmed the inevitability of loss—including the ultimate loss, death itself. The soldier's willingness to risk all for a cause he believed noble (even if he was mistaken) seemed a powerful antidote to the self-seeking calculus governing commerce.

The recoil from comfort led in more disturbing directions as well, toward places in the psyche where not even morality mattered. To Americans whose very sense of selfhood seemed fragmented and frail, aggressive action promised strength and psychic wholeness. To Americans who felt cut off from firsthand experience, it promised immersion in "real life." The Christian and even the nationalist frameworks dropped away; risk became its own reward. Courage and endurance became ends in themselves. This was not quite a cult of death, but when combined with the cult of sacrifice, it came very close. Nihilism—and eventually fascism—fluttered at the edges of militarism.

Perhaps the most prominent purveyor of this worldview was Oliver Wendell Holmes Jr. In some ways he had earned the right to it. Wounded at Ball's Bluff, Antietam, and Fredericksburg, he led men into battle against hopeless odds and watched his best friend die. For the rest of his long life, he kept his bloodied uniform in his closet and disdained the absolutist idealism that led to uncompromising crusades. Yet Holmes fell into his own form of idealism—an apparently apolitical martial spirit that resonated powerfully with the needs of a ruling class worried about its own weakness and eager for regenerative strife. Holmes was nothing if not eloquent. At Keene, New Hampshire, on Memorial Day 1884, he articulated the perspective that would become a patrician creed:

> Through our great good fortune, in our youth our hearts were touched with fire. It was given to us to learn at the outset that life is a profound and passionate thing. While we are permitted to scorn nothing but indifference, and do not pretend to undervalue the worldly rewards of ambition, we have seen with our own eyes beyond and above the gold fields the snowy heights of honor, and it is for us to bear the report to those who come after us.

Holmes's language captured some key elements in the developing cult of martial virtue. "The snowy heights of honor" were accessible to men in gray as well as blue—to anyone who transcended "the worldly rewards of ambition," who clambered "beyond and above the gold fields." The contrast between money-worship and the martial ideal was crucial. Since the war had ended, moralists had fretted about the proliferation of men on the make and the corrupt politicians who served them. Established elites, especially in the Northeast, feared that irresponsible wealth had parted company from public duty. Invocations of wartime heroism, they believed, might lance the boil of luxury and regenerate commitments to the larger good.

Yet Holmes himself had no faith that war could promote this kind of moral reformation. The best it might accomplish was to produce "a race fit for headship and command." Morality had nothing to do with it. We fight "because we want to realize our spontaneity and prove our power for the joy of it," he said. Spontaneity, power, and joy—this was an amoral regeneration. Holmes delivered his most famous paean to war on Memorial Day 1895, when he addressed the Harvard graduating class on "The Soldier's Faith." Among the many strengths of that "faith," Holmes believed, was that it protected young men against the "temptations of wallowing ease." Symptoms of softness were everywhere, particularly "the doctrine that evil means pain, and the revolt against pain in all its forms"—a revolt that in his view included socialism, sentimental literature, and societies for the prevention of cruelty to animals. For Holmes these were the products of an overprotected populace, peaceful and prosperous.

The antithesis between prosperity and public morality was a familiar trope, but Holmes was determined to move beyond conventional cant. Ascending to a crescendo, he announced that "the faith is true and adorable which leads a soldier to throw away his life in obedience to a blindly accepted duty, in a cause which he little understands, in a plan of campaign of which he has no notion, under tactics of which he does not see the use." In its very vacuity, Holmes's rhetoric suggests just how thoroughly the martial spirit had been emptied of political or moral content during the decades following the Civil War. What soon became apparent was how easily apolitical militarism could be adapted to various ideological agendas.

THE MARTIAL ETHIC turned organized violence into a regenerative rite. There were a number of opportunities to perform it during the years following the Civil War. On the Great Plains and in the Rocky Mountains, the U.S. Army completed the conquest of aboriginal Americans, which had begun centuries before. The army's mop-up operation accelerated in intensity during the 1880s, culminating in 1890 in the massacre at Wounded Knee, South Dakota, where federal troops with Hotchkiss cannons faced off against unarmed Indian men, women, and children. (Twenty-three soldiers won Congressional Medals of Honor for that day's work.) The same era witnessed the emergence of class war in the cities of the Northeast and upper Midwest. The long depression that followed the Panic of 1873 touched off widespread wage-cutting and layoffs. When desperate workers organized to protect their jobs and took to the streets in protest, frightened business elites demanded military protection. City and state governments formed local units of a National Guard to stem the labor strife of the 1880s, urging gilded youth to cultivate heroic manliness by defending the sanctity of property. By the end of that decade, massive armories brooded in major cities, testimony to the domestic uses of the martial ideal. Apologists for revitalizing violence could dignify any form of slaughter, even the lynchings, torture, and other forms of terrorism that Southern whites deployed to reassert racial dominance. But ultimately the war song with the widest influence was the hymn to imperial adventure, which sounded faintly and fitfully in the 1880s and rose to a fortissimo in the 1890s. From the imperial perspective, the extension of American power to the Caribbean and even to the farthest reaches of the Pacific would reaffirm the heroism of the rising generation. The regeneration that began in the individual heart would be spread—by force, if necessary—to the entire world. And with it would come *"the creating of more and higher wants,"* which, according to Josiah Strong and others, defined civilization.

What was especially striking about the post–Civil War martial ethic was its comfortable coexistence with commerce. For centuries moralists had identified Mammon and Mars as mortal enemies. Holmes and his contemporaries presented their militarist views as a warrior's critique of a business civilization, contrasting the heroism of the boys in blue (and gray) with their venal descendants in a "Gilded Age." The term was Mark Twain's and Charles Dudley Warner's, the title of their novel of 1873, and it came to characterize the epoch for many Americans, then and since. Yet the hypocrisy, the greed, the corruption, the obsession with quick money—all these qualities of the age cohabited with militarism far more easily than most devotees of martial virtue would have imagined. To be sure, a few patricians openly promoted the marriage of militarism and money, imagining that battlefield courage might stiffen a ruling class to a chivalric defense of capital; this was John Hay's fantastic scenario in his novel *The Bread-winners* (1884). But not until the end of the century, in the imperialist sermons of Theodore Roosevelt and Albert Beveridge, did militarist rhetoric catch up with the commercial realities of public life. And even those imperialists, for all their forthright celebration of war as the engine of American economic expansion, prettified the process in the ethereal language of progress and civilization.

This modern martial ethic, merging commerce and courage, arose during a period of remarkable continuity in American military policy. From the 1870s through the early 1900s, U.S. soldiers fought a series of brushfire wars against various dark-skinned "natives" who were poorly armed and hopelessly out-manned but often determined to fight for independence to the last man. The conquest of the Indians in the trans-Mississippi West marked the consolidation of the inland empire; the suppression of the Cuban and the Filipino independence movements signaled the beginning of a new kind of American empire, one based less on occupation of thinly settled areas than on intervention in populous states. While the shift from occupation to intervention embodied the transformation of the United States from a settler society to a global power, there were striking continuities between Indian wars and imperial wars.

One such continuity was the legal framework for domination. In 1871 the U.S. Supreme Court ruled that Congress could override old Indian treaties by passing new laws; in the years after 1898, in the Insular Cases, the Supreme Court provided a similar carte blanche to Congress, allowing it to pass laws governing the new colonial possessions of Cuba and the Philippines. There were also continuities in military personnel. Many Civil War veterans fought in the Indian wars (including many black veterans, known to the Indians as "buffalo soldiers"), and many veterans of the Indian wars in turn found themselves fighting Filipino insurgents in the jungles of Mindanao. The unbroken path of service was especially prominent in the officer corps. General Nelson Miles, who had fought at Fredericksburg, Chancellorsville, and Appomattox, took command of the U.S. Army in the West after General George Armstrong Custer and his men were massacred at the Little Bighorn in 1876; twenty-two years later, Miles participated in the Cuban campaign and led the U.S. invasion of Puerto Rico.

Strategy and tactics stretched back to the Civil War. The treatment of civilians as belligerents, the effort to eradicate a whole way of life—the total-war approach dominated, whether the enemies were Confederates, Indians, or Filipinos. "During the [Civil] War did anyone hesitate to attack a village or town occupied by the enemy because women and children were within its limits?" Sheridan asked Sherman in 1873. "Did we cease to throw shells into Vicksburg or Atlanta because women and children were there?" The questions were rhetorical, meant to justify similar attacks on Indian women and children.

Still, there was a critical departure. The difference between fighting Confederates and fighting Sioux or Filipinos was that for the dark-skinned foes the scorched-earth policy became a strategy of deliberate extermination. General William T. Sherman wrote Grant in 1867, after Indians had killed off an entire army unit of eighty men: "We must act with vindictive earnestness against the Sioux, even to their extermination, men, women, and children. Nothing else will reach the root of the case." That is how the army proceeded against the Indians for the remainder of the century. Commanders in the Philippines, confronting elusive guerrilla fighters who blended in with village life, also found themselves embracing comparable exterminationist goals—as in the notorious order of General Jacob Smith to kill any Filipino who could carry a rifle. When asked to clarify, he said: anyone over ten. As the historian John Fiske observed in the chapter on the Pequot War in his *Beginnings of New England* (1889), when fighting savages, one had to fight savagely. Racism reinforced the continuity between counterinsurgency wars of internal and external empire.

Like post–Civil War militarism, the late-nineteenth-century ideology of race was endlessly adaptable to the purposes of power. Henry Adams recalled the conventional social science of the Gilded Age: "[R]ace ruled the conditions; conditions hardly affected race; and yet no one could tell the patient tourist what race was, or how it should be known." Muddled at its core, racist thought fostered a range of attitudes, from desire to uplift the little brown brothers to fascination with their exotic vitality to rage against their bestial savagery and ultimately to a negation of their very humanity.

The various strains of racism differed in their virulence. Paternalist uplift, often carried abroad by Christian missionaries, was saturated with racist condescension, compatible with imperial domination, and infused with universalist hubris. Nothing would do, for missionaries, but the conversion of the world. The Rev. Josiah Strong put those aspirations powerfully. His evangelical idiom blended romantic Protestant perfectionism with Anglo-Saxon supremacy and perpetual progress, all in a tone of millennial expectancy:

. . . the world is evidently about to enter on a new era . . . in this era mankind is to come more and more under Anglo-Saxon influence, and Anglo-Saxon civilization is more favorable than any other to the spread of those principles whose universal triumph is necessary to that perfection of the race to which it is destined; the entire realization of which will be the kingdom of heaven fully come on earth.

Equating Anglo-Saxons with Anglo-Americans, Strong recast the old idea that America was "God's New Israel" into an imperial mold. The dream of redeeming the world became central to the American sense of nationhood in subsequent decades.

Vitalist racism was more ambivalent, acknowledging the mysterious power of the primitive but seeking to incorporate it into agendas of white-male revitalization. Sometimes vitalist longings spilled over the banks of respectability. Admiration for primitive vitality animated breathless travelers' accounts of "swarthy bodies shining in the white sunlight." Sheer strength and energy became a source of excitement for Americans abroad or at home. The consequences could be destabilizing. The imagined barbarians' exotic sensuality and noble savagery sometimes undermined the civilizers' assumptions of superiority. While any genuine challenge to dominant norms was halting and half-conscious, the emergence of popular primitivism marked the beginnings of a reversal of values that unfolded in the 1890s and throughout the new century. Just when white Americans were murdering the last remnants of Indian resistance at Wounded Knee, and lynching scores of African-Americans throughout the South, they were also discovering new vitality in those despised racial groups.

Both vitalists and paternalists, for all their racist arrogance, at least acknowledged the common humanity they shared with supposedly backward peoples. Naturalist racism severed that bond, equating native populations with wild animals. This reflex acquired significant cultural authority. The American Museum of Natural History, established in New York City in 1877, presented exhibits of Asian, African, and North American peoples alongside reptiles, fishes, and lions. Still, even the evocation of native peoples' animality could sometimes have comparatively benign consequences. Contemplating the forcible removal of the Sioux from their hunting grounds in the Black Hills, Captain Frederick Benteen (who served with Custer) objected: "I am a Southerner, and I have noticed that you may take a negro far away from home, but he will always have an inclination to return." The same feeling, he concluded, "actuates the salmon"—and the Sioux. Christianity was not the only intellectual tradition that could foster feckless attempts at kindness toward allegedly inferior beings.

What emerged from this conceptual muddle was a racial ideology that orchestrated narratives of Anglo-Saxon progress—civilization of backward peoples on the outskirts of settled society, revitalization of an overcivilized bourgeoisie in the metropolitan centers, negation of whole continents and cultures to create those white spaces on maps that focused the projection of imperial fantasy and power. The young Theodore Roosevelt was adept at invoking those themes. Coming of age in the 1880s, Roosevelt was primed to be receptive to the emerging revival of martial virtue. To Theodore's endless regret and embarrassment, his father was one of many affluent Northerners who paid a substitute to avoid the Civil War draft; on his mother's side were two Confederate uncles. What could be more appealing than a trans-sectional ethos of military heroism?

Theodore Roosevelt became the poster boy for white-male renewal—especially among the Anglo-American elite, the effete "better sort" whom Roosevelt scorned for their decadent and effeminate ways. A nearsighted, asthmatic boy, he turned his own struggle to overcome weakness into a lesson for an entire "leadership class." The struggle began early. When "Teedie" was twelve, a doctor told him that one must "make one's body," or one's mind would languish. The boy vowed, "I'll make my body." He began to devote himself to exercise, inaugurating a regime of frenetic activity that he never abandoned. His classmates at Harvard remembered him racing about the Yard, all noise and bustle—a combination of aggressive physicality and unremarkable intellect. His quest for physical regeneration inspired his foray into the Black Hills in the early 1880s. When a foulmouthed bully in a Dakota saloon taunted him repeatedly as "four-eyes," the well-bred Easterner could take it no longer: "As I rose, I struck quick and hard with my right just to one side of the point of his jaw, hitting with my left as I straightened out, and then again with my right . . . When he went down he struck the corner of the bar with his head . . . he was senseless." In what would become a central pattern of revitalization for upper-class men, frontier experience provided fresh opportunities for virile self-assertion.

The problem was that those opportunities were becoming harder to find. Most men, even among the more affluent, did not have the resources or leisure to embark on extended junkets to the Wild West. And the West was not as wild as it used to be. So the trick was to keep moving, seeking new worlds to test oneself against and (one hoped) to conquer. Young Roosevelt's developing outlook melded the mop-up operation on the frontier with the dawning possibilities of overseas empire. Both were part of a grand world-historical pageant of progress, which he defined in the opening lines of *The Winning of the West* (1889–96), "During the past three centuries the spread of the English-speaking peoples over the world's waste spaces has been not only the most striking feature in the world's history, but also the event of all

others the most far-reaching in its effects and importance." Negating Indian lands as "waste spaces," Roosevelt created conceptually vacant lots for
white acquisition.

This rhetorical move allowed him retrospectively to applaud the Sand
Creek massacre of 1864, when Colonel John Chivington's cavalry surprised
a sleeping Cheyenne village, setting it on fire and slaughtering the inhabitants, nearly all women and children. It was, Roosevelt wrote, "on the whole
as righteous and beneficial a deed as ever took place on the frontier." Echo-
ing the naturalist reductionism of the American Museum of Natural History
(on whose board he served), Roosevelt characterized Indian life as "but a
few degrees less meaningless, squalid, and ferocious than that of the wild
beasts with whom they held joint ownership." Little wonder he felt comfortable asserting (at least privately) that "I don't go so far as to think that
the only good Indians are dead Indians, but I believe nine out of ten are,
and I shouldn't like to inquire too closely into the case of the tenth." Urbane
exterminism flowed easily from the assumption that whole populations
were little more than infestations of potentially valuable real estate.

The link between negation and extermination characterized both the Indian wars and the later wars for empire. Eventually Roosevelt himself would
locate the lineage of overseas empire in the advance of "English-speaking"
settlers across the North American continent: returning the "waste space"
of the Philippines to the Filipinos, he said, would be like giving back Arizona to the Apaches. In either case, reversing the march of progress was
unthinkable.

TR's career reveals how it was possible for an Anglo-Saxon to admire the
barbarian vigor of peoples he deemed racially inferior to his own. If overcivilization was the sickness, careful primitivism was the cure. Roosevelt
articulated this point of view: "Over-sentimentality, over softness, in fact
washiness and mushiness are the great dangers of this age and of this
people," he wrote to the psychologist G. Stanley Hall in 1899. "Unless we
keep the *barbarian virtues*, gaining the civilized ones will be of little avail."
By "barbarian virtues" Roosevelt meant courage, stoicism, and endurance—
everything that constituted the physical side of conventional manliness.
These values could easily be pressed into the service of empire.

From the imperial view, evidence of Western superiority was irrefut-
able. A signature scene in the literature of colonization involved the confrontation between dumbfounded natives and Western technology. Clocks,

compasses, magnets, photographic equipment, matches, telescopes, bilge pumps—all became tokens of the white man's mystifying power. When such encounters occurred in actuality, they often had a significant impact. In 1880, for example, a contingent of Sioux braves ventured across the border from Canada (where they had taken refuge from U.S. Army pursuit) to meet with Nelson Miles in Montana. There they encountered a telephone, which terrified them. Miles reported that when they heard distant friends speaking Dakota through the receiver, "huge drops of perspiration coursed down their bronze faces and with trembling hands they laid the instrument down." Awed by their enemies' sorcery, these strong warriors became advocates of peace.

Despite the whites' technological superiority, there was nothing inevitable about either their westward advance or their overseas expansion: both were the result of particular policies promoted by men with power, animated by popular motives. Often those motives were mercenary. Manifest Destiny and money cohabited comfortably. The paternalist commitment to civilizing the barbarians was often little more than a veneer over desires for valuable resources and investment opportunities. Rarely was this clearer than during the 1870s, when Grant adopted an Indian policy of paternalist assimilation, only to see it crumble quickly under pressure from clamorous economic interests. Like many other Americans, Grant believed that the red man was "vanishing," but that in the interval before his disappearance he might be persuaded (not coerced) to embrace the civilizing influences of Christianity and property ownership. Yet Grant's Indian Commissioner Edward Smith proved unable to sustain his commitment to Indian property-ownership amid the gold fever that erupted around the Black Hills in the late 1860s and early 1870s. The Indians' title to the land had to yield to the greed of the whites. "What shall be done with these Indian dogs in our manger?" the *Yankton* (SD) *Press & Dakotan* demanded in 1868. "They will not dig gold nor let others do it."

The newspapers' bafflement betrayed a fundamental difference in attitudes toward the land. It was a question of roaming versus owning. To ask the Indians to settle in any particular place was like asking rivers to run backward, Chief Joseph said. Confronted with the sight of Indians selling off the Black Hills in 1876, turning their sacred hunting grounds into a commodity, Crazy Horse was baffled. "One does not sell the earth on which the people walk," he insisted. Sitting Bull was equally incapable of conceiving of land as a commodity: at a Sioux Council Meeting, he mockingly proposed getting a scale and selling the earth at so much per pound. These Indian "dogs in our manger" would eventually be dispossessed of their land by force. When that dispossession was virtually complete in 1887, the Dawes Act officially reaffirmed the goal of Indian property ownership, but by breaking up and privatizing Indian lands, the law made even more real estate available to white settlers. Uplift and rapacity coexisted.

The condition of the Indian remnant was recorded by Eastern tourists. One was Mrs. Frank Leslie, the wife of a prominent magazine publisher, who gazed at a devastated people from the window of her private railroad car. As she and her party headed west from Salt Lake City in 1877, Mrs. Leslie reported that the "noble savage . . . now begins to be frequent and importunate at every station. There are women clothed upon with filth of every shade and texture, woven or skinny . . . and about half of them carrying upon their backs a formless and silent burden, which, for filthy lucre, they would unstrap and bring forward. . . . The 'braves' if they will excuse the sarcasm of so calling them, were somewhat more repulsive than the women and children, being equally dirty and more dangerous . . . Many of the women had their faces painted in Turner-esque style of coloring, and begged vociferously for money, which they clutched with no pretense of gratitude or pleasure."

Mrs. Leslie's contemptuous account overlooked the war of extermination that had reduced the Indians to begging. The conflict was then entering its final stages, which were marked by particular ferocity. The destruction of Custer and his men provoked a furious counterinsurgency campaign against the remaining Indians on the Plains. Federal troops swarmed through the Black Hills, chasing the Sioux and Cheyenne into Canada and killing or confining any resisters. Within a few years after the Battle of the Little Bighorn, Crazy Horse was dead and Sitting Bull had fled to Canada with federal troops in hot pursuit. Finally, facing starvation, Sitting Bull surrendered at Fort Buford, Dakota Territory, on July 20, 1881, along with another surviving Sioux chief, Crow King. Sitting Bull gave his rifle to his six-year-old son, telling him to surrender it to the major in charge of collecting them, saying that he wanted to be remembered as the last of his tribe to give up his weapon. Crow King, having already turned in his own rifle, asked the correspondent from the *Chicago Times* for two dollars so he could buy dolls for his daughters. Sitting Bull and his Sioux were assigned to farm twelve acres near Standing Rock. They had no agricultural tradition, and Sitting Bull could never quite get the hang of using a hoe.

The image of this proud Sioux chieftain scratching clumsily at the soil embodies the pathos of paternalist assimilation. Hunters and warriors could not be turned into farmers overnight. The dispossessed Indians were left bereft of even the mental categories they needed to know how to proceed. L. A. Huffman's photograph of a Cheyenne family huddled beside their government meat ration captures their plight. Better, most Americans thought, to avert their eyes from that sad sight and gaze instead at a mythic alternative.

SITTING BULL WAS more successful in his later career, when he turned to show business. Indeed, he had shown a theatrical flair soon after he surrendered, riding down the Missouri River on the *General Sherman*, wearing a pair of green goggles, pleading histrionically for his people, and shaking hands with the curiosity seekers who crowded onto the boat at every stop. In subsequent years he allowed himself to be exhibited at the Philadelphia YMCA and all manner of other public places—though white audiences remained ambivalent, sometimes boycotting the events to protest (actual or imagined) Sioux atrocities. Another last-ditch resister, the Apache chief Geronimo, followed a similar path. After years of bitter struggle against Miles and his men in the Southwest, he finally surrendered in 1886. A decade or so later, he had become a Christian and a celebrity, appearing at a number of world's fairs and riding in President Theodore Roosevelt's inaugural parade in 1905. We can only speculate about what these men thought they were doing, what their performances signified to them or to their people. We know more about white audience reactions.

With respect to white audiences, the larger pattern is significant: the nearly instantaneous transformation of frontier history into mass-marketed entertainment and popular mythology. The most striking example was Frederick Jackson Turner's address to the American Historical Association's annual meeting at Chicago in 1893, "The Significance of the Frontier in American History." Turner used the official closing of the frontier in 1890 as the jumping-off point for his claim that the encounter with the wilderness reshaped the European settler into an American individualist—tough, independent, resourceful, manly. "This perennial rebirth, this fluidity of American life, this expansion westward with its new opportunities, its continuous touch with the simplicity of primitive society, furnish the forces dominating American character," Turner wrote. In becoming American, the pioneering settler became more like the native population, at ease in the wild, even as he displaced the natives through his relentless westward advance. The closing of the frontier meant that there were no more Indians to displace, no more indigenous "barbarian virtues" to emulate, and no more "perennial rebirth."

Turner's imaginary frontier had been preceded by less scholarly examples of mass-marketed mythology. One was the career of William Cody, a Union Army veteran from Iowa who set up shop as a railroad grading contractor after the war. Once, when his men demanded fresh meat, he shot eleven buffalo in quick succession. The soldiers stationed nearby, to protect the advance of the railroad from Indians defending their land, were impressed by Cody's prowess. They took to calling him "Buffalo Bill." Within a few years he was the subject of a dime novel and a stage melodrama. He was also a scout for the army troops trying to drive the Sioux out of the Black Hills. Three weeks after Custer and his men were killed at the Little Bighorn, Cody shot a Cheyenne chief in the head, scalped him, and shouted: "The first scalp for Custer!" He quickly realized the theatrical possibilities of what Roosevelt would call "the winning of the West." In 1882 Cody organized "The Old Glory Blowout" in Omaha, Nebraska, an event combining stunts on horseback with a staged hunt for buffalo. The show's success convinced him to expand. By 1886, he was filling such venues as Madison Square Garden with his "Buffalo Bill's Wild West, America's National Entertainment." The show, structured as "the drama of civilization," epitomized the march-of-progress mythology beloved by Roosevelt and other empire builders. It unfolded in five set pieces: moving from primeval forest and prairie to cattle ranch and mining camp. But the fifth act was pure sensationalist spectacle: a reenactment of Custer's Last Stand.

Buffalo Bill's Wild West captured the contradictions of the emerging regenerative creed. Playing to urban crowds hungry for fantasies of adventure, it melded martial heroism and frontier manliness with industrial logistics and shrewd salesmanship. The West that Cody celebrated was hardly "wild"—it was the West of the revolver, the repeating rifle, and the railroad, all profitable commodities and triumphant expressions of the American manufacturing system. As at so many other points in this epoch, a chivalric ethos sanitized violence in the service of profitable business.

The clearest illustration of that process was the career of George Armstrong Custer himself, especially its posthumous phase. During the decades after the Little Bighorn, the man was celebrated as a veritable Chevalier de Bayard, a gallant knight *sans peur et sans reproche*—the personification of the martial valor that would regenerate American men, redeeming them from the corruptions of commerce. But in fact Custer was quite at ease in the speculative carnival that characterized Wall Street and Washington during the Gilded Age, and comfortable as well with corporate patrons. The mythmakers who presided over his ascension to martyrdom performed some of the cultural work done by post–Civil War militarism: celebrating his allegedly apolitical chivalry, they cleansed his moral meaning of any connection with money and power.

Custer would not have been anywhere near the Black Hills had it not been for the Northern Pacific Railroad, which managed to persuade the Grant administration to provide U.S. Army protection for its surveying expedition along the Yellowstone River in 1873. The presence of the U.S. Army in the region was a direct response to the demands of mining and railroad interests. The discovery of gold in the Black Hills made the building of a railroad a matter of some urgency—at least as far as its directors were concerned. Custer was on board. After the surveying expedition ended, the Northern Pacific hired him to advertise their interests by promoting the Black Hills as an agricultural utopia and pastoral dreamscape. In 1874, Grant appointed him to head an army expedition to the Black Hills, where he remained, with occasional trips back east, until his calamitous end two years later. He became involved with several speculative mining ventures in the area his regiment was patrolling, the sort of covert collusion between business and government that epitomized the seedier aspects of the Gilded Age. In February 1876 he requested an extension of his leave to attend to his affairs on Wall Street, in effect choosing his financial interests over his responsibility to his regiment. His request was turned down. Four months later Custer and all his men were dead. Fifty years on, Custer's widow, Elizabeth, still remembered the responsibility of "the Northern Pacific, to protect whose right of way my husband and his men had died. . . ." But few other Americans remembered; Custer had long before been disinfected of commercial associations, inserted into a tableau of innocence and sacrifice.

The initial public responses to news of the battle at the Little Bighorn were shock, disbelief, and rage. Word spread that the Indians had been led by a mysterious swarthy youth called "Bison," who had studied military science at West Point—nothing else could explain the triumph of savages over a crack U.S. cavalry unit. John Hay (later author of *The Bread-winners* and Theodore Roosevelt's secretary of state) wrote a bitter poem, "Miles Keogh's Horse," about the sole survivor of the battle; it was "calculated to make people kill Indians," as he confided to a friend. Hay was outraged by advocates of Indians' rights, such as Helen Hunt Jackson, whose book *A Century of Dishonor* (1881) had begun to focus remorse among educated Easterners. "I think H.H. should be a Ute prisoner for a week," Hay wrote. (Given common assumptions about Indian practices, the implications were that "H.H." should be raped and brutalized routinely.) Even Whitman penned a lugubrious "Death-Sonnet for Custer." Across the land, newspaper editors gnashed their teeth. To be sure, some criticized Custer's rashness, but most viewed the comparatively unimportant engagement as an epic struggle between civilization and barbarism. To many, the chevalier *sans peur et sans reproche* became an emblem of sectional reconciliation and the hero of an emerging race-based empire. "The North alone shall not mourn this gallant soldier. He belongs to the whole Saxon race," announced the *Richmond Whig*. Custer's apotheosis was under way.

During the next several decades, among many middle- and upper-class observers, the death of Custer became a kind of Christlike sacrifice—redeeming morally sluggish Americans from their commercial comfort and bourgeois torpor. Even Custer's most appalling actions, such as his participation with Philip Sheridan in the massacre of an entire Indian village on the Washita River, appeared in popular culture as a rescue of white women captives from a fate worse than death at the hands of howling savages. "Frank, brave, and humane, quick-witted and self-controlled, he was the beau-ideal, to use the old phrase, of the soldier," an *Atlantic Monthly* review of Elizabeth Custer's memoirs observed in 1888. "He remained young, and the geniality and freedom and warm attachment that made him popular as much as his ability" were evident in his wife's recollections. Elizabeth's efforts to canonize her husband did not go unrewarded. By the 1890s he had achieved iconic status, as a lithograph by Otto Becker of "Custer's Last Fight" (based on a painting by Cassily Adams) hung in thousands of saloons, courtesy of Anheuser-Busch Brewing Company. A reigning imperial tableau was set in place: innocent representatives of civilization, surrounded by screaming savages and soon to be massacred altogether—a set of images that called for vengeance.

The most striking evidence of Custer's apotheosis and of the eventual triumph of the militarist mythology was the contrast between Grant's indifference toward Custer and Roosevelt's admiration for him. Much to Elizabeth's annoyance, Grant took no formal notice of the disaster at the Little Bighorn. Indeed he viewed the battle (correctly) as the unfortunate result of an ambitious officer's overreaching. To the veteran of the Wilderness campaign and the siege of Petersburg, the casualties at the Little Bighorn were hardly worth noticing, and the strategic significance of the battle was virtually nonexistent. Roosevelt, whose only military experience was the comic-opera charge up San Juan Hill, took Custer more seriously, as a moral exemplar to youth. Elizabeth was grateful. "President Roosevelt once said that General Custer's name was a shining light to all the youth of America. It was worth living on to hear a great President say that and to know that a great people think it." For Roosevelt, Custer embodied the courage to plunge ahead even when confronted by overwhelming force. This was the key to his enduring significance. "Far better it is to dare mighty things," TR wrote, "than to take rank with those poor souls who neither enjoy much nor suffer much, because they live in the gray twilight that knows not victory nor defeat."

This was the militarist creed at its most vacant—the exaltation of risk as a regenerative agent, without regard to its object or its cost to others, including the soldiers under one's command. Contrasted with Grant's dismissal of Custer, Roosevelt's effusions underscored the distinction between the professional soldier and the poseur. They also revealed the transition from the memory of actual war to the fantasy of its imaginary effects.

The militarist creed played a major role in revitalizing the hegemony of the ruling class during a period of critical stress. In the 1880s, as biracial insurgencies spread across the South and labor protest erupted repeatedly in the North, chivalric posturing began to provide legitimacy for the violent reassertion of existing (but sometimes precarious) power relations—lynchings and other forms of racial terrorism in the South, the killing of striking workers in the North and West. The emergence of popular militarism sanctified the deployment of domestic militia for the purpose of keeping order at home, and the creation of an imperial navy and army for keeping order abroad. Of course the order was largely rhetorical. The use of military force to promote access to raw materials, markets, and investment opportunities in fact created a good deal of upheaval and bloodshed. But for the beneficiaries of a capitalist economic system that depended on "creative destruction," the line between order and disorder was not always easy to draw.

This was the imperial synthesis, contradictory but powerful, that emerged from the shadow of Appomattox and extended a broad appeal to middle- and upper-class Americans of all regions. But not everyone, even among the more privileged, embraced militarist renewal. Not everyone drew the same lessons from the Civil War. Indeed, some of our most creative minds resisted the martial ethic and sought less conventional models of heroism—models rooted in lived experience rather than the platitudes of millennial nationalism.

JANE ADDAMS WAS born in 1860. Her mother died when Jane was two and a half; her father became the focus of her adoration—and she of his. He was a prominent local mill owner and public figure, a member of the Illinois assembly and friend of Abraham Lincoln. "I never could hear that name without a thrill," Jane recalled. John Addams considered Lincoln "the greatest man in the world" and wept like a child when the president died. Jane grew up in a house steeped in memories and fantasies of heroism. Browsing in her father's library, she gravitated to tales of great men—Washington, Jefferson, Cromwell, Franklin, Napoleon, Plutarch's *Lives*. Her father paid her 5 cents each for reading and reporting on them. Heroism, she was allowed to imagine, was not entirely a male prerogative.

During the election campaign of 1872, President Grant and Governor Lyman Trumbull paced the grounds with John Addams, trying to win his support for their presidential bids. "We felt on those days," Jane recalled, "a connection with the great world . . . [one] much more heroic than the village world which surrounded us." Heroism implied power and even sometimes the willingness to shed blood, as John Brown had done. "I always had a secret sympathy," Jane later wrote, "with [Brown's] impatience and his determination that something should . . . happen." Attending Rockford Female Seminary, young Jane yearned for a "career that demanded larger self-sacrifice, even martyrdom, a close cousin of, but different from, heroism," as her biographer Louise Knight writes. Amid the comforts of an affluent Victorian girlhood, she felt cut off from "real life." "You do not know what life means when all the difficulties are removed!" she complained to a friend. "I am simply smothered and sickened with advantages. It is like eating a sweet dessert the first thing in the morning." After her father died in 1881, Addams feared she had lost her sense of moral purpose and drifted into neurasthenia. She was treated in Philadelphia by Dr. S. Weir Mitchell, who lectured her on her selfishness.

The problem, for Addams, was not simply suffocating affluence or oppressive patriarchy, but culture itself—especially the anemic genteel variety that sealed people off from the palpitating actualities of experience. In 1883, as a young woman passing through the East End of London on an omnibus, Addams looked down on a mob of starving people, swarming around two hucksters' carriages and clutching at the rotten food for sale. She recalled Thomas de Quincey's account of riding on the top of a speeding mail coach, seeing two lovers loitering in the road ahead, and being unable to warn them until he had remembered the appropriate quotation from the *Iliad*—"the great cry with which Achilles alarmed all Asia militant." De Quincey concluded that his classical studies had unfit him for effective action in the actual world. Addams, confronted with another disturbing scene from the top of a bus, came to the same conclusion about herself.

Neurasthenia, for her, was no vacation from self-accusation. She spent several years battling fatigue, insomnia, eyestrain, and other (probably psychosomatic) ailments, constantly berating herself for being "self-absorbed and priggish," and finally emerging from depression when she was able to formulate an alternative to her father's conventional notion of heroism—"one that included space for failure and interdependence," as Knight observes. This was the opening that put Addams on the way to the founding of Hull House, which became a community center for local democracy in Chicago, and a model for similar settlement houses throughout the country. Hull House also became an arena for a new kind of heroism, one that flourished beyond the shadow of Appomattox. Settlement-house work, like social reform in general, became an alternative to militarism for romantic young professionals who sought regeneration through authentic experience. Certainly it worked for Addams: observers described her during the early Hull House years as "keen, alert, and alive in every fiber." War was not the only way to grasp "real life." While other Progressives combined commitments to reform and empire, Addams followed a divergent path, toward anti-imperialism.

Mark Twain challenged the martial ethic more directly. When the editors of the *Century* invited him to contribute to their "Battles and Leaders of the Civil War" series in 1885, Twain penned "The Private History of a Campaign That Failed"—a forceful counterpoint to the bloviation that characterized most of the contributions to the series. The piece was a witty and ironic account—part memoir, part fabrication—of young Sam Clemens's two weeks as a Confederate irregular on the Missouri frontier at the start of the war. He and his pals in Hannibal got together one dark night and constituted themselves as a militia unit they called the Marion Rangers. They were scared young pups full of false bravado, shirking every opportunity to confront any hint of danger.

It was all boyish high jinks and low comedy until they heard hoofbeats one night when they'd been warned of a Union ambush. Someone yelled "Fire!" Clemens pointed his rifle at the shadowy horseman and pulled the trigger. A man fell from the horse; he was neither armed nor uniformed. His shirtfront was covered with blood and he mumbled for hours about his wife and children until he died. "The thought shot through me that I was a murderer; that I had killed a man—a man who had never done me any harm," Mark Twain wrote. "That was the coldest sensation that ever went through my marrow." Later when he learned that five of his friends had fired too, he felt less responsible, but still he could not get the dead man out of his mind. In the end, the incident "seemed an epitome of war; that all war must be just that—the killing of strangers against whom you feel no personal animosity; strangers whom, in other circumstances, you would help if you found them in trouble, and who would help you if you needed it." Rather than a naïve pacifism, these musings suggested Mark Twain's honest attempt to face a primal reality of impersonal, total war—a reality concealed by the cloudy rhetoric of martial regeneration. Twain's anti-imperial stance arose from his commitment to rooting his beliefs in lived experience.

The same can be said of William James. He and Holmes had been best friends in their youth, and much of James's intellectual career involved the formulation of alternatives to Holmes's amoral celebration of risk. Many of James's concerns were summed up in a single lecture, which he delivered at nearly the same time, in nearly the same place, as Holmes's tribute to "The Soldier's Faith." One April night in 1895, several hundred people gathered at the Harvard YMCA to hear James ask: "Is Life Worth Living?" The philosopher was in top form. His reputation had soared since the publication in 1890 of his two-volume *Principles of Psychology*, which both established the academic legitimacy of the discipline and revolutionized many of its assumptions. In three years he would be invited to give the Gifford Lectures at Edinburgh University, which would result in *The Varieties of Religious Experience*. Beyond *Varieties* lay his philosophical explorations in radical empiricism and pragmatism. But despite the wide range of his curiosity, nearly all his preoccupations were present in that YMCA lecture. Asking "Is Life Worth Living?" allowed James to gesture toward all his major themes—the centrality of chance, choice, and moral struggle; the pragmatic value of religious belief; the fascination with "wildness" as well as with its redemption. Unifying them all was the visceral urgency embodied in James's title. No one could mistake this lecture for an academic exercise. Everything, for James, boiled down to the question of how to escape the enveloping fear that life was essentially meaningless—how to get out of bed in the morning and get on with the business of living. This was the kind of courage that interested him. Its enemy was not cowardice but ennui.

"My words are to deal only with that metaphysical *tedium vitae* which is peculiar to reflecting men," James announced. It was especially peculiar to James's generation of educated Americans, for whom positivistic science had blown like a frigid wind across the intellectual landscape—dispelling the comforting warmth of inherited faith, reducing reality to the precisely observable and measurable, challenging familiar ideas of morality and freedom. James insisted that the positivist case against religious faith was not proven. It was still intellectually permissible to believe in "the existence of an unseen order of some kind in which the riddle of the natural order may be found explained." What was no longer possible was the old dogmatic certitude—but that was less a loss than a gain, an opening to the enchanting world of "maybe." It was a world where almost anything was possible, even a heterodox god—a finite, unfinished deity-in-process who needed human beings as much as the other way around. Uncertainty was the key to the ethic of maybe; "not a victory is gained, not a deed of faithfulness or courage is done, except upon a maybe," James said. Risk was the essence of life.

While Holmes reduced risk to battlefield heroics, James's conception was subtler. For him the risk of belief in an "unseen order"—religious belief— was the bet with the biggest payoff. James characterized the stakes starkly: "If this life be not a real fight, in which something is eternally gained for the universe by success, it is no better than a game of private theatricals from which one may withdraw at will. But it *feels* like a real fight—as if there were something really wild in the universe which we, with all our idealities and faithfulnesses, are needed to redeem." Betting on belief brought revitalization in this world rather than salvation in the next. This activist reworking of Pascal's Wager lay at the core of James's thought. He subjected religious truths to the pragmatic test, evaluating them with respect to their consequences—which, at least in his own case, made life worth living.

But why did life have to be "a real fight" in order to be worth living? The question pushes us back into the biography of a man who sat out the "real fight" of his generation, the Civil War, while his best friend and two of his brothers went and were wounded. James lived in the shadow of Appomattox, too. More than almost any American of his generation, he was fascinated by personal energy and its sources of renewal. He longed for manly testing; he challenged the flight from pain. But unlike Holmes, whose stoicism never transcended the celebration of soldiers' valor, James took his own exploration of physical courage in more profound directions. He sought to recover the stratum of hardness in the Christian tradition, the tragic sense of irredeemable "world-pain" that could not be wished away by flabby utilitarian formulations. And he never equated masculinity with martial virtue. On the contrary: when the next war came, James would reject imperialism; ultimately he would seek "a moral equivalent of war." While he, too, longed for regeneration, he defined it more capaciously and humanely than most of his contemporaries.

Jane Addams, William James, and Mark Twain preserved creative alternatives to the discourse of renewal through war. Other visions of political regeneration aspired to create a cooperative commonwealth, an alcohol-free America, or a Kingdom of God on earth—or all three. Some were more benign than others. Some challenged dominant norms; others reinforced them. All had to grapple with the vagaries and demands of the marketplace.

The decades after the Civil War saw the emergence of a freewheeling entrepreneurial society, where capital was unregulated by government and government was manipulated by businessmen to serve their own ends. Crafty speculators, long demonic figures in republican lore, became figures of public fascination and covert admiration—Jay Cooke, the plunger; Jim Fisk, the spender; Jay Gould, the plotter. The great trust builders of the middle and later nineteenth century—Cornelius Vanderbilt, Andrew Carnegie, John D. Rockefeller—enjoyed greater respectability, but they too were little more than freebooting robber barons, in Matthew Josephson's famous phrase. They squeezed competitors dry, smashed unions, and bribed legislatures wholesale. Concentrated capital was responsible only to itself, a raw power that profoundly shaped public policy, influencing every branch of government at every level. Money talked—not for the first time in American politics, but more authoritatively than ever before. No wonder chivalric poseurs succumbed to its insinuations.

CHAPTER 2

The Mysterious Power of Money

✦

Even amid the speculative mania of the Gilded Age, the spread of a money economy was uneven and slow. Farmers and small tradesmen still often resorted to barter. For many Americans in the 1870s, cash was scarce and money exuded an aura of mystery. It could be quantified into apparently precise amounts, yet it remained abstract and arbitrary, a spectral power. This was especially so when it took the form of capital at interest. More than a century earlier, in "Advice to a Young Tradesman" (1748), Benjamin Franklin had summarized the magical power of money to reproduce itself: "Money can beget money, and its offspring can beget more, and so on. Five shillings turned is six, turned again it is seven and threepence, and so on, till it becomes a hundred pounds. The more there is of it, the more it produces every turning, so that profits rise quicker and quicker." Franklin's aphorisms were common currency among Gilded Age Americans. But most could merely dream of quick profits, and only a handful could make money beget money.

Those fortunate few were the capitalists who transformed the American landscape and social order, provoking fascination and fury among the wider population. Despite their attempts to align themselves with the forces of stability, the titans of capital could never quite shake their association with social upheaval. They were magicians of money—to master its mysteries was to exercise an occult power. Nearly all the most successful either had capital to start with or else figured out how to acquire and increase it from an early age. This did not necessarily require hard work, but it did require shrewd bargaining, inside dope, and friends in high places. The spectacle was rarely edifying, but it could be made to seem so. A life of commercial chicanery could be repackaged as a noble assault on adversity. Even P. T. Barnum titled his life story *Struggles and Triumphs*. This was the sort of moral posturing that has given Victorians a bad name. Leading capitalists (including Barnum) shared a fundamental insight with their severest critics (including

Karl Marx): they knew that capital, not labor, was the key to economic success. During the first Gilded Age, as in more recent times, moralists penned
paeans to work while the rich went about their business, largely oblivious to
conventional pieties.

The rest of the population remained divided in mind, fascinated by
money but fearful of its corrupting effects. The fascination was all but inevitable. A country lurching headlong into industrial development presented
myriad opportunities for the ambitious or the merely greedy. Absence of
Old World constraints meant the magic of money was potentially democ-
ratized. Longings to experience its transformative effects could be more
widely satisfied. Any white male, at least in principle, could take a shot at
the main chance. Men and women both could participate in the promise
of regeneration through purchase—the fantasy at the heart of the embryonic consumer culture, the faith that paralleled (and sometimes parodied)
the older promises of salvation. Peddlers fanned out across the countryside,
selling patent medicines and other products that exuded an aura of the mysterious and a prospect of personal transformation.

Still, old suspicions died hard. In popular and often anti-Semitic tradition, money was associated with secret deals, sharp practice, invisible
wealth acquired through trickery and guile rather than productive labor.
The retail experience of commerce provoked mixed feelings as well. To suspicious customers, selling could seem to be a form of seduction, and peddlers to bring a sexual charge to their transactions with female consumers.
Peddlers were often Jews, whose ethnic identity—combined with their mobility and marginality—intensified anxieties about their motives. For many
Americans, well into the post–Civil War era, the very act of participating in
a market economy was fraught with ambivalent fantasy. Whether it involved
speculation in mining or real estate or paper, or simply retail purchase, engagement with the market evoked dreams of sudden self-transformation,
and fears that the transaction was nothing more than a trick.

ANXIETIES SURROUNDING THE spread of a market economy focused on the figure of the confidence man, the trickster who manipulated
appearances to bilk the unwary and pocket the change. Schemes for making
big money overnight pervaded American market culture from earliest colonial days; the European settlement of the New World, despite all the talk
about godly communities and holy commonwealths, was mostly little more

than a series of risky real estate speculations. But while fascination with fast money was not new, it reached a kind of crescendo during the Gilded Age. So it was altogether fitting that Colonel Beriah Sellers, the protagonist of the novel that gave the age its name, was a purveyor of can't-miss investment scams for everything from Tennessee land to eyewash—a quintessential manipulator of appearances, as Mark Twain and Charles Dudley Warner observed in *The Gilded Age* (1873): "The Colonel's tongue was a magician's wand that turned dried apples into figs and water into wine as easily as it could change a hovel into a palace and present poverty into future riches." This confidence man brings nothing but disaster in his wake for the credulous Squire Hawkins and his son.

The Gilded Age was one of many warnings against misplaced confidence in nineteenth-century American literature, ranging from formulaic moral tracts to the multiplying subtleties of Herman Melville's *The Confidence Man* (1857). As early as 1842, Charles Dickens had found American society pervaded by an atmosphere of "Universal Distrust," and the shape-shifting protagonist of Melville's novel, in his guise as a barber, posts a sign in his shop: "No Trust"—in contemporary parlance, no credit. Yet the other side of universal mistrust was a well-nigh universal need for trust. American entrepreneurs depended heavily on borrowed capital to finance business ventures, as Twain and Warner acknowledged in their ironic peroration: "Beautiful credit! The foundation of modern society. Who shall say that this is not the golden age of mutual trust, of unlimited reliance upon human promises?" Ambitious businessmen were valued in accordance with how much they could be "trusted"—how much, that is, they could persuade a bank to lend them. Indebtedness signified membership in the community of the creditworthy, as the young John D. Rockefeller concluded delightedly after he had been trusted by a Cleveland bank for $2,000. Twain and Warner cite "a distinguished speculator in lands and mines" who remarked: "I wasn't worth a cent two years ago, and now I owe two millions of dollars." The parody left the point intact: an expansive economy required a nearly "unlimited reliance upon human promises."

Yet as the authors of *The Gilded Age* knew, those promises often proved false, and the loans they spawned went bad. A great deal of waste, fraud, and corruption went into the making of the modern American economy, and much of it was concentrated on Wall Street. Railroad stocks, the high-tech stock of the day, epitomized the lurching inefficiency of economic advance. Throughout the 1870s and 1880s, railroads were ridiculously over-capitalized; their stock sold for top dollar while their roadbeds disintegrated and their locomotives lay rusting in ditches. In 1884, *Moody's* reported that $4 billion worth of railroad stock was pure water, in the idiom of the day—that is, artificially inflated beyond its stated ("par") value. But value was an elusive concept. From one point of view, stocks' values depended on what investors would pay for them. In any case, the railroad builders pressed on: between the Civil War and the stock market crash of 1893 they laid 150,000 miles of new track. The transcontinental railroads in particular—the Union Pacific, the Northern Pacific, the Texas and Pacific—continued to capture investors' fancy. Their inflated prices expressed the imperial aspirations of Wall Street financiers after Appomattox.

Out in the countryside, attitudes toward venture capitalism were more complex. During the post–Civil War years, as never before, high-rolling speculation provoked ambivalent fascination among the American populace. Wall Street was a madhouse, a witches' cauldron, critics charged; predatory traders evoked Hobbesian visions of nihilism. Yet there was an undeniable if crude vitality about some of the more fabulous plungers: the tubby womanizer Jim Fisk, a king of the dudes whose "flash" drew a thousand mourners to his funeral; the ferocious Cornelius Vanderbilt, who preferred ruining rivals to suing them. Some, like Vanderbilt and Daniel Drew, a psalm-singing Methodist who made millions by selling watered stock, exuded a risk-taking virility that transformed them from confidence men (at least in the public eye) to Napoleons of finance. Others, like Jay Gould, a sly and secretive man who raised exotic orchids, epitomized the effeminate deceitfulness associated in the male imagination with money manipulators. Whatever their personal style, these capitalists financed a huge industrial explosion even as they systematically corrupted the polity, watering stock and bribing legislatures wholesale, preaching laissez-faire while they depended on government for loans, land, and subsidies.

Such hypocritical freebooters could never be more than temporary heroes. After the stock market crashed in September 1873, the country slipped into five and a half years of the worst depression in its history. Hordes of unemployed men thronged the highways in search of work, while those who kept their jobs faced draconian wage cuts. The big-shot speculators' cultural stock plunged almost as quickly as their portfolios. Even Jay

Cooke, who had made himself into a war hero by mass-marketing Union war bonds, became a target of public scorn when his deeply overextended Northern Pacific securities collapsed in price, touching off the panic that led to the crash. By 1877, the Wall Street money men were in bad odor with the rest of the country.

Yet even while the 1870s depression reinforced the seedy reputation of speculators, a new and even more mysterious form of money manipulation was emerging in the commodities markets of the Middle West. Their epicenter was the Chicago Board of Trade (founded in 1848), where traders transformed the solid realities of wheat, corn, cattle, and hogs into airy abstractions with unpredictably fluctuating money value. The new practice of trading in "futures" involved betting on the prospective rise or fall in the price of beef or pork, without ever having to deliver the steak or bacon. A successful bet could produce plenty of hard cash, but the rules of the game remained opaque to the uninitiated. A guidebook to the Chicago Board of Trade, published in 1891, put the matter bluntly: "from this [visitors'] gallery a perfect view may be had of the operations on the floor, operations which it would be impossible to describe, and impossible for the average visitor to understand." Seldom had the power of money to beget money been so flagrantly mystified.

The alchemical promise of sudden self-transformation gave money a centrifugal force and a corrosive edge. It could dissolve settled communities and social bonds, send young men spinning off from their ancestral seats in search of fresh possibilities, clothe reprobates and rakes in raiments of respectability. A universal standard of value, money was also a universal solvent of other standards of value. Custom, tradition, morality—all dissolved, as Karl Marx and Friedrich Engels said, "in the icy waters of egotistical calculation." This was the heartless world from which, moralists urged, the Victorian home could be a haven. Still, the market had more alluring connotations as well. Since the early Middle Ages, the marketplace had been associated with openness to unsettling experience, to encounters with the strange, the foreign, the new. Exotic spices, silks, oils, and elixirs offered unfamiliar forms of sensuous enjoyment, possibly even personal transformation. Peddlers and other trickster figures proliferated on the margins, evoking visions of an endlessly liminal self—a self in constant transition from one identity to another. The marketplace exuded a carnival spirit of excess. Indeed, in European towns the market was often located on the same town square where carnival itself was held, where the Lord of Misrule was crowned and traditional hierarchies upended.

When market exchange spilled over the boundaries of a particular time and place, as it did in the fluid expansive economy of the mid-nineteenth-century United States, sales were not confined to Saturdays on the square. The carnival was in town all the time. American society began to approximate Melville's vision—a milling mob of conniving confidence men and questing consumers, rendered credulous by their dream of magical self-transformation through purchase. Money was more than merely a means of keeping people afloat, more even than the key to new realms of pleasure; it was also a mechanism for reinventing the self. It financed fresh starts, new sets of surface appearances.

In a mobile, anonymous society, apparently trivial impressions acquired heavier cultural weight. How often, in late-nineteenth-century literature and life, does an article of clothing hold the key to a transformation of one's condition in life? One thinks of the new suit that signified Horatio Alger's Ragged Dick had achieved respectability, the soft gloves that embodied sensuous experience and status ascent for Theodore Dreiser's Sister Carrie, or the light brown hat coveted by the young Hamlin Garland—his emblem of longings for escape from a bleak prairie boyhood. Fashion, so often dismissed as mere superficial display by moralists, turned out to be an instrument for refashioning the self.

Often the promise of personal transformation went deeper, toward an inner alchemical change, a regeneration. Indeed, by the mid-nineteenth century, patent-medicine advertising began to resemble a materialist version of the Protestant devotional literature surrounding the conversion experience. Testimonials from satisfied customers resembled the cries of the converted, rescued from spiritual torment. Many advertisements asserted that before ingesting the elixir in question, the patent-medicine customer had suffered from boredom, lassitude, apathy, and overwhelming depression—the dark night of the soul that Protestant believers experienced before conversion. But in the patent-medicine literature, the root of this soul-sickness was physical, and so was its remedy. A Childs catarrh tonic advertisement from 1877 promised nothing less than relief from despair: if catarrh is allowed to persist, untreated by Childs, "the patient becomes nervous, his voice is harsh and unnatural; he feels disheartened; memory loses her power; judgment her seat, and gloomy forebodings hang overhead,—hundreds, yea, thousands in such circumstances feel that to die would be a relief—and many do even cut the thread of life to end their sorrows." The point is not that everyone took this hyperbole literally but that the language of rebirth had begun to refocus from soul to body, and from religion to commerce. Selves could be revitalized through consumption as well as conversion. So the advertising industry claimed.

Not everyone was convinced. Believing Christians insisted that there was no regeneration apart from conversion; the patent-medicine version was little more than parody—reinvention, if anything, rather than rebirth. And while money allowed for the reinvention of the self, it also threatened the cherished belief that there was any true or enduring sense of self apart from the realm of manipulated appearances. The animating impulse of Protestantism was a distrust of display and ritual as foolish mummery that only distracted the believer from the direct encounter with God. From this view, the truly regenerated self was a sincere and transparent self, whose outward conduct corresponded perfectly with his inner experience of grace. By the mid-nineteenth century, the Protestant desire for individual sincerity had been extended through the encounter with market exchange into a vision of social transparency, of a society of plain speakers who said what they meant and meant what they said.

At about the same time, theology and morality merged in the Protestant ethic of disciplined achievement. The sincere self was also a hardworking self—so hardworking, in fact, that he produced his own success, his own social identity. He was, in short, a self-made man. For moralists, this paragon of autonomy provided a crucial centripetal force against the centrifugal energies of markets and monies. The ideals embodied in self-made manhood, it was hoped, would diffuse throughout society and stabilize the sorcery of the marketplace, contain its carnival spirit. Yet the sorcery kept resurfacing. After all, ascent to the lordship of capital required more than diligence—and less than sincerity. Success was a slippery business. Titans of industry, who seemed the apotheosis of solidity and reliability, turned out at crucial moments to be confidence men.

AMONG THE MOST remarkable magicians of money was the steel magnate, Andrew Carnegie, whose companies eventually gave birth to the world's first billion-dollar corporation, United States Steel, in 1901.

Carnegie, an out-of-work weaver's son, was one of the few rich Americans who could claim to be a self-made man. But, to his credit, he refused to do so, locating the source of his wealth, indeed of any millionaire's wealth, in "the community." By which he meant he was in the right place at the right time: Pittsburgh in the 1870s, when the shift from iron to steel was about to take off. But there was more to it than that. From the outset, Carnegie had a knack for ingratiating himself with corporate mentors and turning them into dependable cronies. In fact he had become a very rich man even before he got into the steel business, mainly by capitalizing on inside tips and timely stock sales.

Carnegie was born in 1835, in the upstairs room of a weaver's cottage in Dumfermline, Scotland. His father was never too ambitious, but his mother was headstrong, and when the linen trade collapsed in the late 1840s she packed the family off to Allegheny City, Pennsylvania (near Pittsburgh), where some Carnegie cousins had already settled. Her thirteen-year-old son began work as a bobbin boy and later a boiler attendant at a cotton mill. Embarrassed by his broken-down dad, he became a mama's boy—prim, priggish, and eager to move from the factory floor to the office. He took a job as a telegraph messenger boy, filled in for an off-duty operator, and quickly demonstrated his good ear. He won a job as a full-time "smooth operator" when he was still only fifteen, receiving a bonus of a dollar a week from six Pittsburgh newspapers for copying transatlantic dispatches. That money "I considered my own," Carnegie remembered. "It did not go to the family support. It was my first capital."

The way to increase one's capital was to become a company man. The Pennsylvania Railroad was discovering the importance of the telegraph to its operations, and Tom Scott, the Western Division superintendent, hired Carnegie as his personal operator. As Carnegie's biographer David Nasaw observes, the younger man "tied himself to Scott's coattails and never let go." The relationship soon began to bring rewards. Well positioned in an industry that was about to take off, Scott could invest in companies that were poised to benefit from the railroad business. One of these was the Adams Express Company. Scott loaned Carnegie the money to buy ten shares at $50 each. Carnegie received guaranteed dividends of $10 a month—a 24 percent return on his investment.

The arrival of his first dividend check was a revelation. "I shall remember that check as long as I live," he wrote in his autobiography. "It gave me the first penny of revenue from capital—something that I had not worked for with the sweat of my brow. 'Eureka!' I cried. 'Here's the goose that lays the golden eggs.' " He showed the check to his friends, all of whom were amazed by the magic of investment capital: "How money could make money, how, without any attention from me, this mysterious golden visitor should come, led to much speculation on the part of the young fellows, and I was for the first time hailed as a 'capitalist.' " It was the first of a series of deals that made Carnegie a rich young man. His earliest and most lucrative enterprises involved manipulating money; only later did he turn to making steel. The man who would come to personify productive industry began as a beneficiary of crony capitalism.

Still in his twenties, Carnegie learned the art of insider trading. With Scott and Scott's boss J. Edgar Thomson, he bought shares in the Woodruff Sleeping Car Company just before it was enriched by a contract with the Pennsylvania Railroad. The pattern was in place: Carnegie avoided risky railroad stocks and instead invested in companies that supplied the railroads' needs: coal, wood, iron, oil. Carnegie soon was flush and ready to move into the Pittsburgh iron business. As the railroad frenzy accelerated after Appomattox, Carnegie refined the arts of insider trading. He maneuvered to make his iron company the beneficiary of sweetheart deals between the Pennsylvania Railroad and its suppliers, such as the Keystone Bridge Company. He accumulated capital by trading shares in overcapitalized companies and skimming profits from inflated stock prices. He set sail for London, selling Pennsylvania Railroad bonds to Baring Brothers and J. P. Morgan's father, Junius—raising money for roads that were unbuilt and unnecessary, acquiring a reputation less as a builder than as a broker.

Technology and tariff policy combined to turn Carnegie in a new direction. He had toyed with various steelmaking methods, but none had panned out. When the tariff of 1870 placed a duty of $28 a ton on imported steel, though, the federal government opened unprecedented opportunities for American steelmakers to sell in a protected market. In 1872, Carnegie toured Henry Bessemer's steel plant in Sheffield, England. That was enough for him. He was ready to invest in Bessemer steel. He built a steel plant in Braddock, Pennsylvania, outside Pittsburgh, and with a born crony's talent for flattery named it after his old boss at Pennsylvania, the Edgar Thomson Works. When the Panic of 1873 hit, Carnegie sold all his interests in other businesses and focused on the E.T. plant. Demand for steel rebounded and then soared.

The shift from iron to steel combined with the resurgent railroad boom to underscore Carnegie's accuracy regarding the source of his wealth: the "community"—the convergence of a particular place and a particular historical moment. Pittsburgh had everything a budding steel magnate could want: rivers and railroads for transporting raw materials and finished goods, an abundant supply of skilled and unskilled labor (increasingly, the Slavs, whom locals labeled "Hungarians"), and easy access to tons of coal, which could be turned into coke to heat Carnegie's blast furnaces. The big coke man in Pittsburgh was short in stature—and mean as hell. Carnegie early on recognized Henry Clay Frick as a potential rival and sought to form alliances with him, eventually bringing him into the steel business as manager of his Homestead plant and partner in the enlarging firm of Carnegie Steel. Throughout the 1880s, despite dips in the business cycle, Carnegie's steel business was riding high, increasing its productivity by over 800 percent. Much of this was squeezed directly out of the workers by keeping wages low, hours long, breaks infrequent, and the threat of layoffs constant.

Other titans' success was equally dependent on manipulating money. Consider John D. Rockefeller Sr. He specialized in the extraction and refinement of oil, certainly a key ingredient in the stew of industrial revolution. He supplied Americans of modest means with kerosene—"the poor man's light." But he made most of his money by shrewdly deploying large amounts of capital to squeeze rivals and purchase legislatures. He loved the game of capitalism, but he always played with loaded dice, as his critic Ida Tarbell observed. Rockefeller's pious rectitude concealed his diffusion of moral responsibility through the complex delegation of authority. Secrecy and deception were central to his success, and he learned how to orchestrate those skills at new levels of subtlety. In the corporate and legal labyrinths of the late nineteenth century, one can see the notions of truth and innocence beginning to be transformed into the notions of credibility and deniability. Though Rockefeller and his generation remained attached to a Protestant moral idiom, their institutional creations rendered it less applicable to everyday life. Anyone who blocked his implacable will to profit was overwhelmed through secrecy, deception, and the brutal exercise of market power. And if the facade of deniability cracked, this paragon was perfectly willing to prevaricate under oath, as he did in testifying before

Judge Kenesaw Mountain Landis in 1907, when Standard Oil was on trial for taking illegal rebates.

Ultimately Rockefeller's confidence games proved wildly successful. At its height, his fortune outstripped those of all the other robber barons—even Carnegie's, by a hair. By 1913, Rockefeller's net worth totaled nearly a billion dollars, or 2 percent of the U.S. gross national product; a comparable share today would give Rockefeller a net worth of $190 billion, or more than triple that of the richest man in the contemporary world, Bill Gates. To be sure, Rockefeller was ultimately more than a mere accumulator. His world-view was softened by his embrace of the doctrine of stewardship. "God gave me my money," he asserted; the implication of this apparent arrogance was that the money was not his to keep: he was only its temporary steward, charged with distributing it to worthy causes and recipients. This belief was the spiritual engine of his later career in philanthropy. But Rockefeller did not make that shift in earnest until his retirement in the 1890s.

The younger Rockefeller was less concerned with giving money away than with systematically acquiring it. His father, William "Doc" Rockefeller, was a smooth-talking purveyor of trinkets and magic elixirs—the sort of shape-shifting confidence man who flourished on the margins of the mobile mid-nineteenth-century marketplace. His absences and infidelities provoked his son's resentment, but his flamboyant displays of cash impressed the boy with the magical power of money. Flashing it constantly, Bill made money seem (his son's biographer observes) like "God's bounty, the blessed stuff that relieved all of life's cares." John D. Rockefeller, the quintessential "rational capitalist," was animated from the outset by a fascination for money as a kind of fetish object. The key to his success was managing his secret passion. "I was a young man," he remembered, "when I got my first look at a bank-note of any size." His employer in Cleveland showed it to him and then put it in the safe. "As soon as he was gone I unlocked the safe, and taking out that note, stared at it with open eyes and mouth, and then replaced it and double-locked the safe. It seemed like an awfully large sum to me, an unheard of amount, and many times during the day did I open that safe to gaze longingly at the note." The origins of the Standard Oil Trust could be traced to a young man's erotic longings for money.

But Rockefeller knew that fitful longings were insufficient; he was determined to make the "blessed stuff" predictable. Money may have been magical, but like other forms of magic it could be controlled, directed.

That was what John discovered when he first lent money at interest: the results astounded him. "The impression was gaining ground with me that it was a good thing to let the money be my slave and not make myself a slave to money," Rockefeller recalled. Fine words, but the task was easier described than done. To harness money's unpredictable power required calm, unrelenting concentration—which Rockefeller possessed in preternatural abundance. Throughout the decades following the Civil War, Rockefeller steadily expanded his domination of the oil industry, from the pump to the pipeline to the country store. Creating a successful monopoly, he removed the risk from a risky business—at least for Standard Oil and its shareholders.

Rockefeller's mastery of the market mirrored his mastery of self. From childhood to old age, he was obsessed with control: of himself, of his environment. Even his admirers, such as the journalist William O. Inglis, admitted there was "something bordering on the superhuman, perhaps the inhuman," in Rockefeller's "unbroken, mechanical perfection of schedule." Reacting against his father's unreliability, he embraced his pious mother's Protestant ethic with a fervent and lifelong enthusiasm.

Rockefeller embodied the contradictions of Christian capitalism in the Gilded Age. Like other forms of Protestantism, his Baptist faith celebrated sincerity and demonized deception, envisioning a righteous community of plain-speaking believers who treated each other fairly and honestly, who said what they meant and meant what they said. Yet Rockefeller's success depended on the deceitful manipulation of appearances, on conforming to the letter while evading the spirit of the law. The world of Standard Oil was governed by the motto of his partner Henry Flagler: "Do unto others as they would do unto you—and do it first." This was Christianity in reverse. Rockefeller used his mother's religiosity to cloak conduct as dishonest and selfish as his father's.

Yet Rockefeller also epitomized the virtues of the self-made man—the paragon that moralists habitually invoked to exorcise the demon of his alter ego, the confidence man. In many ways one could hardly find a fitter exemplar of the pieties in Victorian advice literature. Rockefeller's relentless work habits, his rigid self-discipline, and his obsessive thrift all made him a model of the upright businessman. So did his determination to shield his family from the corruptions of "the world." His wife and children occupied a separate domestic realm, defined sharply against the amoral chaos of the market. When business drew him away from the hearthside, he wrote his wife longing letters, declaring that "the world is full of Sham, Flattery, and Deception and *home* is a haven of rest and freedom." It was a standard formulation, the stuff of Sunday sermons and domestic tracts, and betrayed no hint of awareness that its author was himself a master of deception. Rockefeller's divided self drew neat divisions between market and morality, combining secret passion with calculating reserve.

Despite vast differences in personal style, Carnegie and Rockefeller had much in common. Eventually both men turned to systematic philanthropy, contributing to the common good even as they disregarded it in their business practices. Both shared a tendency to conflate their own interests with those of society and indeed humanity at large, as well as a talent for self-deception that dissolved moral ambivalence in a warm bath of ideological certitude. In this they were no different from other captains of commerce in their own time and ours. Both publicly disdained speculation; both privately profited from it. Both proclaimed their devotion to free-market principles while they depended on government support, ranging from tariffs and other subsidies to state-sponsored violence. Both distanced themselves from the decisions of their subordinates; neither had a clue what life was like for the typical worker in any of the enterprises they owned. Privilege underwrote their calm as they stood at the center of the storms sweeping through American economic life. This was not how most businessmen experienced the Gilded Age.

NOT MANY AMERICAN men, even among the comparatively prosperous classes, were as able as Carnegie and Rockefeller to master the tensions at the core of their culture. Success manuals acknowledged the persistent problem of indiscipline, the need to channel passion to productive ends. Often the language of advice literature was sexually charged. In *The Imperial Highway* (1881), Jerome Bates advised:

> [K]eep cool, have your resources well in hand, and reserve your strength until the proper time arrives to exert it. There is hardly any trait of character or faculty of intellect more valuable than the power of self-possession, or presence of mind. The man who is always "going off" unexpectedly, like an old rusty firearm, who is easily fluttered and discomposed at the appearance of some unforeseen emergency; who

has no control over himself or his powers, is just the one who is always
in trouble and is never successful or happy.

The assumptions behind this language are fascinating and important to
an understanding of middle- and upper-class Americans in the Gilded Age.
Like many other purveyors of conventional wisdom—ministers, physicians,
journalists, health reformers—authors of self-help books assumed a psychic
economy of scarcity. For men, this broad consensus of popular psychology
had sexual implications: the scarce resource in question was seminal fluid,
and one had best not be diddling it away in masturbation or even nocturnal emissions. This was easier said than done, of course, as Bates indicated,
since men were constantly addled by insatiable urges, always on the verge of
losing self-control—the struggle to keep it was an endless battle with one's
own darker self. Spiritual, psychic, and physical health converged. What
Freud called " 'civilized' sexual morality" fed directly into the "precious
bodily fluids" school of health management. The man who was always " 'going off' unexpectedly, like an old rusty firearm," would probably be sickly
as well as unsuccessful—sallow, sunken-chested, afflicted by languorous
indecision (which was how Victorian health literature depicted the typical
victim of what was called "self-abuse").

But as this profile of the chronic masturbator suggests, scarcity psychology had implications beyond familiar admonitions to sexual restraint.
Sexual scarcity was part of a broader psychology of scarcity; the need to
conserve semen was only the most insistently physical part of a much more
capacious need to conserve psychic energy. As Bates advised, the cultivation
of "self-possession" allowed you to "keep your resources well in hand, and
reserve your strength until the proper time arrives to exert it." The implica-
tion was that there was only so much strength available to meet demanding
circumstances and achieve success in life. The rhetoric of "self-possession"
had financial as well as sexual connotations. To preserve a cool, unruffled
presence of mind (to emulate Rockefeller, in effect) was one way to stay
afloat on the storm surges of the business cycle.

The object of this exercise, at least for men, was personal autonomy—
the ownership of one's self. Only in the United States was it "comparatively
easy" for a middle-class man to achieve pecuniary independence, observed
a *Harper's* contributor in 1894. To do so, "a man must steadily earn an excess of what will provide for his daily wants; he must employ his mind, be

commonly educated, capable of some self-discipline. He must be, in short, what the mass of Americans are in intelligence and enterprise, and what they are not in thrift and monetary appreciation." Slow accumulation was preferable to sudden riches, which were likely to turn business into passion, and passion finally into monomania. A "manly man" did not fear poverty or disaster except as it affected his wife and children—for their sake, investments had to be chosen conservatively. The bottom line was to underwrite the larger aim of independence: "no man can be otherwise independent who is not pecuniarily so." The dependent man "must smile on those he hates, he must extend his hand where he would strike, he must speak pleasantly with a curse in his throat, because he is ever seeking work . . . he wears dependence like a yoke." Independence, in contrast, kept a man "dignified and self-respecting, above the need of asking for favors, above all the inevitable meannesses of poverty." Thrift and forethought, in other words, were necessary (though not sufficient) to manliness.

But it was impossible to separate manliness from womanliness, or from the larger context of a culture that was created and transmitted in large part by women. According to the dominant Victorian ethos in the post–Civil War decades, the home—the domain of the mother—was supposed to provide many contradictory services to the bourgeois family. It was to be a haven from the market and a school for entrepreneurial success, a refuge for authentic feeling and an arena for status display. Despite official claims, there was never any way to isolate the bourgeois household from the corrosive powers of cash.

So it should come as no surprise that the Victorian household was a major contested terrain when it came to the meaning of money. Husbands and wives alike were entangled in issues of saving and spending. Generally the struggle was unequal, given the typical (though not universal) male control over the money supply. Still, it was a struggle, and both sides had accusations to make. Imprudent investments as well as improvident housekeeping could start the family on the road to ruin. Cigars and stag outings could waste as much money as ball gowns and silver slippers. From either partner's point of view, the citadel of thrift—the bourgeois household—was under siege.

Thrift, a keystone of the Protestant ethic, faced challenges from several quarters. In most cities, the sporting crowd was a constant presence, tempting family men away from their firesides to fritter away small fortunes with cards and dice. This at any rate was the great fear shared by custodians of

conventional morality, and there was no doubt much truth to it—sharpers
fleeced many men of whole paychecks or more, with ruinous consequences
for themselves and their families. Gambling was part of a larger fascination
with getting rich quick—the same instinct that drove men to join the speculative frenzy of the stock market in search of overnight wealth, or to crowd
into Nevada gold camps in search of a "lucky strike." As Henry Ward
Beecher observed, "a Speculator on the exchange, and a gambler at his
table, follow one vocation only with different instruments. . . . Both burn
with unhealthy excitement . . . they have a common distaste for labor . . .
neither would scruple in any hour to set his whole being on the edge of ruin,
and going over, to pull down, if possible, a hundred others." From the viewpoint of scarcity psychology, any sort of prolonged excitement was probably
an unhealthy depletion of limited vital energy. The most flagrant exploitation of this "unhealthy excitement" was the lottery, which demoralized the
poor with its false promises of instant success, encouraging their "neglect
of business and general shiftlessness." Hence by 1890, lotteries had been
forbidden in all nations that considered themselves enlightened and every
state in the Union except Louisiana, from which a state lottery continued
to extend its appeal. The siren song of something for nothing was never
completely silenced.

The appeal of fashion was equally seductive, and equally injurious to
thrift. Since the eighteenth century, republican moralists had railed against
the noxious influence of extravagance in dress. By the post–Civil War era,
the misogynist assumptions of this critique had become explicit. In the male
humor and (often female) criticism of the late nineteenth century, chuckle-
headed women, piling up frivolous purchases, taken in by "the shams of the
shops," became stock figures. But fashion was more than a symptom of female silliness. It was part of a larger social picture, an increasingly fluid and
mobile society, with five hundred classes instead of four (as one observer
put it in *Good Housekeeping*, glancing across the Atlantic to England)—a
society where people were constantly seeking advance through the clever
deployment of display.

Contrary to Thorstein Veblen's claims, the rise of conspicuous consumption was not simply about status striving and "pecuniary emulation." The
meanings of consumption were multiple, idiosyncratic, and personal; many
were responses to the promise of self-transformation associated with market exchange. Men and women both were attracted to that promise, but as

commerce and entertainment merged in major cities, women embraced the new possibilities with particular avidity. Women of all classes were out and about more in the new downtowns, shopping in department stores, lunching in tearooms, attending the theater and (eventually) the movies. The rise of an urban consumer culture opened a wider (though more openly commercial) public sphere for women—not only wealthy dowagers staging extravagant entertainments, but women of moderate means who always liked to window-shop, and sometimes liked to buy. Fashion was becoming a feature of the mass market. By the 1880s, observers in Chicago and elsewhere were noticing a new breed of "American girl"—young women who seemed forthright, articulate, and quite able to take care of themselves (thank you). They were an early expression of the new commercial public sphere.

Advocates of thrift were having none of it. For them (as for Veblen), fashionable consumption was reducible to status display. Upward social mobility (or the desire for it) was a complex and ever-present menace to frugal ways. Status-striving was pervasive. It was by no means confined to women; though they were often blamed for it, they claimed in response (with justification) that by organizing fashionable entertainments and attending charity balls they were only doing what their husband's position required them to do. Whether the husband in question was an executive or a shipping clerk, status-striving was a temptation for man and wife, and it was held responsible for busting many a family budget.

By the late nineteenth century the high cost of appearances was having dire consequences. In 1886, a *Good Housekeeping* contributor named C. S. Messinger compared the expenses of five families in varying economic circumstances "to arrive at a clear estimate at what might be cut out of our expenditure and not interfere with comfort or health." An alarming number of men he knew—"brain workers"—had died in early middle age, succumbing to "the strain of trying to live at an expensive rate, and at the same time to make savings against old age." They made the savings, all right, but did not live long enough to use them. Their frantic lives and early deaths were becoming a typical pattern among "our nervous ambitious American race." What Messinger claimed to discover was that no matter what their income, all five households were sufficiently nourished and decently dressed; the increase in expenditure as one went up the economic scale was due to the expense of higher social position. This was the burden of the well-to-do—or would-be well-to-do—an unnecessary "source of much anxiety to breadwinners" at the upper end of the income scale. While fretting primarily about the rich, Messinger expanded his findings to an all-encompassing conclusion. The lesson was clear, he said: "We want too much."

It was one thing to lament excessive wants among the working class, who were supposed to be cultivating contentment with their lot, and quite another to find the same fault among the middle class, who were supposed to be improving themselves. The critique of middle-class desire posed potentially subversive questions about the dynamic of dissatisfaction at the core of market culture, about the very possibility of sustaining a stable sense of self in a society given over to perpetual jostling for personal advantage. The ruinous results of status-striving led advocates of economic thrift to advocate psychic thrift as well.

By the 1880s, the need to conserve scarce psychic resources was a commonly voiced priority among the educated and affluent. Beard's *American Nervousness* had identified "the chief and primary cause" of neurasthenia as "modern civilization," which placed unprecedented demands on limited emotional energy. "Neurasthenia" and "nervous prostration" became catchall terms for a constellation of symptoms that today would be characterized as signs of chronic depression—anxiety, irritability, nameless fears, listlessness, loss of will. In a Protestant culture, where effective exercise of will was the key to individual selfhood, the neurasthenic was a kind of anti-self—at best a walking shadow, at worst a bedridden invalid unable to make the most trivial choices or decisions. Beard and his colleagues—neurologists, psychiatrists, and self-help writers in the popular press—all agreed that nervous prostration was the price of progress, a signal that the psychic circuitry of "brain workers" was overloaded by the demands of "modern civilization."

While some diagnoses of this disease deployed electrical metaphors, the more common idiom was economic. Popular psychology, like popular economics, was based on assumptions of scarcity: there was only so much emotional energy (and only so much money) to go around. The most prudent strategy was the husbanding of one's resources as a hedge against bankruptcy and breakdown. In 1885, *Good Housekeeping* presented the cautionary tale of two sisters, Louisa and Lydia, who took turns caring for their aged invalid mother until Louisa broke down, a victim of nervous prostration. "Louisa lived on her principal, I on my interest," Lydia explained. "The secret of health, as of wealth, is to lay by a little each day." Psychic saving was as important as financial saving; psychic wastrels could bankrupt themselves (even with a noble aim) and succumb to neurasthenia. The sufferer from nervous prostration "has not kept his books balanced with the minute care which Nature always employs in the management of her accounts," wrote a *Harper's* contributor in 1891. "He has hoped . . . that she was at least as careless, or as weakly indulgent as he, and that some few things might be overlooked or happily forgotten. But Nature's ways of business are not . . . the curving and yielding lines of benevolence and charity, but the rigid and straight ones of truth and justice." The key to contentment was not the satisfaction but the reduction of overblown wants—to the point where we take "a positive pleasure . . . in seeing shops loaded with innumerable things that we do *not* want and wouldn't have if we could." Psychic thrift promised relief from the endless cycle of dissatisfaction and desire.

But this attitude remained a decidedly minority strain—the sort of outlook that gave rise to various Simple Life movements at the turn of the century (and indeed ever since). What was much more common, if one could afford it, was the headlong race for success interrupted by periodic "breakdowns." This was the emerging pattern among the educated professionals during the Gilded Age—"brain workers" ranging from professors and poets to stockbrokers and investment bankers, including the circle of lieutenants around J. Pierpont Morgan. No one better personified this manic-depressive pattern than Morgan himself, who lurched through most of his life at a manic pace, piling up rare books and objets d'art, pursuing innumerable amours, and brilliantly managing his own investments not to mention (sometimes) the rest of Wall Street's as well. Yet even the Promethean Morgan ("Pierpont Morgan is apparently trying to swallow the sun," Henry Adams once quipped during one of Morgan's financial escapades) ran out of psychic fuel on a regular basis and "broke down utterly." The remedy for these episodes was almost always "a long sea voyage." Nice therapy if you could get it. The neurasthenia epidemic spread far beyond the precincts of J. P. Morgan & Company, afflicting a broad swath of middle- and upper-class American men and women—many of whom could not afford to disappear for months on a long sea voyage.

The epidemic of nervous invalidism embodied more than businessmen's desires to recharge their batteries and get back to work. It suggested longings for a more profound regeneration. Occasionally they were uttered openly. Characterizing "Invalidism as a Fine Art" in 1888, a *Harper's* contributor presented his own protracted rest cure as an opportunity to cultivate sensibilities neglected since early childhood—almost an intimation of immortality. Part of the change was a widening of perception: "The invalid, like the poet, and like all acute, sensitive beings, is remarkable not for seeing differently, but for seeing more than does the rest of the world. He endows everything about him with personality." The armchair, the cane, the pillow, the medicine bottles become a circle of "silent friends."

Mental expansion follows. "Repose and hope, accurate observation, philosophy and fancy—our fine art has much to bestow on the willing and ready recipient." He embarks on a life "stripped of superfluities," meeting only "necessary" people on "the plainest and most informal terms. He tells them the truth and they speak to him with equal disregard of rhetoric. The simple, the unsophisticated, the primary are presented to his thoughts." It is a return to an ur-state of innocence: "For the period of his confinement he is forced to live honestly as a saint, purely as a little child, bravely and patiently as a soldier." It is the closest thing to the fantasy of the clean slate—and certainly a respite from moral demands of any kind. "It is a paradise, an intermediate state between sickness and health, where there is neither judgment nor condemnation, neither temptation nor struggle." When he finally arises from bed, his legs beneath him again, it is a scene of rebirth. "He has chipped his shell, burst his cocoon. It was worth all the being ill, he tells you, to be born again in this fashion."

Being reborn through a self-allowed regime of lassitude was idiosyncratic, though important as a limiting case. Few Americans had the leisure or the inclination to engage in this kind of Wordsworthian retreat. Most considered neurasthenia at best a temporary respite, at worst an ordeal. They strained, if ambivalently, to be back in harness.

The manic-depressive psychology of the business class mimicked the lurching ups and downs of the business cycle. In both cases, assumptions of scarcity underwrote a pervasive defensiveness, a circle-the-wagons mentality. This was the attitude that lay behind the "rest cure" devised by the psychiatrist Silas Weir Mitchell, who proposed to "fatten" and "redden" the (usually female) patient by isolating her from all mental and social stimulation. (This nearly drove the writer Charlotte Perkins Gilman crazy, and inspired her story "The Yellow Wallpaper.") It was also the attitude that lay behind the fiscal conservatism of the "sound-money men" on Wall Street and in Washington—the bankers and bondholders who wanted to restrict the money supply by tying it to the gold standard. Among the middle and upper classes, psyche and economy alike were haunted by the common specter of scarcity. But there were many Americans for whom scarcity was a more palpable threat.

AT THE BOTTOM of the heap were the urban poor. To middle-class observers they seemed little more than a squalid mass jammed into tenements that were festering hives of "relapsing fever," a strange malady that left its survivors depleted of strength and unable to work. The disease was "the most efficient recruiting officer pauperism ever had," said a journalist investigating tenement life in the 1870s. Studies of "the nether side of New York" had been appearing for decades, but—in the young United States at least—never before the Gilded Age had the story of Dives and Lazarus been so dramatically played out, never before had wealth been so flagrant, or poverty been so widespread and so unavoidably appalling. The army of thin young "sewing-girls" trooping off in the icy dawn to sweatshops all over Manhattan, the legions of skilled mechanics forced by high New York rents to huddle with their families amid a crowd of lowlifes, left without even a pretense of privacy in noisome tenements that made a mockery of the Victorian cult of home—these populations began to weigh on the bourgeois imagination, creating concrete images of the worthy, working poor.

Among the worthiest of tenement dwellers were the wounded Civil War veterans scraping by on pensions. "The Pensioner's apartment," in the journalist Edward Crapsey's account of a New York tenement house in the 1870s, was "composed, in the parlance of the place, of 'a room and a bedroom.' The room was about twelve foot square, and eight feet from floor to ceiling. It had two windows opening onto the court, and a large fireplace filled with a cooking stove. In the way of additional furniture, it had a common deal table, three broken wooden chairs, a few dishes and cooking utensils, and two 'shakedowns,' as the piles of straw stuffed into bed-ticks are called; but it had nothing whatever beyond these articles. There was not even the remnant of a bedstead; not a cheap print, so common in the hovels of the poor, to relieve the blankness of the rough, whitewashed walls. The bedroom, which was little more than half the size of the other, was that outrage of capital upon poverty known as a 'dark room.' By which it is meant that it had no window opening to the outer air; and this closet had no furniture whatever except two 'shakedowns.'" Nine people lived here: the Pensioner, 35, his wife and three children, a woman lodger with two children, and an eighteen-year-old boy named Buster, who paid 15 cents a night to "'stretch on the boards without any shakedown whatsumdever.'" Yet the Pensioner considered himself fortunate. He received $15 a month from the government, for an arm he lost at Spotsylvania. "It was enough to keep body and soul together and he could not complain," Crapsey reported. The Pensioner's stoic fortitude was shared by his wife, who "scoured the rough floor white" and kept three small children clean, innocent, and guileless. Crapsey developed a grudging respect for this "uncouth creature," and as for the Pensioner himself, could only declare him "a hero!"

He was a special sort of hero. His injury prevented him from striving for success and sanctioned his stoic acceptance of his fate. In contrast, able-bodied men of all classes were expected to be up and doing. Despite mounting evidence to the contrary, economic failure was still widely associated with moral failure—especially the failure to stay in harness, day after day. The mysterious power of money, the capacity of capital to create or eliminate jobs, simply disappeared from much commentary on "the labor problem." The sanctity of plodding diligence remained the keystone of the bourgeois cathedral. When the *Atlantic Monthly* profiled "Three Typical Workmen" in 1878, it evaluated each in accordance with his work habits. One was a shoemaker, wounded at Antietam, a reformed drunk with seven children and $5-a-month disability pay from the federal government. He eked out a living doing piecework in a small factory town for $1.50 a day, barely above subsistence, with no savings for times of illness. Yet the shoemaker imagined that "in a year of steady work and close economy he can pay off all he owes." Of one thing he was certain: "It takes a deal of hard work to keep this world going on, and it seems to me these labor reformers only make things worse [by agitating for a shorter workday]." The second worker was a lifelong abolitionist and a common soldier who became an officer in the Union Army; after the war he worked as a farmer and carpenter and failed repeatedly at everything he tried, done in by his dreamy habits of mind, his penchant for romantic utopianism and abstract speculative thought. He was a kind and generous man, but "he is poorly fitted for a world where effects depend on causes, and most good things have their price in toil." The third worker was a penniless orphan who at sixteen went to work as a farm laborer, accumulating enough savings to buy his own "nearly worthless" farm, enriching the land over ten years with horse manure he swept from the streets of a neighboring town, and eventually achieving a level of prosperity that made him nervous. He did not want to get too comfortable, so he was preparing to move on, find another piece of hardscrabble land that he could bring to life. He too hailed the regenerative powers of work, admitting that "I am sometimes almost frightened to find how fast the weeds will grow in a fellow's disposition with a little idleness. All sorts of unprofitable and dreamy thoughts come up and get stronger and stronger. It will not take long to feel meddlesome and envious and sour and discontented. I believe I should soon be a savage if it were not for hard work." From this view, disciplined labor was the core of the civilized self. What went without saying was that it was also the sine qua non of success.

Moralists defined "the labor problem" as idleness, fantasizing that workers were free agents and overlooking the structural causes of unemployment. This required a determination to ignore the impact of frequent financial crises, most obviously the long-term consequences of the Panic of 1873. Throughout the 1870s and 1880s, industrial workers endured the periodic pain inflicted by the business cycle on an unregulated workplace: recurring wage cuts and prolonged unemployment, displacement by machinery or cheaper labor, unrelenting physical demands and frequent danger, sometimes even dismemberment and death. Consider the example of New York City longshoremen, who throughout the Gilded Age and indeed as late as the 1910s had no moving cranes and were expected to operate as human machines, handling two-hundred-pound bags of coffee, three-hundred-pound bags of sugar, five-hundred-pound bales of cotton, and hogsheads of tobacco that weighed twice that. This was casual gang labor, each job lasting only as long as the turnaround of a single ship. No wonder longshoremen—like other laborers, skilled and unskilled—groped for ways to mitigate the harshness of their daily lot. No wonder they sought security through solidarity.

The working-class worldview played counterpoint to liberal individualism and the Protestant ethic. Throughout the post–Civil War decades, workers who were drawn into the ever-widening sphere of industrial wage labor came mostly from the rural periphery of Europe or North America, from communities bypassed or steamrollered by the engines of modernization. These migrants brought with them a sense of fellow feeling that survived in the workplace, sustaining the importance of pals, kin, connections, even working couples—longshoremen, for example, who knew each other's moves without verbal communication. The larger point was that the group was more important than the individual; individualism was an ideology for the rich and well-born—or so it seemed, at any rate, to the working stiffs who crowded into saloons in Pittsburgh, Baltimore, Chicago, and other industrial cities, buying each other rounds of beer, sustaining an ethic of mutuality and reciprocity.

The ethic of mutuality was increasingly important in the workplace, where employers were demanding ever-increasing productivity by closing up the pores of the working day. As Marx observed in *Capital* (1867), under capitalism, to "be a productive laborer is . . . not a piece of luck but a misfortune." Looking out for each other, workers stigmatized the hogs, rooters, and boss's pets who broke the piece rate and allowed quotas to be raised. Facing escalating demands, experienced workers generally agreed that they would rationally restrict output in a spirit of "unselfish brotherhood." This was a question not only of quality of life, but of actual survival, especially over the long haul. Tom Benyan, a Welsh-born miner near Pittsburgh, was asked how he had survived sixty-five years of toil. "Oh, they can't kill you with work if you have sense enough to go slow," he said. Having sense enough to go slow depended partly on skilled workers' craft knowledge, which allowed them to set their own pace. As the adage had it, the manager's brains were under the worker's cap. Craft was a resource for resistance.

Skilled workers believed in the redemptive powers of their own labor, its capacity to regenerate individual and society alike. They took pride in themselves and their participation in the honorable army of producers—people who produced economic value through their own efforts, unlike the "parasites" (lawyers, bankers, brokers) who merely manipulated abstractions or other people's money. The opposition between producers and parasites depended on a labor theory of value, which held that loading ships, laying railroad tracks, drilling tunnels, and making steel were the actual means of creating wealth in society. Real value, from the producerist view, derived not from the mysterious power of money but from the sweat of the workers' brow.

This producerist outlook evoked Jeffersonian republicanism in its distrust of concentrated power. It pervaded the universalist ideology of "free soil, free labor, free men" that inspired the antislavery movement and the Republican Party before the Civil War. Productive labor was a badge of manliness and personal dignity, as the *Atlantic*'s "typical workers" made clear.

While this view was easily assimilated to individualism, it also preserved a radical edge. The producerist link between labor and dignity promoted criticism of the economic status quo, beginning with slavery but continuing after the war. Producerist values undergirded Henry George's enormously influential *Progress and Poverty* (1879), which proposed to undermine the power of rentier capital through a "single tax" on the unearned increment in the value of land. A producerist worldview also animated the emerging labor movement, especially its challenge to Gilded Age employers' definition of productivity.

During the decades after the Civil War, workers' resistance to indignity increasingly focused on the demand for an eight-hour day. "You keel yourself. Twelve hours long time," a steel worker in Cleveland cautioned a newcomer who had started in at full tilt. The dialect in the quotation suggests an increasingly important development in the labor history of the period: the influx of a foreign-born working population. Eventually this would fragment the producerist vision, as manly behavior would be defined in ethnic terms and labor solidarity would splinter along racial lines. Already in the 1870s and 1880s, skilled workers were largely native-born, or else Northern or Western European, while the ranks of common laborers were swelled (in the Northeast and Midwest) by newer immigrants from Southern and Eastern Europe as well as African-American migrants from the battered South, and (in the Southwest and far West) by Mexicans and Chinese. These were the outliers in the emerging labor movement; they would prove notoriously difficult to organize. They were isolated by language barriers, scorned by skilled workers (often on racial grounds), and even more footloose than the rest of the working population.

The mobility of the workforce during the 1870s and 1880s was not a matter of choice. Necessity was more important than desire in the creation of the "tramp problem," which respectable commentators discussed with increasingly fretful urgency as the lurching business cycle repeatedly threw masses of men out of work, adding them to the army of casual laborers that took to the roadways every spring and fall in search of seasonal employment. It was not the case, a textile mill owner in Woonsocket, Rhode Island, observed in the 1880s, that workers were on the move because they had "as roving a disposition as the Tartars"—though this, he acknowledged, was the universal assumption among the more comfortable classes. "They go, it is true, where they can get the best employment, and the best wages, but few remove because they are fond of changing their locations." Much work was seasonal. Railroad gangs on the Western plains could expect to work from March or April to November or December; then they headed back to Chicago, where they cut ice, shoveled snow, or found other odd jobs to get through the winter. Even in good times, life was a matter of constant moving from job to job.

Working-class women were forced to move frequently too, though for different reasons. They were less able to work even semi-consistently for pay: they made less money for the same job and often worked themselves to exhaustion trying to meet production norms set by men. They also had caretaking responsibilities within the family, and it was that familial role that most often required their mobility, as they had to travel to care for sick or aged relatives. Though they worked for pay when they could, they were more tightly tied to the household, which for the working class as well as the business class was woman's domain.

Consider the experience of Emily French, a "hard-worked woman" whose diary we happen to have for the year 1890, when she worked as laundress, seamstress, general domestic, and seller of subscription books. We know the bare bones of her earlier life. Born Emily Eliza Rood in Michigan in 1843, she eloped at fifteen with Marsena French of New York; the couple had nine children. From Michigan they moved to Anamosa, Iowa, where her husband had a clothing business and later went to medical school. They bounced around the Midwest for a decade and a half, with French flailing about at farming and various businesses and at one point declaring bankruptcy. By 1884 they had established a homestead at Elbert, Colorado; Emily's younger, disabled sister Annis took the adjoining piece of land. The sisters hopefully expected an inheritance from their father; when they lost in court to his second wife, Marsena French lost interest in the marriage and divorced Emily in 1889. That same year her youngest child died and a severe drought settled on the high Colorado plains. Emily was in a hell of a mess. She hid her surviving children from French in Denver, rented half a double log cabin with Annis in Elbert, took in the neighbors' washing, and fought her ex-husband for the title to Annis's land. Annis herself was a burden: she was dirty and smelled constantly, especially after she had "benastied" herself. Emily pitied her but frequently lost patience. "She tries to help me, poor girl, but she is a carless [sic] *nobody*." There was "no use to try to make a companion of her, she is so *dull*."

Emily herself was resourceful, if desperate. She rigorously maintained the appearance of respectability, making dresses for her daughter in the latest, puffed-sleeve fashions, yearning for a home while she worked as a live-in cook for a vile man named Larkin. By April she was in Denver, determined to buy a lot and build a house—a plan she put in motion by persuading "the head men of the church" to sign her note for $500. By May she was back in business, taking in sewing, mending, and washing. One of her customers, John Lawson, became her suitor—and for a while, she thought, the answer to her prayers for economic security. The courtship heated up, for a month or so, then cooled when John left town on business and rarely if ever answered Emily's letters. He reappeared in her life over the next several months, repeatedly raising her hopes, but ultimately disappointing her. Meanwhile Emily was getting desperate for more work, more income to meet the first payment on the note. Offered $35 a month for the job of cook at a mountain resort called the Buffalo Creek Hotel, she drove forty-one miles in the rain to take it. She was the only cook on the premises, and with so little help, "oh dear I shall die," she said. She quit after one day, and managed to find work as a nurse to a new mother, Mrs. O'Brien, in Dake (pop. 200), the site of charcoal kilns for nearby smelters. Apparently Emily was expected to take care of both the bedridden mother and the baby, along with all the meals and laundry. Sickly and impatient, Mrs. O'Brien complained constantly of Emily's inadequacy and eventually fired her as a nurse but not as a laundress. Emily, who could not meet house payments on the pittance she made from washing diapers and nightshirts, fled back to Denver. She tried a week making suits at A. Z. Solomon's sweatshop, and found the piecework "awful"—"I cannot earn my salt," she concluded ruefully. Soon she was back in domestic service, in the household of a Denver plumbing contractor and his wife.

Before long, Emily's employers were carping at her, their children, and each other; shouting matches became slapping matches, accompanied by slamming doors and wailing babies. Cooking, washing, and caring for this ill-tempered crew earned Emily $20 a month—not enough to continue meeting the payments on her house. She may have left Denver by 1892; sometime between 1893 and 1894 she married a Mr. Varney and, as a consequence, lost her legal claim on any title to the homestead she had owned with Marsena French. A "hard-worked woman" on her own, who wanted to support children and maintain respectability, was often forced to live in fear—straining to meet creditors' demands, enduring verbal and some-times physical abuse from employers and ex-husbands. Emily's daughter Olive was equally vulnerable. She hired out as a maid to a Mrs. Anfinger, who took "to abusing her, refused her the use of the water closet, such a mean trick." The home was no refuge from the perversities of class and power relations. Yet Emily yearned above all else for a home of her own. Flawed as it might be, the domestic sphere still seemed to shelter possibili-ties for regeneration. For the working class as well as the bourgeoisie, the home occupied a unique if contradictory social space—in the market but not of it, an expression of the power of money but also a promise of escape from it.

Like the bourgeois home, the working-class home illuminated the com-plexities of class privilege in a country officially committed to denying that class even existed. The domestic sphere was the sphere for spending as well as saving money—the former was a source of pleasure and a sign of status ascent; the latter was a moral command at the center of the secularized Prot-estant ethic. In Packingtown as well as on Chicago's North Shore, husbands and wives sat across kitchen tables, sorting out the meanings of extrava-gance and thrift.

Thrift had different meanings for the poor and working class, who were expected to accept their lot in life, than it did for the middle class, who were expected to be moving up in the world, and for the upper class, who were pressed into high expenditures to maintain their social posi-tion. Reining in one's desires to match one's social station was too static an agenda for those who wore white collars to work, but it was all very well for working folk. Or, at least, so many Americans assumed, even among the working class. But not everyone was so sure.

Through the business downturn following the Panic of 1873, advocates of sound money management considered the plight of the working-class majority. In 1879, the *Atlantic Monthly* surveyed the situation of working-men's wives. What emerged was a portrait of resourceful women, who had borne the "anxiety and suffering" of the long depression with more patience and courage than their "depressed and injured" husbands had been able to muster. These women were often knowledgeable and pragmatic. They pointed out the difficulty of saving when there was no safe repository, when banks frequently failed and securities were likely to decline in value. But they also upbraided other working people for their inability to live within their means.

Some were as hard on their own class as any bourgeois moralist could be. Indeed, one wife wondered, maybe working people simply weren't fit to accumulate wealth the way their economic superiors did. Interest on savings and investment might be fine for business people, she said, "but for working people it does harm, and not good. Many of our class are excited and dazzled by the thought of their money increasing, and as they say, 'piling up while they sleep,' so that they often risk losing the whole of it by lending it to men who are not to be trusted, or venturing into wild speculations." The dream of easy money gives workers "unreasonable hopes for the future, and leads them to desire above all things to escape from the necessity [of work]." Better to be useful and happy as we are, doing the necessary work of the world, than to try "to rise to positions which are not suited to us" by going into debt for expensive pianos and clothes for our children and teaching them to want what they cannot have.

What do working people need? another was asked. "They need discipline, the power and habit of self-restraint and self-direction in nearly everything, but especially in their use of money." In a country like ours, full of resources, "they might all be rich, but they are so impulsive and extravagant that most of them are in debt, and are often pressed and harassed by their inability to pay their notes." Systemic indebtedness kept the poor under, but the root of their woe was personal improvidence. So it seemed to moralists of varying backgrounds, even humble ones. The working-class household sheltered a complex collection of sentiments, not all compatible with one another: a mutualist ethic of communal responsibility and an individualist desire for upward mobility, anchored by a stoical resignation to one's social fate.

But for many working-class Americans during the 1870s and 1880s, stoical resignation became impossible. The Gilded Age saw a series of massive nationwide strikes that ended up as pitched battles between labor and capital—factories and freight cars torched and smoldering; angry workers squaring off against heavily armed police, militias, the National Guard, and the U.S. Army; a crackle of gunfire; men, women, and children dead. As federal troops were withdrawn from the South, they were reassigned to put down strikes in Chicago and other Northern cities. Civil war gave way to class war.

THE FIRST BATTLE of that new conflict was the Great Railroad Strike of 1877, which engulfed towns and cities from Baltimore and Pittsburgh to Chicago and St. Louis, leaving millions of dollars' worth of property destroyed, dozens of people dead, and dissident workers bloody but unbowed. The background of the strike was the long depression; the proximate cause was the railroad men's desire to protect profits in a time of business contraction and cutthroat competition. They wanted to redirect the federal government's attention from Southern politics to railroad finances; that was one reason so many of them helped to broker the Compromise of 1877. At the same time, with stock prices stagnant, they were feeling the need to cut costs. Tom Scott, who headed the Pennsylvania Railroad (and the Texas and Pacific), was involved in both the compromising and the belt-tightening. After successfully brokering the compromise, he faced a challenge from Rockefeller, who was trying to squeeze out a Pennsy subsidiary. The shock waves from their struggle rippled through the railroad industry, showing how unregulated competition between capitalists could have catastrophic consequences for labor (as well as for the small businessmen who lacked the capital to compete with the big boys). Slashing rates to meet his rival, Scott covered the costs by firing hundreds of workers, cutting wages 20 percent, and doubling the length of trains without adding any crews. The Baltimore & Ohio took comparable measures.

Workers reacted quickly. On July 17, 1877, engineers in Martinsville, West Virginia, refused to run the trains. When the governor called out the state militia and they tried to move a train, workers blocked it. Gunfire broke out. A striker and a militiaman fell dead. News of the struggle spread down the B & O line from Baltimore to the Midwest. Violence escalated. Confrontations erupted in Pittsburgh, Chicago, and other cities.

Affluent Americans evoked apocalyptic visions. "Since last week the country has been at the mercy of the mob," John Hay wrote his father-in-law from Cleveland on July 24, "and on the whole the mob has behaved rather better than the country. The shameful truth is now clear, that the government is now utterly helpless and powerless in the face of an unarmed rebellion of foreign workingmen, mostly Irish. There is nowhere any firm nucleus of authority—nothing to fall back on as a last resort. The Army has been destroyed by the dirty politician, and the state militia is utterly inefficient. Any hour the mob chooses, it can destroy any city in the country—that is the simple truth." Under pressure from frightened men of property, and determined to refute the charge of corruption, governors called for local militia, the National Guard, and the U.S. Army. As soldiers fired on their fellow citizens, railway cars burned, and strikers lay dead in the streets, newspaper editorialists called for a "regular army large enough to be of prompt service in such emergencies." Workers and their sympathizers drew different conclusions. In Terre Haute, Indiana, the young Eugene Debs watched in shock as federal troops fell upon a peaceful crowd of protesters. At that point he began his odyssey from producerist moralism to socialism, and eventually became the leader of a vigorous, homegrown Socialist Party.

As the sense of menace subsided, bourgeois moralists took stock of "the strike and its lessons." The Rev. Henry Ward Beecher was a representative figure, an outspoken abolitionist and supporter of John Brown before the Civil War. His postwar career revealed the Republicans' increasing use of free labor ideals as a defense of economic privilege. His sermons summarized the regnant mix of laissez-faire and natural law—the chaos of unregulated economic life contained (at least rhetorically) by the stasis of unchanging principle. "Are the working men of the world oppressed?" he asked. "Yes, undoubtedly, by governments, by rich men, and by the educated classes—not because of selfishness and injustice but because it *must* be so. Only in the household is it possible for strength and knowledge and power not to oppress weakness and ignorance and helplessness." This was "a great natural law": "no being against being, or little being against much being, must always kick the beam. The volume of power that is in any class must have scope and operation." Lest anyone misunderstand that last statement, Beecher quickly added that "the American idea recognizes no classes. . . . There is no rich class before the law, and there is no working class before the law; and in the intense sense in which the term 'class' is now coming to be used in the controversies of the day it is un-American, it is unphilosophic, it is undemocratic, it is false. We are all common citizens, having the same liberty as one another; and he who classifies men and seeks to antagonize them is an enemy of the country and of his kind." For Beecher and his comfortable audience, the "American idea" was clear: "God gave me my right to liberty when he gave me myself; and the business of government is to see that nobody takes it away from me unjustly—that is all." This was the worldview that left unprotected labor at the mercy of unregulated capital.

It was also the worldview that—in the interests of protecting employers' liberty—sanctioned state-sponsored violence. During the next several decades, the government deployment of armed force in the interests of the propertied classes would become almost commonplace. Local elites assembled various military and paramilitary forces in the defense of social order: federal troops, supplemented by increasingly professionalized urban police, state militia, and National Guard units. These were the heroes lionized and fantasized by John Hay in his novel *The Bread-winners* (1884)—chivalric defenders of capital. It was an impressive array of armed might, but hardly reassuring to property owners who felt increasingly besieged. The vision of armed class conflict seemed the shape of things to come.

Of course industrial workers had their own strong reasons for feeling besieged. They were caught in the throes of business upheaval, as entrepreneurs struggled to stay afloat amid persistent low prices, frequent economic crises, and rampant business failures. Lack of liquidity meant many a captain of industry had to go down with his ship. Employers cast about frantically for ways to lower the cost of production: wage cuts, speedups, stretch-outs. Unions they considered a menace, and they sought to break them at every opportunity. The more farsighted aimed for longer-term managerial efficiency, through the adoption of new machinery or a more subdivided system of labor. Some of these strategies could be combined, and all of them were threatening to workers.

Just how threatening became apparent in the confrontation between Rockefeller and the Coopers' Union, also in 1877. The union struck to protest a series of pay cuts, and this gave Rockefeller the opportunity to break them. His managers introduced barrel-making machinery and hired a variety of strikebreakers, including some inmates of the Pittsburgh prison. They also mobilized the Cleveland police, who waded into a crowd of strikers wielding nightsticks and cracking heads. Eventually the union died, along with the workers' hopes for protection from their employer's power.

The real problem for workers, and the reason that labor strife intensified throughout the 1880s and early 1890s, was that wage cuts were part of a comprehensive managerial strategy aimed at more efficient productivity (the strategy Marx dissected in *Capital*). In the wake of the events of 1877, when labor uprisings everywhere were suppressed by policemen and soldiers firing into crowds of protesters, industrial workers felt increasingly desperate. It was about this time that the Knights of Labor emerged, presenting itself to workers as their shield of protection. Mobilizing respect for productive labor into a producerist ideology, the union aimed to shelter all kinds of "producers" in one big organization that would resist the rapacity of "parasites." The Knights refused to exclude anyone on the basis of skill, race, or sex; they eventually included farmers and even small businessmen in their army of producers.

But membership in the Knights was especially important to industrial workers. The organization enabled them to resist their bosses' offensive and retain their dignity. In less than a decade the Knights attracted more than 700,000 members. They had brought the republican and producerist traditions into the industrial workplace, telling factory operatives that "no pride of craft, no caste of trade should separate you"—a capacious message that "had a special meaning for workers who had no craft," as the historian David Montgomery writes. Indeed the Knights made the only serious effort to organize unskilled factory operatives before the 1930s.

The bosses, meanwhile, were determined to press their advantage. Between 1879 and 1884, Cyrus McCormick Jr. adopted a typical managerial strategy at his Reaper Works in Chicago: replace as many skilled workers as possible with machines, speed up the work of the rest. Other innovators followed suit; in Chicago, they were not only the industry leaders in meatpacking, men like Gustavus Swift and Philip Armour, who perfected the "disassembly line," but also the captains of commerce in more marginal businesses, such as woodworking and cigar-making. These trades were dominated by German immigrants, many of them freethinkers and socialists, maybe even anarchists. Catholic and Protestant clergy fretted about these people but the radicals became more and more influential, embracing common cause with the Knights of Labor and sharpening the edge of labor discontent as the city slipped into economic depression during the mid-1880s. This was the background to the Great Upheaval—the strikes that proliferated in Chicago and other cities during the spring of 1886, strikes that were supported by the Knights as well as more radical elements, and that—against the bosses' speedup—demanded an eight-hour day.

This was a movement for a freer, better way of life. The Knights began and ended their convocations with "The Eight-Hour Song":

> We want to feel the sunshine;
> We want to smell the flowers;

We are sure that God has willed it.
And we mean to have eight hours.

Employers were just as determined to deny this demand, so the men walked
out by the thousands.

The strikes eventually spread into the general conflagration of May 1,
1886, when sixty thousand workers walked off their jobs—maybe as many
as forty thousand in Chicago. McCormick's factory was one of the strikers'
targets; he shut it down and locked out the union workers until he could
hire scabs to replace them, which was almost immediately. On May 3, when
strikers attacked scabs departing the factory, two hundred massed Chicago
policemen were on the premises and began firing into the crowd. Four strikers were killed. August Spies, a German socialist, was there and was outraged. He and his comrades organized a protest meeting for the next day in
Haymarket Square. When the time came, the place was packed. Spies and
other speakers demanded justice; the crowd roared its agreement. Then a
solid phalanx of a hundred and seventy-six Chicago policemen advanced on
the protesters, ordering them to disperse. From among the crowd a bomb
flew toward the policemen, landing in their midst. Seven died; dozens more
were injured. The police began firing into the panicked, milling multitude;
three civilians were killed and scores wounded. The prosperous classes in
Chicago and indeed throughout the United States shook with fear and outrage. Eight German workers, all labeled "anarchists," were accused of the
crime; eventually five (including Spies) were hanged. "[T]his republic has
just executed five men for their opinions," the novelist William Dean Howells wrote his father. An influential editor at the *Atlantic* and later *Harper's*,
Howells had publicly appealed for clemency, noting that the accused men
were fairly indictable only for conspiracy, not for murder. Their crimes were
unproven; only their "frantic opinions" were known, he observed, and holding unpopular views— however unsound or even potentially dangerous—
was hardly a capital offense. Howells's courageous stand unleashed a flood
of outrage against him, and no one else of his stature stood up to the popular cry for the anarchists' blood. The evidence against the condemned men
was flimsy to nonexistent but feelings ran high and the respectable classes
demanded vengeance (in the name of justice), melding class fears with xenophobia. As one editor put it, "The enemy forces are not American [but]
rag-tag and bob-tail cutthroats of Beelzebub from the Elbe, the Vistula, and

the Rhine." Still, the foreign origin of the "anarchists" offered cold comfort to propertied Americans with something to lose. Class conflict was real, and it was intensifying. Capitalists themselves were making sure of that.

Carnegie and Frick, for example, were at the cutting edge of managerial innovation. They were determined to put workers on two twelve-hour shifts rather than three eight-hour shifts, a concession the union had won a few years previously. The elimination of one entire shift would throw hundreds of workers out of work and reduce the remaining ones to beasts of burden. Carnegie simply could not grasp the deadening impact of the twelve-hour day. Management kept trying to impose it, workers kept resisting it—in flush times, when steel prices were rising, the resistance sometimes succeeded. From the workers' perspective, their labor was directly responsible for business profits. Like other unions, the Amalgamated Association of Iron and Steel Workers wanted workers to be recognized as partners with capital, to share profits and to exercise some control over the pace and process of their labor. From the viewpoint of management, this was simply out of the question.

Carnegie and Frick were determined to lower wage costs per capita as well as the number of workers. They started at the Homestead plant, near Pittsburgh. When the Homestead contract expired in 1892, the management proposed draconian wage cuts of 15–18 percent, and for some workers as much as 35 percent. The union-busting strategy was already in place. Management would begin by making impossible demands, and when the union refused them, lock out the workers and bring in the sheriff's deputies or the hired guns of the Pinkerton Detective Agency (or both). After a brief pause, the managers would reopen the plant under armed guard and invite workers to return as individuals. Those who refused would be replaced by scabs.

The plan worked, but it was a messy business. The workers were not the free-floating, free-bargaining individuals of capitalist fantasy. They believed they were part of a particular community, in a particular place. When the Pinkertons invaded, arriving on barges one July morning, they were not allowed to disembark. Led by such figures as Billy Foy, an Englishman and former head of the local Salvation Army, and Mother Finch, a white-haired saloonkeeper and veteran of forty strikes, the residents of Homestead met the Pinkertons with muskets, pistols, fireworks left over from the Fourth of July, and a Civil War cannon. The Pinkertons fired into the crowd; the crowd fired back. Six strikers and two Pinkertons were killed. The Pinkertons finally surrendered at five p.m. and were forced to run through a gauntlet of angry workers and their wives to the opera house, from which they were rescued the next day by sheriff's deputies. The workers held the plant until Frick persuaded the governor of Pennsylvania to send in the National Guard, who recaptured the factory and ended the battle of Homestead.

Carnegie and Frick succeeded in crushing the union, but in the process provoked an outpouring of public anger—including a failed attempt on Frick's life by the anarchist Alexander Berkman. Frick had been on the premises, serving as field general and focus for popular outrage. Carnegie, who had approved Frick's strategy, kept his distance and tried to strike an Olympian pose. Sojourning at Loch Rannoch hunting lodge in Scotland throughout the summer of 1892, he was surrounded by stags' heads and servants in livery. He refused to discuss Homestead with reporters; instead he created his own fantasy version of events, insisting that the Homestead workers had cabled him in July 1892: "Kind Master, tell us what you wish us to do and we shall do it for you." Despite exhaustive efforts, no historian or biographer has ever found any evidence that this cable existed. Safe in his own delusions, Carnegie still failed to keep Homestead from becoming a symbol of the exploitation of labor by capital.

Yet Homestead was also an economic triumph for Carnegie Steel. The unions were driven out of the steel industry; twelve-hour shifts became the norm; workers were denied grievance rights and even occasional breaks. The pores in the working day were filled. Even during the hard times of the 1890s, profits rose steadily while wages fell and machines replaced men. Between 1892 and 1897, the workforce at Homestead declined by 25 percent. Carnegie Steel was in high gear, dominating the market. And the key to its dominance was its victory over labor.

No wonder workers developed their own class-conscious version of producerist thought, which defined them as heroic producers confronting commercial parasites—knights of labor challenging lords of capital. The Knights of Labor became the most formidable labor organization of the 1880s, the big tent that sheltered producers and gave them the strength to fight parasites. The Knights were involved in most of the major labor disputes of the Gilded Age, and sought common cause with farmers—who also increasingly considered themselves aggrieved producers, plundered by parasitical bankers, brokers, and other magicians of money.

As class conflict sharpened, even academic economists began to pay attention. A few suspected that, when it came to the needs of big business, the ideal of minimal government was more honored in the breach than the observance. Tariffs, state subsidies, and credit guarantees (not to mention the use of state-sponsored violence)—all made a mockery of the laissez-faire creed. Nor did all economists agree that employers were simply obeying natural law when they pursued draconian labor policies. Those who took Christian morality seriously questioned its compatibility with laissez-faire capitalism. A week after his first Christmas abroad in 1878, the young economist Henry C. Adams confided to his diary: "If it was right for Christ to take the cloak away which covered the sins of men, it is right for me to do the same for that which makes mere men think their own acts of injustice are not their acts but the outworking of laws beyond human control. Nothing in the economic world is beyond the control of men and men must waken up to the control of those laws." A response (in effect) to Beecher's invocation of natural law, Adams's confidence was also a Copernican moment in the history of economic thought, foreshadowing the transatlantic revolution that would occur over the next several decades—the effort to tame laissez-faire capitalism by the creation of a regulatory, welfare state.

From the 1870s into the early 1890s, the welfare state was still a mere gleam in the eye of a young Christian socialist. But a few winds of change were unsettling stale doctrine. Antimonopoly sentiment was gradually spreading, as the popularity of Henry George's "single tax" and the growth of the Knights of Labor suggested. In 1890, suspicion of monopoly power led to the passage of the Sherman Anti-Trust Act, which empowered the federal government to dissolve business "combinations in restraint of trade." And in 1894, the Chicago journalist Henry Demarest Lloyd published a book exposing Rockefeller and other predators, bearing a title that aligned antitrust reform with republican tradition: *Wealth Against Commonwealth*.

Still, concentrated capital set the boundaries of permissible debate. The Supreme Court proved particularly helpful to business interests, eviscerating the Sherman Act by excusing offenders on technicalities, and defining labor unions as "combinations in restraint of trade." Equally important was the Court's gradual redefinition of the Fourteenth Amendment as a substantive defense of corporate property rights. The culmination of this process was the Court's decision in *Santa Clara County v. Southern Pacific Railroad* (1886), which extended the definition of the word "persons" in the Fourteenth Amendment to include legal persons—i.e., corporations. What began as a measure to confer rights on ex-slaves became a boon for big business.

Despite the public hostility, the frequent strikes, the business failures, and the long depression, the magicians of money were still managing to make it. Without always consciously setting out to do so, they were creating the foundations of monopoly capitalism. Economic indicators were good. Throughout the Gilded Age, a high savings rate (18–20 percent) meant much investment capital was available. A positive balance of trade, with exports exceeding imports, emerged in 1876–80—the first time this had ever happened for five years in a row. The shift in the balance of trade was the beginning of a long-term trend: there were only three years until the 1970s when the United States failed to export more than it imported. Yet as low prices persisted through the 1880s and into the 1890s, economists and other commentators traced them to the continuing problem of overproduction. The mantra of overproduction led to a search for overseas markets, intensifying in the 1880s and 1890s. This was a way of killing two birds with one stone—an imperial solution—flattening the curves in business cycle and raising workers' wages, in the process reducing "industrial disturbances."

It is about this time that we see the beginnings of the search for social comity through increased abundance. Edward Bellamy's *Looking Backward, 1887–2000* (1887) was the managerial utopian version of this bland but benign ideal—a consumer culture presided over by philosopher-king experts. During the next several decades, Bellamy's utopia would inspire many blueprints for a managerial welfare state. But in the 1880s his vision was still idiosyncratic. A more popular idea was that abundance would be achieved through empire—first the internal empire of the trans-Mississippi West, which would provide the safety valve of cheap lands that would siphon off restless workers; then the external empire of investment opportunities abroad that would create new markets and new wealth for all our citizens. So, at any rate, the empire boosters began to claim. Both internal and external empire would be guarantors of abundance, and abundance in turn would bring about social peace. The rhetoric of empire accompanied the rise of monopoly capitalism, as mergers and other centralizing strategies grew increasingly successful. While capital grew more organized, labor grew more fragmented along ethnic and occupational lines; the producerist vision gave way to a more pragmatic, less morally charged trade unionism. More and more Americans were touched by metropolitan, corporate-sponsored culture. Among urban consumers, at least, the mysterious power of money became less mysterious, more available for spending—though the promise of self-transformation preserved its magical power.

Economic centralization brought more remote areas into contact with the vagaries of the market. Chicago offered the key example here, reaching out its tentacles of power across the hinterlands but also shining its bright lights, attracting young moths in search of bright new selves. The consolidation of capital in cities led toward a new sense of possibility for some rural folk but to insecurity or at least uncertainty for many more. The power of money continued to baffle and outrage those who felt uninitiated to its mysteries. Indeed it was "the money question" above all others that began to hover over the politics of the 1880s. In state after state, farmers and other debtors in need of cheap money faced off against sound-money men. Both sides were in search of stability, or claimed to be. Farmers were at the mercy of unpredictable world markets as well as equally unpredictable weather. They were damned if they did and damned if they didn't. Monetary policies did not help. Tight money encouraged old anti-Semitic fantasies about the dark deeds of (allegedly) Jewish moneylenders, but also inflicted real hardship on smallholders throughout the Midwest and South. Events were building toward a nationwide confrontation between producers and parasites, but that epic battle would not occur until the 1890s. Meanwhile, whatever their other differences, farmers and workers alike could find themselves agreeing that laissez-faire capitalism was not all it was cracked up to be.

Changes were under way that would transform that mythology. Sound-money men had to yield certain assumptions over time. They had always had to battle the common (and correct) perception that money was a fluid and amorphous entity rather than a fixed and stable one, a perception that fostered suspicion among the populace while it created opportunities for confidence men. During the Gilded Age, more Americans began to think like confidence men. A sense of the fluidity of money began to take hold among the wider population. Americans, unlike Europeans, readily invented and accepted such alternatives to cash as the postal money order (1864) and the traveler's check (1891). The trickster acquired new legitimacy in the advertising trade, which sought professional status as the servant of emerging corporations. Under the influence of national brand-name advertising,

Americans developed new "needs" to be met by industrial by-products that included Vaseline and Crisco, as well as agricultural by-products from the pigs prepared by Swift and Armour. The "chromo-civilization" denounced by Edwin Godkin of *The Nation* in 1870 was a proto-consumer culture, which was also spread by department stores in the cities and patent-medicine peddlers in the countryside. All this culture lacked was enough consumers with cash in their pockets to make it a national phenomenon. Yet even on that front, proto-Keynesian economists in *Gunton's* magazine and elsewhere were challenging the assumptions of scarcity at the heart of conventional wisdom, arguing that constantly rising wages might be a good thing for the economy as a whole. The sorcery of the market began to be stabilized by new managerial systems, new secular idioms of control.

At the same time, and more subtly, one begins to see challenges to the psychology of scarcity, suggestions of a more openly fluid self, a self that might be capable of endless growth (just as the economy might be capable of endless growth). This thought was not exactly new; indeed, it was rooted in certain enthusiastic strains of liberal and evangelical Protestantism. But it received new and flamboyant expression in the late nineteenth century, above all in the alluring and fascinating figure of Sarah Bernhardt. She became an icon embodying widespread and sometimes contradictory longings for release, regeneration, revitalization, harmony. Eventually those longings would be met, however inadequately, by therapies and expert management (the partial fulfillment of Bellamy's vision), as well as by the prospect of imperial adventure. Religious desires for regeneration would be repackaged in secular containers—a managerial ethic of peak performance, a martial ethic of disciplined sacrifice. The rationalization of regeneration would create the core of the dominant culture in the twentieth-century United States.

But this would take time. During the 1880s and 1890s, the shape of the social order seemed very much up for grabs. Indeed, it was not even clear that there would be a social order much longer. For some among the frightened affluent, the barbarians were already at the gates. Anxious Americans cast about for idioms of control, conceptual and ethical frameworks that would provide some basis for certainty in an uncertain world. Self-made manhood and natural-law economics were available but increasingly problematic in a society convulsed by class conflict and dominated by irresponsible capital. Amid moral and intellectual confusion, scientific racism emerged as a key legitimator of hierarchy and guarantor of epistemological security.

All kinds of innovation could be confidently undertaken if racial hierarchies remained in place. Dreams of abundance through empire arose from a solid faith in Anglo-Saxon supremacy. For many old-stock Americans, of all classes, belief in racial superiority provided the promise of bedrock reassurance and cultural renewal. But for African-Americans and other minorities, scientific racism was the enemy of promise.

CHAPTER 3

The Rising Significance of Race

✦

One baking-hot Georgia afternoon in 1877, the Methodist minister Atticus Haygood took the Macon and Brunswick Railroad from Jesup to Macon and chanced upon a memorable scene. "The smoking car," he recalled, "was packed full with a rare and racy, if not rich crowd of lumbermen," returning home to Macon after delivering a load of timber to Brunswick. "We saw a very black negro and a fair-haired youth drinking alternately out of the same black-bottle," Haygood wrote. "They sat promiscuously and drank, smoked, laughed, sang, whistled, and danced together. One young fellow knew the potent notes and they sang 'fa, so, la' while he beat time. . . . He sings a sort of wild tenor we used to hear at camp-meeting." The scene typified the easy race-mixing that characterized everyday life in parts of the rural South into the 1880s. Hunting, fishing, cooking, shucking corn, tending to the sick and midwifing babies—all involved cooperation and sometimes camaraderie between the races.

Consider another scene, a country picnic at Pitman's Mill, Georgia in 1896. A young boy named Mell Barrett was about to listen to an Edison talking machine for the first time. "With the tubes in my ears, the Pitchman was now adjusting the needle on the machine. . . . My excitement increased, my heart was pounding so I could hardly hold the tubes in my ears with my shaking hands. . . . 'All Right Men, Bring Them Out. Let's Hear What They Have to Say,' were the first words I understood coming from a talking machine. . . . The sounds of shuffling feet, swearing men, rattle of chains, falling wood, brush, and fagots, then a voice—shrill, strident, angry, called out 'Who will apply the torch?' 'I will,' came a chorus of high-pitched, angry voices . . . [then] the crackle of flames as it ate its way into the dry tinder . . . My eyes and mouth were dry. I tried to wet my lips, but my tongue, too, was parched. Perspiration dried from my hands. I stood immobile." What Mell Barrett heard was several black men being burned alive, after they had confessed at gunpoint to an interracial rape. It was one of hundreds of such lynchings that scarred many parts of the South between the late 1880s and the early 1900s—a mass ritual of racial revitalization through violence.

The difference between these two scenes underscores the transformation of race relations in the Gilded Age South. The earlier period was hardly an era of biracial harmony, characterized as it was by systematic white efforts to drive blacks from public life. Yet as the lumbermen's frolic suggests, even after Reconstruction, as white Democrats returned to power, race relations remained fluid among the folk. By the 1890s, the fluidity was gone. Lynching was only the most brutal and sensational example of a concerted white effort to reassert absolute dominance by drawing the sharpest possible boundaries between the races. This effort was part of a campaign by the prosperous to purify the Southern body politic, rendering it fit for inclusion in the parade of economic progress. In sum, it was all too appropriate that the first sound young Mell Barrett heard from that modern marvel, the talking machine, was the baying of a lynch mob. Southern lynching in the 1890s, like the incandescent racism that spawned it, was a product of modernity.

To be sure, the consciousness of racial difference had existed for centuries, at least since the earliest European encounters with the dark-skinned inhabitants of the New World. But there was something profoundly different about the racism of the late nineteenth century—it was more self-conscious, more systematic, more determined to assert scientific legitimacy. The whole concept of race, never more than the flimsiest of cultural constructions, acquired unprecedented biological authority during the decades between Reconstruction and World War I.

The rising significance of race reflected a much broader impulse to seek solid foundations in a world that seemed awash in uncertainty. The movement for "sound money" sought to tie ephemeral paper to the "intrinsic value" of gold. Modern racism provided similar solidity to personal identity, in a secularizing market society where most forms of identity were malleable and up for sale. Biological personhood created a new bottom line, more reliable, more resistant to change than the arbitrary manipulation of surface effects for self-advancement. Sheer physicality beckoned, as a counterweight to the confidence games of the market and the ethereal ideality of late Victorian culture. Protestant dreams of regeneration acquired palpable, bodily form. The quest for physical vitality spread among the sedentary middle and upper classes, especially among men. In the republican political tradition, manhood had long been a key criterion of moral worth, but the increasingly systematic organization of work made the achievement of manliness at once more elusive and more urgent. The gospel of muscular Christianity spread by the Young Men's Christian Association, the growing popularity of college football, and the emerging fascination with weight lifting and bodybuilding—all reflected the reassertion of white manhood against the enervating impact of a desk-bound existence.

But to focus on physical being alone was not enough. Biology was not, after all, an entirely reassuring basis for identity; indeed, in its reductionist formulations it threatened to turn human beings into twitching automata. Mere physicality evoked the specter of Darwinian nature, the reduction of human beings to animals involved in an amoral struggle for existence. With apes for ancestors and Hottentots for cousins, white men needed more precise definitions of what it meant to be human, and what it meant to be civilized. Racial categories embodied a widespread taxonomic impulse to impose an apparently rational grid on the anarchic varieties of nature. In a land where self-making was supposedly a way of life, personal identity became tethered increasingly to origins. For many citizens of the republic during the decades following the Civil War, being an American increasingly came to mean being a Caucasian.*

This was not simply an exercise in black and white. Various races required sorting and categorizing. Indian people embodied the remnants of savagery yielding to civilization, vanishing into a rosy afterglow of nostalgia, evoking sentimental tribute as "the first Americans." Meanwhile the arrival of new Americans—wave after wave of non-Anglo immigrants—demanded more complicated taxonomies. Popular ethnology created scientific legitimacy for familiar prejudices: the brutish Celt, the treacherous Sicilian, the conniving Jew. Yet hierarchies remained unstable. In Boston, the Irishman could be a simian lout, discomfiting the Anglo-Saxon elite by trading votes for drinks in the local saloon; but in San Francisco he could be a defender of American labor, demanding the exclusion of cheap Chinese competition.

* The word "Caucasian" was coined by Johann Friedrich Blumenbach, a professor of medicine at the University of Göttingen, in his doctoral thesis of 1775. It was based on a single skull in Blumenbach's collection, which came from the Caucasus Mountains in Russia and resembled (he believed) the crania of Germans. From this conjecture came the category that by the mid-nineteenth century was synonymous with "white."

Over time, racial categories revealed a complex blend of fluidity and rigidity. Eventually, even the most despised European immigrant groups would find ways to become American by claiming common membership in the Caucasian race, implying in effect that whatever else they were, they were not yellow, brown, or black. This strategy was less available to Mexican-Americans (already by definition a "mixed breed") and not available at all to Asian- or African-Americans. But for Slavs, Celts, Jews, Italians, and other European minorities, the equation of American and Caucasian offered escape from the discourse of Anglo-Saxon supremacy. As early as 1898, during the Spanish-American War, Irishmen, Jews, and other immigrants asserted their Americanism as fervently as any Anglo-Saxon. Still, the assimilation of recent immigrants took time, and throughout the half-century following the Civil War, racial distinctions among Europeans preserved a powerful emotional charge—powerful enough to sustain a movement for immigration restriction that eventually resulted in the National Origins Act of 1924. This act created quotas for European immigrants (2 percent of the number from each country that had been in the United States in 1890) and excluded Asians altogether.

Racist thinking proved remarkably resilient—compatible with the latest science, resonant with widespread longings for renewal. As evolutionary metaphors pervaded popular ethnology, racial theorists adapted static taxonomies to the emerging emphasis on change across generations. Hereditarian schemes of progress proliferated. For several generations, people who considered themselves "progressive" nourished fantasies of "perfecting the race" through selective breeding and enforced sterilization of the unfit. Yet even this perfectionist project harbored a primitivist countercurrent—a suspicion that dark-skinned folk preserved a primal energy that overcivilized white people needed somehow to reclaim.

In this pervasively racist atmosphere, one could hardly expect African-Americans to flourish. The bottom category in every taxonomy, the supposed laggards at the rear of the evolutionary march, African-Americans could expect little help from their erstwhile Northern liberators. The federal abandonment of Reconstruction allowed Southern white supremacists to create new racial boundaries, to destroy the widening sense of possibility that had opened up after emancipation. But the Jim Crow agenda was not accomplished overnight. Vernacular race-mixing survived, as the boys on the Macon and Brunswick line revealed. Ultimately, white supremacy required more than such strategies of containment as segregation and disenfranchisement; it also drew strength from a vision of racial regeneration—a vision that acquired its most palpable form in the auto-da-fé of lynching.

Yet black people dreamed of their own revitalization. Even in this worst of times, they still struggled to retain a foothold in political and civic life. Despite the terrorist tactics of the white supremacists, African-Americans continued to vote, hold office, and participate in political life in many parts of the South well into the 1890s. To be sure, some said the hell with it (especially young males) and lit out for the territory. But others stood and fought.

THE YEAR 1877 marked a new phase in racial politics—a reassertion of white power on a variety of fronts. The best-known event was the compromise that ended Reconstruction. In February, congressional Republicans and Democrats cut the deal that gave Hayes the presidency in exchange for the withdrawal of federal troops from the South and the appropriation of public money for railroads and other internal improvements in many parts of the ravaged Confederacy. Forging an alliance between capitalists on either side of the Mason-Dixon Line, the compromise also ensured the return of white supremacy throughout the former slave states—though the full restoration would take twenty years to work out. The details of the compromise were less important than its coincidence with a broader rise in race consciousness. Yet, even after federal withdrawal, black people still held their own in many parts of the South.

One was low-country South Carolina, which Thomas Wentworth Higginson revisited (along with Virginia, North Carolina, Georgia, and Florida) in 1878. Higginson had commanded a black regiment during the war, and for three years afterward he had headed the Union force that occupied the coastal region. On his return to the South ten years later he felt like Rip Van Winkle, blinking in astonishment at the changes that had occurred in his absence. Former slaves had bought farms, learned to read, acquired beds and other furniture—including tables where they could sit at family meals ("a step toward decent living," in Higginson's view). Black people valued their public schools and counted on their own votes to maintain them, rather than Northern aid. Higginson had heard from Northern friends that the white South had a "covert plan for crushing or re-enslaving the colored race." He did not believe it. Given the "impulsive and ungoverned" nature of Southern whites, it was "utterly inconceivable that such a plan, if formed, should not show itself in some personal ill usage of the blacks, in the withdrawal of their privileges, in legislation endangering their rights. I can assert that, carrying with me the eyes of a tolerably suspicious abolitionist, I saw none of these indications."

Instead he saw a "colored militia" in Charleston (while Connecticut had refused to incorporate one), "colored police" in Charleston, Beaufort, and Jacksonville (while he knew of no Northern city that had any), and blacks in first-class train cars in Virginia and the Carolinas (while, only a few years before, "one of the most cultivated and ladylike-colored teachers in the nation" was ejected from a streetcar in Philadelphia). As for black suffrage, Southern whites accepted it as Northerners "accept the ignorant Irish vote,—not cheerfully, but with acquiescence in the inevitable . . . Any powerful body of voters may be cajoled to-day and intimidated to-morrow and hated always, but it can never be left out of sight." If abuses existed, the remedy lay in using the voting power of blacks. Meanwhile, Higginson thought, Northerners could rest assured that the civilization of the Old South had been annihilated, replaced by new preoccupations with "business, money, financial prosperity." Poverty was the benign spur that was making energy and industry fashionable among the young men.

Higginson described white-black relations that still preserved some possibility for the oppressed minority. That could hardly be said of white-red relations. Though people in isolated frontier communities still feared that "the savage is over the border" (in the words of a song from the Mexican War era), the national consensus was that the Indians were on the way out. Those who survived were expected to "vanish" as a people by blending in with property-owning whites. Indians themselves had other ideas; even the Crow and others who collaborated with the white invaders tried to piece together the shreds of a distinct tribal tradition despite the devastating loss of their fundamental ontological assumptions. But from the conquerors' point of view, by the late 1870s the Indians were indeed a vanishing race, poised on the brink of becoming a cultural icon. Dying in fact, they were reborn as myth.

The owl of Minerva flew at dusk. As the cultural historian Alan Trachtenberg has shown, Indians acquired their metaphorical grandeur at a historical moment when the question "what does it mean to be an American?" was acquiring a racial charge of unprecedented power and complexity—and when, in a land of supposedly self-made men, origins were becoming a crucial source of social identity. While many white Southerners strained to contain and thwart the aspirations of freed blacks, old-stock Northeasterners recoiled from hordes of would-be "new Americans," mostly Catholics and Jews from Southern and Eastern Europe.

Religious differences took racial form. Anti-Catholicism persisted from the antebellum era, deriving new strength from Protestant fears of the priest-ridden immigrant masses. Anti-Semitism surfaced in novel ways, focusing on such allegedly "racial" traits as "ostentation" and "incivility." In July 1877, the Jewish banker Joseph Seligman was refused service at the United States Hotel in Saratoga, New York. It was a straw in the wind of upper-class bigotry, and perhaps, as well, in the gale of Jew-hatred that was about to begin blowing from the East—beginning with the Russian pogroms of 1881. Racial hostility cut across class solidarity.

This was especially apparent among white working-class men, whose rhetoric of manliness often subordinated class to color. Even in the summer of 1877, when railroad strikes swept from Baltimore to St. Louis and class consciousness among workers reached unprecedented heights, white labor leaders' claims of common cause with blacks were accompanied by rank-and-file murmurs against "naygurs" and their supposedly baneful influence on work rules and wage scales. Skilled workers in San Francisco were equally convinced that the Chinese depressed everybody's pay by living in squalor, on next to nothing. Racist assumptions were embedded in working-class culture (as in American culture generally): Slavs were oafish, Jews larcenous, Negroes indolent—though the belief in black people's alleged laziness combined paradoxically with disdain for "nigger work," labor that was too hard and dirty for white men.

Hostility toward blacks was part of the elaborate racial hierarchy established by the white working class. Indeed much of the time, African-American workers were simply invisible, beneath notice, as in a ditty called "The Puddlers' Jubilee" that described the celebration of a union scale contract by iron puddlers. The song reflected the dominance of skilled trades by Northern Europeans:

There were no men invited such as Slavs and "Tally Annes,"
Hungarians and Chinamen with pigtail cues and fans.

No, every man who got the "pass" a union man should be;
No black sheep were admitted to the Puddlers' Jubilee.

These sorts of distinctions could be risky. Outside the working class, sometimes even in it, Irishmen and Germans could be excluded from the charmed circle of the Anglo-Saxon. In the wake of the strike wave of 1877, *Harper's Weekly* called for a war against the radical Irish labor organization the Molly Maguires, in much the same language that was used against American Indians. This would be a race war, the magazine said, of the civilized Anglo-Saxon against the barbarous Celt. In California, though, the Irish had an easier time laying claim to full American status, by defining themselves against non-Caucasians. The San Francisco Workingmen's Party, founded in solidarity with the striking railroad workers in the summer of 1877, quickly shifted its base from labor to race. In the Thanksgiving Day Parade that same year, the Workingmen's Party contingent was dominated by anti-coolie groups rather than labor organizations. It would not be long before the Chinese were being charged with encouraging the spread of opium addiction, introducing oral sex to America, and seducing white women by the cartload—not to mention driving down the wages of artisans. Inter-racial competition for jobs stoked subtler fears, and white men banded together. In December 1877, the Order of Caucasians was founded in San Francisco. Pledged to "drive the Chinese out of California," the organization was a powerful assimilative agent, transforming Irish and Germans into respectable republican producers, when back east they would have been deemed little more than drunken hooligans.

Racial animosities flared in an atmosphere of multicultural fluidity, economic scarcity, and sexual rivalry. Attitudes arising from visceral hostility acquired a veneer of scientific objectivity. Race theory was nothing new, but in the late nineteenth century it mutated into multiple forms, many of them characterized by manic urgency, sexual hysteria, and biological determinism. Taxonomists had been trying to arrange various peoples in accordance with skull shape and brain size for decades; popularized notions of natural selection accelerated the taxonomic project, investing it more deeply in anatomical details. The superiority of the Anglo-Saxon—according to John Fiske, the leading pop-evolutionary thinker—arose not only from the huge size of his brain, but also from the depth of its furrows and the plenitude of its creases. The most exalted mental events had humble somatic origins. Mind was embedded in body, and both could be passed on to the next generation.

The year 1877 marked a crucial development in this hereditarian synthesis: in that year, Richard Dugdale published the results of his investigation into the Juke family, a dull-witted crew that had produced more than its share of criminals and mental defectives. While he allowed for the influence of environment, Dugdale emphasized the importance of inherited traits in the Juke family. If mental and emotional traits could be inherited along with physical ones, then why couldn't superior people be bred like superior dogs or horses? The dream of creating a science of eugenics, dedicated to improving and eventually even perfecting human beings, fired the reform imagination for decades. Eugenics was a kind of secular millennialism, a vision of a society where biological engineering complemented social engineering to create a managerial utopia. The intellectual respectability of eugenics, which lasted until the 1930s, when it became associated with Nazism, underscores the centrality of racialist thinking among Americans who considered themselves enlightened and progressive. Here as elsewhere, racism and modernity were twinned.

Consciousness of race increasingly pervaded American culture in the Gilded Age. Even a worldview as supple as Henry James's revealed its moorings in conventional racial categories when, in *The American* (1877), James presented his protagonist, Christopher Newman, as a quintessential Anglo-Saxon but with echoes of the noble Red Man, with the same classical posture and physiognomy. There was an emerging kinship between these two groups of claimants to the title "first Americans." The iconic American, from this view, was a blend of Anglo-Saxon refinement and native vigor. While James only hints at this, in less than a generation such younger novelists as Frank Norris and Jack London would openly celebrate the rude vitality of the contemporary Anglo-Saxon, proud descendant of the "white savages" who subdued a continent. It should come as no surprise that their heroes were always emphatically male. The rhetoric of race merged with a broader agenda of masculine revitalization.

THE IDEAL OF manliness was central to the late-nineteenth-century political universe, as important to the black leader Frederick Douglass as it was to the Republican Theodore Roosevelt and the Socialist Eugene Debs.

In Terre Haute, Indiana (where Debs grew up), as in many other American villages and towns, manhood was a matter of taking responsibility for one's family and community, embracing citizenship, playing a public role. And manhood had specific, racially charged meanings for recently freed black slaves as well as for skilled white workers. Being born male was not enough: to "be a man" one had to reject servility, to declare one's independence.

Declarations of manly independence took strikingly various political forms. In the 1880s, the *Dallas News* declared that radical groups talked "too much about regulating capital and labor . . . and too little about freeing capital and industry from all needless restraints and so promoting the development and diffusion of a high order of hardy manhood." Manliness, from this view, was indistinguishable from laissez-faire individualism. At the same time, the rhetoric of manhood was central to the more communitarian aims of the labor movement, in particular the Knights of Labor's efforts to promote the solidarity of manly producers against the assaults of effete parasites. Being a man, however one defined it, was essential to successful participation in public life. Clearly women had no place in politics, according to the conventional (male) wisdom. "It would be no more deplorable to see an angel harnessed to a machine than to see a woman voting politically," said John Boyle O'Reilly, a popular poet and editor of the *Boston Pilot*. O'Reilly was an Irish Catholic, but he spoke for the Protestant majority too. Politics was part of the strife of the world, from which women were to be excluded. Yet despite their exclusion from electoral politics, for decades women had been participating in the broader public life in ever greater numbers. Jane Addams and the settlement-house movement were part of a long-term trend that began with the early suffragists and abolitionists. Critical social movements were often led by intrepid women. But into the 1890s, they still faced entrenched opposition from white men.

Whether black men were to be excluded from politics as well, despite their gender, remained a contentious issue. African-Americans' struggle to stay in politics was part of a larger effort to claim manhood. For them as for other racial minorities, the achievement of manliness involved conformity to conventional mores. Consider the young Booker T. Washington's account of an Indian boy's experience at the Hampton Institute in Virginia in 1881: "His long hair and moccasins he has long since forgotten, and instead of the weak, dirty, ignorant piece of humanity that he was, with no correct ideas of this life or the next—his only ambition being to fight the white man—he goes back a strong, decent, Christian *man*, with the rudiments of an English education, and hands trained to earn his living at the carpenter's bench or on the farm." This vision of a native yeomanry was the stock-in-trade at Hampton as well as Washington's own Tuskegee. It was a kind of manliness that had changed little since Jefferson's time, except to include (however grudgingly) a wider range of skin colors.

But other notions of manhood were changing in the Gilded Age, especially among the white middle and upper classes. By the 1880s, muscular Christians were sweeping across the land, seeking to meld spiritual and physical renewal, establishing institutions like the Young Men's Christian Association. The YMCA provided prayer meetings and Bible study to earnest young men with spiritual seekers' yearnings, gyms and swimming pools to pasty young men with office workers' midriffs. Sometimes they were the same young men. More than any other organization, the YMCA aimed to promote the symmetry of character embodied in the phrase "body, mind, spirit"— which a Y executive named Luther Gulick plucked from Deuteronomy and made the motto of the organization. The key to the Y's appeal, a *Harper's* contributor wrote in 1882, was the "overmastering conviction" of its members: "The world always respects manliness, even when it is not convinced [by theological argument]; and if the organizations did not sponsor that quality in young men, they would be entitled to no respect." In the YMCA, manliness was officially joined to a larger agenda.

For many American Protestants, the pursuit of physical fitness merged with an encompassing vision of moral and cultural revitalization—one based on the reassertion of Protestant self-control against the threats posed to it by immigrant masses and mass-marketed temptation. The chief temptation was alcohol, dispensed in saloons that in the East were hotbeds of immigrant corruption (so it was said) and in the West were franchises operated by the major breweries, strung out in the towns along the railroad lines as they headed west across the plains.

When dreams of personal salvation melded with broader social agendas, the racist and xenophobic dimensions of Protestant revitalization became more apparent. Prohibition was an appealing instrument of social control for respectable Anglo-Saxons, North and South. Offended or frightened by the unseemly pleasures of the sporting crowd (which, according to common assumptions, included footloose free blacks as well as liquored-up Irishmen and beer-swilling Germans), Protestant moral reformers embraced Prohibition as a means of allaying racially inflected fears of social disorder—of keeping the unwashed classes sober, self-disciplined, and on time for work.

To be sure, social control was not the whole story of Prohibition. There were other, more compelling arguments against alcohol, especially localist and feminist ones. Small towns resented the incursion of saloons franchised by national breweries; women who were economically dependent on men needed sober and nonviolent breadwinners. And however parochial the moral reformers' outlook may have been, their racism remained tempered by the same Christian universalism that gave rise to their self-righteousness. For them, liberation from alcohol would eventually become a program of regeneration for all. The Christian idea that every human being was created in God's image—however imperfectly honored—was always an inconvenience for hard-core racists.

Yet as early as the 1880s, older Christian ideas had ceded significant ground to scientific racism. This ideology provided new criteria for drawing boundaries between the human and the subhuman—an increasingly difficult problem as Darwinian ideas became popularized. It also injected a visceral urgency into the rhetoric of the regenerated self.

ALONGSIDE THE OLD duality of body and soul, scientific racists created a new racial hierarchy, with the Caucasian at the pinnacle and the Negro barely a rung above the orangutan. As early as 1860, only a few months after the publication of Darwin's *Origin of Species*, P. T. Barnum exploited the fascination with racial categories by exhibiting a light-skinned African-American man he called a "Nondescript." (The word first appeared as a noun in the 1860s, defining "a person or thing that is not easily described, or is of no particular class or kind.") The Nondescript both enticed and eluded the Victorian urge to pigeonhole people, but the manner of his presentation had a more sinister significance as well. Barnum's implicit suggestion that this black man might not even be a human being made the Nondescript a convenient "missing link" in the Great Chain of Being or in the process of Darwinian evolution. In subsequent decades, this would be the role implicitly assigned to Negroes in the most "advanced" racial thought of the age.

The pseudoscience of race provided legitimacy for white Southerners' fear of the "new negro," who had never known the supposedly civilizing influence of slavery. Paternalist agendas of uplift survived, but the dominant image of the Negro shifted from Sambo to the black beast—from irresponsible but educable child to subhuman menace. This was not an exclusively Southern development. The idea that freed blacks were retrogressing to savagery surfaced in intellectually respectable venues, North and South. In 1884, Nathaniel Shaler, a professor of natural science at Harvard (and later dean of the Lawrence School of Science there), asserted in the *Atlantic Monthly* that blacks and whites had evolved profoundly different race traits over eons of time: white people were endowed with organizational skills; black people were imitative. The proximity of the races promoted by slavery had given blacks the opportunity to imitate whites, and to become sufficiently like them to survive. After emancipation, Shaler asserted, that strategy was no longer available to black people; he predicted that "there will naturally be a strong tendency, for many generations to come, for them to revert to their ancestral conditions." That meant retrogression to a savage state.

Southern whites took retrogression theory and ran with it. In 1884, the same year that Shaler warned about the "The Negro Problem" in the *Atlantic*, the historian Philip Alexander Bruce proposed his own notion of black retrogression (he called it "regression") in the *New York Sun*. Bruce came from an old Virginia planter-class family, and he clung to the paternalist hope that the Negro might be saved from savagery if Southern whites would step up to their tutorial responsibilities. But by 1889, when he published *The Plantation Negro as Freeman*, Bruce had abandoned any vestigial paternalism and become a full-fledged radical racist. He could see nothing ahead but catastrophe: continued reversion of blacks to the "original African type," leading eventually to a race war—with the whites, of course, victorious.

Despite his apocalyptic vision, which seems hysterical to contemporary eyes, Bruce possessed intellectual legitimacy; he was a respected historian with access to national media. His views on the dangers of black retrogression were shared, in various forms, by men with scientific credentials, north of the Mason-Dixon Line: Walker Francis Willcox, professor at Cornell and chief statistician for the U.S. Census; Edwin Drinker Cope, professor of zoology and comparative anatomy in the University of Pennsylvania; Frederick L. Hoffman, statistician for the Prudential Insurance Company and author of *Race Traits and Tendencies of the American Negro*, which was published by the American Economic Association in 1896. Radical racism was eminently respectable.

But what was really important about the image of the black beast was less its intellectual legitimacy than its resonance with the racial views emerging among many white Southerners. Academic theories gave voice to vernacular prejudice. In 1889, Marion Butler, the editor of the *Clinton* (North Carolina) *Caucasian*, recommended to his readers the views of "Prof. Shaler (of 'Cambridge')" who had observed that freed blacks were "sinking back to the conditions of barbaric Africa. Prof. Shaler is the author of the new and probably correct theory for explaining the unprogressiveness of the negro, namely that his animal nature so preponderates over his intellectual and moral natures, that in the age of puberty, when the animal nature developes [*sic*], that the moral and intellectual qualities are clouded by the animal instinct and not only cease to develop but really retrograde." When the sober voice of science warned against the Negro menace in our midst, men like Butler reasoned, who could deny the necessity that whites fight back? Two years after his editorial reference to Shaler, Butler defended a local lynching as "justified by public sentiment, if not by law. A more fiendish deed [than the one that provoked the lynching] has not been attempted in our community for many years."

The "fiendish deed"—which almost certainly never occurred—was the alleged rape of a fifty-five-year-old white woman by a black man. Sex (or the fantasy of it) was the crucial piece in the puzzle linking radical racial theory to the rising tide of lynching that engulfed many parts of the South from 1889 through the first decade of the twentieth century. Between 1882 and 1888, throughout the United States, 595 whites were lynched, compared to 440 blacks. In 1889 the ratio shifted to 76 whites and 94 blacks, and three years later the discrepancy had nearly doubled: 69 whites were lynched, and 162 blacks. For the next decade and a half, about 85 percent of all lynching victims were African-American men in the former Confederate states. This carnage occurred in the wake of major political setbacks for blacks—not only the reassertion of white power at the local level but the crucial decision by the U.S. Supreme Court in the Civil Rights Cases of 1883: that the Civil Rights Act of 1875 was unconstitutional, because the Fourteenth Amendment applied only to the states, and that private segregation, by individuals or companies, was legal under the Constitution.

Lynching was more than the manifestation of white power in the wake of black defeat. It was a violent reaffirmation of white community, a ritual that served to exorcise sexual anxieties and overcome class conflict. In a sense it was the most extreme form of what W. E. B. DuBois called the "public and psychological wage" paid to white workers to compensate for their low monetary wages. The constant reaffirmation of their racial superiority allowed white workers to overlook their "practically identical interests" with black workers and abandon any hope of economic democracy in exchange for membership in the community of white men. In the flickering light of the flames, as the victims howled for mercy, landlord and tenant could forget their economic differences and become righteous white men together.

Lynching and interracial rape were twinned rhetorically if not in actual fact. Through the post–Civil War decades, white men's sexual fears and fantasies increasingly focused on the mythical black beast. A major piece of evidence for Negro retrogression, Bruce claimed, was the alarming increase in the rape of white women by black men. He was untroubled by the absence of evidence for this supposed spike in sex crimes. On the contrary, he made the manufactured crisis an excuse for a lurid description of how desire for white women reduced black men to beasts. "There is something strangely alluring and seductive to them in the appearance of a white woman; they are aroused and stimulated by its foreignness to their experience of sexual pleasure, and it moves them to gratify their lust at any cost and in spite of every obstacle." The Southern countryside, Bruce claimed, was swarming with black sexual predators: no wonder white women were afraid to venture abroad. This imagined epidemic of sex crime spread fear among the women, outrage among the men, "and not unnaturally, for rape, indescribably beastly and loathsome always, is marked, in the instance of its perpetration by a negro, by a diabolical persistence and a malignant atrocity of detail that have no reflection in the whole extent of the most bestial and ferocious animals." Black beastliness posed a challenge to white manliness.

Lynching was a reassertion of the link between whiteness and manliness, and a ritual regeneration of both. Repeatedly, Southern white men— senators, journalists, even jurists—invoked the protection of white womanhood to justify the torture, dismemberment, hanging, or burning of black men who may or may not have actually committed any crime at all (and who in any case had never been given a trial). Economic conflicts and rivalries were as important as sexual tensions in fomenting the kinds of white hostility that led to lynching, but no one can deny the obsessive sexual language that pervades much of the white racial discourse (and especially the discourse surrounding lynching) during these years. Imbibing the potent brew of race and sex, Southern white men merged manliness and whiteness, redefining manhood in racial rather than occupational terms. And whether work or sex created the conflict that led to the lynch mob, its main mission was the reassertion of white manhood.

While white Southern churches were scandalously silent about lynching, they contributed little or no support to the theory that justified it: Christianity and radical racism remained uneasy bedfellows, especially when it came to systematic violence and blood sacrifice. Missionaries and race theorists came together more easily in the rhetoric of empire. Protestantism and Progress marched westward together, fulfilling the imperial destiny of Anglo-Saxon civilization.

By the 1880s, this belief in inexorable advance was the common sense of the comfortable classes. The Panglossian John Fiske, writing in *Harper's* in 1885, resurrected the antebellum slogan of "Manifest Destiny" and applied it to an imperial age. Religion and race melded in Fiske's account of English conquests. Thus "the conquest of the North American continent by men of English race was unquestionably the most prodigious event in the political history of mankind" and Wolfe's victory at Quebec "the greatest turning point as yet discernible in all modern history." The clash of Catholicism and Protestantism would prove which tradition gave rise to the "higher and sturdier political life. The race which should here gain the victory was clearly destined hereafter to take the lead in the world." When the Protestant "race" won, the English "seed of civilization" was able to grow unchecked in American self-government.

This led eventually to separation from the mother country. Yet the American revolution was not a struggle with "a civilization of inferior type" like the French; it was "a struggle sustained by a part of the English people in behalf of principles that time has shown equally dear to all. And so the issue only made it apparent to an astonished world that instead of *one*, there were now *two* Englands, prepared to work with might and main toward the political regeneration of mankind." And indeed, no end was in sight: "the work which the English race began when it colonized North America is destined to go on until every land on the earth's surface that is not already the seat of an old civilization shall become English in its language, in its religion, in its political habits and traditions, and to a predominant extent in the blood of its people." The Anglo-Saxon people could look forward to a "stupendous" future when "four-fifths of the human race will trace its pedigree to English forefathers, as four-fifths of the white people" in the United States do.

While Fiske melded religion and race, the Congregational clergyman Josiah Strong added commerce to the imperial mix. In *Our Country* (1885), he asked: "What is the process of civilizing but the *creating of more and higher wants?*" Commercial enterprise would follow the missionary and ensure that "the millions of Africa and Asia are some day to have the wants of a Christian civilization." And "with these vast continents added to our market," surely the United States would become "the mighty workshop of the world, and our people 'the hands of mankind.'" What ensured this outcome, Strong asserted in *The New Era* (1893), was the innate superiority of the all-conquering Anglo-Saxons. The religious life of this race was "more vigorous, more spiritual, more Christian than that of any other." Their civilizing mission was unstoppable. "Is there any room for doubt that this race, unless devitalized by alcohol and tobacco, is destined to dispossess many weaker races, assimilate others, and mold the remainder, until, in a very true and important sense, it has Anglo-Saxonized mankind?"

Strong's synthesis struck a responsive chord: *Our Country* became a best seller, and Strong was appointed secretary of the American Evangelical Alliance, the organization in charge of Protestant missions overseas. The desire to convert the heathen was perfectly compatible with dreams of conquest. When a missionary was expelled from a country, as E. L. Godkin of *The Nation* wrote, he gave "the impression of a furious animal robbed of his prey." Strong had the predatory mind-set that was suitable for missionary work. When white people had settled all of North America and driven the aboriginal inhabitants to extinction, he predicted, "then will the world enter upon a new stage of its history—*the final competition of the races for which the Anglo-Saxon is being schooled.* If I do not read amiss, this powerful race will move down upon Mexico, down upon Central and South America, out upon the islands of the sea, over upon Africa and beyond. And can anyone doubt that the result of this competition will be the survival of the fittest?" Strong knew the wide currency of that potent phrase, which Darwin had borrowed from Herbert Spencer and which was providing another layer of legitimacy for schemes of racial domination. Science and religion seemed to point in the same direction: Progress and Providence were one.

Yet the synthesis remained precarious. Physical prowess, the basis of national supremacy, could not be taken for granted. Strong acknowledged in passing that Anglo-Saxons could be "devitalized by alcohol and tobacco." Racial superiority could be undone by degenerate habits. Even the most triumphalist tracts contained an undercurrent of anxiety, rooted in the fear of flab. The new stress on the physical basis of identity began subtly to undermine the Protestant synthesis, to reinforce the suspicion that religion was a refuge for effeminate weaklings. The question inevitably arose, in some men's minds: What if the YMCA and muscular Christianity were not enough to revitalize tired businessmen and college boys?

Under pressure from proliferating ideas of racial "fitness," models of manhood became more secular. Despite the efforts of muscular Christians to reunite body and soul, the ideal man emerging among all classes by the 1890s was tougher and less introspective than his mid-Victorian predecessors. He was also less religious. Among advocates of revitalization, words like "Energy" and "Force" began to dominate discussion—often capitalized, often uncoupled from any larger frameworks of moral or spiritual meaning, and often combined with racist assumptions. The aspiring novelist Frank Norris wanted to write about "man with his shirt off, stripped to the buff and fighting for his life," revealing the strength and tenacity that (Norris believed) were intrinsically Anglo-Saxon. The young Norris inhaled deep drafts of Anglo-Saxon supremacy from Rudyard Kipling and a racial interpretation of literature from Lewis Gates, his chief mentor at Harvard. Racism shaped manly revitalization in late-nineteenth-century America, from the streets of San Francisco to the Harvard Yard.

The emerging worship of force raised disturbing issues. Conventional morality took a backseat to the celebration of savage strength. After 1900, in the work of a pop-Nietzschean like Jack London, even criminality became a sign of racial vitality: as one of his characters says, "We whites have been land-robbers and sea-robbers from remotest time. It is in our blood, I guess, and we can't get away from it." This reversal of norms did not directly challenge racial hierarchies, but the assumptions behind it led toward disturbing questions. If physical prowess was the mark of racial superiority, what was one to make of the magnificent specimens of manhood produced by allegedly inferior races? Could it be that desk-bound Anglo-Saxons required an infusion of barbarian blood (or at least the "barbarian virtues" recommended by Theodore Roosevelt)? Behind these questions lay a primitivist model of regeneration, to be accomplished by incorporating the vitality of the vanquished, dark-skinned other. The question was how to do that and maintain racial purity.

This was the tangle of white obsessions that "non-whites" had to face in Gilded Age America. The "non-white" category included some European immigrants as well as Asians and African-Americans. The difference was that while the Chinese were eventually excluded and black people were gradually segregated, Europeans (if they stayed) had a fighting chance of assimilating into the emergent definition of what it meant to be "an American"—that is, a Caucasian. But this would take decades, and would become more difficult as the dominant stream of European immigrants began to flow from Southern and Eastern Europe rather than from Northwest Europe and the British Isles. Italians, Poles, Hungarians, Russian Jews—all these groups seemed strange and threatening to the American native-born. The pervasive resort to biological metaphors turned the nation into an organism and inferior immigrant "races" into a menace to it. By 1893, the previously ebullient Strong warned: "There is now being injected into the veins of the nation a large amount of inferior blood every day of the year." Even Social Gospel ministers were thinking with the blood. No wonder many immigrants preferred not to settle permanently in the United States and just kept moving: to Canada or Latin America, or back to their point of origin.

BEFORE 1890, NEARLY all immigrants arrived in New York City at Castle Garden, on the Battery. Approaching Castle Garden on lower Broadway, in the 1870s, one observer began to see little clusters of new arrivals, "walking slowly along the sidewalk, and bestowing a look of wonder on everything they saw." A German woman said of the "new magnificent" Equitable Building, "'Das muss der Palast sein [That must be the palace],' an opinion that seemed to be instantly shared by her companions. For a city without a 'Palast' of some kind is an impossibility in Germany." Crowds thickened as one approached the disembarkation point, "the passage was so blocked up with vehicles, peddlers of cheap cigars, apple-stands, and runners from the different boarding-houses and intelligence-offices that abound in the neighborhood." Among these last were the hordes of confidence men ready to fleece the unsuspecting greenhorn just off the boat. Not everyone just off the boat was entirely alone, though. Some had kin awaiting them in the Reception Room of the main building on the Battery. There one could witness a "blushing" Irish girl in the arms of her "faithful sweetheart," who sent for her after a three-year separation. "There is kissing and crying and squeezing, and applause from the by-standers, who for the moment forget that they themselves in a few minutes will probably do the same thing."

Such scenes were repeated endlessly throughout the second half of the nineteenth century. Between 1855 and 1890, eight million immigrants came through Castle Garden. After 1890, the entry point shifted to Ellis Island, where procedures became more formal and bureaucratic; the move coincided with the growing predominance of "new immigrants" from Southern and Eastern Europe. But through whichever entrepôt they entered, immigrants depended on staying mobile and getting help from kin. They were far more than the "huddled masses yearning to breathe free" of assimilationist lore. Usually they moved as part of a group (or at least a couple) and not individually. A Polish immigrant's letter to his brother in the old country (though it comes from the post-1900 era) typifies the pattern for the entire half-century after the Civil War:

> Dear Brother Waclaw:
> . . . I inform you about an offer from which you will perhaps profit. My old boss told me today that he had much work, so perhaps I know some carpenters, and if so I should send them to him. I told him that I had a brother carpenter (i.e. you) who was working, but if the work would be steady, I could bring him. He answered that he hoped to have steady work. So, I advise you to come dear brother . . . we could live here in the foreign land together. . . . We could meet him in South Chicago and speak about the business while drinking a glass of beer.

Despite the convivial beer, the emphasis on work as the key motivation was crucial. From a global perspective, the United States during this period was not a haven for the downtrodden but one point on the periphery of expanding world capitalism. Imbalances of supply and demand in the labor markets, in various places, at various times, kept immigrants on the move. Assimilation was not the only or even necessarily the best option: often immigrants returned and repatriated to their country of origin, or moved to someplace else—as many Italians did to Buenos Aires. Like the swelling army of tramps, which was also becoming ubiquitous and worri-some to respectable Americans, the growing mass of immigrants was made up of people in constant motion, swarming over vast territories in search of employment.

Indeed, the tramp and the immigrant were often the same person. Ad-dressing "The Tramp—His Cause and Cure" in the *Independent*, the soci-ologist Franklin Sanborn observed that "the two movements, as they show themselves in America—immigration and tramping—are but varieties of the same species. Both come under the general name of *migration*; and so great are now the facilities given to the poor and vicious for migrating within our own land, or from other countries to this, that it becomes important to . . . consider them in their locomotive condition." What begins as a laudatory im-pulse to better one's state in life "soon becomes a mere aimless ramble, or else degenerates into land-piracy. The lustful, thieving, or murderous tramp is a land-pirate—an outlaw as dangerous as the highwayman of ocean, who must be extirpated." The tramping tendency was characteristic of immigrants, and transmissible to the next generation. Two-thirds of Massachusetts tramps are foreigners or foreigners' children, Sanborn claimed. Out of every thousand mobile immigrants, a few tramps are formed, and from the immigrants' prog-eny, "thrown upon the public for support by the death, desertion, intemper-ance or imprisonment of their parents, the army of street-arabs and roadside beggars is largely recruited." To the comfortably settled classes, a mobile mass of mostly foreign indigents was hardly a reassuring prospect.

The engine that kept migrants and immigrants in motion was the inter-national market for labor. The half-century after the American Civil War was a crucial epoch in the globalization of capitalism. Open labor markets were the key to the expansion of capital beyond national boundaries. A huge inflow of immigrants created a reserve labor supply that served em-ployers' interests by dampening down wages. Men who could be easily re-placed would not so easily go on strike. The cure for the chronic American labor shortage—an abundant supply of cheap immigrant labor—threatened workers who were already on the premises. Or so they (understandably) thought, as they watched employers use immigrants to break strikes and lower wages, often pitting one despised minority against another. Bitter in-terethnic rivalries undermined the fitful prospects for working-class solidar-ity. Then as now, talking about race was a way of not talking about class, and historians have long pointed to ethnic fragmentation as one reason socialism never had the political clout in the United States that it did in Europe. As racism and nativism intensified among the Anglo-Saxon majority, so did minorities' sense of their Irishness, say, or their Jewishness. Zionism and Irish nationalism were just two of the most obvious examples of the ethnic self-consciousness—what we now call "ethnicity"—that took root during this period. The construction of race-based community proceeded on many and various fronts.

Every inclusion constituted an exclusion. White ethnic solidarities were especially hard on African-Americans, who were less able to count on kin networks to get jobs and who were kept out of craft unions either systematically or informally. Power and prejudice combined to keep many of them on the Southern plantation, whose owners preferred local blacks to European immigrants. According to one South Carolina planter, Swedes and Germans constantly found excuses to stay out of the sun while they consumed huge quantities of food; they were not worth what it cost to board them. "I am now done with white labor," he announced. "The Immigration Society of New York send to us (down South) the offscouring of the earth—penitentiary birds and lunatics out of their asylums. . . . I think this immigration business one of the grandest humbugs of the day." Rationales for excluding immigrants varied from one region to another. The Chinese Exclusion Act of 1882 was the most flagrant and formal rationale, and the only federal one until the National Origins Act of 1924.

Despite its national reach, the Chinese Exclusion Act reflected distinctly regional tensions. Between 1850 and 1882, 322,000 unskilled Cantonese arrived in San Francisco to work on the railroads, plantations, and ranches of California and the Great West. They shared a migrant-workers' mentality: most planned to return to their families in China when their labor was no longer wanted. With them, especially in the early years, came a trickle of Cantonese merchants and skilled artisans who pursued commercial ventures in San Francisco and other cities, creating the "Chinatowns" that became nodes of the exotic for Westerners. In the nativist imagination, Chinese immigrants were the source of strange cuisine, seductive drugs, and diabolical sexual practices; but most important, they were cheap labor. They provoked deep resentment among the blacks (who had little political clout) and the Irish (who had a lot). By the late 1870s, the Chinese constituted one-fifth of the state's population of 600,000, and the bitter rivalry between Chinese and Irish workers in San Francisco had erupted into open warfare.

The *New Englander* magazine identified the casus belli by applying the laws of political economy: when labor is scarce and capital abundant, wages tend to rise; when labor is abundant and capital scarce, wages fall. In an old country where all the land is already apportioned and production is restricted, the law of Malthus applies: wages will drop to starvation levels. But in a country with an unlimited supply of land, both profits and wages may be great. So they were in California, until the labor supply was "abnormally increased" by the importation of the Chinese, which affected common laborers directly and all other workers indirectly. "After the disturbance caused by the suddenness of the increased supply of labor had eased, the results would approximately be—a great increase in the wealth of capitalists and land-owners, diminished wages in the hands of those who were laborers before the coming of the Chinese, cheapened products for the community at large, except perhaps in the case of food, and increased development of the country." Wages might eventually rise to where they were before, except that there seemed no limit to the number of Chinese who might emigrate. "China may be likened to a vast reservoir of labor, California to a partial vacuum, and communication once opened between them, the current of labor once started, equilibrium will only be reached when the rate of wages is reduced so low . . . that inducements to emigrate are counterbalanced by the annoyances and difficulties." The increasing population would keep prices up and wages down. Capitalists would become "irresistible masters," the Chinese "almost their slaves," and American workers the "poor whites" of tomorrow. American laborers simply could not compete with the Chinese except by lowering their standard of living: "The food and shelter an Irishman gives to his pig would suffice for the wants of a Chinese; and while this is so the Chinaman can compel the Irishman to descend to the level of his pig."

As if this scenario were not degrading enough, the *New Englander* warned that the Chinese also posed a political threat. If they decided to become naturalized U.S. citizens, the political consequences would be catastrophic—nothing less than an "inversion of races." Since they were almost all adult males, they nearly equaled the legal voters of California. With only a small increase in numbers, they could take over the government, including public education. They could teach "their own views of science, religion, and morals. They would have the same right to compel American scholars to listen to the institutes of Confucius, that a Yankee majority has to compel

Irish children to listen to the Protestant Bible." Given this apocalyptic prospect, it should come as no surprise that the *New Englander* concluded by wondering whether our "experiment of the peaceful mingling of the races in one republic" might be at odds with the doctrine of natural selection, which if allowed to operate in California would eliminate the Chinese by exposing them to their natural enemies, the Irish laborers. Wasn't it time to lighten the ship of state by jettisoning our sentimental ideals of democracy and human equality, the *New Englander* asked, and acknowledging (as our white Southern brethren appear prepared to do) that "self-government is not a characteristic of all races"?

The sheer strangeness of Chinese culture reinforced Americans' suspicions. Mrs. Leslie visited a Chinese theater and concluded that the play was "like a feverish dream," filled with "grotesque figures" performing "ferocious and monotonous gestures," accompanied by sounds that could only be described as "frightful discord." To be sure, the affluent visitor to San Francisco could locate fashionable Chinese shops where, as Mrs. Leslie observed, the atmosphere was "redolent of sandalwood and Oriental perfumes," and the high-caste merchants were "altogether different from the Chinese laundry-men from whom we, of the Atlantic Coast, take our ideas" of China. But for every "reposeful" merchant there were ten stupefied opium addicts, their heads lolling, their eyes "glazed and lifeless." As a signal of readiness for self-government, this would never do.

There were those, mainly Easterners, who defended the Chinese—usually by contrasting their calm, clean, and disciplined habits with the wayward ways of the Irish. The Chinese, they pointedly said, made superb domestic servants and common laborers, while "the Irish immigrant" has "always hated any race and any nationality that has been brought into competition with him in common labor." Some defenders of the Chinese even took the high road, invoking democratic principles: "The Declaration of Independence and its sequel, universal suffrage, may be grievous blunders, but we are positively committed to them until a new idea is born," announced *Potter's American Monthly.* "The thing must now be fairly tested, not by locking the back door against the Mongolian, and barring the front door against the African, but by throwing wide all the entrances of this new home of man"—even if white people eventually lost control.

This was an idiosyncratic view, thoroughly out of tune with dominant desires for racial revitalization. The argument for exclusion (the one that soon prevailed) drew strength from a potent mixture of race and economics. The cause of Chinese exclusion quickly acquired political and judicial legitimacy. *In re: Ah Yup* (1878), a U.S. Circuit Court decision, denied a Chinese man's application for citizenship and established "Caucasians" as a legally recognized racial group. This was a key event in the redefinition of Americans as white people, a development that would eventually allow for the racial assimilation of European immigrant groups. Its impact would be gradually felt over the next several decades, as narrow and rigid categories sometimes revealed greater fluidity and capaciousness. Pressed by San Franciscans, Secretary of State James G. Blaine betrayed this tendency when he took up the issue of Chinese exclusion in 1879, casting it as a racial Armageddon. "Either the Anglo-Saxon race will possess the pacific slope, or the Mongolians will possess it," he warned. Blaine was politically savvy enough to know that the war against the Chinese was being led by the Irish—was this merely a slip of the tongue, or was he implicitly anointing the Irish as honorary Anglo-Saxons? With their agitation for Chinese exclusion, the Irish took a major step toward full membership in the American community.

Cultural, racial, and economic anxieties fed a visceral fear and animosity that spilled over regional boundaries and eventually led to the Chinese Exclusion Act of 1882. But the war on the Chinese was not over. In February 1885, when Chinese factions fell to fighting among themselves in Eureka, California, the city council held an emergency meeting and voted to expel all the Chinese from town: they had twenty-four hours to clear out. This was the first of many ethnic cleansings undertaken by white citizens in small towns throughout the mountain West. Some months later, a massacre of Chinese railroad workers in Rock Springs, Wyoming Territory, touched off a wave of similar mob actions. Charles Francis Adams, the president of the Union Pacific Railroad, ordered disciplinary action against the white railroad workers; the Knights of Labor demanded that all Chinese be fired. White workers' standard of living continued to slip, thanks to management's determination to cut labor costs. But coolies made a convenient scapegoat.

Despite the persistence of conflict, the Irish had played a major role in promoting Chinese exclusion; their success opened their door to full Americanism a little wider. But real assimilation was still a long way off. European immigrants faced not only the vagaries of the labor market but also the perversities of Anglo-Saxon racism. Even in the earlier years, when immigrants came mainly from Northern and Western Europe, the Germans and (especially) the Irish were held up for scorn. Suspicions of popery ran deeply in Protestant America, animating a pattern of invidious distinctions with secular as well as religious significance. Walter Rauschenbusch, Washington Gladden, and other Social Gospel Protestants contrasted the sedative effects of Roman Catholicism with the regenerative effects of Protestantism. From the Protestant view, Irish Catholics' propensity for obedience allowed unscrupulous politicians (as well as authoritarian priests) to lead them around by the nose.

By 1877, 25 percent of New England was Roman Catholic, largely due to Irish immigration, Anglo emigration to the West, and "most ominous," the *Independent* reported, a soaring Catholic birthrate. The question was no longer far-fetched: "Will New England Become Catholic?" The magazine rallied native-born Protestants to more vigorous procreative habits, and warned that the growing Catholic population would need careful education to assimilate. A Catholic New England, the *Independent* concluded, "would be something vastly superior to any known Catholic country, we do not doubt . . . Its priests are self-denying, useful Christian teachers, doing their utmost to develop a faulty system, and exercising an influence which is healthfully repressive of vice, if not as educational in intelligence and right religion as one could wish. Though we fear a Catholic New England, we have more fear of a population outgrowing Catholicism, restive under religious control, like that in Pittsburgh, which Bishop [John] Tuigg has cut off from the Church." The church hierarchy's disapproving response to labor violence made one thing clear: Catholic obedience to authority was preferable to working-class agitators' contempt for it. As conflict between labor and capital flared into open warfare, radicalism replaced religion as the chief source of nativist fears.

Persistent preoccupations with race gave political anxieties a palpable, physical form. By the 1880s, Celtic caricatures were recast from the familiar simian features in Thomas Nast's cartoons of Irish machine politicians to the murkier figure of the Irish labor radical. Nevertheless, physiognomy remained destiny. Consider John Hay's portrait of the Irish union organizer Andy Offitt in *The Bread-winners* (1884). His "was a face whose whole expression was oleaginous. It was surmounted by a low and shining forehead covered by reeking black hair, worn rather long, the ends being turned under by the brush. The moustache was long and drooping, dyed black and profusely oiled, the dye and the grease forming an inharmonious compound. . . ." Offit had "one of those gifted countenances which could change in a moment from dog-like fawning to a snaky venomousness." The slippery unreliability of this character was embodied in his physical form.

Hay's foray into physiognomy was vicious enough, but soon immigrants stranger than Irishmen began to crowd into lower Manhattan and fan out across the countryside. Surveying the changes in immigration during the 1880s, the young Woodrow Wilson spied a descent from the "sturdy stock" of Northern Europe to "men out of the ranks where there was neither skill nor energy nor any initiative of quick intelligence"—men, that is, from Southern and Eastern Europe. In Wilson's formulations as elsewhere, allegedly racial characteristics melded with mental and moral ones. The British observer James Bryce captured the conventional Anglo-Saxon wisdom when he described a typical scene in New York during the run-up to an election in the late 1880s. He reported that "droves of squalid men," accompanied by the local Democratic machine organizer from Tammany Hall, were marched before the magistrate to register to vote. Illiterate, unkempt, and undisciplined, they were "not fit for the suffrage," Bryce concluded, melding class prejudice with ethnocentric fears. Concern that unfit immigrant "races" would undermine the foundations of the republic underlay patrician agitation for limiting immigrants' access to entry, which began in earnest with the foundation of the Immigration Restriction League in 1892.

Where supposedly racial differences were small enough, the possibilities for assimilation were greater. And what were called racial differences were often indistinguishable from cultural differences. The Irish and the Germans were disappointingly prone to Catholicism and alcohol, but the best of them displayed the bourgeois virtues. Even in the shantytown that immigrants had constructed west of Central Park in midtown Manhattan, a *Scribner's* contributor reported in 1880, many of the inhabitants scrimped and saved, planted gardens, kept pets, and in general sought to sustain a stable domestic life. Young couples conducted "decent and sober" courtships at home—even if home was a tumbledown shack. Irish-German interplay provided occasion for Anglo-Saxon bemusement. Juliet Mulvany "is spanked and put to bed for making mud-pies with Romeo Guggenheim. Romeo dies not for her, but growing older, turns to a maiden of his own people, and visits her on Saturday nights." As he leaves, "small boys throw tomato cans at him and chorus: 'Sho'! Sho'! Lottie Bierbaum's got a beau!'" Immigrants could be funny and charming as well as threatening. Another path to assimilation, by way of local color and literary sentimentalism, was beginning to appear.

But sentimentality benefited some groups more than others. By the late 1870s, from the native-born Protestant point of view, a divide had already opened between Northwestern Europe and the rest of the continent. Italians, for example, were routinely described as "squalid" and "uncleanly"—in contrast to the well-kept English and Germans. A *Scribner's* writer described an "immigrant's progress" by narrating the passage of Honest Giles—an exceptionally literate carpenter—and his family from their English village to Castle Garden and eventually his new home, "a broad expanse of untilled land" somewhere in the Great West. This was fulfillment, but the effort to get there had been excruciating—especially the Atlantic crossing in steerage, where "a cleanly, thrifty English or German woman is berthed next to a filthy Italian woman. Mrs. Giles thinks her bed would be hard enough, even though it were isolated, but her misery is intensified by the presence of a dreadful hag in the next berth." Distaste for Italians was exacerbated by their distance from whiteness; even more than the Irish, they were the "niggers" of the European immigrant world. The White League in New Orleans affirmed that assumption in 1891, when they tortured and hanged eleven Italian immigrants who had been accused of conspiring to murder the police chief. Newspaper opinion was unanimous nationwide: the "sneaking and cowardly Sicilians" got what they deserved. "Our own rattlesnakes are as good citizens as they," the *New York Times* declared.

The White League was a terrorist organization that had originated in resistance to Reconstruction; the lynching underscored the continuity between antiblack and anti-immigrant racism, as well as the racial ambiguity of swarthy Sicilians. Apparently difficult to characterize as either black or white, Italians posed a challenge to citizens bent on color-coded categories. It would take several decades before Italians were considered culturally white enough to assimilate. Certainly in the Gilded Age, the superiority of Northern European immigrants was taken for granted by received opinion; indeed they were the ones who mostly quickly became "Americans"—down to and including their adoption of nativist attitudes.

The saga of the Danish-American photographer and journalist Jacob Riis provides a good illustration of this trend. The very title of his memoir—*The Making of an American* (1901)—epitomizes his assimilationist zeal. His tale fit the mythic model of the upward-striving immigrant as ambitious individualist. Unlike most of his contemporaries, Riis emigrated alone, though with romantic aspirations to send for his childhood sweetheart when he could support her. He arrived at Castle Garden in 1870. "It was a beautiful spring morning . . . my hopes rose high that somewhere in this teeming hive there would be a place for me. What kind of place I had myself no clear knowledge of. I would let that work out as I could. Of course I had my trade [carpentry] to fall back on, but I am afraid that this is all the use I had thought of putting it to. The love of change belongs to youth, and I meant to take a hand in things as they came along. I had a pair of strong hands and stubbornness enough to do for two; also a strong belief that in a free country, free from the dominion of custom, of caste, as well as of men, things would somehow come right in the end, and a man get shaken into a corner where he belonged if he took a hand in the game."

For the next few years, Riis took a hand in things as they came along. He began as the greenest of greenhorns. Thinking he would encounter Indians and buffalo on Broadway, he bought a big revolver and strapped it to his hip, until a policeman warned him it might easily be stolen, and that it was in any case not à la mode in Manhattan. He headed west, joining a crew who contracted to work at Brady's Iron Works on the Allegheny River; nearly all the men deserted at Pittsburgh. "Not one of them, probably, would have thought of doing it on the other side [i.e., in Europe]. They would have carried out their contract as a matter of course. Here they broke it as a matter of course, the minute it didn't suit them to go on." This was the underside of the vaunted American freedom. Riis built miners' huts in East Brady, Pennsylvania, where he suffered "horrible homesickness" for the flatness of Denmark; he tried coal mining there as well, and was terrified by the silence and dark, not to mention nearly killed by a falling boulder. After knocking about for some time in western Pennsylvania and Ohio, never holding a job long, he returned to New York in frustration, nearly starved in the street, and in a climactic moment resolved to rid the city of the noisome slums where he had almost died.

But by the time he had reached middle age, Riis may have established some distance from his younger self. Certainly he had embraced conventional bourgeois moralism. Straggling down the road from New York to Philadelphia, where he had relatives he believed might help him out, the young Riis found himself on "the great tramps' highway, with the column moving south on its autumn hegira to warmer climes." Though he had often been forced to fall in with tramps, the older Riis claimed he found them distasteful and kept his distance. "As for the 'problem' they are supposed to represent, I think the workhouse and the police are quite competent to deal with that, provided it is not a Tammany police," he huffed. "It does not differ appreciably from the problem of human laziness in any other shape or age." Moral blinders narrowed Riis's perception, preventing him from seeing how many tramps were simply immigrants. The settled, successful journalist had forgotten that the locomotive condition was at the heart of the immigrant experience.

Whatever Riis's shortcomings as a social observer, no one could accuse him of laziness. After resting two weeks with his friends in Philadelphia, he reported, "I was none the worse for my first lesson in swimming against the current, and quite sure the next time I would be able to breast it." He headed for western New York, where he worked at a variety of jobs: making cradles, felling trees, running a "wheelbarrow express" delivery service, hunting and trapping muskrats, and lecturing to workmen on the "formation and development of the earth." (Foundering on the explanation of longitude, he soon lost his audience.) He worked as a cabinetmaker in Buffalo, but quit when his boss kept cutting his piece rate. He joined a gang laying railroad track but found he didn't have the strength or stamina for it; the Irishmen he worked with tried to protect him from the most demanding tasks, but eventually the heat, the work, and the foreman were too much even for them. Riis had to leave. He tried business, working as a "drummer" (a traveling salesman) for a furniture factory in the oil fields of western Pennsylvania, selling irons for a Midwestern firm and managing its Chicago office. Back in New York, he studied telegraphy at a technical school, and a chance encounter with the owner of the school led to a job at a news agency. "So began my life as a newspaper man," Riis recalled.

For years he had longed to go into the newspaper business, convinced that "a reporter's was the highest and noblest of all callings: no one could sift wrong from right as he, and punish the wrong." Riis's belief in "the power of fact" to right wrongs led to his career as a crusading Progressive journalist. Like many of his contemporaries he assumed that the mere exposure of an evil would lead to its elimination. And like most other Progressives of Northern European background, he embraced the dominant culture's attitude toward the new streams of immigrants arriving from Southern and Eastern Europe: a blend of fascination and repulsion. Reporting from the

Lower East Side in the 1880s, he reveled in hierarchical taxonomies and zoological parallels (especially feline): the Chinaman, for example, was as clean and cunning as a cat, the Italian as inoffensive as a child if his fur was not stroked the wrong way. Riis's transformation from struggling immigrant to nativist flaneur typified the ironies of the assimilation process: in this case a Northern European, whose Caucasian credentials were impeccable, quickly began affirming received racial categories.

Many immigrants' experience involved a delicate pas de deux of competing desires—longings to join the mainstream but also to reassert race pride in the face of scientific racism, renewed nativism, and competition from other ethnic groups. During the late nineteenth century, just as the Irish were being admitted to full membership in the white republic, they were also developing an unprecedented sense of ethnic solidarity—an outlook prodded by Protestant hostility and animated by a Catholic devotional revolution that put even businessmen on their knees. Jews, in the wake of the Russian May Laws and the pogroms of 1881, increasingly embraced race as a basis for unity, especially in the ideology of Zionism: a distinct people, some Jews began to say, needed a distinct homeland. Emma Lazarus, an upper-class American Jew of German extraction, celebrated the Americanization of the "huddled masses yearning to breathe free" in her paean to the Statue of Liberty, "The New Colossus" (1883). But she played a variation on the theme of distinctiveness in *An Epistle to the Hebrews* (1887). Judaism, she announced, was both a race and a religion, and Jews themselves were a wonderful "fusion of Oriental genius with Occidental enterprise and energy." For outsiders as well as insiders, categories of race played a critical role in sustaining social identity.

Still ethnic solidarity had its limits, especially when it faced the potent engines of assimilation that John Wanamaker and other department store magnates were installing in major American cities. Wanamaker and his contemporaries were clear: the department store was not only a machine for selling goods; it was also a machine for acculturating immigrants—for creating a standardized "American look" as a criterion for social acceptance. Advertising for national-brand-name goods, which was also coming into its own in the late nineteenth century, complemented the influence of department stores. The criteria for attaining the "American look" were becoming predictable, almost formulaic in the emergent consumer culture. Over several decades, the younger generations of European immigrants would gradually acquire the knack of looking American. Ethnic differences would preserve importance but would yield gradually in the public realm to the homogenizing power of whiteness. Color would be the master key to cultural acceptance, and "American" would be virtually synonymous with "Caucasian."

As immigrants began to blend in by fits and starts, blacks were more systematically segregated and excluded from participation in public life. Still it would be a mistake to treat the Jim Crow South as an inevitable development, or to read its imminent triumph back into black life of the Gilded Age. Even into the 1890s, in some parts of the South, black men voted, held office, organized unions, denounced injustice, demanded public services, cut deals, and took bribes.

In short, they were involved in politics in all the ways that white men were. It is important to see the post-Reconstruction history of African-Americans not as a swift and inevitable descent to a nadir but as a period when freed people struggled, sometimes successfully, to sustain the meaning of black emancipation against the relentless reassertion of white supremacy. It was also a time that remained fluid with possibilities, for the fortunate few who could follow Booker T. Washington's gospel of self-help, and for those on the fringes of the old Confederacy. Black people, too, embraced the locomotive condition—migrating from the upper South to work in the cotton fields of the Delta and the turpentine camps of the piney woods, or from the red clay hills of rural Georgia to work in the barbershops and bordellos of Atlanta. At first fitfully, then more steadily, a stream of black migrants began to flow toward Northern and Midwestern destinations, as well. Out of desperation and desire, black people embarked on their own efforts to reinvent themselves as free people, even as the white supremacist counterrevolution sought to shut down their options.

ONE BRISK APRIL day in 1879, a steamboat moored at Wyandotte, Kansas, on the Missouri River near Kansas City, to discharge an unlikely cargo of black men, women, and children. As they stood on the wharf, shivering in the wind, one Eastern journalist noted, "a sort of dumb awe seemed to settle upon and possess them. They looked like persons coming out of a dream." Within two weeks, more than a thousand such migrants had arrived in Wyandotte County alone, and within a year, in various Kansas towns, somewhere between fifteen thousand and twenty thousand more. Most came from Mississippi and Texas, the rest from Tennessee, Louisiana, Alabama, and Georgia. They had not left the South willingly, they said, but they were never going back. The reporter summarized their reasons: "They assert that there is no security for their lives and property in their own homes; that the law and courts are studiedly inimical to them and their interests; that the exercise of the electoral franchise is obstructed and made a personal danger; that no facilities are accorded them for educating their children; that their family rights and honor are scoffed at and outraged, as in the slave days; and finally—and this is the most frequent complaint—that they are so unjustly and unfairly dealt with by white land-owners, employers and traders, that it is impossible to make a living." The restoration of white supremacy hurt black people in many ways, but the most immediate and pressing damage was economic.

The attempt to start over in Kansas met with mixed success. The first winter was exceptionally mild. " 'God seed dat de darkeys had thin clothes,' was the remark of one of their preachers, 'an' he done kep' de cole off.' " This was a blessing, but other problems remained. Though a solid minority of the migrants had tools and teams of horses, only a handful had somehow managed to accumulate enough capital to set up farming on their own land. To be sure, the freed people showed extraordinary courage and tenacity. Kansans acknowledged that they "seem able to make a feast on what would haunt white persons with visions of starvation," but neither their ingenuity at making do nor their capacity for hard work could create economic independence. Their skills were spotty, and not always suited to northern conditions. Even a seasoned plantation cook could not simply walk into a Kansas kitchen and prepare breakfast; routine cuisine in the Deep South could be exotic on the Plains. Like European immigrants, most migrants were forced to support themselves with casual labor, hoeing beans or flipping pancakes, dependent on the vagaries of the market and the weather. Despite its abolitionist tradition, Kansas was no promised land for blacks.

Still, the West held an appeal, especially for young black men. Consider the case of Nat Love, who became known as Deadwood Dick. Born into slavery in 1854 in Tennessee, Love recalled his early life choices as self-made manhood or starvation. His father was "a sort of foreman of the slaves," his mother the plantation cook; both faced incessant demands that prevented them from paying much attention to their children. "I received very little attention from any of the family; therefore necessity compelled me at an early age to look after myself and rustle my own grub," Love recalled. He rustled his own liquor too. Before his voice had even changed, he and his sister and brother unearthed a jug of wine their mother had made and hidden. "I suppose I acquired the taste for strong drink on this occasion," Love wrote. Along with a taste for liquor he also developed an ability to drink huge amounts without getting drunk.

He grew up fast. The war came, the master left to fight in the Confederate Army, and when he returned he never told his slaves they were free. When they finally learned, Nat's father was immediately determined to be an independent farmer. He rented twenty acres from his former master and planted corn and tobacco. At this time the Love family was destitute, Nat recalled: "without food or money and almost naked, we existed for a time on the only food procurable, bran and cracklins." Just when they seemed about to turn a corner, Nat's father died and Nat was forced to shoulder adult responsibilities. "Although I was the youngest, I was the most courageous," Nat maintained with characteristic modesty. "Always leading in mischief play and work. So now I took the leadership and became the head of the family . . . I put on my best rags and searched for work." When he was cheated by one employer, Nat remembered, "I hit him in the head with a rock and nearly killed him"; after this, he announced, "I felt better." It was one of his first lessons in "self-dependence and life's struggles." Here was an unexpurgated version of the self-made man.

Unlike many self-made men (or at least their mythical representations), Love achieved success not by plodding diligence but by harnessing the energy, courage, and resourcefulness required for adolescent high jinks—hunting rabbits, battling other boys with rocks for weapons—to more pragmatic ends. His most successful such stunt was breaking in colts for employees on a horse ranch, while their boss was at church. Nat received ten cents a head, and a taste for the sort of life he would live on the Plains. Like many young men, black or white, he was restless. "I wanted to see more of the world and as I began to realize there was so much more of the world than what I had seen, the desire to go grew on me day to day. It was hard to leave mother and the children, but freedom is sweet and I wanted to make more of the opportunity and my life than I could see possible around home. Besides I suppose I was a little selfish as mortals are prone to be." Luck intervened. Nat won a raffle, split the hundred-dollar prize with his mother, and—after an uncle had promised to stay with her—took off.

Fifteen and green, he headed for Kansas. In Dodge City, after demonstrating his riding skills, he was hired by a Texas cattle ranch that already employed several "colored cowboys." On the Fourth of July, 1876 (ten days after Custer's Last Stand), in Deadwood, Dakota Territory, Nat acquired the nickname Deadwood Dick by dominating all the roping and shooting contests held that day. For the next fifteen years, he knocked around the Great West, always landing on his feet. He survived blizzards, range wars between cattlemen and farmers, the death of his Mexican sweetheart, capture and adoption by Yellow Dog's tribe of "halfbreeds" (as well as successful escape from them)—and a bout with "bad whiskey" that left him trying to rope a cannon at Fort Dodge, Kansas. (An embarrassing moment, but one Nat characteristically turned to his advantage by noting that Bat Masterson himself came to his defense.) He outlived Billy the Kid and the buffalo herds, but by 1890 his old life was over. He married, but settling down didn't appeal, and he became a Pullman porter to continue his traveling ways.

The life of Nat Love was not as idiosyncratic as it seems. Westward migration was one path available to restless Southern blacks, and if farming didn't work out, more venturesome possibilities awaited, especially for young men. Staying on the premises made less and less sense as white rule was reasserted in state after state. Still, many Southern blacks did stick it out, seeking to sustain some semblance of public life, even as disenfranchisement and lynching took their toll.

By the 1880s, public life in many Southern states was a cesspool of corruption. The buying and selling of votes was common among both parties and both races. Even after the restoration of white rule, Republican strength persisted among white people in the uplands and black people in the low country. Democrats sometimes succeeded in bribing or bullying blacks into voting for them. Party lines and racial boundaries were not yet cast in concrete, as they would be under Jim Crow. In black majority districts, "fusion" became the order of the day: white Democrats held office in exchange for ceding control over local patronage to Republicans, who were usually black. Fusion helped account for the black postmasters, school superintendents, and other public officials who kept their offices well into the 1890s, especially in tidewater Virginia and eastern North Carolina. Fusion also left electoral politics entirely dominated by force and fraud. White elites had regained control, but at the cost of rampant corruption and near-anarchy. White supremacy lacked legitimacy, and triumphant claims of "redemption" were overshadowed by the swelling public sense that politics had nothing to do with real life.

Reactions to political unreality varied widely. "The nihilism of the common man might be expressed in an excessive devotion to bird dog and shotgun," the historian C. Vann Woodward later wrote, "or in the towns and cities by heedless absorption in money getting and progress." But during the 1880s and early 1890s, more direct resistance to the unreality of Southern politics was still possible. Insurgencies flared across racial lines. The sugar country of Louisiana, where black people constituted a majority, was a node of labor unrest and a fertile field for Knights of Labor organizing. In 1880 a strike broke out among the sugar workers. The Democratic governor, Louis Wiltz, called out the state militia, and white officials in St. Charles arrested fourteen black "ringleaders" for trespassing. The justice of the peace announced that the men had to be disciplined because "the great arm of the great wheel of agriculture is the nigger. Next is the mule." But in St. John's, the black sheriff John Webre made no arrests, and one justice of the peace joined the strikers, while the black state senator Henry Demas tried to mediate between the workers and the employers. African-Americans were still actively involved in local government, and this helped the sugar strikers. The strikers held out for some time, declaring, "the colored people are a nation and must stand together," demanding a dollar a day, and even drawing up a "constitution" specifying workers' rights and responsibilities. Eventually the white militia arrived and the strike leaders were arrested and jailed.

Still, unrest continued in various pockets of lower Louisiana, and the Knights of Labor began trying to establish themselves there. By 1886, they were fanning north from New Orleans, organizing workers against the Louisiana Sugar Planters Association. Amid growing popular demands to break up big holdings, the planters cut wages in the fall of 1887. The Knights called a strike for November 1, and 90 percent of the workers walked out. It was the start of the grinding season and the cane was vulnerable to spoilage. Some planters gave in. But the Democratic governor sent two companies of state militia, with a Gatling gun, to evict the strikers and guard against "any insurrection of the negroes." After their confrontation with the militia, the evicted strikers poured into the local towns, especially Thibodaux. The planters, led by Taylor Beattie, complained of "idle negroes" clogging the streets and organized a "peace and order" committee, which persuaded the sheriff to declare martial law and seal off the town. No black people were permitted to leave. Early in the morning of November 23, white vigilantes massacred the trapped strikers, killing more than fifty of them. Months later, local "regulators" were still terrorizing blacks. The Knights soon disappeared from the sugar country. A similar pattern appeared in Arkansas, where the Knights successfully organized black cotton-pickers until they were overwhelmed and scattered by state violence.

Yet the insurgent spirit kept erupting in various Southern places. The liveliest was Virginia. After the Civil War, farmers in the Old Dominion diversified, turning to truck and grain farming in the old tobacco districts; African-Americans bought small plots from big white landowners who needed liquid capital and seasonal wage labor. Virginia soon had the largest percentage of black landowners in the old Confederacy. At the same time, Virginia politics boiled in a ferment of possibilities, as a biracial insurgency called the Readjuster movement rose to power in the 1880s. The Readjusters backed a readjustment of the state debt to favor the 95 percent of the population that did not hold state bonds. This was precisely what conservative Democrats feared: a mass movement rooted in discontent with policies that served the narrow interests of white elites—a movement likely to appeal to hill-country plain folk and Southside blacks alike.

The Readjusters were led by the former Confederate general William Mahone, who built a powerful biracial machine by using trade-offs and filling black quotas, and who ascended to the U.S. Senate for one term in the 1880s. The Readjusters funded public services, especially public education, with a generosity hardly seen in the Old Dominion before or since. But they were constantly challenged by racist badgering. Democrats played on white fears of "negro rule," especially in black majority counties like Pittsylvania, where Danville is located. In Danville, during the run-up to a state election in 1883, Democrats evoked visions of uppity Negroes trying "to *force ladies* from the pavement." The Saturday before the election, a street altercation left four blacks dead and roving bands of whites patrolling the area. Three days later, the Democrats won—barely.

Insurgencies continued to crop up in many Southern states, creating a potential biracial audience for the agrarian radicalism that would animate the Farmers' Alliances in the 1880s and the Populist Party in the 1890s. What the agrarian rebels could make of that audience, amid the politics of white supremacy, remained to be seen. Politics, insurgent or establishment, was not foreclosed to blacks in the Gilded Age, but was increasingly fraught with difficulties. Too often, pursuing an ambition in the political field involved picking your way around dead bodies.

With respect to everyday life, though, there was at least some good news for black people, even at the nadir of their fortunes. They continued to acquire land, especially in the upper and border South. Their civic and associational life thickened, as black churches, schools, benevolent societies, and religious journals proliferated. It was also during this period that a black professional class began to establish itself in Richmond, Durham, Charleston, New Orleans, and other Southern cities. And there were less tangible cultural developments as well. African-American music flowered in vernacular forms, first gospel and later a new secular hybrid, inextricable from the railroads and the mobility they spawned: the blues.

So much for the good news. The bad news was the emergence of a nearly solid phalanx of white racism, much of it bearing scientific legitimacy. Of course it was always possible for African-American intellectuals to deride the discourse of Anglo-Saxon supremacy—to challenge the silly equation of brutality and aggressiveness with civilization. But nearly all, even the young W. E. B. DuBois, spoke from their own romantic racialist perspective on the essential virtues inherent in their race. Few nineteenth-century African-American intellectuals were any more willing than their white counterparts to take on the epistemological category of race. In any case, the main racial problems were more palpable than theoretical. They involved the immediate threat of violence and the long-term constraints posed by the Jim Crow regime—which by the 1880s was under construction in many parts of the South.

Jim Crow was a way to sanitize and rationalize the dream of racial renewal through violence. During the 1880s, the white middle and upper classes became disgusted with the wholesale corruption and frequent violence of electoral politics. Some began openly to suggest that the only way to make white supremacy legitimate was to make it legal—to disenfranchise black people with laws rather than guns. Mississippi led the way in the disenfranchisement movement, whose leaders presented it as a straightforward campaign against corruption. "The old men of the present generation can't afford to die and leave the election to their children and grandchildren, with shot guns in their hands, a lie in their mouths and perjury on their lips in order to defeat the negroes," warned one Mississippian. Newspaper editorialists agreed: "There must be devised some legal defensible substitute for the abhorrent methods on which white supremacy lies," as one put it. State after state followed Mississippi, which in 1890 rewrote its state constitution to include literacy tests, poll taxes, and other measures designed to deny the vote to blacks (and sometimes to poor whites as well). Formal disenfranchisement would be a way of making white supremacy (and elite rule generally) seem legal, rational, and modern. But it would not be fully accomplished until the late 1890s.

Along with disenfranchisement, the other half of the Jim Crow agenda was segregation, which began on Southern railroads. By 1891, eight Southern states had created separate but allegedly equal cars; soon this would become the norm throughout the region. Not all black people accepted these developments calmly. One of the most vigorous resisters was the young Ida B. Wells, who later led a nationwide campaign against lynching.

Wells was born in Holly Springs, Mississippi, in 1862, the eldest of eight children; her father was a carpenter, her mother a cook. After emancipation, they managed to accumulate enough resources to buy a house. Both parents died of yellow fever when Ida was fourteen. She took charge of her remaining five siblings and passed the exam for a country schoolteacher—a position that brought in $25 a month. On the weekends she went to town to do washing, ironing, and cooking for white folks. Eventually the whole family moved to Memphis to live with an aunt.

Ida Wells was an educated young woman with a profession and she didn't like the taste of Jim Crow. In 1884, traveling back from Memphis to her teaching job in Shelby County, Tennessee, Ida took the ladies' car, as usual. The conductor returned her ticket, saying he couldn't accept it in that car. When he told her she would have to move, she recalled, "I refused, saying that the forward car was a smoker, and as I was in the ladies' car I proposed to stay. He tried to drag me out of my seat, but the moment he caught hold of my arm I fastened my teeth in the back of his hand. I had braced my feet against the seat in front and was holding to the back, and as he had already been badly bitten he didn't try it again by himself. He went forward and got the baggage man and another man to help him and of course they succeeded in dragging me out. They were encouraged to do this by the attitude of the white ladies and gentlemen in the car; some of them even stood on the seats so they could get a good view and continued applauding the conductor for his brave stand." She got off the train rather than change cars, still clutching her ticket. Her linen duster was torn but otherwise she was unhurt.

Wells sued the railroad and won $500 in damages, but the state supreme court reversed the local ruling. This was an early consequence of the U.S. Supreme Court's 1883 invalidation of the federal Civil Rights Act of 1875—the decision that permitted racial discrimination by private corporations and individuals. By the time the case was decided against her, Wells had secured a teaching position in Memphis, which was a good thing because it allowed her to pay the court costs. "None of my people seemed to feel that it was a race matter and that they should help me with the fight. So I trod the winepress alone."

It is difficult to blame her people. As resistance to the emerging Jim Crow regime seemed increasingly futile, the frankly accommodationist views of Booker T. Washington appeared to hold out more promise than the angry resistance of Ida Wells. Washington epitomized the marriage of manliness and black uplift. As a student at Hampton Institute, young Booker came profoundly to admire the founder, the former Union general Samuel C. Armstrong, as well as other Northern philanthropists, like Robert C. Ogden. Washington was inspired by Ogden's "strong, fresh, clean, vigorous physique" as well as his earnestness and dedication.

These sorts of models put Washington on the road to creating his own stern ethos of self-help, which he would put into practice at Tuskegee beginning in the 1880s. Washington's gospel grounded mental and moral progress in material life and habit; few things were more important in uplifting the race, he believed, than the bath, the toothbrush, and the second sheet. His vision of uplift owed much to Armstrong, who had grown up in Hawaii, where his parents had been missionaries. Armstrong believed that Southern Negroes were like Polynesians. Playful and indolent, they needed to be taught to put away childish things, to still their dark laughter, and to channel their energies into practical, industrial pursuits. That all sounded about right to Washington.

By the 1890s he had become the leading spokesman for his race—certainly as far as whites were concerned. Washington secured his primacy at the Atlanta Exposition of 1895, where he was one of the featured speakers at the opening ceremonies. Succeeding his mentor Armstrong at the podium, Washington stood "straight as an Indian chief," according to one white journalist. Clearly he was enough of a realist to know that his people were fighting for their very existence. You cannot simply discard the colored people of the South, for they constitute fully one-third of the region's population, he told the assembled audience (which included blacks as well as whites). To his fellow blacks, he said: "Cast down your bucket where you are"—there will be a place for you in the New South if you work hard. To the white power structure, he said, give us a chance—this is our country too. Then he came to his conclusion. "In all things that are purely social we can be separate as the fingers, yet one as the hand in all things essential to mutual progress." The place went wild. Members of the audience, black and white, rushed the stage to congratulate the young orator.

In retrospect, the scene is tinged with irony and sadness. Washington's words epitomized the dilemma of black leadership, caught between a rock and a very hard place. It is difficult to put oneself in Washington's position, as lynchings multiplied and disenfranchisement proceeded apace. But it is necessary, out of fairness to him. Many historians have judged Washington harshly. Yet his dream of oneness in "mutual progress" was doomed by forces far stronger than any one man. It was his bad luck that his endorsement of segregation, which started as a desperation gambit, ended as a signature for the Jim Crow era.

Black dreams of freedom fell prey to white drives for racial regeneration. For the white majority, race became a reassuring social category, creating solid ontological ground for a culture in flux, relaxing class tensions by reviving the antebellum vision of a democracy for white men only. Yet racial appeals alone could not ensure democracy or end monopoly privilege. From the Kansas prairie to the clay hills of Georgia, farmers—white and black—were beginning to stir. Demanding justice, they began to organize. Eventually agrarian radicals transformed interest-group farm politics into a redemptive crusade—a movement aimed at nothing less than the restoration of real democracy in a plutocratic age.

CHAPTER 4

The Country and the City

✦

Henry Grady was about as far from being a farmer as any young man could be. Clean-shaven, buoyant, and boyish, he used his post as editor of the *Atlanta Constitution* during the 1880s to preach the gospel of the New South, singing the praises of the region as a fertile field for Northern investment capital. His pulse quickened with visions of the transformative power of money. "It is a revelation to any provincial to enter the gallery of the stock exchange and gaze upon the floor below," he reported from New York. A glimpse of frenetic trade "kindles the blood of an onlooker as any battle would." This was the ferocious energy, Grady believed, that would set Southern backwaters thrumming with the rhythms of commercial life.

Yet even Grady indulged in dreams of bucolic escape. His biographer Joel Chandler Harris, chief editorial writer for the *Constitution* and creator of his own pastoral fantasies in the Uncle Remus stories, recalled that Grady would withdraw into his office, instructing his secretary to tell all his callers that he had "gone to his farm." As Harris recalled, "The farm was a dream, but he no doubt got more enjoyment and profit out of it than a great many prosy people get out of the farms that are real."

The "prosy people" on real farms were not impressed. Tom Watson was their spokesman in the Georgia state legislature. Son of a failed cotton farmer, he still harbored a Jeffersonian commitment to the nobility and desirability of life on the land. But he knew how hard it was. "It takes these city fellows to draw ideal pictures of Farm life—pictures which are no more true to real life than a Fashion plate is to an actual man or woman," he told the legislature in 1888. "In Grady's farm life there are no poor cows. They are all fat! Their bells tinkle musically in clover scented meadows & all you've got to do is hold a pan under the udder & you catch it full of golden butter. In real life we find the poor old Brindle cow with wolves in her back & 'hollow horn' on her head & she always wants to back up where the wind won't play a tune on her ribs & and when you milk her you get the genuine 'blue milk'. . . ." Watson went on to cite the economic woes that added to the everyday hardships of rural life: tariffs that raised the price the farmer paid for essential equipment; railroad rates that made it prohibitively expensive to ship goods to market; banking and monetary policies that put credit out of reach of all but the wealthiest landowners; and (in the cotton South) a crop-lien system that kept farmers mired in helpless dependence on local merchants. Add to this list the unpredictable vagaries of weather and prices and the conclusion was clear: it would take more than honeyed words to soothe the mind of the troubled farmer.

The gulf between the urban booster's "dream farm" and the hardscrabble reality was one of many variations on the archetypal contrast between country and city. In the Anglo-American literary imagination, those two poles have often been deployed rhetorically to make a moral point. Jeffersonian tradition posed agrarian virtue against urban vice, and generations of orators viewed the city with suspicion, as the source of the "effeminate" luxury that would undermine republican virtue. During the post–Civil War years, Tammany Hall and other urban political machine rose to power through the wholesale purchase of immigrant votes, reinforcing familiar fears of the undisciplined mob among respectable (and often rural) Americans. From their standpoint, the city was the source of corruption, dissipation, extravagance, and deception, a devil's playground swarming with painted women and confidence men—no place for a plain-spoken Protestant.

Yet the stereotypical perspective could be reversed. By the 1880s, it was equally possible to sentimentalize urban life while dismissing rural ways. National advertising glamorized brand-name products in elegant metropolitan settings. A whole new vocabulary of contempt came into use among the smart and up-to-date: the sturdy yeoman became a hayseed, a yokel, or a hick. A generation of young people, typified by such writers as Theodore Dreiser and Hamlin Garland, came of age hating the drudgery of farmwork and the parochialism of village life, and dreaming of escape to the enchantments of the metropolis—which often turned out to be as much a mirage as any agrarian fantasy. Then there were those privileged few (Henry Grady was one) who began to imagine they could have it both ways: the excitements of urban commerce and the respite of a rural retreat.

Powerful as all of those fantasies were, they shared a fundamental flaw. Whether one sentimentalized the country or the city (or both), the antithesis between them concealed the complexity of their interdependence. Part of this complexity involved the accelerated movement of populations set off by the explosive expansion of capitalism during the late nineteenth century. Cities were magnets for migrants, nodes of an international labor market that attracted rural workers from the fringes of the industrial world—creating an Irish working class in London, a Hungarian working class in Pittsburgh, an Italian working class in Buenos Aires, and a black working class in Birmingham, Alabama. Yet the boundless prairies of the "Great West" preserved a powerful pull as well. Necessity and fantasy kept people in motion. Migrants were motivated by actualities of desperation and dreams of regeneration.

The city's force was centrifugal as well as centripetal. By the 1880s, Chicago had become the distribution hub for the entire Midwest, transforming raw materials into finished products and sending them by rail across the nation—lumber for the farmhouses of the Great Plains, dressed meat and packaged cereals for the kitchen tables of the urban Northeast. Farmers depended on distributors to get their goods to market; distributors depended on farmers to get them something to distribute. But unequal power could upset the balance; the railroad could charge what it wanted when it was the only game in town. So could the bank. The situation was worst in the South, where cotton farmers faced the monopoly power of local merchants as well as distant railroads and banks. Caught in the coils of the crop-lien system, most Southern farmers were forced to neglect subsistence crops, devoting every square foot of ground to the marketable crop of cotton and using what they grew as collateral for usurious loans from the storekeeper who controlled access to seeds, tools, fertilizers, and food.

Boundaries between city and country were blurred by such arrangements. A village merchant could exercise power across the counter as ruthlessly as any corporate overlord ensconced in an executive suite. Face-to-face relations were no guarantee of community. Exploitation took many forms. A complex web of money and power bound cities, towns, and villages with the people who worked the land. To focus only on the contrast between the exciting (or corrupt) city and the desolate (or virtuous) country was to ignore power relationships, to take the politics out of the picture.

Yet to emphasize the gap between country and the city was not simply an evasive exercise: dreams of bucolic stillness or urban energy stemmed from motives more complex than mere escapist sentiment. City and country were mother lodes of metaphor, sources for making sense of the urban-industrial revolution that was transforming the American countryside and creating a deep sense of discontinuity in many Americans' lives during the decades after the Civil War. If the city epitomized the attraction of the future, the country embodied the pull of the past. For all those who had moved to town in search of excitement or opportunity, rural life was ineluctably associated with childhood and memory. The contrast between country and city was about personal experience as well as political economy.

By the 1880s, though, even rhetoricians as clever as Grady found it difficult to avoid political controversy when they discussed rural life. A variety of insurgent movements swept across the American countryside, challenging the inequalities of power at the heart of the urban-rural divide—Greenbackers, Readjusters, Farmers' Alliances, and finally Populists. Whatever their concerns, all these movements shared a common concern with credit. They wanted to wrest control of the money supply from private bankers and put it in the hands of the people, to be administered by their elected representatives. They wanted a democratically managed currency, flexible enough to expand with a growing economy and fund the farmers' needs. And for a while they convinced themselves—and their frightened opponents—that they just might get what they wanted. The troubled farmers' cry became, for a moment, a creed of redemptive transformation.

REVERENCE FOR THE man of the soil was rooted in the republican tradition. In his *Notes on the State of Virginia* (1785), Jefferson articulated the antithesis that became central to agrarian politics (and to the producerist worldview in general)—the contrast between rural producers and urban parasites. "Those who labour in the earth are the chosen people of God, if ever he had a chosen people, whose breasts he has made his peculiar deposit for substantial and genuine virtue," he announced. "Corruption of morals in the mass of cultivators is a phenomenon of which no age nor nation has furnished an example. It is the mark set on those, who not looking up to heaven, to their own soil and industry, as does the husbandman, for their subsistence, depend for it on the casualties and caprice of customers. Dependence begets subservience and venality, suffocates the germ of virtue, and prepares fit tools for the design of ambition." Small wonder, from this view, that urban centers of commerce seemed to menace the public good. "The mobs of great cities," Jefferson concluded, "add just so much to the

support of pure government as sores do to the strength of the human body."
Jefferson's invidious distinctions echoed through the nineteenth century, fu-
eling the moral passion of agrarian rebels. Watson, among many, considered
himself a Jeffersonian.

There were fundamental contradictions embedded in Jefferson's conceptions of an independent yeomanry. Outside certain remote areas in New
England, most American farmers were not self-sufficient in the nineteenth
century—nor did they want to be. Many were eager participants in the agricultural market economy, animated by a restless, entrepreneurial spirit.
Indeed, Jefferson's own expansionist policies, especially the Louisiana Purchase, encouraged centrifugal movement as much as permanent settlement.
"What developed in America," the historian Richard Hofstadter wrote,
"was an agricultural society whose real attachment was not to the land but
to land values." The figure of the independent yeoman, furnishing enough
food for himself and his family, participating in the public life of a secure
community—this icon embodied longings for stability amid a maelstrom of
migration.

Often the longings were tinged with a melancholy sense of loss. The
popular poet James Whitcomb Riley captured the nostalgia felt by many
Americans who had left a rural childhood to make their way in the world.
"Oh, it sets my heart a clickin' like the tickin' of a clock," he wrote in 1883,
"when the frost is on the punkin and the fodder's in the shock." Agrarian
roots were recollected in a burgeoning regionalist literature. "Local color"
writers as different as Mark Twain and Sarah Orne Jewett evoked the appeal
of rural communities left behind by industrial development—Twain in his
constant return to the "soft, reposeful summer landscape" of his Missouri
boyhood, Jewett in her representations of preindustrial pockets in New
England. In *Deephaven* (1877), Jewett described a deserted farmhouse, a
familiar sight across the region in the post–Civil War decades, with characteristic precision: "that fireless, empty, forsaken house, where the winter sun
shines in and creeps slowly along the floor; the bitter cold is in and around
the house, and the snow has sifted in at every crack; outside it is untrodden
by any living creature's footstep. The wind blows and rushes and shakes
the loose window-sashes in their frames, while the padlock knocks—knocks
against the door."

For those with Jeffersonian sympathies, abandoned farms were disturbing evidence of cultural decline. As a *North American Review* contributor

wrote in 1888: "Once let the human race be cut off from personal contact with the soil, once let the conventionalities and artificial restrictions of so-called civilization interfere with the healthful simplicity of nature, and decay is certain." Romantic nature-worship had flourished fitfully among intellectuals since Emerson had become a transparent eye-ball on the Concord common and Whitman had loafed among leaves of grass. By the post–Civil War decades, romantic sentiment combined with republican tradition to foster forebodings. Migration from country to city, from this view, was a symptom of disease in the body politic. Yet the migration continued. Indeed, nostalgia for rural roots was itself a product of rootlessness. A restless spirit, born of necessity and desire, spun Americans off in many directions—but mainly westward. The vision of a stable yeomanry was undercut by the prevalence of the westering pioneer.

Hamlin Garland's father was a pioneer par excellence. He could never seem to stop packing up his household and heading over the next hill, toward the setting sun. Young Hamlin spent his early childhood in Green's Coulee, on the La Crosse River in western Wisconsin; life was primitive though food was plentiful and friends were near. But his father was irritated by the hilly land and stumps, eager for change, and confident of success in Iowa. His mother "was not by nature an emigrant,—few women are." She was content with gentle slopes, good neighbors, her kinfolk nearby. "From this distance," Garland wrote fifty years later, "I cannot understand how my father brought himself to leave that lovely farm and those good and noble friends."

But he did it again and again. He bought land in Iowa where the woods and the prairie met, but that did not satisfy him; within a couple of years the family was heading west again, toward the open grassland of Mitchell County, Iowa. "My heart filled with awe as well as wonder," Garland recalled, when he first found himself surrounded by prairie. "The majesty of this primeval world exalted me. I felt for the first time the poetry of the unplowed spaces." His father had no time for exalted reflections. "'Forward march!'" the Union Army veteran shouted. "Hour after hour he pushed into the west, the heads of his tired horses hanging ever lower, and on my mother's face the shadow deepened, but her chieftain's voice cheerily urging his team lost nothing of its clarion resolution. He was in his element."

Life on the prairie was hard, and the Garlands kept moving. On one farm, an unexpected windstorm turned their carefully pulverized fields into a blizzard of soil; on another, a plague of chinch bugs destroyed what would have been a bumper crop of wheat. Disgusted by this calamity, Garland's father determined once again to go pioneering and leave a neighborly round of life. It was 1880; the last of the Cheyenne and Sioux were being driven from the Black Hills, and the very word "Dakota" had a magical appeal to would-be settlers. Hamlin was twenty. In retrospect he decided that "our going was of a piece with the West's elemental restlessness." The westering impulse was inexorable: "The border line had moved on, and my indomitable Dad was moving with it." Their neighbors threw the Garlands a party, a combined silver-wedding celebration and send-off. Young Hamlin had to flee the painful scene of farewells, "bitterly asking, 'why should this suffering be? Why should mother be wrenched from all her dearest friends and forced to move away to a strange land?'"

The gender divide between the Garlands was stereotypical but real: the wife attached to settled community; the husband driven westward by an insanely restless will. The pattern repeats itself in innumerable memoirs, including Laura Ingalls Wilder's multivolume account of her family's travels from one "little house on the prairie" to another.

But not all pioneers fit this pattern. William Larrabee was an army officer found guilty of deserting his post in the Dakota Territory and sentenced to two years in a federal prison; he and his wife, Mary, managed to get the sentence changed to "ten years of life on the prairie," keeping a relay station for mail carriers on the Fort Totten Trail in Dakota Territory. In the fall of 1876, soon after hearing of the Little Bighorn massacre, the couple moved to a log house near the James River valley. The setting was sheltered by hills and open to the east; it was "a good place for raising stock," Mary observed. They were surrounded by wildlife in abundance: geese, ducks, prairie chickens, sandhill cranes, and herds of antelope. But there were no white people closer than Fort Totten, thirty miles away. Indian women were friendly and visited frequently, but "Oh, how homesick I get for the sight of a white woman's face," Mary wrote in May of 1877. She had just given birth to a baby boy, "the first white child born in Foster County." Mary endured six more years of isolation before a family of white settlers moved in a couple of miles away. The father in the new household worked for William, who had been appointed postmaster. "At last Foster County is coming into its own," she wrote in 1883. "New settlers are coming in droves." Railroads and real estate developers led the way. "Another townsite is planned in this county and is called Carrington after Henry Carrington of Toledo, Ohio, of the Carrington Casey Land Company. This will bring in the settlers and soon we will see a shack on every quarter section."

Mary was right. Within a few weeks she reported that "two passenger trains have reached Carrington and many who wished to come on the first train could not even find a foothold on the cars—men swarming over the tops of cars and clinging to the railings on platforms." Migrants managed to survive the bitter winter of 1883–84 by huddling in railroad cars, living on leftover provisions and jackrabbits they killed. When spring came, Carrington flourished again. Mary noted "a beautiful new hotel . . . which is run in great style." There was a growing clientele for it, "as many rich people from the east are coming to buy land." The scene in Carrington was repeated often across the prairies and the Great Plains; the West still attracted hordes of settlers hoping for a fresh start and investors eager for a fast buck.

But for other migrants, the blank slate was less appealing than the settled community. And even the Garlands sometimes stayed long enough in one place to allow a town to develop around them. Town life, Garland recalled of himself and his siblings, "tended to warp us from our father's designs. It placed the rigorous, filthy drudgery of the farm-yard in sharp contrast with the care-free companionable existence led by my friends in the village, and we longed to be of their condition. We had gained our first set of comparative ideas, and with them an unrest which was to carry us very far away." Enrolling in a seminary in Osage ("hardly more than a high school"), Garland encountered books and ideas and began to imagine escape to a wider world.

"Going West" was the theme of Garland's graduation oration, but in fact he would move in the opposite direction. He spent one awful winter in Dakota, tending his father's store during the day and studying Hippolyte Taine's laws of literary development at night while he tossed on his bunk, restless with longing. Then he headed for Boston, birthplace of his paternal grandmother and (he decided) the site of his self-education. Garland's destination suited his genealogy and his genteel taste, but most ambitious young Midwesterners looked toward Chicago.

IN LITTLE MORE than a decade, Chicago had rebounded from the fire of 1871. By the 1880s its pulsating vitality was proverbial. "Chicago has become an independent organism, growing by a combination of forces and opportunities beyond the contrivance of any combination of men to help or hinder, beyond the need of flaming circulars and reports of boards of trade and process pictures," Charles Dudley Warner wrote in 1888. "It has passed the danger or the fear of rivalry, and reached the point where the growth of any portion of the great Northwest, or of any city in it, . . . is in some way a contribution to the power and wealth of Chicago." It was the Rome of the Great West; all (rail)roads led to it. Its population would soon reach a million; its annual trade value had already passed a billion.

No wonder so many young people flocked to Chicago. Indeed, Warner wrote, the "striking feature of the town is 'youth,' visible in social life as well as in business." Partly this was a matter of tone, the youthful "vim and spirit" that even the elderly displayed. But also it was a matter of demographics: "the great Eastern universities" were simply pouring their young men into Chicago. All their energy was bent toward money-getting rather than more exalted pursuits, but "if the men of Chicago seriously take hold of a culture, they will make it hum," Warner predicted. And they would be assisted by "a type known in Europe and the East as the Chicago young woman, capable rather than timid, dashing rather than retiring, quite able to take care of herself."

All this youthful vitality, actual or imagined, made Chicago attractive to many young Midwesterners who had never been near one of "the great Eastern universities." Theodore Dreiser was one. He was an impressionable boy of twelve when his family moved briefly to Chicago; the city posed a sharp contrast to the drab Indiana towns where he and his family had been scraping by, pinched by poverty and the father's fanatical Catholicism. Theodore was enraptured by the city's sensual panorama. "I was lost in a vapor of something so rich that it was like food for the hungry, odorous and meaningful like flowers to those who love. Life was glorious and sensate, avid and gay, shimmering and tingling," he recalled in his memoirs. "The spirit of Chicago flowed into me and made me ecstatic. Its personality was different from anything I had ever known: it was a compound of hope and joy in existence, intense hope and intense joy."

Whether Dreiser actually felt this way at twelve is an open question, but it was the way he came to write about the city, and the way he imagined its appeal to the appetites of young "life-hungry" migrants (as in *Sister Carrie*). At the same time, he recalled, he was reduced to tears by his inability to manage the job of cash-boy in a dry-goods store. Life was not all beer and skittles, even in the Magic City. Within a few years he returned and came to know the darker side of city life: the constraints imposed by tedious and demanding jobs, the shabby frame houses that fell apart in a few years, the pervasive stench of "sour beer or stale whiskey or uric acid or sewer gas out of broken mains or poisonous vapors from some distant paint factory or glue works, but always one or the other or all in combination." "In truth," he concluded, "I have never seen more picturesque or more terrible neighborhoods than Chicago contained at that time."

While Chicago inflamed the imaginations of aspiring novelists, it also played a more prosaic though equally powerful role as economic hub of the great Midwestern hinterland. Through the 1880s, lumber companies continued to cut white pines in the Great North Woods of Wisconsin and Michigan and float them by barge down Lake Michigan to Chicago; lumber mills sliced them into boards and sent them on flat cars as far west as the Rockies. At about the same time, cattle and pigs were being shipped by the million into the feedlots, stockyards, and slaughterhouses of Chicago, from which they emerged as dressed meat that was sent in refrigerator cars as far east as Long Island.

The story of the meat industry reveals the interdependence of country and city with exceptional clarity. It began in 1873, when Joseph Glidden invented barbed wire. Before then, fencing long distances on the grasslands had required too much wood to be economical; after then, the livestock industry (which included English and Scottish land syndicates as well as representatives of Eastern capital) could begin to transform thousands of acres of grassland into pasture. It was only a short step from pasture to feedlot— the systematic fattening of steers and pigs, who were then slaughtered and separated on the continuously operating disassembly line. Gustavus Swift and Philip Armour aimed to control this process in every phase—grain elevators, feedlots, slaughterhouses, packinghouses. Combining horizontal and vertical integration, they centralized control, steamrolled small competitors, and created what was called the Beef Trust.

The creation of the Beef Trust was part of a much broader development that helped conceal the actual ties between country and city: the rationalization of natural processes in accordance with the demands of capitalist productivity. Sometimes, as in the clear-cutting of the Great North Woods or the destruction of the buffalo, the assertion of human dominion was simply a matter of laying waste to nature. But other times, as in the transformation of the hinterland from local ecosystems to monoculture, the rationale of efficient productivity for market was more clearly at work. Efficiency required the rationalization of time and space, as was revealed on November 18, 1883, when railroad officials persuaded Congress to create four standard time zones. (Previously every town and hamlet had kept its own local time, a practice that wreaked havoc with railroad scheduling.) Railroads freed human transportation from reliance on energy from easily exhausted sources (such as horses) as well as from all but the most extreme weather. This technological conquest of time and space left city dwellers less aware of how dependent they remained on inconstant nature and the people who wrested a living from it.

The distribution of dressed meat revealed how technology enabled sales to a national market and distanced urban consumers from the origins of their food. Just as the Beef Trust insulated its shareholders from the vagaries of the market, the refrigerated freight car insulated its products from the vagaries of nature (weather, spoilage, vermin). The refrigerated car paralleled the steam-powered grain elevator: both allowed the meatpackers to fragment a single entity (a steer, a pig, a bushel of wheat) into multiple commodities with varying markets. The consequences for the consumer were convenience but also adulteration, as manufacturers strove to eliminate waste and throw nothing away, creating the cliché that they "used everything in the hog except the squeal." The consequence for farmers, as they became dependent on selling to one centralized corporation, was greater vulnerability to the unpredictable fluctuations of the market—and no alternatives to that single corporation's terms. The working Midwestern farmer was not a beneficiary of the Beef Trust; nor did he find Chicago quite as dazzling as young Dreiser did.

By the late 1880s, natural and market forces combined to create unprecedented hardship for farmers in much of the Chicago hinterland. They were battered by blizzards, bankers, and brokers; their profit margins were squeezed down to nothing by high railroad rates, tight money, and mounting indebtedness. When they got lucky and raised a bumper crop of corn or wheat, their prices plummeted. Commodities markets were as menacing and unpredictable as the weather. Not that farmers were merely passive victims. Part of their predicament was created by their own speculative fantasies, which were shamelessly encouraged by railroads and local boosters, and which led them to overextended borrowing for land at inflated prices.

"Most of us crossed the Mississippi or Missouri with no money but with a vast wealth of hope and courage," a Kansas official later recalled. "Haste to get rich has made us borrowers, and the borrower has made booms, and booms made men wild, and Kansas became a vast insane asylum covering 80,000 square miles." When the boom collapsed in the late 1880s, the farmers were left with huge mortgages on overvalued land. The situation was a severe instance of a chronic condition: Midwestern farmers lived on the edge in good times and bad.

Southern farmers faced these problems and many more peculiar to their region. The shadow of Appomattox lingered for decades. Much of the countryside had already been laid waste, less by entrepreneurs (though they were gearing up), than by invading Union armies and heedless agricultural practice. As late as the 1890s, Northern travelers were appalled as they peered through railroad windows at miles of desolation—leached-out soil, gullied hillsides, collapsing unpainted shacks. This was no prosperous hinterland, and there was no single city serving it. Instead there were a handful of port cities (Norfolk, Charleston, New Orleans) ravaged by the war, their harbors cluttered with sunken ships and nautical detritus, and a growing number of inland towns (Atlanta, Raleigh, Memphis), linked by a gradually expanding railroad network. The rhetoric of boosters like Grady concealed a systematic pattern of elite domination.

THE ENTIRE REGION was in thrall to Northern capital, trapped in the typical pattern of a colonial economy—selling cheap raw materials to a world market and buying expensive manufactured goods from protected industries at home. Agriculture was plagued by land monopolies, absentee ownership, soil mining, and the one-cash-crop fixation. All these problems had originated under slavery and intensified after its abolition. The key to the new system of elite dominance was the crop lien, which kept much of the rural population, black and white, in peonage.

The Compromise of 1877 ended Reconstruction, sealed the alliance between Northern and Southern conservatives, and ratified the shifting emphasis of Northern policy from the political and missionary to the economic and exploitative. Federal land policy reflected the change: between 1877 and 1888, the average size of Southern parcels sold increased dramatically over the average for the previous ten years. Forty acres and a mule was now a sentimental slogan; the big shots were on top. Among the absentee landlords were Northern lumber syndicates, which began to slice through Southern pine forests at a brisk clip—often using convicts leased to them by impoverished state governments. The convict lease system was yet another way that slavery could continue in all but name.

Northern capital could not have swept so swiftly through the South had it not been for the collaboration of Southern business elites. The men who "redeemed" state governments from carpetbag rule were eager to play the role of junior partner in the lumbering, railroad, textile, and other industries that began transforming the South in the 1880s. Their rhetorical devotion to the "Lost Cause" and the supposed glories of the old order were the syrup that made the medicine of modernization go down. As early as the summer of 1877, when railroad strikes threatened to rip the Northern class structure apart, Southern publicists saw their opportunity. The *Raleigh Observer* addressed the "panic-stricken, mob-ridden States of the North," promising that "Money invested here is as safe from the rude hand of mob violence as it is in the best U.S. bond." When the economic depression finally began to lift in 1879, money poured into railroad construction across the old Confederacy. Scores of smaller local lines were swallowed by larger regional and national ones. The colonial character of the enterprise surfaced with particular clarity on May 30, 1886, when the Lackawanna & Northern Railroad set an army of eight thousand men to work adjusting the Southern track gauge to fit the national standard—which was also the Northern standard—in a single day's intensive labor. The sweating and straining of those men embodied the desperation of the South (or at least its business leaders) to conform to Yankee expectations.

Infusions of Northern capital began to transform the countryside. A wide variety of villages, towns, and cities sprouted from the Tidewater to the Piedmont. The North Carolina railroad village of the late 1870s offered one example of a common type. The coming of the railroad gave the enterprising local merchant an excuse to build a flimsy shanty for a railroad station, in exchange for the railroad agreeing to stop its daily passenger train. If signaled, the train would stop, discharge a single passenger or a box or barrel for the merchant, but rarely take anything on board. There might be three white families of importance near the station, the journalist Walter Hines Page recalled; then the settlement dwindled down the road to a dozen Negro shacks, one Baptist church, one Methodist, and an intermittent school. Newer kinds of towns appeared with the rise of the textile industry. The number of textile workers in the region more than doubled in the 1880s (from 17,000 to 36,000) and so did the percentage of steam-powered mills (from 17 to 47 percent). Cotton mills were magnets for impoverished rural folk. Dozens of tiny mill towns began to appear, the workers' cabins arranged in serried ranks around the mill, in a kind of parody of the old plantation order. At the same time, more prosperous midsized towns popped up as distribution hubs for textiles, lumber, or tobacco. By the 1880s, in places like Winston-Salem, North Carolina, or Augusta, Georgia, one could see significant signs of new wealth—Victorian mansions with telephones and indoor plumbing, smart downtown stores with plate-glass display windows.

Yet even among the genteel white population, the effects of the war were still felt. One example was the plight of Gertrude Clanton Thomas (1834–1907), daughter of a wealthy planter in Augusta, Georgia. She was educated at Wesleyan Female College in Macon, Georgia, and married Jefferson Thomas, a Princeton graduate, in 1852. She bore ten children, seven of whom survived longer than five years. Thomas was a privileged young blade with no head for the business of cotton-planting. When Gertrude's father died in 1864, she did not receive the handsome inheritance she was expecting, because her husband had borrowed heavily against it. The defeat of the Confederacy meant further financial distress, bankruptcy, and lost property for the Thomas family. Her husband deteriorated steadily in body and mind in the years following the war. By New Year's Eve 1878, Gertrude was staring into a financial void. "The absorbing thought is how shall we live?" she confided to her diary. "If I can succeed in procuring a situation, this time next year I shall be earning something for my children." She managed to secure a job teaching at the local school and kept the family afloat by carefully husbanding resources. Her diary is filled with detailed lists of expenses. "Everything is so low that a great deal can be bought for a small amount of money but oh the scarcity of money—the war times was nothing to it." Despite the dearth of cash she put enough aside ($15) for her son Jeff to buy a suit. That was satisfying.

Still the feeling of lost status could be painful. "I have no driver and my carriage is so shabby that I never use it except to drive to Ma's and then it is put in the stable and never driven on the street . . . The consequence will be that I shall cease to go after a while in the carriage." A few weeks later she had come up with the alternative of riding in her aunt's carriage:

"It may be foolish to admit it but I do not like to walk upon Broad Street. I have always been accustomed to driving and it is the only way I like to go." Chafing against the constraints of cash, she prayed: "'heavenly father do pray keep me from being covetous. Keep me from the sin of envy.' I searched my own heart and I was ashamed of myself. I must say this much in defence. I can stand poverty for myself but oh my children!" Night after night, she cried for their lost opportunities. Her daughter Mary Belle could not travel "North with Ma or to Catoosa springs with her Aunt Mamie"; her son Jeff had to forgo Athens College (the University of Georgia) and go to work "clerking for a Chinaman by the name of Loo Chong. It was the only situation he could obtain. He only gets a salary of three dollars a week." Meanwhile her husband remained morose, profane, financially inept, and perpetually in debt. Gertrude, like a good Southern lady, apparently confined her complaints to her diary.

The Thomases' story of downward mobility provided a counternarrative to the tale of progress told by Henry Grady and other New South boosters. Even with a background of privilege, many families struggled and slid into genteel poverty as the agricultural economy remained deflated. But the boosters' vision of town opportunities had something to it. Widowed and unmarried women found opportunities in the city that were unavailable in the country: sewing, domestic service, mill work, schoolteaching. Married black women found work as maids, but their husbands had to head out of town—to the harvests, the railroads, the turpentine and lumber camps. (The result was a rise in the percentage of female-headed households among urban blacks.) For the most fortunate among the young black women, urban life could be a great leap forward—for Millie McCreary, for example, a teacher in the Atlanta Female Seminary, whose life by the 1890s included ice cream sodas, ball games, and a male friend with a "wheel" (a bicycle). The opportunities of the city were uneven but genuine.

This was especially true for forward-looking young white men on the make. Mark Twain caught their character in *Life on the Mississippi* (1881). They were, he wrote, "Brisk men, energetic of movement and speech; the dollar their god, how to get it their religion." This was a sharp swerve in cultural style from the misty-eyed custodians of Confederate valor. Towns were nodes of the commercial spirit. Opportunism and quick action counted. The businessman was "wide-awake"—he looked at his watch often, swearing under his breath. He was always in a hurry, always keeping a sharp eye out for the main chance. Henry Belk personified the type. He started a chain of department stores that dominated several North Carolina downtowns by the end of the 1880s. And he knew how to get attention for his products, arranging (for example) for a man to lead a large-uddered cow through the streets of Charlotte, advertising BELK'S FOR THE BEST SHOE VALUES IN TOWN — THIS IS NO BULL. Belk was thoroughly at home with the compulsive cleverness that characterized the infant industry of national advertising.

So was his fellow North Carolinian, James Buchanan Duke, the founder of the American Tobacco Company. When a young inventor named James Bonsack showed Duke a machine he had designed, a Rube Goldberg device that could turn out hundreds of cigarettes in a matter of minutes, Duke knew his production problems were solved. He could produce more than enough cigarettes to saturate the market; the challenge was how to market them. He installed the machines in his factories and moved his business operations from North Carolina to New York, from which vantage he could oversee marketing strategies. (They included offering trading cards with every pack, featuring baseball stars and scantily clad actresses.)

But the South did more than produce cigarettes, Coca-Cola (formulated in 1886), and other consumer products. It also purchased them. Even rural poverty was no bar to a spreading commodity civilization. To be sure, the use of cash advanced only fitfully in certain areas. As late as 1897, the New York Cash Store in Greenville, Alabama, advertised in the local newspaper that "we will take in exchange for goods, country produce, particularly Eggs, Chickens, Bees Wax, Dry Hides, Peas, Corn meal, and anything else that we can dispose of. If you have any cash you might bring that along." But the yen for commercial commodities was pervasive. Traveling salesmen, or "drummers," were everywhere, linking city wholesalers to rural or small-town stores. The writer Harry Crews remembered his family in South Georgia: "They loved *things* the way only the very poor can. They would have thrown away their kerosene lamps for light bulbs in a second. They would have abandoned their wood stoves for stoves that burned anything you did not have to chop." Even packaging had its uses—children's nightgowns made from flour sacks, for example. "It was not unusual to see the baby asleep in his crib with the words 'The Best in the World' printed on his little nightgown," a woman from Virginia's Eastern Shore remembered of her childhood in the 1880s. Commerce penetrated the countryside in a multitude of ways.

The politics of commerce were embodied in Grady's New South Creed, a merger of Jeffersonian ideas of minimal government with the Gilded Age religion of money-worship. Public service, from this view, existed only to promote the interest of private investment, which, if allowed to penetrate the countryside, would ensure prosperity for all. And most of the investors came from above the Mason-Dixon Line.

Grady shamelessly sucked up to Northern capital, assuming and asserting that the best (white) men of both sections could bury the bloody shirt, put the recent unpleasantness of the Civil War behind them, and make common cause in the interests of economic progress. When he addressed the New England Club in 1886, he shared the platform with William Tecumseh Sherman—who, he said, "is considered an able man in our parts, though some people think he is a kind of careless man about fire. . . ." One can only imagine the appreciative men's club chuckle that swept through the well-fed audience.

Then Grady got down to brass tacks, persuading the crowd that Southerners meant business. "We have sowed towns and cities in the place of theories, and put business in place of politics," he said. "We have . . . wiped out the place where Mason and Dixon's line used to be, and hung out a latchstring to you and yours. . . . We have fallen in love with work. . . . We are ready to lay odds on the Georgia Yankee as he manufactures relics of the battlefield in a one-story shanty and squeezes pure olive-oil out of his cotton-seed, against any down-easter that ever swapped wooden nutmegs for flannel sausages in the valleys of Vermont." Invoking stereotypes of chicanery, Grady distanced himself from the vices of commerce. He and his audience knew they were there to promote *legitimate* business, which was consistent with Christian morality and even Southern honor.

A key criterion of legitimacy was commitment to a "sound money" policy, and Grady was as committed to it as any bearded conservative. The moral core of sound money was a fundamentalist faith that paper currency represented intrinsic value, which could only be redeemed in gold. The deep, almost religious attachment to the gold standard was rooted in bondholders' desire to stabilize the arbitrary fluctuations of monetary value by tying it to a supposedly timeless benchmark. A less abstract motive was their interest in maximizing the value of the debt they held. Young or old, devotees of Southern development combined entrepreneurial zeal with rentier cunning.

New South men and Bourbon aristocrats differed mainly in cultural style; politically they were all conservative Democrats, as at ease as their Northern counterparts with bondholders and bankers. When Grover Cleveland won the election of 1884, the joy was general among the business class of Atlanta. The shadow of Appomattox seemed finally to be receding. Businessmen poured into the streets, capering with joy, saturating bloody shirts with oil and setting them ablaze. Grady burst into the state House of Representatives, grabbed the gavel from the Speaker, and declared the House adjourned in the name of Grover Cleveland. His vision of a New South seemed on the cusp of realization.

Out in the countryside, though, no one would have claimed that an economic millennium was at hand. The growth of Southern cities reflected rural impoverishment as much as urban prosperity. "In a declining or decaying state, with agriculture on the wane and the social order disturbed," Lewis Harvie Blair wrote of Virginia in the 1880s, "there is a constant influx into the cities—where there is more life and activity, more society, and especially more security." First "the younger and more ambitious desert the villages and the country because they have a lessening field for their energies; professional men of all kinds do the same; families of means and culture, tiring of a country life constantly becoming harder and more unsocial, follow next; then follow the timid, who dread the relaxations of legal restraint upon the improvident and badly disposed, and then those seeking the advantages of education, which constantly diminish in such a state." Finally, "the mechanical and laboring people, who find work becoming scarcer and wages smaller and more uncertain, also flock to the cities, where, if anywhere, work is to be found. And thus it is that cities grow in decaying countries." The desolation of the countryside was a problem in political economy.

CONDITIONS IN THE countryside were exacerbated by monetary policy at both the federal and state level. The Civil War had been financed with paper currency—"greenbacks," as the dollars were called because of the green ink with which they were printed. But in 1875, the Grant administration persuaded Congress to authorize the resumption of specie payment—that is, to return to paying coin for government obligations. The problem, for the general public if not for bondholders, was that the dollar had appreciated sharply in value since the war. While the Civil War had been fought with 50-cent dollars, its cost would be paid in 100-cent dollars. Taxpayers would pay the difference to the banking community, which held the bonds. Ordinary citizens would suffer while investors grew rich.

Overall monetary policy was more gradual: keep the money supply stable, while population and production increased. The contraction of the money supply meant debtors had to pay their obligations in an appreciated currency; those who had borrowed 50-cent dollars would have to pay them back at double their value. So farmers and other debtors took a view of money that was more skeptical than their creditors' faith in its intrinsic value. On the contrary, the indebted classes argued, money was nothing more or less than a flexible instrument of value designed to meet society's needs for economic development. A democracy should allow the people to manage their own currency, through their representatives, in accordance with their needs. Government, from this "fiat money" view, should be able to control the money supply in the public interest. In effect, fiat money supporters acknowledged the arbitrary value of money and aimed to harness it for democratic ends. This vision of currency reform inspired Greenbackers, Populists, and eventually even some Democrats, while it scared the daylights out of sound-money men.

Still, the investing classes kept the reins of policy. Despite the severe business downturn of the 1870s, the fiscal conservatives in power remained committed to contracting the currency. They demonetized silver in 1873, removing silver dollars from circulation and ensuring that gold would be the only coin in circulation once specie payment was resumed. But the achievement was ambiguous and the gold standard not as pristine as the most fervent "gold-bugs" would have liked.

Partly this was a result of bad timing. The return to gold coincided with Wall Street panic, deflationary downturn, and the discovery of silver deposits in Nevada, Colorado, and Utah. Western silver-mine owners began referring to the demonetization of silver as "the Crime of '73," and indebted farmers took up the epithet, too, as they felt the tightening pinch of "sound money" and looked to inflation for relief. Southern and Western congressmen, under pressure from the odd coalition of miners and farmers, eventually produced the Bland-Allison Act of 1878, which required the government to reintroduce silver into the money supply by purchasing limited amounts. Since secretaries of the treasury continued to purchase the minimum silver required by law, the Act had almost no effect on the money supply. Free and unlimited coinage of silver remained a compelling goal for many among the indebted classes. "Free silver" was a catchy phrase, but it distracted critics of monetary policy from the questions at the core of currency debate: who would control the money supply? And to what ends?

Sound-money men evaded those questions, too, by wrapping the interests of rentier capital in the rhetoric of natural law, or Southern honor. Fiscally conservative policies at the federal level were repeated and reinforced at the state level—particularly in the former Confederate states, which had been accumulating huge public debts since antebellum days. In Virginia the question of funding the state debt was at the top of the political agenda. The old Whigs who reclaimed power after Reconstruction styled themselves the "Funder Conservatives." They were dominated by mercantile, banking, and railroad interests, and they were determined to do right by the states' creditors—bondholders like themselves—even if that meant paying them off in dollars worth twice as much as they were worth when the bonds were sold. This would have been hard enough anytime, but it proved all but impossible during the grim years after the Panic of 1873. The social costs of the Funders' fiscal orthodoxy were calamitous. To meet interest payments alone the state had to take draconian measures, sharply raising taxes on real and personal property, drastically cutting public services—especially schools. Those measures provoked opposition from planters in the tidewater, yeomen in the piedmont, and African-Americans throughout the state.

The battle lines over monetary policy in Virginia typified the nationwide conflict between the country and the city. Increasingly, the two major parties became beholden to urban industrial and financial interests. The election of Cleveland in 1884 made clear that Democrats were as committed as Republicans to deflation, hard money, the creation of privately owned banks, and the maintenance of a protective tariff. While skilled urban workers might at least support the tariff, farmers could find nothing to endorse in either major-party platform. As the largest interest group within the indebted classes, farmers badly needed to bring dissident voices into public discourse. No wonder agrarian radicals led the turn toward insurgent politics. Thanks largely to them, the several decades after Reconstruction marked the golden age of third-party insurgencies in American politics.

The stirrings of agrarian insurgency first became apparent in the campaign of 1878. Disaffected Southern Democrats in Arkansas, Texas, and Louisiana broke with their party, running as Independents and joining forces with the newly formed Greenback-Labor Party (and even, sometimes, with Republicans). Seeking common ground for the indebted classes, the Greenbackers took on sound-money doctrines directly, declaring a government-controlled paper-money supply to be "the people's currency, elastic, cheap, and inexportable, based on the entire wealth of the country." But they were not a one-issue party. Along with their commitments to inflation and a democratically managed currency, the Greenbackers aimed to protect "the needs of small producers." They opposed monopolies, denouncing concentrated wealth and power as well as "ring rule" in the legislatures by a corrupt alliance of industrial and commercial interests.

The insurgents needed votes badly enough to seek support from Republicans, including black ones. This was most apparent in Texas, where the Greenback insurgency made a strong bid for state power in the 1878 campaign. Texas Republicans fused with the Greenbackers, and many rural blacks went along, especially in counties where black people made up more than one-third of the population. But in the cities, black Republicans split their ballots to avoid voting for Greenbackers. Accusations of fraud broke out and mistrust spread across the racial as well as the rural-urban divide. Two years later the Texas Greenback convention was lily-white. This would not be the last time that race would trump class in the politics of agrarian radicalism.

Racial anxieties were entwined with regional hostilities. Business and political elites on both sides of the Mason-Dixon Line aimed to distract popular attention from economic issues by constantly referring to the war and its aftermath. In the South, for whites, that meant a politics of fear— fear of the return of "carpetbag rule," fear of the return of federal troops, fear of the "Negro menace"—all of which, it was hoped, would herd the Southern masses into the arms of conservative Democrats. In the North it meant the maintenance of wartime animosity toward the old Confederacy among the voters of the Midwest, in the hopes of heading off a revived alliance between the South and the West. According to the antislavery-agitator-turned-Republican-operative William Lloyd Garrison, the lesson of the 1878 campaign (when Republicans won almost everywhere outside the South) was "The bloody shirt! *In Hoc Signo Vinces.*"

When rhetoric failed, fraud was available. In the South, poll taxes were used to disenfranchise poor people of both races, and mainstream Democrats were doing everything they could to make public life into a private men's club. A farmer in Georgia, on learning that two-thirds of the white voters had been removed from the jury rolls in his county, gave vent to his frustration. "We would like to know to what clique we must belong, and whom we must allow to do our thinking. To whom must we pull off our hats, and whose boots must we lick to be counted worthy to serve on the jury?" This was the political vision of Southern elites—and, *mutatis mutandis*, of their Northern counterparts—a deferential society run by crony cliques in the interests of capital. The role of the state in creating that social structure cannot be underestimated. Indeed, federal and state governments alike proved instrumental in securing elite domination. Whether the project was disenfranchising blacks, breaking unions, or muzzling dissent, the rule of law proved pliant, yielding to intimidation, fraud, or force whenever existing power relations were challenged.

Still, hope kept erupting. Agrarian radicals were not ready to accept their exclusion from public life. In the early 1880s, Virginia became a key battleground in the struggle between insurgents and established elites—a struggle that would set the pattern for many more in the decade to come. William Mahone's Readjusters wanted to readjust the state's debt to broaden prosperity and promote economic growth among the mass of the people, black and white. When Mahone ran for the United States Senate in 1880 at the head of the Readjuster ticket, he courted black Republicans by pledging to abolish the whipping post and the poll tax, and by protecting the public schools. Readjusters won a majority in the state legislature, which was where senators were chosen until 1913. Mahone entered the Senate and proceeded to amass federal patronage from President Chester Arthur, whose party was encouraging Southern independent movements to challenge Democratic hegemony. By the time the local elections of 1881 rolled around, Readjusters were poised for victory. Black voters embraced them in droves; by the end of election day, the governorship and both houses of the state legislature were in Readjuster hands. Among the legislators were fifteen African-Americans. Through the early 1880s, Readjuster rule brought unfamiliar policies to the Old Dominion. The state government lowered real estate taxes, raised corporate taxes, chartered labor unions and fraternal organizations, regulated the power of banks, railroads, and tobacco companies, undermined the courthouse cliques, repealed the poll tax, abolished the whipping post, and provided additional funds for schools. Black schools proliferated, staffed by black teachers, who received pay equal to whites. The state also appropri-ated funds for a black state college and black insane asylum. If this was not utopia, it was at least a remarkable interlude. Not again for nearly a century would Virginia politicians provide as many public services as fairly to the entire state population.

Readjuster rule was soon brought down by Virginia Democrats deploying the familiar strategies of race-baiting and fraud. But Mahone had demonstrated what insurgents could do by connecting monetary reform to a wide range of egalitarian and anti-monopoly policies. They could challenge the notion that government was a private (white) men's club; they could widen the public sphere by creating common ground among the indebted classes, linking farmers and laborers, even blacks and whites. Of course these alliances were shaky and easily toppled. But they provided political outsiders—people who had never imagined themselves acting effectually in public—with a glimpse of what an insurgency could do. As the historian Lawrence Goodwyn has argued, this was a crucial moment in the creation of a "movement culture": a mass of insurgents becoming visible (to themselves and others) as political actors for the first time.

Farther west, the Farmers' Alliances had embarked on a similar project. The organization began in Texas, Arkansas, Louisiana, and Kansas as a counterforce to the feelings of isolation and impotence that enveloped the countryside in the 1880s. Dividing into Northern and Southern Alliances, the farmers nevertheless soon began to see themselves as part of a huge and effectual national movement—and not merely another interest group scuffling for narrow gain. A key moment in this broadening process was the Great Southwest Strike of 1886, when the Alliance tried to reach out to the Knights of Labor. Jay Gould had set out to crush the Knights of Labor on his Missouri Pacific Line. When his general manager H. M. Hoxie fired a union leader for missing work to attend a union meeting (something the railroad had given him permission to do), the Knights walked out. The strike spread from East Texas throughout the West, igniting a series of skirmishes between strikers and Pinkertons or militiamen (or both). Everyone was armed, in this frontier class war. W. R. Lamb, the head of the Montague County (Texas) Alliance, urged the Southern Alliance to back the Knights, insisting that the farmer was not a businessman but a worker, like the members of the Knights of Labor. The age of the independent yeoman, he believed, had been brought to an end by monopoly power. Many Farmers' Alliance leaders shared Lamb's perception; said one, Evan Jones: "We extend to the Knights of Labor our hearty sympathies in their manly struggle against monopolistic oppression."

The language of manliness melded rural and urban discontent in a producerist worldview. Producerism reaffirmed the ties between farmers and workers, underscoring their common attachment to "manly" ideals of economic independence and identifying their common enemies as bankers, speculators, and loan-sharking merchants—parasites who produced nothing but made money only by manipulating it, sucking the lifeblood from the honest labor of farmers, mechanics, and small proprietors. These groups together constituted "the producing classes."

Skeptical liberals as well as cynical capitalists have dismissed the producerist worldview—especially its agrarian version—as the outlook of ignorant bumpkins about to be steamrollered by modernity, enraptured by nostalgic fantasies of a lost agrarian utopia, and given to provincial xenophobia. The indictment is an unfair caricature, but there is a grain of truth to it. On occasion the agrarian producerist critique of moneylending became infected with anti-Semitism, or bogged down in literalist epistemology, primitive economics, and parochial morality. Still, there were times when only a producerist mentality could do justice to the ironies of capitalist development—such as the overcapitalized railroads of the 1880s, whose stock prices soared while their bridges collapsed and equipment fell apart. Sometimes literalist notions of reality constituted a salutary corrective to Wall Street fantasy. More important: producerist economic thought, however simple in its origins, was leavened by egalitarian impulses that eventually fostered a sophisticated challenge to laissez-faire orthodoxy.

But the great Southwest Strike was about power, not ideas. In the end Gould outlasted the strikers and drove the union from the road. Unions were nowhere as well organized as farmers in the 1880s; nor were they as able to solidify a democratic base (at least not until the formation of industrial unions in the 1930s). The dream of a farmer-labor coalition faced cultural and economic difficulties in any case: farmers were old-stock Protestants who favored temperance reform and eventually prohibition of alcohol; industrial workers were increasingly members of ethnic minorities who liked to hang out in saloons; free trade was the farmers' slogan, while tariffs were the workers' friend (or at least many of them believed so). Still, these were by no means insurmountable obstacles, and the idea of rural and urban workers making common cause continued to animate populist protest throughout the twentieth century.

DESPITE THE FAILURE of the Southwest Strike, it had shown the Farmers' Alliance that they were becoming a political organization. S. O. Daws, a Texas organizer, summarized the strategy when he said the Alliance should "call each neighborhood together and organize anti-monopoly leagues . . . and nominate candidates for office." The opposition to monopoly led to specific policy implications, which farmers first spelled out when they met in August 1886 in the dusty little farm town of Cleburne, Texas. Their immediate concern was challenging the dominant pattern of land sales. Scottish and English cattle syndicates as well as American railroads had bought up huge swaths of land for speculative purposes, leaving little public domain for settlement. Issuing a statement that became known as the Cleburne Demands, the Alliance insisted that speculative land be taxed, that foreigners be prevented from speculating in American land, and that speculators be required to sell land titles to settlers. Most important was their call for a federally administered national banking system, with the United States Treasury issuing legal-tender notes (greenbacks) that "shall increase as the population and business interests of the country expand." Concern for a federal currency and credit system was at the core of the Farmers' Alliance program.

That preoccupation led to their most innovative proposal, the subtreasury plan. Its progenitor was C. W. Macune, a handsome and articulate man who was born to be a political organizer. Growing up in Wisconsin in the 1850s, an orphan at ten, Macune had bumped around the Midwest, "reading" for the professions in the nineteenth-century fashion and landing on the Texas frontier in the 1870s. By 1886 he had risen to prominence in the Alliance and had begun creatively to address the farmers' central problem of credit. His solution was to combine a flexible government-issued currency with the cooperative marketing arrangements that farmers had tried to set up as an alternative to dependence on merchants and trusts. Cooperatives had failed because private bankers had refused them credit. Under the subtreasury plan, the United States Treasury would underwrite the cooperatives, providing farmers credit at low interest by issuing them federal subtreasury certificates (greenbacks) for their crops, which would then be stored in government-owned warehouses, or subtreasuries. Released from the endless cycle of debt and dependency, the farmer could choose the optimum time to sell. In one fell swoop, the plan eliminated usurious merchants, commercial banks, and mortgage companies from American agriculture, providing citizens access to reasonable credit by shifting control of the money supply from commercial banks to the United States Treasury. Heretical as it may have seemed to laissez-faire ideologues, Macune's subtreasury plan embodied a central tenet of republican tradition: the management of national resources to serve the public good.

Despite that broad appeal, the farmers' movement spread unevenly. From the outset the Southern Alliance was bigger, better organized, and more radical than the Northern Alliance. As early as 1888 the Southerners scored a significant victory over the makers of jute-bagging, who had formed a trust in St. Louis and colluded to double jute prices. Tom Watson urged farmers to boycott jute and use cotton bagging instead. "It is useless to ask Congress to help us, just as it was folly for our forefathers to ask for relief from the tea tax, and as they revolted . . . so should we." Thousands of farmers embraced the boycott and took to wearing cotton-bag suits as a sign of protest; on Alliance Day at the Piedmont Exposition in Atlanta, a double wedding was performed with both couples decked out in cotton bagging. Within months the jute trust caved in and reduced their prices. Southern farmers were jubilant. For once the plain people had come together, had acted in concert. The movement culture spread as poor folk confronted a novel sight: themselves, acting effectually in public.

Hopes soared across the countryside. Through the late 1880s and into the early 1890s, the Farmers' Alliance movement spread like a prairie fire from the South into the Midwest. Southern farmers may have been scruffier and more radical than their Midwestern counterparts, but the two groups had common grievances. Cheap Russian wheat and cheap Egyptian cotton depressed their prices on the international market; railroads gouged them to pay the dividends on watered stock; tight money kept them in thrall to bankers and merchants. Midwestern farmers shared Southerners' distrust of "the town clique."

As the Alliance advanced across the plains, the political gap widened between the country and the city. In Cowley County, Kansas, for example, town folk continued to vote Republican while farmers flocked in droves to the new Independent ticket. Indeed, Kansas was one of the states where the Farmers' Alliance began to take on the characteristics of a regenerative mass movement—described by various observers as "a pentecost of politics," "a religious revival," and "a crusade." Along with stump speeches by Macune and other orators, Farmers' Alliance meetings featured long parades of wagons stretching for miles, decorated with evergreens to symbolize the "living issues" of the Alliance rather than the dead tariffs and bloody shirts of the existing two-party system. The plain people could see themselves acting politically en masse. In Kansas as elsewhere, farmers fired up by the experience of participatory democracy began to take matters into their own hands. The insurgent culture produced insurgent politics. In Harper County, Kansas, the Alliance demanded stricter usury laws; in Brown County they protested "the extortions of the binding twine trust" and proceeded "at once to the erection of a co-operative manufactory for binding twine." This was how a democratic social movement was born.

Still, the Alliance had to overcome the power of regional and racial mistrust. Little more than twenty years earlier, Midwesterners and Southerners had been killing each other at Fredericksburg and Chickamauga. Old resentments died hard, as Garrison understood when he recommended the bloody shirt to Republican orators. At the same time, the two regions' shared evangelical ethos began to acquire greater strength and political significance, bringing old antagonists together on common cultural terrain. The emergence of Protestant moral reform in both sections focused on the redemptive power of the family and the destructive effects of drink. In the trans-Mississippi West, men got drunk in saloons, which were often franchises backed by corporate breweries—outposts of the national market economy in remote communities; in the South, men got drunk on Main Street, in grocery stores that were groggeries as well—familiar community spaces for male camaraderie. Despite these different social contexts, reformers in both regions agreed that the death of demon rum would promote national as well as personal renewal.

By the 1880s the dream of regeneration through the prohibition of alcohol had begun to ferment even in the old Confederacy, where temperance societies had to outgrow their antislavery roots before they could acquire a popular following. Women provided the prime source of support. In the South as elsewhere, they were the victims of dissolute husbands at home and the spectators of male drunkenness on every public occasion. When Frances Willard of the Women's Christian Temperance Union swept through the former Confederate states on a speaking tour in the 1880s, women flocked to her lectures and embraced her cause, forming local chapters of the WCTU. As in the North, the Prohibition movement offered many Southern women their first real chance to participate in public life.

Willard was the perfect apostle to conservative women in the South, as elsewhere. Far from dismissing domestic ideals of womanhood, she insisted on the interdependence of the private and the public, the home and the world. And she infused her politics with her Methodist Christianity. Indeed, she was inspired to support women's suffrage through a conversion experience, which occurred when she was preparing to give a temperance lecture one Sunday morning in Columbus, Ohio. "Upon my knees alone, in the room of my hostess, who was a veteran [temperance] Crusader, there was borne in upon my mind, as I believe, from loftier regions, the declaration, 'You are to speak for woman's ballot as a protection to the home and tempted loved ones from the tyranny of drink,' and then for the first and only time in my life, there flashed through my mind a complete line of argument and illustration," she later recalled. The voice spoke to her in 1876; for nearly twenty years she articulated that "line of argument and illustration." For Willard, temperance and women's suffrage worked hand in glove: by increasing electoral support for temperance legislation, female suffrage would liberate drunkards from enslavement to alcohol, cleanse the home of inebriating poison, and allow women's redemptive influence to suffuse the entire society.

Southern men were not immune, either, to the appeal of rebirth through sobriety. Sam Jones, a reformed drunk and Methodist minister, began preaching temperance sermons to all-male audiences in Memphis in 1884. "Hundreds of men wept like whipped children," a reporter noted, as Jones told them they had nobody to blame but themselves for their sins against self-control. Soon he was packing them in from Richmond to New Orleans. The emphasis on personal responsibility for one's own salvation created common ground for evangelicals in every region; what gave them a common political cause was the national Prohibition movement, which extended the temperance struggle's scope and reach, demanding unconditional surrender by the liquor interests and making personal morality a federal responsibility. Kansas pointed the way by including the prohibition of alcohol as part of its state constitution in 1880.

But the national Prohibition movement did not really catch fire until 1900. For most rural folk in the 1880s and 1890s, political economy mattered more than cultural politics. The question for agrarian rebels was: could the Northern Farmers' Alliance and the Southern Farmers' Alliance work together? In 1889, when the two groups convened at St. Louis, hopes for full consolidation were dashed, but the Kansas, South Dakota, and North Dakota delegations broke off and joined the Southern Alliance—which soon became known as the National Alliance, or simply the Alliance. True to producerist tradition, the Alliance opened its membership to mechanics as well, acknowledging the presence of the Knights of Labor at the convention. The St. Louis convention adopted a capacious platform that included the subtreasury plan as well as public ownership of telegraph lines and railroads and an expanded money supply based on the free coinage of silver. As Watson and other Alliance leaders knew, inclusiveness was the key to building a broad national movement.

In that spirit, the delegates elected Leonidas L. Polk their president. He was the one agrarian leader who provided the single best hope for sectional reconciliation. A North Carolina Unionist who had opposed secession, Polk had "gone with his state" and fought for the Confederacy. But he was no misty-eyed Lost Cause devotee. "Not the war of twenty-five years ago . . . but the great struggle of today between the classes and the masses . . . is the supreme incentive and object of this great political revolution," Polk told a cheering Alliance convention at Indianapolis in 1891. By then it was apparent that the "revolution" of the plain folk had replaced old sectional solidarities with new national ones—at least among the white farmers.

The inclusion of the black farmers was more problematic. The Colored Farmers' Alliance was founded in East Texas in 1886. Its leader was a white Baptist minister and former Confederate officer named R. M. Humphrey. The group expanded gradually, opening cooperative exchanges in New Orleans, Norfolk, Houston, Mobile, and Charleston. The Colored Alliance was present at the St. Louis convention, but on the fringes. Black people were understandably wary about joining up with white farmers: they knew that crop liens and hard money—damaging as they were—were less pressing threats than night-riding terrorists and systematic disenfranchisement. Still, white Alliance leaders made sustained efforts to cross the color line. Henry Vincent was one, a scion of abolitionists and editor of the pro-Alliance newspaper *American Nonconformist*, in Winfield, Kansas. Vincent persistently urged the broadest possible base for the Farmers' Alliance, praising the Knights of Labor for their racially integrated convention in Richmond, Virginia, and urging the farmers to take a comparably inclusive approach.

Of course it was far more politically difficult for white Southerners to take a similar stance. Yet Tom Watson did. As early as 1882, when he was running for the Georgia state legislature, he courted the black majority in MacDuffie County. At that point African-American voters were manipulated and intimidated but not yet disenfranchised. Watson won the endorsement of black Republicans by promising free schools and an end to the convict-lease system. Though Watson sought to distance himself from the official Republican platform, his opponent accused him of trying to steal the black vote by endorsing Republican policies. Watson won anyway. He introduced bills to investigate the convict-lease system and to allow tenants legal standing to contest landlord's claims against them. Neither bill went anywhere, but Watson was establishing himself as a voice for the dispossessed—both black and white.

As he rose to prominence, Watson remained committed to bridging the racial divide by emphasizing the common economic grievances of the poor. "Here is a tenant—I do not know, or care, whether he is white or black, I know his story," Watson would say. "He starts in and pays $25 for a mule, 1,000 pounds of cotton for rent, and two bales for supplies. By the time he pays for that mule, and the store account, and the guano, he has not enough money left to buy a bottle of laudanum, and not enough cotton to stuff his old lady's ear." Poverty and dependence cut across the color line. Watson repeatedly called for a union of black and white farmers, denouncing disenfranchisement and demanding political equality between the races. While he sought to calm white anxieties by disavowing "social equality," Watson insisted that "the accident of color can make no difference in the interests of farmers, croppers, and laborers." Racial divisions, contrary to Grady and other white supremacists, had no place in the making of public policy; class divisions did. To the extent that the Alliance advanced this idea, Polk might be pardoned for calling the agrarian revolt a "revolution."

AS ECONOMIC CRISIS deepened throughout the Cotton Belt and across the plains, the perversity of market-based distribution became impossible to ignore—or at least impossible for farmers to ignore. In January 1890, a dairy farmer from western Kansas noted the cruel irony that his neighbors were "burning corn for fuel, while coal miners and their families in another section of our land are famished for food." Across the South and Midwest, the Alliance mobilized campaigns for independent candidates. In the election of 1890, they met with remarkable success, even at the federal level. Two senators and at least fifteen representatives owed their elections to Alliance backing.

In December 1890 the Alliance reconvened at Ocala, Florida, to reaffirm its political principles. The Ocala Platform contained the familiar Alliance planks—the subtreasury, a flexible money supply, free silver, tariff reduction, government supervision (and, if necessary, ownership) of "the means of public transportation and communication"—and added some new, more explicitly egalitarian ones, including a graduated income tax and the popular election of senators. (Until the passage of the Seventeenth Amendment in 1913, U.S. senators were chosen by the state legislatures.) A month later the Alliance met again in Indianapolis and requested that all congressmen elected with Alliance support "decline to enter into any party caucus called to designate a Candidate for Speaker, unless adherence to principles of the Ocala Platform are made a test of admission to said caucus." This was a prescription for a congressional insurgency.

All through the winter and spring of 1891, as the Alliance-backed congressmen settled into Washington life, the question that dominated discussion was: should we form a third party? The Indianapolis resolution made fidelity to the Ocala Platform a precondition for continued Alliance support. Yet some Southern Democrats were reluctant to break with the white man's party, the powerful political organization that was consolidating its rule throughout the region. As the session neared, debate raged, cloakroom conversation heated, and delegates discovered where their loyalties lay.

The die-hard Alliance men were led by Tom Watson of Georgia and "Sockless Jerry" Simpson of Kansas. Hamlin Garland, now thirty-one, observed them from the gallery, where he was gathering material for an essay in *Arena* magazine. His book of short fiction, *Main-Travelled Roads*, had just been published, and had been praised by none other than William Dean Howells for its bleakly realistic portrayal of Midwestern farm life. For Garland, Simpson and Watson played fascinating variations on the country themes he knew well. Simpson acquired his sobriquet during a political campaign against a Republican dandy, of whom he observed that "princes wear silk socks," while he, a poor countryman, had none. Soon farm women throughout the Midwest were knitting socks for him. According to Garland,

Simpson was "about fifty years of age, of slender but powerful figure"; he wore "old-fashioned glasses, through which his eyes gleam with ever present humor." Lacking formal education, he was "naturally a studious man," who thought for himself, made up his own mind, and spoke his convictions plainly. When he was called out of order for characterizing a senator as an "iniquitous railway attorney," Simpson said, "Well, I will withdraw that. I am a new member and do not know your rules. But that is the way we talk in Kansas. We are plain speaking people." Here as elsewhere in our history, the Protestant tradition of plain speech (for all its literalist naïveté) provided a strong ethical basis for political critique—as well as a refreshing contrast to the banal pomposity of official discourse.

Along with Simpson, Garland found Watson the most remarkable of the agrarian radicals. "He speaks with a touch of the dialect of the South, and wears a soft hat in the southern way. . . . He is small and active. His face is perfectly beardless and quite thin. His eyes are his most remarkable feature, except possibly the abundance of dark red hair, pushed back from his face." About Watson's politics, Garland waxed enthusiastic: "His life of hard work and suffering has made him a commoner and a radical—'a dangerous man' to some of the Southern people,—but a very moderate and fair-tempered reformer to me. He is simply one more of the scores of similar young radicals and commoners of my acquaintance. He not only types the best economic thought of the young South,—he leads it. He stands for the further extension of the idea of liberty." This was a fine alternative, in Garland's view, to the more familiar rural attitude of resignation, the outlook he had seen so much as a child.

In early 1891 Watson and Simpson led a group of ten who began to caucus on their own. This was the beginning of the People's—or Populist—Party. Support for the Populist agenda spread quickly in hard times. As low prices and tight money persisted in the countryside and employers hired thugs to break strikes in Homestead, Pennsylvania, Coeur d'Alene, Idaho, and other industrial towns, the Populist assault on privilege acquired a resonance beyond the agricultural districts. It caught the imagination of a variety of reformers—single-taxers, Socialists, feminists, Social Gospelers—who were increasingly appalled by the mounting social costs of laissez-faire capitalism and were looking for some humane policy alternatives. The more hopeful even envisioned a cooperative commonwealth.

The *Arena* magazine became a forum for reform thought, and in 1892 Tom Watson published an essay there that asserted the Populist Party's determination to build a biracial coalition in the South. The People's Party, wrote Watson, said this to white and black farmers alike: "You are kept apart that you may be separately fleeced of your earnings. You are made to hate each other because upon that hatred is rested the keystone of the arch of financial despotism which enslaves you both. You are deceived and blinded that you may not see how this race antagonism perpetuates a monetary system which beggars both." Watson described the role of race hate in class hegemony more succinctly than most politicians, before or since. Yet despite the incisiveness of Watson's critique, the biracial coalition had already revealed some strains. In 1891 the Colored Alliance called a cotton pickers' strike, which collapsed with embarrassing speed. Whites began to distance themselves and the Colored Alliance's membership began to decline. This was a straw in the wind. Racist mores and laws prevented blacks from coming together in public, from engaging in the visible collective action that gave impetus to democratic movements. White power and paranoia blocked Populist efforts to create a biracial coalition.

But in early 1892, Populist leaders remained hopeful, and eager to make connections with other reformers who would endorse the Ocala Platform. At a general reform conference in St. Louis in February 1892, L. L. Polk was elected conference chair and head of the People's Party. He welcomed the delegates by announcing that "The time has arrived for the great West, the great South, and the great Northwest, to link their hands and hearts together and march to the ballot box and take possession of the government, restore it to the principles of our fathers, and run it in the interests of the people." The republican dream of a restored commitment to the public good, like the millennial hope of a cooperative commonwealth, acquired urgency from the delegates' sense that the nation was poised on the brink of catastrophe. No one caught the mood of apocalypse better than Ignatius Donnelly of Minnesota.

. . . we meet in the midst of a nation brought to the verge of moral, political, and material ruin. Corruption dominates the ballot box, the legislatures, the Congress, and touches even the ermine of the bench. The people are demoralized. . . . The newspapers are subsidized or

muzzled; public opinion silenced; business prostrate, our homes covered with mortgages, labor impoverished, and the land concentrating
in the hands of capitalists. The urban workmen are denied the right
of organization for self-protection; imported pauperized labor beats
down their wages; a hireling standing arm, unrecognized by our laws,
is established to shoot them down, and they are rapidly degenerating
to European conditions. The fruits of the toil of millions are boldly
stolen to build up colossal fortunes, unprecedented in the history of
the world, while their possessors despise the republic and endanger
liberty.

When Donnelly finished, the place was pandemonium. He was quickly
surrounded by adoring throngs. The Populist platform, which restated the
Ocala principles, was whooped through, and a presidential nominating convention scheduled for July 4, 1892, in Omaha. Polk was the obvious choice
to bring the South and the West together, but he died suddenly on June
11. The convention nominated James Weaver, a former Union general from
Iowa, for president, and James Field, a former Confederate general from
Virginia, for vice president—to balance the ticket. Weaver was a less attractive candidate than Polk, especially in the South. Old Confederate Democrats, those supposed Southern gentlemen, pelted the candidate and his
entourage with rotten eggs; one hit his wife in the head. Still he pressed on
gamely and ultimately garnered more than a million popular votes (out of
twelve million cast) and twenty-two electoral votes. Populists won twelve
new seats in Congress.

Tom Watson was not among them. He fought hard, enlisting the fervent
support of both races. One of his leading black supporters was H. S. Doyle,
a young Baptist preacher, who made sixty-three speeches for Watson. When
Doyle was threatened with lynching, Watson installed him in his own home,
where two thousand white farmers protected him. In that time and place,
probably no man could have come closer to creating a genuine biracial coalition than Tom Watson. Georgia Democrats stole the election with brazen
effrontery, stuffing ballot boxes wholesale, intimidating and manipulating
voters of both races. Despite these flagrant crimes, Populists remained fired
with encouragement and fervently committed to their cause. But the charismatic Watson's defeat suggested the magnitude of the task before them.

Currier and Ives, "Across the Continent: Westward the Course of Empire Takes its Way." Print, 1868.

L. A. Huffman, "5 Minutes Work." Stereo photograph, Jordan, Montana, 1882.

Otto Becker, "Custer's Last Fight." Lithograph, 1896.

L. A. Huffman, "Two Moon's Tepee, Lame Deer Valley." Photograph, 1896.

Solomon Eyting, "Among the Tenement-houses During the Heated Term—Just Before Daybreak." Print published in *Harper's Weekly*, 1879.

T. de Thulstrup, "The Anarchist Riot in Chicago—A Dynamite Bomb Exploding Among the Police." Print published in *Harper's Weekly*, May 15, 1886.

"Scene of a Lynch at Clinton, Alabama, August 1891."
Photograph published in Ida B. Wells, *United States Atrocities: Lynch Law*
("Lux" Newspaper and Publishing Company: London, 1891).

Nat "Deadwood Dick" Love. Photograph, 1907.

Louis Sullivan, Union Trust Building (detail), St. Louis, Missouri, 1893.

New York Stock Exchange, Broad Street, 1903. Photograph by Irving Underhill, 1908.

Carry Nation. Photograph, ca. 1901.

Edward Van Altena, Theodore Roosevelt in Africa with dead rhino.
Lantern slide, 1909.

Sarah Bernhardt. Photograph, ca. 1895.

Gertrude Hoffman as Salome. Photograph, 1908.

Celebrity Art Co., "I Love My Wife, but OH! You Kid." Postcard, 1909.

Harry Houdini in handcuffs and a straitjacket, hanging 100 feet above Broadway, New York City. Photograph, ca. 1916.

CHAPTER 5

Crisis and Regeneration

◆

On May 1, 1893, the World's Columbian Exposition opened its gates in Chicago. Within days it was a sensation, attracting swarms of tourists from around the country and abroad. The notion of a World's Fair was itself nothing new. For decades, the modernizing nations of the West had been staging grand expositions to celebrate their imperial aspirations and achievements, to affirm their place at the cutting edge of progress in the characteristic Victorian manner—by accumulating and displaying tons of stuff. The Chicago World's Fair followed suit but claimed to redeem the jumble by subordinating it to neoclassical ideals of balance and harmony.

"Not Matter, But Mind; Not Things, But Men" was the official motto of the fair, repeated often by the architect Daniel Burnham, its head designer. Burnham assembled a team of architects and artists with impeccable neoclassical credentials as well as powerful ties to the patronage establishment. Nor were they short of self-esteem. "Look here, old fellow," the sculptor Augustus Saint-Gaudens burst out to Burnham at a planning meeting, "do you realize that this is the greatest meeting of artists since the fifteenth century?" Saint-Gaudens, Burnham, and their colleagues and patrons all believed that they could discipline the furious, expansive energies of American capitalism with the cool ideality of neoclassical hierarchies, values, and tastes. Class and race conflict dissolved in the neoclassicist vision of regeneration through art and culture—a dream of universal unity that reinforced the developing discourse of empire.

The fulfillment of the planners' imperial agenda was aptly dubbed the White City. The core of it was the Court of Honor, a cluster of plaster temples assembled around a lagoon lit by hundreds of incandescent lights. The chaste buildings were crammed with the latest products developed by Westinghouse, Krupp, General Electric, and other burgeoning trusts—traveling cranes, artillery pieces, dynamos. Radiating outward from the Court of

Honor were less formal structures housing less powerful enterprises, such as the Agriculture and Fisheries Buildings and the Women's Building.

At the farthest fringe was the Midway Plaisance, where (as Burnham noted) "no distinct order is followed, it being instead a most unusual collection of almost every type of architecture known to man—oriental villages, Chinese bazaars, tropical settlements, ice railways, the ponderous Ferris wheel, and reproductions of ancient cities. All these are combined to form the lighter and more fantastic side of the Fair." The Midway Plaisance revealed some features of the emerging civilization that could not be easily assimilated to neoclassical ideality—the "ponderous Ferris wheel" that embodied the first stirrings of mass-marketed entertainment; the "tropical settlements" that had already been colonized by European empires and were soon to be claimed by an American empire, too. Despite their apparent disparity, tropical settlements and Ferris wheels would both contribute to the rise of an imperial way of life in America.

Though the Midway was the most popular site at the fair (largely due to the fetching belly dancer who called herself Little Egypt), few literate observers spent much time discussing its carnal pleasures. Most hovered on the edges of the Court of Honor, rhapsodizing about the redemptive powers of art—as the planners had hoped. Yet ultimately the fair slipped away from its organizers' intentions, revealing a central irony: the future belonged to the consolidated force of capital, and not to the flimsy neoclassical structures that temporarily housed it. The period from the Chicago World's Fair to the merger wave of 1897–1903 marked a key moment in the shift from the chaotic laissez-faire capitalism of the Gilded Age to the corporate, managerial capitalism of the Progressive Era and beyond. The laissez-faire ideal had been compromised for decades by business dependence on government subsidies; Populists and later Progressives aimed to excise the hypocrisy by increasing government's power to represent the public interest against private gain, creating a countervailing force against monopoly capital. They were gradually and fitfully successful, but ultimately unable to sustain the revival of commonweal that they craved. Plutocracy was refined but not destroyed; meritocratic ideals made class hierarchies more flexible but also more resilient. Established elites developed their own successful strategies of self-renewal, as they collaborated selectively with the new world of ambitious immigrants, parvenu plutocrats, imperial adventurers, and Progressive reformers.

The drive for renewal through empire lay at the core of this cultural transformation, but other movements played a role as well. Populist desires to create a cooperative commonwealth combined with Social Christians' longings to usher in the Kingdom of God on Earth; the result was a steady stream of insurgent sentiment that survived electoral defeats in 1896 and 1900 and continued to animate Progressive reform after the turn of the century. The give-and-take of legislative compromise gradually blunted radical critiques and led reformers toward regulation rather than confrontation. Millennial dreams yielded to managerial techniques as utopian visions were translated into practical policies. Progressive reformers laid the foundations of the welfare state and vindicated the role of government in protecting the public good from private greed.

Yet the wealthiest Americans managed to fend off the most serious challenges to their privilege, compromising with the reformers at crucial points, and diffusing the insurgent spirit by embracing a broad agenda of self-renewal that merged psyche and society, the personal and the political. The imperial expansion that began in 1898 provided unprecedented revitalization for established elites—a global field of opportunities for physical and moral testing, not to mention profitable investment. Eventually the revitalized rich refashioned a role for themselves as directors and managers of the emerging American empire. But no one could have predicted that in 1893.

ON MAY 5, 1893, four days after the opening of the World's Columbian Exposition, bad news spread on Wall Street soon after the Stock Exchange's opening bell. The National Cordage Company, the "rope trust," had gone belly-up—hanged itself, as wags said. In less than an hour, the *New York Times* reported, traders had embarked on a frenzy of selling: "the floor might have passed for a corner in Bedlam." Waves of financial panic broke throughout the economy: within weeks, hundreds of banks failed, and hundreds of thousands of men lost their jobs. The worst depression the country had ever seen enveloped the land for the next four years.

Few were spared hard times. For farmers it was more of the same: bad weather meant poor crops and low volume; good weather meant bumper crops and low prices. In fall 1893, a Methodist minister told his missionary conference of conditions at harvesttime near Lincoln, Nebraska, where "an honest Methodist farmer" rolled up to the grain elevator with a hundred bushels of wheat, the yield of twenty acres. He received $31 for it. "With this he paid his taxes and half of his grocery bill, and went home without dinner because there was not a nickel left in his pocket." Out-of-work men took to hunting and trapping full-time, but there was only so much wild game to go around, especially in agricultural areas where habitats had been cleared for crops. With their families skipping meals and facing slow starvation, fathers struck out across the countryside in search of work. The ranks of the tramp army swelled.

The depression was a cross-country and cross-class catastrophe. Even the well-heeled were pinched. During the summer of 1893, panic ripped through the rentier class in the urban Northeast. A patrician intellectual and scion of two presidents, Henry Adams was summoned home from Europe in July to save the Adams Family Trust from mismanagement by his inept brother John. When Henry arrived, he reported to his friend John Hay, "I found Boston standing on its head, wild with terror, incapable of going to bed and brushing its weary old tusks in the morning; all this only because no one could get any money to meet his notes." Economic collapse had a multiplier effect: creditors might fail when debtors could not meet their obligations.

Prominent businessmen scrambled to raise money to keep their enterprises afloat. "I suppose that it will be somewhat troublesome to raise the money for the payment of notes by the Carnegie Mill," wrote Blanche Ames to her husband Adelbert in August 1893. A Radical Republican governor and congressman from Mississippi during Reconstruction, by the 1890s Ames was a successful flour-mill owner in Lowell, Massachusetts. But even Ames was short of cash in the summer of 1893, and his wife (the Union general Ben Butler's daughter) wanted to help him sort out how to raise some. "Of course Carney [a client] owes us plenty of money, but we don't know if he will pay it now," she observed, wondering, "would it not be well, Del, to enquire of Baldwin [their banker] if it would be possible to raise money on a second mortgage on the Chicago building? Perhaps money is not so tight there as here."

But money was tight everywhere, as were the multiplier effects of its tightness. At Yale, enrollments shrank as students' fathers failed and tuition went unpaid. The dwindling student population spelled disaster for New Haven tradesmen—especially the high-grade tailors, who became "rabid pessimists" by the winter of 1894. Harvard began firing faculty at about the same time. The impact of mass unemployment spread from office and factory to household. Despite the pressure to keep up middle-class appearances, housekeepers were forced to reduce or eliminate servants. As opportunities in domestic service declined, the ranks of applicants for it were swelled by unemployed factory and shop girls and "typewriters" who had lost office jobs. "An advertisement for a second girl last week brought a besieging crowd of seekers for the place," the *New York Times* reported on Christmas Eve of 1893. "The would-be employer was overwhelmed. They were at both doors at once; they filled the basement and the upper hall, and stood outside. Among them were many to whom such service was new or long discarded." Milling crowds of job seekers often included the educated, refined, and respectable, reduced to scuffling for survival along with working-class folk.

Even when they touched bottom, acknowledging helplessness was hard—especially for people who had never known the pain of severe want, or if they had, were convinced they had put it behind them. In November 1893, an Ohio paper reported that "a perfectly steady man, member of a leading church in Cleveland, and who last year gave $100 for charity, was recently obliged to go to the Bethel for help." Out of work since July, he had exhausted his savings, had been without food for two days, and finally could stand it no longer. For him as for so many of his contemporaries, only desperation could justify seeking charity—and even then it was a source of shame. At a 5-cent restaurant on Bleecker Street in lower Manhattan, established by the New York Christian Industrial Alliance, a genteel middle-aged woman, tightly wrapped in a faded shawl, hesitated at the door when she saw the place was filled by men and boys. An attendant came forward and asked if he could serve her a bowl of stew. "Yes, sir," she said, "I would feel greatly obliged to you—I have the money you know—for a little something to eat, such as you usually serve for 5 cents." She counted out the warm, moist coppers she had been gripping so tightly and was served separately from the male crowd, on a box behind the counter. She had returned to her old neighborhood, dramatically changed since her childhood by the influx of immigrants, because she knew no one would recognize her. But she was hardly alone in her shame. "Many well-dressed persons, mainly young men, were at the counter," a reporter observed. "Some few even wore kid gloves, and they buried their faces in their soup bowls when they caught anybody looking at them." They had been brought to the same level as the "seedy and red-faced men" around them, all gobbling stew greedily, "so hungry that they seemed in danger of eating the spoons and saucers."

The scene was repeated often during the years following the crash, in scores of American cities, as municipal governments, churches, and other private charities tried to stem the tide of starvation. Sometimes desperate hunger bred lawlessness. In August of 1893 in Buffalo, New York, a mob of unemployed Polish ironworkers, "having exhausted the resources of the Poormaster," took to looting the stands and stalls of the outdoor Broadway Market. The police arrived, arrested ten of the ringleaders, and stayed on the premises for several days to try to reinstate calm. When masses of hungry people assembled for free food, panic could provoke police violence. An Italian immigrant woman recalled one such incident in Chicago in the winter of 1893, when she was a young girl: "The city hall was giving food to the people. The people were standing in line on Clinton Street. We used to get for one week a piece of salt pork and some dried peas and a loaf of bread and some coffee or some tea. Sometimes we stood there half the day and when it's our turn they had no more left to give. One day I was standing there early, early in the morning . . . Us poor women were frozen to death; and there was such a storm with the snow and the wind! Eight o'clock, when the door opened, all the people were pushing to get in. There came the police with their clubs and they were yelling like we were animals. Then one of the police hit the woman next to me in the head with his club. I didn't see her, but I don't think she pushed. The people behind me were pushing, that's all. When I saw that, I said, 'Better I starve before I let that policeman hit me!' And I ran home from that line. And I never, never went there again."

Usually the bread lines were peaceful. Men hung their heads, loitered about, and eventually left hurriedly with a loaf thrust inside their jackets—though always, a few could not wait and began tearing into it ravenously. Women were more stoical, less outwardly perturbed, deftly folding a loaf or two into their aprons and bustling on their way. The shame of charity was especially strong for men. Pride knew no class barriers. Even the destitute were reluctant to accept what looked like a handout. They seized almost any opportunity to avoid it—shoveling snow from stoops and pavements, chopping and sawing wood, pawning household objects of even minimal value—anything to pick up a little cash. Some, in despair at their inability to support a family, committed suicide. Others committed petty crimes—such as the unemployed carpenter who threw a brick through a Brooklyn shop window so he could be sent to Sing Sing, where he could get fed. The decision to seek charity was charged with anxiety, as a letter to a local relief committee in New York City, dated December 29, 1893, made clear:

Dear Sir:

It is with deep sorrow and reluctance that I am compelled to address you, but the love of my two children and wife, who are now without food, and no fire, prompts me to do as I am doing.

I am a painter, but, unfortunately, out of work for the last eight weeks, and how we have lived during that time God only knows. My rent is long overdue, and I don't know how long they will have the shelter that is now over their heads. One of the children goes to school, and most times without anything to eat. If any ladies or gentlemen know of any work, no matter how menial, I would gladly accept it.

A visit of inspection will find what I say is true, and my neighbors will tell you that I provide for my family when I work. I am temperate and will give satisfaction to anybody that gives me employment.

I am very sorry to have to ask any aid, but my little ones crying for bread nearly drive me mad.

Hoping you will not pass this appeal by,
I remain, truly, yours

—— ——.

The painter's insistence that he would pass inspection was revealing. Respectable opinion distinguished sharply between deserving and undeserving poor. Charitable organizations tried to enforce the distinction by poking around the households of the indigent, searching for evidence of idleness, lasciviousness, or intemperance. Unconditional almsgiving was thought to be so degrading to the recipient that many charitable organizations created miniature public-works projects for the poor, paid them a pittance, and charged them an equally modest sum for their coffee, stew, and bread. Thus was born the "5-cent restaurant" of the period.

Still, so many people were so obviously destitute through no fault of their own that the narrow version of the Protestant ethic—the stress on individual responsibility for one's economic fate—was difficult to sustain with the old confidence. By August 1894, hard times had dragged on for over a year, and familiar assumptions were shifting. When an unemployed street-car employee named McClean from Englewood, New Jersey, stole a purse from a Mrs. Sedgwick, the victim decided to look into the thief's circumstances. Discovering that McClean was the sole support of an aged father, a wife, and a two-month-old baby, and that the household had been on the verge of starvation for weeks, Mrs. Sedgwick requested that the indictment be dismissed. The district attorney agreed: "The distress which impelled this defendant to attempt the commission of this crime charged against him, the harrowing destitution of his family, and the abundant evidence of his previous good character, showing that this condition was the result of sheer misfortune and not bad conduct, seem to show that he was not in a condition of mind to form the intent necessary to a crime."

By admitting that poverty, even crime, might arise from "sheer misfortune" rather than merely "bad conduct," the district attorney signaled a major shift in moral sensibility—a recognition that hard times (and the business cycle fostering them) were beyond any individual's control. Though many moralists continued to blame the poor for their own fate, the mass poverty of the 1890s had nothing to do with the morality or immorality of the jobless, and everything to do with the structural weaknesses of the Gilded Age economy.

THE COLLAPSE OF the 1890s had been developing for decades. It expressed the fundamental flaws of an economy based on unregulated capital markets and entrepreneurial frenzy. National Cordage—the company whose failure sparked the panic—was a characteristic Gilded Age enterprise: an overcapitalized, overextended company built on a rickety network of promissory notes (to repay debt) and gentlemen's agreements (to restrict competition). Few of those documents were worth a hoorah in hell. Railroads were as mismanaged as rope manufacturing and as vulnerable to tremors in the business cycle, with far more calamitous consequences for the economy as a whole. Indeed, it was the failure of the Philadelphia and Reading Railroad in February that sent the first storm signals to Wall Street. Over the next several months, hundreds more railroads declared bankruptcy, including the Northern Pacific, the Union Pacific, and the Santa Fe. Each of these employed more people and capital than all of the U.S. armed forces combined.

The impact of all this was undeniable, but the sound-money men who represented the investing classes thought they had a more compelling explanation for the depression: the impact of the Sherman Silver Purchase Act. Faced with a choice between accumulating silver certificates (which might become worthless in the event of a policy change) and trading them in for gold (which could be counted on to retain value), investors on both sides of the Atlantic chose gold. As foreign investors sent gold home and depleted U.S. reserves, the dollar's value fell. By late 1892, the *Commercial and Financial Chronicle* was already noting "the lack of confidence which our policy is causing Europe to feel in our financial stability. No more foreign capital comes to the United States and as fast as Europeans can dislodge their holdings in America they take their money away." From the bankers' view, the source of the collapse was the unstable currency created by the monetization of silver and the remedy was obvious: repeal the Sherman Silver Purchase Act.

President Cleveland agreed. For him and for other fiscal conservatives, gold was like the "natural laws" beloved of laissez-faire economists: a solid foundation of value that one could depend on amid the centrifugal flux of market forces. Little more than a month after the Wall Street crash, Cleveland called a special session of Congress to repeal the Silver Purchase Act. Defenders of silver, suspecting they were doomed, swung into action anyway. All summer long, they sweated and plotted. The cause drew strange bedfellows. One anomalous adherent was Henry Adams: despite his rentier status, he had inherited his family's republican distrust for men of mere trade, and especially for the Boston bankers of State Street; to this animosity he added a virulent fin de siècle strain of anti-Semitism. Still, as he and his brother Brooks sat up late talking silver, night after hot night in August of 1893, they began to grasp what few of their class had even dimly sensed: there was nothing "natural" about sound-money doctrine, or even laissez-faire capitalism.

Most backers of silver were more egalitarian and tolerant than the Adams brothers. Their leader was a young second-term congressman from Nebraska named William Jennings Bryan, who brought the insurgent spirit into the Democratic Party and eventually into the contest for the presidency. The advocates of sound money were led by a very different sort of man, John Pierpont Morgan, a banker born to wealth who knew how to increase it but who also believed that privilege entailed some responsibility for the public

good. Bryan's populism and Morgan's paternalism embodied two characteristic responses to the crisis of the 1890s, powerfully at odds but not, in the
long run, altogether incompatible. Still, the long run took two decades to
materialize. In the meantime the two men epitomized bitterly antagonistic
strains in American political culture.

Bryan imbibed a blend of politics and religion with his mother's milk.
He was born in 1860 in Salem, Illinois, a town boasting such signs of progress as a new railroad and a Methodist women's college, but surrounded
by farmers fretting about tight money and mounting debt. His father was a
practicing lawyer and prominent figure in the state Democratic Party. His
mother was competent and devout, a leading member of the local Women's
Christian Temperance Union. Young Bryan himself seemed fated for oratory from the outset: at the age of four, he began to give "little talks" to his
playmates from the front steps of his house. At thirteen he attended a revival
of the Cumberland Presbyterians, who rejected Calvinist notions of "election," holding out salvation to all while condemning dancing, drinking, and
similar profane sports. This was the combination of liberal theology and
conservative morality that Bryan would favor throughout his life.

Young Bryan's career sputtered briefly, then caught fire. After several tedious years of practicing law in Jacksonville, he visited a law school chum in
Lincoln, Nebraska, and "caught a vision" of "a new country." He packed up
his young family and headed west. Soon after he arrived in Lincoln, he began introducing himself to every Democratic leader in the state. The party
was poised between the laissez-faire Bourbon establishment and the insurgent Farmers' Alliance; the key issue dividing them was how much (if any)
government intervention to demand on behalf of the dispossessed. Bryan
took his time deciding which faction to support, but hard times helped
make up his mind. Blizzards and other bitter weather were ruining crops
and compounding the farmers' financial woes. The Alliance spoke directly
to their desperation, arraying the producers of the prairie against the parasites of Wall Street. Bryan was raised in that rhetorical tradition, and threw
in his lot with the Alliance Democrats.

Bryan began to deploy producerist rhetoric as a young activist in the
campaign of 1888, stumping statewide on behalf of Democratic candidates.
Addressing discontent with simple force, he perfected his speaking style.
Returning one night from the northwest corner of the state, he awakened
his wife, Mary, to share his excitement. "Last night I found that I had power

over the audience," he said. "I could move them as I chose. I have more than usual power as a speaker. . . . God grant that I may use it wisely." He knelt by the bed and prayed. The boy orator was already melding grandiosity and humility, on his way to becoming the Great Commoner.

In 1890 Bryan ran for Congress. It was a propitious moment. Local Farmers' Alliances were coalescing into the People's Independent Party, aka the Populists. Running as a Democrat, Bryan wanted to take the lead of a prairie insurgency. He attacked tariffs, trusts, and the gold standard. He waffled on Prohibition so as not to alienate his working-class constituency in Omaha. Stopping in saloons, he had his aide buy beers all around while he himself quaffed soda water. He won in a walk, the second Democratic congressman in Nebraska history. Soon he became known as an opponent of trusts and an advocate of low tariffs and free silver. A Democrat in Washington, he continued consorting with Nebraska Populists.

Bryan was already known as an agrarian radical (at least by the standards of the Congress) when he rose one stifling afternoon in August 1893 to defend the Silver Purchase Act. No one had ever heard him go on with such eloquence for so long (three hours) about the injustice inflicted by fiscal austerity. Bryan was outraged, denouncing the proposed repeal as a deflationary move that would only exacerbate the economic depression. Asking, "Can you cure hunger by a famine?" he delivered a series of proverbial couplets, such as: "The poor man is called a socialist if he believes that the wealth of the rich should be divided among the poor, but the rich man is called a financier if he devises a plan by which the pittance of the poor can be converted to his use." The speech was a sensation, provoking ecstasy in the countryside and dark fulminations on Wall Street.

But the white-shoe boys on Wall Street won easily in the end. After months of debate, the Act was repealed. The money supply contracted further; indebted farmers and dispossessed workers became more desperate. And still the weather remained squally on Wall Street. But the solution to Wall Street's problems—at least from the Street's point of view—could be found in one man, J. P. Morgan. By the 1890s, Morgan was already a legendary character, having acquired more authority than any banker before or since.

He was a generation older than Bryan, and a lot richer. Born in the panic year of 1837, Morgan was the son of Junius Morgan, a Hartford dry-goods merchant who had retreated from the nasty weather on Wall Street to the comparative calm of retail trade. Young John Pierpont was a sickly child, tormented by mysterious seizures until his adolescence. Throughout his life he was convinced that some strange affliction had him in his grip, and that if it disappeared in one form it would reappear in another. So in his fifties, when he developed the rhinophyma that disfigured his nose, he never had it fixed, out of fear that the seizures would return. This zero-sum physiology merged with the scarcity psychology and economics of the Victorian bourgeoisie. There was only so much health, energy, and money to go around. These assumptions underwrote Morgan's sound-money principles as well as his frequent long vacations, which he justified as a means of regenerating his shattered nerves. Like many members of his class (including his own partners, as well as intellectuals like Henry Adams and William James), Morgan oscillated between a drive for disciplined achievement and a longing for passive withdrawal. A psychic boom and bust paralleled the lurchings of the laissez-faire economy.

The Morgan family gave those tensions a local habitation and a name. Junius was obsessed with his son's character, constantly seeking ways to shape it properly—teaching the boy about business, overseeing his reading habits and his pocket change, providing him with glimpses of European history and culture, arranging the acquisition of foreign languages. His mother had little to do with him. She made nervous exhaustion a way of life, lapsing into invalidism and cranky self-absorption. Young Pierpont navigated between them, enduring long absences in boarding schools while his family moved from Hartford to Boston and his father became a rising star in the New England banking community. Pierpont's youthful diaries revealed him to be an obsessive record-keeper, seeking to erect barriers against what he could not control: his family's constant moving, his mother's moods, his own seizures, acne, and rheumatic fever.

Another reassuring source of order was Morgan's early faith in a personal savior, and the providential allotment of rewards and punishments in this world as well as the next. This has always been a comforting doctrine for the affluent. Morgan remained a devout Low Church Episcopalian all his life, convinced that salvation came not by works but by faith in the atoning death of Christ. He was too much the worldly sensualist to epitomize the Protestant ethic, as his contemporary Rockefeller did; but there is no question that Morgan, too, considered himself among the saved. For both men, Christianity validated wealth and power.

By the time he was nearing his majority, Morgan was already convinced that he inhabited a well-ordered cosmos and that he might master it if he tried. Fortunately for him, his father's star had become visible in London, where the Bostonian George Peabody owned a bank that was highly regarded by conservative investors. Peabody made it his business to certify the value of the securities that he underwrote. A bachelor, he needed an heir, and he picked Junius. At the time nobody realized that he had founded a dynasty.

Young Pierpont soon matched and then superseded his father's shrewdness in investing. From his early career on, he had an extraordinary grasp of international markets as well as of local opportunities. His capacity to keep the big picture in focus reinforced his conviction that he and his father were engaged in public service. When the Civil War broke out, he had no doubts about hiring a substitute to serve in the Union Army. Service to the bank was a form of service to the Union. That was the assumption behind Morgan's great work of the post–Civil War decades: the financing and stabilizing of the nation's astonishing industrial growth, especially its railroads.

The crash of 1893 made it clear that Morgan still had work to do. In his view, the wave of railroad failures only demonstrated what he already knew: the free market in railroads was too free. The field was cluttered by inferior players, sometimes nearly bankrupt and just limping along. The responsibility of the bankers was to discipline the industry by strengthening the lines whose earnings indicated they deserved strengthening, allowing them to eliminate or absorb the weaker ones and confirming the "natural monopoly" of the most efficient road in a particular region. But railroads had a public character. They depended for their very existence on state charters, land grants, and rights-of-way; they constituted the common arteries of transport for the entire nation. Should such an obviously public resource be under the control of private bankers? Critics like Bryan wondered. The question never crossed Morgan's mind.

Responding to the crisis of the 1890s, he developed an organizational method so innovative and ingenious that it became known as "Morganization." It involved shifting the balance of a firm's securities from debt to equity, from mortgage bonds requiring annual interest to stocks that depend on company earnings. To persuade investors to trade in their safe, high-interest notes for riskier equity instruments, the Morgan bankers offered preferred stocks, which took precedence over common stocks: the railway company had to pay dividends on the preferred stock first, at a specified rate. The Morgan syndicate took its own payments in common stock, indicating Morgan's confidence in the railroad's long-term profitability.

The Morganization of the railroads in the 1890s portended a broader Morganization of the American economy. As more and more enterprises were reorganized and consolidated under the control of Wall Street investment banks (Drexel, Morgan and Kuhn, Loeb, among others), the sorcery of the capital markets began to stabilize. Wall Street began to service the capital needs of business generally, and white-shoe bankers cultivated an unaccustomed air of sobriety and responsibility.

But Morganization did not occur overnight, and during the months and years following the panic the evidence for stability was hard to find. The repeal of the Sherman Silver Purchase had not stopped the drain on U.S. gold reserves. By January 1895 they had fallen to $35 million. Morgan was worried. He cabled his brother-in-law: "We all have large interests dependent upon maintenance sound currency U.S." (The unexamined "we" was a characteristic touch of a man who conflated his own interests with those of society at large.) Morgan arranged to head an international banking syndicate that would buy $65 million worth of U.S. government bonds, paying in gold. He also gave Cleveland his personal guarantee that he would control the international currency market for the next six months, preventing any further withdrawals from the nation's gold reserves. It was an extraordinary promise, and Morgan kept it. He acted as the unofficial central banker of the United States, and (for a time) of the transatlantic Anglophone world as well. And he brought desperately needed reassurance to the panicky investing classes.

Not everyone was impressed. Morgan's "we" did not include the indebted farmers and unemployed workers who were suffering from deflationary policies. The pain of the people was real, and some of them turned it into political protest. Whether they blamed Wall Street speculators, railroad barons, or the sound-money crowd in Washington for the economic collapse, they were terrified and angered by its consequences. In a letter to the Populist governor of Kansas in 1894, a farm woman captured the seriousness of the situation: "I take pen in hand to let you know we are starving. . . . My husband went away to find work and came home last night and told me that he would have to starve. He has been in 10 counties and did not get no work. . . . I haven't had nothing to eat today and it is 3 o'clock." Not many governors could ignore a letter like that—and certainly not a Populist. Contrary to their critics' dismissive assumptions, Populist anger was not merely the raving of distempered cranks. It was a demand for justice.

THE DEPRESSION OF the 1890s laid bare the deep class divide in American society. Dives and Lazarus confronted each other directly in the winter of 1893–94, as a writer who called himself "a rustic in New York" reported in the *Atlantic*. Dining with friends at a new Fifth Avenue hotel, he wrote, "we had an elaborate repast of many courses and well-selected wines. The room was a little too warm, and a window near us had been opened an inch or two, though the night was cold and wet. Suddenly this window was thrown wide open, and there appeared at it a gaunt man, with matted beard and wild, hungry eyes. He looked at us and at the rich, abundant food, and then he said, in a loud but apparently not excited voice, 'Three days ago I pawned my coat to buy a loaf of bread for my wife and children.' That was all. The head waiter rushed to the window and slammed it down; there was talk of the police; a lady nearby turned pale with fright, and had to be revived by means of a smelling-bottle; then the sumptuous eating and drinking went on as before. But I confess that my uneducated country appetite did not survive this incident. The victuals that the man outside was going without stuck in my throat; champagne itself failed to wash them down."

When a single starving man became part of a social movement, the threat to affluent appetites became more sustained. Through the winter of 1893–94, as employers laid off more and more workers, scattered groups of jobless men formed "armies" led by "generals." The most prominent general was Jacob S. Coxey, a businessman who operated sandstone quarries in Massillon, Ohio, and nurtured egalitarian sympathies for the workingman. In late winter of 1894, Coxey began assembling local unemployed men to march on Washington and demand public-works jobs at government expense. This would become a major part of the New Deal relief effort forty years later, but in 1894, custodians of responsible opinion dismissed it as little more than a dangerous utopian delusion. Indeed, Coxey's army was infused as much by religious fervor as by economic discontent. His aide-de-camp was Carlo Browne, a labor organizer and religious visionary, who declared Coxey's army "the Commonweal of Christ." A hundred men left Massillon on Easter Sunday, drawing crowds and picking up recruits as they trudged eastward. By the time they reached Washington in May, there were more than five hundred of them—nowhere near the hundred thousand that Coxey had predicted but enough to send a ripple of anxiety through the respectable classes. The march's denouement was a disaster: before they could present their petition to Congress, Coxey and his lieutenants were arrested for trespassing on the Capitol lawn, clubbed by DC police, and dragged off to jail. The crowd of bystanders, mostly respectable tourists from out of town, was shocked by the police brutality. The marchers, observers agreed, "have as much right to be here as anybody." The local newspapers confirmed that the behavior of the police was scandalous and unprovoked.

Yet the spectacle of public protest—however justified, however unfairly suppressed—provoked disgust and fear among the custodians of privilege in the national press. To alarmed men of property, Coxey's ragged army seemed a portent of proletarian revolution. Among clerics, only the occasional radical dared raise a sympathetic voice. The Congregationalist Rev. George Herron asserted that "when the divine judgment of history passes between the national legislature of 1894, and the vagabond citizens who were mobbed by the police for bearing this proposition to the Capitol steps, I pray to be judged among the vagabonds."

One might well ask the U.S. Congress, Herron implied: just how menacing could an unarmed crowd of "vagabond citizens" be? Indeed, the army of the discontented was not nearly as unified or powerful as the business classes imagined. Despite the producerist rhetoric farmers and workers shared, the two groups had differing interests and, as immigration accelerated, increasingly different cultural values as well. Labor radicalism and union organizing exuded an aroma of foreignness that sometimes became disturbing to the predominantly old-stock rural population. Most important, farmers were far better organized than workers. By the early 1890s, the Farmers' Alliances and the Populist Party had successfully demanded a place, however precarious, in public debate. The Knights of Labor, meanwhile, had declined after the failure of the eight-hour-day campaign in 1886, and by 1893 had almost disappeared as an effective force. Their egalitarian vision survived among Populists and Socialists, but their organization faded into marginality. As the depression deepened, industrial workers were on the defensive everywhere, scrambling to survive their employers' relentless drive to minimize labor costs, maximize productivity, and smash unions.

The weakness of unions became apparent in June 1894, when employees at the Pullman Palace Car Manufacturing Company, just outside Chicago, decided to go on strike. This was no ordinary labor conflict. George Pullman, who had developed the luxurious railroad car that bore his name, considered himself a model of humane, philanthropic management. He had founded the town of Pullman, where his employees lived and worked, as a paternalistic community, with himself as paterfamilias. Visitors viewed it as a slice of heaven, from which "all that is ugly, discordant, and demoralizing is eliminated." It embodied, they said, "a solution of the industrial problem based on the idea of mutual recognition." A peaceable kingdom.

Yet even in the best of times, the citizens of Pullman were not persuaded that they inhabited a utopia. George Pullman controlled the minutiae of everyday life, down to and including the price of a pound of coffee. The town was "a civilized relic of European serfdom," said William Carwardine, the Methodist minister at Pullman. "We all enjoy living here because there is an equality of interest, and we have a common enemy, the Company, but our daily prayer is, 'Lord, keep us from dying here.'" Despite his philanthropic aspirations, Pullman behaved like any other capitalist during the business downturn, laying off scores of workers and cutting the wages of the rest by 25 percent. When employees sent a delegation to Pullman to protest, he refused to see them and fired several of them outright. At that point the workers finally decided to strike.

Stung by what he viewed as their ingratitude, Pullman was baffled, hurt, and outraged. Jane Addams shrewdly dubbed him "A Modern Lear" in a lecture of that title given to a Chicago conference on social economics. Addams put her finger on the fundamental weakness of paternalism when it came into conflict with market values. The model town of Pullman was also an investment that (its owner decided) had to return 4 percent. To secure that return, Pullman kept rents and prices high even when he cut wages. Like Carnegie, he wore the blinders of the wealthy uplifter. "The theater was complete in equipment and beautiful in design, but too costly for a troupe who depended on the patronage of mechanics, as the church was too expensive to be rented continuously," Addams observed. "We can imagine the founder of the town slowly darkening his glints of memory and forgetting the common stock of experience which he held with his men." Like other men of his class, Pullman had no conception of the moral vitality of the labor movement, of "that conception of duty which induces men to go without food and to see their wives and children suffer for the sake of securing better wages for fellow-workmen they have never seen," said Addams.

Solidarity and self-sacrifice were not part of his picture of the working class. Like King Lear, Pullman could not imagine his beneficiaries as in any way his equals, could not grant them their full humanity as independent beings. So their rebellion left his lofty aims a shambles.

Sympathetic as it may seem to readers today, Addams's critique of Pullman was rejected by mainstream magazines and newspapers, who considered it simply too hot to handle. The Pullman strike had quickly become a national issue, and a major battle in the renewed class war. Pullman workers had recently joined the American Railway Union, which had been started in response to hard times and had elected Eugene Debs its first president. Debs would soon declare himself a Socialist, but he was a far cry from the popular image of the slogan-mouthing radical with a thick German accent. He was a homegrown product of the Indiana Corn Belt, and his democratic, producerist brand of socialism was compatible with many of the more serious versions of Populism.

Debs was, in short, not a revolutionary but a pragmatic politician, and when his union wanted to show solidarity with the strikers by refusing to handle Pullman cars, he advised against it. He was overruled. The railroads dismissed the sympathetic strikers and the union in turn struck the railroads. Trains nationwide quickly came to a halt and fighting broke out between scabs and strikers in the yards at Blue Island, Illinois. Custodians of responsible opinion aligned solidly against labor. "The inhuman and brutal selfishness of the leaders of the American Railway Union is something which disgraces modern civilization," the *Churchman* asserted, summarizing the dominant clerical view. With this kind of hysteria behind him, President Cleveland had no trouble deciding to dispatch federal troops to Chicago, despite the protest of Illinois governor John Altgeld. A federal court issued an injunction against the strikers, accepting the government's argument that the strike created a national emergency by obstructing mail service. Debs and other ARU leaders were jailed for violating the injunction. A year later, the Supreme Court upheld the constitutionality of their imprisonment.

Labor had hit a low ebb. After the catastrophic strike of 1894, unions began to define themselves in less ambitious ways, as instruments of interest groups that could build coalitions with other interest groups. Samuel Gompers headed the American Federation of Labor, which was organized officially along craft lines and unofficially along ethnic and racial lines. Whiteness and manliness continued to complement each other, but the producerist rhetoric waned. Gompers said his philosophy could be summed up in one word: "More." He sought not preservation of producerist values but accommodation to the new world of megacorporations. He accepted management's control over the workplace in exchange for higher wages and shorter hours. But even that limited goal would take years to accomplish.

On the farm, producerist values proved more resilient than in the factory. Agrarian insurgents were faring a little better than striking workers, but not much. Though the Populists were being robbed at the polls, they were still preserving some legitimacy, still fighting the good fight in the political arena. But in the South their opponents had the race card to play. In Louisiana in the mid-1890s, establishment Democrats took to calling the Populist fusion ticket the "Populist-negro social equality ticket." John Pharr, the Populist coalition candidate in 1896, had an anti-lynching plank in his platform. The *New Orleans Daily States* deduced from this that Pharr "inferentially approved" Negroes raping white women. From the other side, black farmers were understandably reluctant to make common cause with white farmers who in more prosperous times might well have been willing to tolerate race-baiting and even indulge in racial terrorism. For blacks, lynching remained a more immediate threat than tight money. And race remained the Achilles' heel of Southern Populism.

Throughout the Midwest as well as the South, Populists debated the question of cooperation with the Democrats. Discussion became heated as fundamental issues arose, especially regarding money. If anyone bothered to stop and think about it, populist monetary thought posed a potentially devastating challenge to orthodox economic theory—especially to the assumption that money represented unchanging worth. "There is no more reason that the material in a dollar should have an intrinsic value equal to a dollar than that the yardstick should possess an intrinsic value equal to the value of the cloth that it measures," wrote Stephen McCallin, the editor of the *Topeka Advocate*. "Money as such possesses neither length, nor thickness, and its only value consists of the fact that by law and custom it is the medium by which debts are paid and wealth exchanged." Boldly asserting the core doctrine of fiat money—that cash was merely an agreed-upon convenience— Populists continued to ask the discomfiting question: why shouldn't the money supply be managed democratically, for the public good?

Few Democrats were willing to ask it. They preferred the tepid formula of free silver, the mildly inflationary policy of monetizing two metals rather than one. For the Populists to embrace free silver would mean a fatal watering-down of their doctrines—at least according to the veteran Alliance men, especially in the South. Tom Watson was at their head, digging in his heels against compromise with the Democrats. But as the presidential campaign of 1896 loomed, enough Populists were persuaded by the silver panacea to join the Democrats in nominating a common presidential candidate: William Jennings Bryan.

Bryan had been radicalized by the depression: he spoke out for a graduated income tax and federal insurance on bank deposits; he attacked Cleveland's intervention in the Pullman strike and endorsed the workers' right to form a union and to strike. He was attracting national attention, but his ambitions ran afoul of a Republican landslide in 1894. Setting his sights on the Senate, he won 73 percent of the popular vote but lost in the Republican-dominated state legislature.

Bryan's Senate defeat had been a moral victory. He was the people's choice, and he was poised to assume prominence in a Democratic Party that was leaning to the left, responding to the human cost of Cleveland's disastrous policies. The country was aflame with popular movements of the discontented. In July 1896, many of them descended on Chicago, where the Democratic Party was holding its convention. Inside the hall, free-silverites from the South and West controlled the platform debate; Eastern gold bugs were banned from the floor. The streets outside thronged with suffragists, Prohibitionists, Socialists, and Populists—a motley lot, thought respectable folk, whose ministers invoked the specter of anarchy.

The 1896 Democratic platform decisively reset the party's course, away from laissez-faire and toward Woodrow Wilson's New Freedom and FDR's New Deal. It declared the gold standard "not only un-American, but anti-American," because it placed Americans' welfare in the hands of British bankers (who, sometimes being Rothschilds, were sometimes Jewish—this was the opening to anti-Semitism in Populist lore). It reviled Grover Cleveland for bedding down with J. P. Morgan and criticized the Supreme Court for nullifying the income tax. It demanded government control of the money supply and defended workers' right to strike. The platform was powerful but the speakers were unimpressive, until Bryan stepped up to the podium.

Bryan's speech resonated with republican tradition. Much of its two hours were taken up with the familiar producerist argument that farmers, miners, and other laborers created as much or more wealth than commodity traders or financiers. The nod to labor was an attempt to bring the urban worker on board, but while Bryan lavished praise on farmers he had nothing to say about factory hands or building tradesmen, who could equally well claim producers' credentials. Bryan's agrarian bias would prove fatal to his campaign.

But no one in the hall was thinking about that as Bryan rose to his conclusion. "Having behind us the producing masses of this nation and the world, supported by the commercial interests, the laboring interests, and the toilers everywhere," he said, "we will answer their demand for a gold standard by saying to them: You shall not press down upon the brow of labor this crown of thorns, you shall not crucify mankind upon a cross of gold." He stepped back from the podium, stretched his arms out to his sides, and held the Christ-like pose for five seconds. There were a few moments of silence; then "everybody seemed to go mad at once," the *New York World* reported, "the whole face of the convention was broken by the tumult—hills and valleys of shrieking men and women." The *New York Times*, like much of the established press, imagined the dire social implications at once: "A WILD, RAGING, IRRESISTIBLE MOB" had been unleashed by a demagogue.

Whatever their disagreements about currency reform, the Populists and the Democrats had a charismatic candidate who spoke directly to the plain people. William Allen White, a Republican journalist from Kansas who feared Bryan's demagoguery, nevertheless acknowledged the candidate's importance. "It was the first time in my life and the life of a generation," White wrote, "in which any man large enough to lead a national party had boldly and unashamedly made his cause that of the poor and oppressed." The problem, for the Populists, was the vice presidency. The Democrats nominated Arthur Sewall, a hard-money banker from Maine; the Populists nominated Tom Watson. For Watson the campaign was a humiliating disaster. Bryan ignored him, and throughout the South, Populists supported Sewall and the Democrats in exchange for the promise of local offices. Watson, embittered, withdrew into a long, sodden twilight of race-baiting and rants against popery. Betraying the biracial dream he had once tried to cultivate, he sounded in the end little different from any other white supremacist demagogue of his time and place. It was a sad fate for a Populist warrior.

Bryan was more fortunate and more buoyant. For him the election of 1896 was about far more than the money question. The choice between him and the Republican William McKinley, he believed, was a choice between "two ideas of government"—prosperity from the top down or from the bottom up. He insisted on the protection of a common public interest from rapacious private interests, proposing the regulation of business and other policy innovations in homely metaphors. En route to a campaign stop in Iowa, he saw some hogs tearing up a farmer's field and remembered that one of his jobs as a boy had been to keep the swine tethered to protect the family land. "And then it occurred to me that one of the most important duties of government is to put rings in the noses of hogs," he said. "We submit to restraint on ourselves in order that others may be restrained from injuring us."

Bryan's idiom was grounded in the agrarian vernacular, and it cemented a bond between him and his rural audiences. At thirty-six, he was the youngest man ever to run for the presidency (before or since), and he turned his striking physical presence and endless energy to extraordinary account. For more than three months he gave five speeches a day, taking his campaign to the people by rail (the first time a presidential candidate had done so), shouting himself hoarse to every assembled crowd at every whistle-stop town along the way.

But ultimately oratory was not enough. The hogs were not ready to be reined in. While Bryan roared about the country, trying to sell himself, McKinley campaigned from his front porch in Canton, Ohio, letting his handler Mark Hanna sell him "as if he were a patent medicine," in Theodore Roosevelt's words. Roosevelt knew whereof he spoke: he was one of the dozens of orators Hanna paid to bustle about the country portraying Bryan as a dangerous radical. This was only one of Hanna's innovative strategies. Fund-raising was the most important. Soon after the Republican Convention, Hanna called on leading bankers and corporate executives to bankroll McKinley's campaign. Terrified by Bryan's supposed radicalism, wealthy contributors forked over a record $3.5 million, five times what the Democrats raised and equivalent to $3 billion today (as a comparable percentage of gross domestic product).

Hanna used the money inventively. Besides hiring rhetorical hit men like Roosevelt, he deployed the sort of clever gimmickry that the infant advertising industry was using to sell goods. He printed thousands of phony dollar bills, bearing Bryan's portrait and the slogan IN GOD WE TRUST . . . FOR THE OTHER 53 CENTS—reasserting the Republican claim that a dollar backed by silver would be reduced in value to 47 cents. Other, more straightforward gambits were also in Hanna's tool kit. In what has become a familiar Republican tactic, the McKinley campaign distributed thousands of American flags and flag buttons, implying that their opponents were somehow less than patriotic. McKinley, the last president to have fought in the Civil War, was also the first to be sold with the methods of modern advertising.

Aside from the wiles of the canny Hanna, Bryan confronted more serious problems as well. Agrarian radicalism did not always translate well into industrial settings. Free silver meant little to urban workers, and the tariff protected the corporations who employed them. Bryan's camp meeting style alienated German-American voters, who helped put Illinois and Indiana in the Republican column, along with the upper Midwest, the entire Northeast, and the West Coast. Bryan took the Great Plains and the South, and this was not nearly enough. Despite their defeat, though, the Democrats had departed decisively from their laissez-faire past. Bryan was at the center of this transformation.

Within a few years after the campaign of 1896, the money question faded. Free silver lost resonance as corn, wheat, and cotton brought higher prices on commodities markets and farm debt fell. The discovery of gold in Alaska relieved pressure on the money supply, and a Republican Congress reaffirmed its commitment to the gold standard. The emerging class issue was fear of the trusts—the unprecedented and largely unconstrained economic power concentrated in monopolistic corporations. Manipulation of the money supply seemed a paltry weapon against these behemoths, and radicals grew impatient with Populist panaceas. In certain circles, murmurings about public ownership began to be heard.

Republicans, meanwhile, were moving in the opposite direction. McKinley's winning campaign, like Bryan's losing one, signified an ideological transformation. The party of McKinley and Hanna, of Theodore Roosevelt and Henry Cabot Lodge, was also the party of centralizing capital and expanding empire. McKinley's win affirmed and displayed the consolidation of big-business influence in American political life. Hanna's corporate fundraising solidified the alliance between concentrated capital and the Republican Party. Capitalists, it appeared, were willing to pay the piper if they could expect to hear a pleasing tune. In effect, what had triumphed in 1896 was not the White City but the machines it contained and the power behind them. American politics would never be quite the same.

An anonymous *Atlantic Monthly* article, published while the campaign was still under way, captured the stakes and the consequences of the conflict. It was a brilliant exercise in the creation of cultural hegemony, deflecting economic issues onto a moral plane. The author hoped that the present political campaign would be an occasion for public education: "Besides the lesson of sound money another lesson is forcibly taught—a larger corollary of the same proposition, that financial honesty is the basis of character— the lesson, namely, of the intricate workings and supreme value of credit." Credit is "the instrument and measure of civilization." It fine-tunes our relationship with the global trading community, delicately adjusting "this closely knit world, part to part." Alongside credit, the gold standard has rapidly become part of "the inevitable and irreversible process of social development." "Small wonder" that men who have no concept of credit should respond to the passing of silver with "superstitious fear." All this would be mere silliness except "the alarming fact is that nearly all the groups of malcontents that have hitherto existed separately are now united" with the "unthinking mass of the Democratic Party" behind the free coinage of silver. Whatever ideology they espoused, all could be reduced to a simple complaint: "These malcontents are not as prosperous as they think they ought to be, and they think there is some artificial barrier to their prosperity." It was a politics of envy, nothing more, the author declared.

Causes of the discontent were many. Agricultural profits had shrunk as new machines and methods had increased productivity, requiring fewer farmers and expanding the area under cultivation faster than the demand for what was cultivated. At the same time, the *Atlantic* observed, the farmer had lost dignity and social standing. Once the embodiment of independence and civic virtue in every public utterance, he was now a stock figure for humorists. He had declined from "sturdy yeoman" to "hayseed," and the spread of town fashions through national advertising in newspapers only made his backwardness more painfully apparent to him.

Yet the fundamental source of social disquiet, the *Atlantic* decided, was a widespread defect of character—"a lack of thrift and of a rigid commercial morality." These were difficulties no revival of trade could solve. There were, moreover, regional aspects to this morality play. It was "more than coincidence that the menace to property and credit is most determined" in the South and West, two regions that "have nothing in common but a lack of thrift." The problem with farmers, despite all their railing against Wall

Street, was that they were the looniest plungers of all. "It is not by saving, but by 'booming,' that fortunes are thought to be made" among rural folk, the author claimed; as a result, too often they fell into the habit of "borrowing with only a speculative opportunity to pay." This sort of profligacy could scarcely go unpunished.

"The Political Menace of the Discontented" was more immediate now that the frontier had closed and we had become part of "complex civilization." No longer were we immune to European-style class feeling, and the politics of envy shamelessly stirred it up. In fact, it was all nonsense. "Never since industrial society was organized has there been such a general rise from poverty to comfort" as in the United States in the last thirty years. "There is no more fallacious doctrine than that the rich are becoming richer, and the poor poorer."

The *Atlantic*'s comfortable aphorisms embodied the view that prevailed in the 1896 election. It signaled a culmination of developments that had been in the works for decades. Lincoln's political tradition—free soil, free labor, free men—had by this time disappeared in the cloud of apolitical sentimentality surrounding Father Abraham. The Republican Party became the party of big business. Except for a handful of Progressives, most of its leaders were at ease in the boardrooms and executive suites of the industrial Northeast, and most of its policies served the needs of the emerging corporations. The Democratic Party groped toward more egalitarian policies at the national level while its Southern wing finished the job of black disenfranchisement and voter participation in the South dropped to all-time lows. Below the Potomac, infant ideas of economic democracy could only survive if swaddled in white supremacy. During the 1890s, Jim Crow legislation swept through state after state in the old Confederacy, and the Supreme Court declared in *Plessy v. Ferguson* (1896) that the "separate but equal" rationale for racial segregation was constitutional.

Republicans remained largely oblivious. Lodge's "Force Bill," which would have authorized the use of federal troops to ensure fair elections, had been voted down in 1890; the Force Bill was the last hurrah of the abolitionist tradition. Even without their erstwhile Northern protectors, black people continued to participate in pockets of Southern public life. But not for long. During the 1890s, white supremacists orchestrated a region-wide attack to finish the racist counterrevolution, rewriting constitutions that created an impenetrable labyrinth of obstacles to black voting (and sometimes to poor white voting as well). The rationale was the elimination of corruption, but the consequence was elite white domination.

THE COUNTERREVOLUTIONARIES' MOP-UP operation did not always proceed smoothly. White supremacist Democrats faced some determined last-ditch opposition. The merger between Populists and Democrats at the national level was not always easy to arrange at the local level, especially in the old Confederacy. In certain Southern places, the economic crisis of the 1890s drove Populists and Republicans into each other's arms, creating the strategy of "fusion." By mid-decade, fragile biracial coalitions had elected fusion tickets in Alabama, Georgia, Texas, and—most successfully—in North Carolina, where fusion candidates held the statehouse and the legislature as well as many local offices. Between 1894 and 1898, the fusionist legislature required *The School History of the Negro Race in the United States* to be taught in North Carolina public schools; it also raised money for education and poor relief by increasing taxes on railroads and other corporations, coming closer than any other state legislature to enacting the agenda of agrarian reform.

In the campaign of 1896, the North Carolina Populist leader Marion Butler chose to fuse nationally with the Democrats, locally with the Republicans. It was a successful strategy. North Carolina became the single exception to the Populist failure of 1896. The fusionists sustained their biracial coalition and extended its reach through the black majority counties in the eastern part of the state, electing black officeholders in law enforcement, education, and other areas of governance that required daily interaction with white people. For a time, it was as if the dream of a Reconstructed South had been resurrected under the pressure of economic calamity.

To white Democrats, this was nothing less than their old nightmare of "negro domination." Furnifold M. Simmons, the chair of the state's Democratic Executive Committee and later a U.S. senator, warned his colleagues that they faced a crisis: "NEGRO CONGRESSMEN, NEGRO SOLICITORS, NEGRO REVENUE OFFICERS, NEGRO COLLECTORS OF CUSTOMS, NEGROES in charge of white institutions, NEGROES in charge of white schools, NEGROES holding inquests over white dead. NEGROES controlling the finances of great cities, . . . NEGRO CONSTABLES arresting white women and men, NEGRO MAGISTRATES trying white women and men, white convicts chained to NEGRO CONVICTS, and forced to social equality with them." In the elections of 1898, the Democrats vowed, they would redeem North Carolina from black rule by conducting a statewide drive for white supremacy with the familiar methods of fraud, violence, and intimidation. On November 8, 1898, they succeeded: white Democrats retook the state, ending its brief experiment in biracial politics.

But the job was not quite done. There were many black officeholders in the eastern part of the state, whose seats did not become vacant until the next election, especially in Wilmington—the state's largest, most cosmopolitan city, with a black majority population that was literate, prosperous, and politically engaged. White supremacists in Wilmington craved a completion of the racial revitalization that the election had validated. They had been getting juiced on violent rhetoric for months. The chief rhetorician was Alfred Waddell, a former Confederate officer and U.S. congressman who had seen better days. Everywhere he spoke he deplored the black insolence supposedly encouraged by the fusion regime. "We will not live under these intolerable conditions," the creaking Confederate told a roaring crowd in the run-up to the election. "We will never surrender to a ragged raffle of negroes, even if we have to choke the current of the Cape Fear with carcasses."

The trouble in Wilmington resulted from the statewide white supremacist campaign, but it was also a local instance of the regional hysteria about interracial sex. By the late 1890s the madness had reached a fever pitch among whites, crossing class and gender lines, producing fervid speeches on various public occasions. One such utterance acquired a special significance for Wilmington. On August 12, 1897, Rebecca Latimer Felton rose to address a meeting of the Georgia State Agricultural Society. Felton was the wife and campaign manager of a U.S. congressman and, since 1886, a leading spokesperson for the WCTU. She spoke on "Woman on the Farm," a bland enough topic she had addressed many times before. Yet to the usual catalogue of complaints (more education, less alcohol) she added another: white women's vulnerability to the black rapists who were supposedly roaming the rural South at will. The fault, she declared, lay with Southern white men: they had failed to "put a sheltering arm about innocence and virtue." Felton concluded that if lynching was required "to protect woman's dearest possession from the ravening human beasts—then I say lynch, a thousand times a week, if necessary."

Felton's ravings, which played on every taut string of white male anxiety, were reprinted in newspapers throughout the region. In the summer of

1898, the *Wilmington Messenger* published the speech as part of the state-wide white supremacy campaign. This was too much for Alexander Manly, the editor of the state's only black newspaper, the *Wilmington Record*. Manly was smart and provocative, and determined to point out that the relationship between sex and race was not as simple as Felton claimed. Poor white women were not the passive victims that Felton described: they "were not any more particular in the matter of clandestine meetings with colored men, than are the white men with colored women." Indeed, he said, "meetings of this kind go on for some time, until the woman's infatuation or the man's boldness bring attention to them and the man is lynched for rape." Nor was every alleged rapist a "big, burly black brute," as the newspapers always said. Many were the offspring of white fathers and were "sufficiently attractive for white girls of culture and refinement to fall in love with them, as is well known to all." Manly, the acknowledged mulatto son of an antebellum governor of the state, was personally acquainted with these questions. Of Felton, he demanded nothing more than a color-blind version of the single sexual standard sponsored by the WCTU: "Tell your men," he wrote, "that it is no worse for a black man to be intimate with a white woman than for a white man to be intimate with a colored woman."

Manly's daring was not unprecedented. Ida Wells had been making a similar argument for years in her campaign against lynching and had been driven from the South as a result. But Manly was on the front lines of racial violence, and there are some times when nothing is more incendiary than the truth. Manly's editorial sent white men into paroxysms of rage. Plotting revenge, Wilmington Democrats postponed it until after the election. On election eve, Waddell told white Democrats: "Go to the polls tomorrow, and if you find the negro out voting, tell him to leave the polls, and if he refuses, kill him." The night of the election, white Democrats met en masse, vowing to remove any remaining black officeholders from New Hanover County and to expel the diabolical Manly by force. (Manly had prudently left town weeks before.) The next morning a white mob formed outside the office of the *Record*, set the building on fire, then ran pell-mell through the city's black neighborhoods, scattering poorly armed resistance, shooting unarmed men at random, and sending terrified residents to hide in the woods nearby. The massacre touched off a mass exodus of blacks from Wilmington while it reaffirmed manhood and power for whites. Few were as personally regenerated as Alfred Waddell, who after years of obscurity returned to political life as a leader of the lily-white Democrats.

Republicans, up to and including McKinley, were unmoved by the Wilmington coup d'état, even when a delegation of North Carolina black leaders pleaded for federal intervention to restore blacks to office—blacks who had been legally elected by a biracial coalition. White Democrats' seizure of power in Wilmington was only the most blatant enactment of a scene that took place throughout the South in the 1890s. Most remnants of black participation in politics were eradicated by 1900.

The disenfranchisers were proud of what they had done. Many believed they were part of a broad effort to cleanse the body politic of corruption—a bipartisan national reform movement whose leaders took to calling themselves Progressives. Many white supremacists saw disenfranchisement as only one of many necessary reforms. Felton, for example, was committed to Prohibition, female suffrage, the admission of white women to the University of Georgia, the creation of separate courts for juveniles, and the abolition of the convict-lease system. Felton was atypical only in her gender; once race was off the table, Southern Progressives sounded much like their Northern contemporaries. White supremacists could pass for reformers at a historical moment when assumptions of black inferiority had scientific sanction. More important, Progressives and disenfranchisers alike believed they were engaged in a common project of social and individual purification—a politics of regeneration. The idioms they spoke ranged from the Christian and Socialist language of the cooperative commonwealth to the managerial discourse of the efficient economy. Eventually management would win out with a boost of morality from the prophets of empire. But no one could have known that outcome in the mid-1890s, when reformers of all stripes were scrambling to respond to the crisis of American capitalism, inspired by the hope that a dramatic social transformation was at hand. The shape of American society still seemed up for grabs.

PROGRESSIVE REFORM DID not affect national policy until after 1900, but its origins lay in the longings for revitalization that pervaded late-nineteenth-century American culture. Through the 1890s, most reformers used a common language of personal and social transformation. They wanted to use government to change people's behavior in unprecedented ways: to end class conflict, to control big business, to segregate society, or to sober it up. Some wanted to use it to do all these things. Eventually they would broaden their concerns from local and state to national affairs.

The most powerful visions of political renewal were rooted in Protestant Christianity. In fact it was the religious dimension of reform that underwrote its intensity and its virtually limitless scope. But the political inflections of Christianity could of course vary widely. In *Our Country*, Josiah Strong had warned that the only alternative to Anglo-Saxon moral revival was national collapse. The Rev. George Herron was more effective at recovering the radical edge in Christian tradition, and reviling his ministerial colleagues' abandonment of it. He charged that "the priests who accompanied the pirate ships of the sixteenth century, to say mass and pray for the souls of the dead pirates for a share of the spoil, were not a whit more superstitious or guilty of human blood, according to the light of their teaching, than Protestant leaders who flatter the ghastly philanthropy of men who have heaped their colossal fortunes upon the bodies of their brothers."

Herron could be scathing in his critique of laissez-faire pieties. The celebration of "enlightened self-interest," he wrote in 1894, was "the principle on which Cain slew his brother. It was the seductive whisper of the serpent in Eve's ear. . . . The law of self-interest is the eternal falsehood which mothers all social and private woes; for sin is pure individualism—the assertion of self against God and humanity." He was fond of making assertions that sounded revolutionary—"any wealth that is not the creation of labor is fictitious," or "the people must finally own and distribute the products of their own labor."

Yet he remained vague about how the cooperative commonwealth would come about, and in the end fell back on the familiar Protestant hope of mass conversion. "I see no other hope for our nation, no other redemption for society, than a religious revival such as the world has never known, that shall enthrone Christ in our national ideals, and give men the common will and the power to put the Christ life into social practice." Herron's focus on individual regeneration as the key to social regeneration linked him to other, less radical advocates of "social Christianity"—men like the British journalist W. T. Stead, who in 1894 wondered what would happen *If Christ Came to Chicago* (the Golden Rule would govern the city), or the Rev. Charles Sheldon, who followed *In His Steps* (1897). Long on fervor, the early Social Gospelers pulled up short on policy.

Nevertheless they provided legitimacy for alternatives to laissez-faire and set a new tone in talking about individual morality. The finger-wagging moralism of the *Atlantic*, tracing poverty and discontent to defects of character, became increasingly difficult to justify in the face of mass poverty. Under the pressures of the 1890s depression, even Prohibitionists groped toward a morality more complex than evangelical obsessions with personal responsibility would allow. At the WCTU Convention in 1894, Frances Willard, reversing her earlier stand, announced that we should wipe out poverty first, then booze. "It was only our own ignorance of the industrial classes that magnified a single propaganda and minimized every other so that temperance people in earlier days believed that if men and women were temperate all other material good would follow in the train of the great grace." Other virtues besides temperance were subject to a materialist critique. Settlement-house workers like Jane Addams acknowledged the impact of economic deprivation on the supposedly universal beneficence of thrift.

This was the sort of insight that led to a broader rethinking of charity. As Addams reflected in 1899, a scrupulous charity worker might well suspect "that in holding her poor family so hard to a standard of thrift she is really breaking down a rule of living which they had formerly possessed: that saving, which seems quite commendable in a comfortable part of town, appears almost criminal in a poorer quarter, where a next-door neighbor needs food." Confronted with communal alternatives, the charity worker "feels the sordidness of constantly being obliged to urge the industrial view of life." The more one learned about the lives of the poor, the more platitudes were overturned—consider the "horrors of the saloon," which to the poor may be a place of kindness, free lunch, treating, loans, warmth in hard times, simple sociability. The "industrial view of life" was not adaptable to all social circumstances.

Social Christianity played a crucial role in dissolving the congealed ideology of laissez-faire, especially the moralistic assumption that the poor alone are responsible for their fate. Firebrands like Herron made it clear that true Christianity not only allowed but in some sense required opposition to the comfortable creed of enlightened self-interest. No wonder many of the "new economists" who pioneered the welfare state (John Bates Clark, John R. Commons, John Bascom) considered themselves Social Christians.

Still, there were other important sources of reform thought. One was the rising importance of women—not only prominent figures like Addams and Willard, but legions of teachers, nurses, and social workers who helped to develop a spreading reform culture. Many were inspired by a belief that they could use the values associated with woman's sphere (the bourgeois home) to transform the public realm—to "make the world more Home-like," in Willard's phrase. This was an important and powerful agenda. The domestic realm, however entangled with the market, nevertheless embod-ied a set of alternative values. Familial relationships, however encrusted with patriarchy, resisted reduction to the cash nexus. The bourgeois home may not have been a cooperative commonwealth, but it looked more like one than most other American institutions. The irony was that, though re-formers set out to bring domestic ideals to bear on government policy, they ended by leaving the home more vulnerable to government interventions. Self-control yielded to social control, personal responsibility to public re-sponsibility. The government gained a foot in the door of private life.

Progressive reformers emphasized the importance of a public interest that transcended the opportunistic scuffle of private interests: the formula-tion revealed the roots of their thought in the republican tradition, as well as their debt to the Populists. Like the Populists, Progressives derived their de-votion to the public good from republican ideas of civic virtue, which faced unprecedented challenges in the era of monopoly capital. The muckraking journalist Henry Demarest Lloyd put the matter starkly in the title of his 1894 exposé of the Standard Oil Company, *Wealth Against Commonwealth*. But not all reform thought was homegrown. Some Progressive intellectuals were also profoundly impressed by the welfare-state policies emerging in Berlin and other European centers of social-democratic thought.

In 1895, the sociologist Albion Small articulated an emerging synthesis that proved central to Progressive reform. There were, he believed, two fun-damental principles to social order—the acknowledgment of "the essential similarity of all human beings in capacity for happiness," and the recognition that "not merely public office but private business is a public trust." While the first principle underlay the democratic faith that everyone was entitled to pursue happiness, the widening inequalities under industrial capitalism meant that "we are getting familiar with differences of social conditions which can be contemplated tranquilly only on the implied assumption that some of us are made from finer clay than the rest." The rich man may be in-capable of sensitive feeling or serious thought but may still "ride roughshod over the personal dignity of the unattached proletarian, who with only plain living, may be capable of high thinking." The dignity of the producer also animated Small's discussion of his second principle, the "unwritten law of civilization that every citizen shall be a public servant." Men who cleared land and developed it, who built and operated railroads, banks, or factories, deserved reward for their public service—but not the beneficiaries of overvalued stocks or inherited privilege. "The time will come when men will perceive that it is as monstrous for a father to bequeath to his son a controlling interest in a factory or railroad, as it would now appear for a President of the United States to offer his daughter the city of New York as a dowry." That halcyon day would arrive when the "civic idea" had triumphed over the claims of laissez-faire.

Still, how one defined the public good was open to debate. In the details of policy, Progressives began to demonstrate their departures from Populism. Policy differences were often accompanied by differences in cultural style, which could be rooted in moral conviction. Some Progressives reasserted the Populist and Social Christian assault on privilege with all the old evangelical fervor; others spoke in cooler tones, displacing the rhetoric of social justice with the slogans of efficiency. To be sure, some combined the two modes. Jane Addams, an egalitarian moralist, was also drawn to the managerial ideal of efficiency—if it could be harnessed to public ends. To many Progressives, efficiency was clean and clear; it epitomized an Olympian realm above the pettiness of partisan strife and the corruptions of patronage. Only gradually did it become apparent how easily the managerial ideal could be harnessed to narrow and destructive purposes.

Reformers' emphases varied from place to place. On the whole, the more locally rooted the Progressive politician, the more forthrightly he challenged concentrated wealth and power. Progressive mayors like Sam "Golden Rule" Jones of Toledo and Hazen Pingree of Detroit aimed to implement the "civic idea" in their own backyards, creating government programs to provide the services previously offered (however inefficiently) by corrupt machine politicians—food for the hungry, jobs for the unemployed. In the U.S. Congress, insurgent Progressives in both parties carried on the Populist effort to empower ordinary citizens and curb plutocratic rule by promoting antitrust legislation, railroad regulation, public ownership of utilities, popular election of U.S. senators (rather than election by the state legislatures), and other measures designed to invigorate democratic citizenship. But Progressives with a more cosmopolitan perspective were less interested than the locally based insurgents in social democracy, more comfortable with an imperial foreign policy and with rule by elite expertise. This was the managerial version of Progressivism, which ultimately triumphed at the national level, led by Presidents Theodore Roosevelt and Woodrow Wilson.

What cut across these policy divisions, what brought Progressives together and distinguished them from Populists, was their preoccupation with personal and national purification, and the mingling of the two agendas in the reform imagination. Whether this preoccupation was articulated in religious, moral, or medical idioms, it was the common thread that tied Southern white supremacists with pure-food-and-drug advocates, Prohibitionists, and warriors for empire. The reformers most likely to keep the Populist hope alive were the ones whose humanitarian sentiments reinforced old-fashioned republican concerns about concentration of power—and who subordinated the rhetoric of personal purification to the more capacious vision of a cooperative commonwealth.

For a time, Social Christianity bred an atmosphere of millennial expectancy. In 1901, a Methodist minister in Indianapolis declared that the work of reform must attend to "the entire life of man, individual and social." The Rev. Washington Gladden agreed. "A great work of reconstruction, social, industrial, political, ecclesiastical, has got to be done," he told an audience a year later at the University of Michigan. Inspired by millennial hopes, Social Christians helped lay the foundation for a welfare state. But the vastness and vagueness of their vision betrayed its political limitations. Indeed, by the time that Gladden urged "a great work of reconstruction," other Americans had already found a source of regeneration more satisfying, more visceral and palpable, than the dream of a cooperative commonwealth.

FROM ITS VERY beginnings, the United States had been conducting an expansionist foreign policy—pressing the line of settlement ever westward, claiming thinly settled territories and exterminating their aboriginal inhabitants, buying or seizing contested lands from rival occupiers. But the official closing of the frontier in 1890 signaled an end to settler colonialism and the beginning of something closer (though not identical) to the European variety. The American empire would depend only in part on formal acquisition of foreign colonies. More commonly it would involve periodic military intervention (rather than permanent occupation) and support for governments friendly to American policy. This indirect approach would make it easier for American imperialists to wrap themselves in exceptionalist rhetoric and claim moral superiority to their European counterparts. But the aims of American empire were the same as those of European empire—free access to foreign markets, raw materials, and investment opportunities, all in the name of a civilizing mission that (it was alleged) would bring regeneration to the colonizer and the colonized alike.

From the outset, arguments for empire intertwined economic calculation and teleological fantasy. As early as the 1870s, Southern textile executives craved an open door to China and clothed that wish in a rhetoric of Manifest Destiny. "The march of empire is westward," said the aptly named congressman Hernando D. Money of Mississippi in 1876, asserting that "every people who have enjoyed Asiatic commerce have grown rich and prosperous." So it seemed quite apparent (to Money) that the United States must possess Hawaii as a way station en route to the Far East.

By the 1890s, economic arguments became more sophisticated and more urgent. The economist David A. Wells postulated that the disastrous frequency of business crashes could be traced to industrial overproduction. Mechanization had accelerated the supply of goods beyond the capacity of demand to absorb it. His solution was straightforward: flatten out the curves in the business cycle through market penetration abroad. After four years of depression, the recovery of 1897–98 seemed to bear him out. It was largely based on a boom in exports. "We must have new markets," Henry Cabot Lodge concluded, still reeling from the class war of the early 1890s, "unless we would be visited by declines in wages and by great industrial disturbances of which signs have not been lacking."

What this statement has to do with empire might not be immediately clear. The dominant pattern of American empire involved a (usually Latin American) country developing dependence on the U.S. market for a single cash crop: as Honduras, the first banana republic, became dependent on the U.S. appetite for bananas—to the benefit of the United Fruit Company. For a while at least, though, U.S. manufacturers were concerned not only with extracting natural resources and cheap labor from Latin American and Asian countries but also with making them into markets for their own goods. Expectations were especially high with respect to China, which was declared to be "the New Far West" by business promoters. "In China there are four hundred millions of people, more than five times as many as exist in the United States," one publicist said. "The wants of these four hundred millions are increasing every year. What a market!" This was the sort of assumption that underwrote arguments for acquiring territorial possessions in the Pacific and maintaining an "open door" for investment in China and throughout the Far East. Pacific territories would be coaling stations for our navy and the China trade it protected. Ultimately, the coaling stations remained but the China market did not pan out. The problem, observers agreed, lay in the innate conservatism of the Chinese.

The inhabitants of Latin America, from the imperial view, proved equally indifferent to progress. Unable to develop their own "unimproved" land, they would simply have to yield to whatever great power was willing to turn it to account. As Richard Harding Davis, an upper-class-adventurer-turned-gringo-journalist, reported in 1896: "The Central Americans are like a gang of semibarbarians in a beautifully furnished house, of which they can understand neither its possibilities of comfort nor its use." Indeed, opportunity was far more important than order as a guiding force in American foreign relations during this period, as the historian Walter LaFeber has made clear. American leaders were more likely to stir up revolutionary sentiment—if it served their interests, as in Cuba and Hawaii—than to seek to ensure stability. And their definition of stability was explicitly market-based. When General Leonard Wood was asked when he thought Cuba would be stable, he said: "When money can be borrowed at a reasonable rate of interest and when capital is willing to invest in the island, a condition of stability will have been reached."

The equation of markets and progress defined consumer demand as the engine of human improvement, indeed of civilization itself. This was a characteristic move in the rhetoric of empire, whatever the subject population in question. At the Lake Mohonk Conference of Friends of the Indian, in 1896, Merrill Gates announced that the organization's chief task was to awaken "in the savage broader desires and ampler wants." This was the key to the Indian's cultural ascent. "In his dull savagery he must be touched by the wings of the divine angel of discontent," Gates urged. "Discontent with the teepee and the starving rations of the Indian camp in winter is needed to get the Indians out of the blanket and into trousers—and trousers with a pocket in them, and with a pocket that aches to be filled with dollars!"

There were other, loftier ways of equating capitalism and progress. American sugar planters in Hawaii, having overthrown Queen Liliuokalani's native government in 1893 with the collusion of the U.S. state department, declared themselves a republic and elected the pineapple grower Sanford Dole president. In 1895, Dole characterized this seizure of power as a blow for freedom. "A brief ten years had been sufficient for the Hawaiian nation to break down the hoary traditions and venerable customs of the past," he wrote, "and to climb the difficult path from a selfish feudalism to equal rights, from royal control of all the public domain to present proprietorship and fee simple titles for poor and for rich"—among whom, he might have added, he was fortunate to count himself. Dole and other planters kept up a steady drumbeat for American annexation. Their tone ranged from dry calculation—Hawaii would be "a revenue producing property"—to wet sentimentality: "Some day we shall gather up this pretty string of pearls and throw it merrily about the neck of the beautiful woman who has her handsome head on the outside of the big American dollar; and then they will be beautiful American islands," wrote the California poet Joaquin Miller in 1895.

American politicians were capable of this sort of sentimentality, too. In public, at least, they could insist that their apparently imperial aims were uniquely leavened with moral concerns—in particular a commitment to the spread of freedom and democracy. But in private, their sentiments were less exalted. Writing to Rudyard Kipling, Theodore Roosevelt reviled "the jack-fools who seriously think that any group of pirates and head-hunters needs nothing but independence in order that it may be turned forthwith into a dark-hued New England town meeting." Most "dark-hued" peoples lacked the crucial character trait, he noted elsewhere: "There must be control. There must be mastery, somewhere, and if there is no self-control and self-mastery, the control and the mastery will ultimately be imposed from without."

Roosevelt's obsession with "mastery" revealed the trigger of empire. Behind all the economic calculations and all the lofty rhetoric about civilization and progress was a primal emotion—a yearning to reassert control, a masculine will to power amid the drifting slack waters of the fin de siècle. Admiral Alfred Thayer Mahan invoked the cautionary example of ancient Rome, after it had abandoned its "strong masculine impulse" and "degenerated into that worship of comfort, wealth, and general softness, which is the ideal of the peace prophets of to-day." Mahan was the leading big-navy imperialist, and imperialism was the most important political form of late-nineteenth-century longings for regeneration. Those desires flourished on both sides of the Atlantic, taking shapes peculiar to their surroundings. In the United States, the quest for regeneration through empire reworked ancient Protestant dreams of rebirth into a secular militarist agenda. Yearnings to recapture the heights of Civil War heroism combined with Anglo-Saxon racism, fears of overcivilized decadence, and a providentialist faith in American mission.

The result was an ideological witches' brew. In Europe similar mixtures fostered fascism; in the United States imperial ideology had more benign consequences—for U.S. citizens themselves, if not for their subject populations. The reasons for this divergence are many and complex, but perhaps the most important was the genius of the Constitution's framers in creating the checks and balances that prevented executive tyranny. Still, American imperialist rhetoric, including Roosevelt's, often sounded remarkably proto-fascist. Like the ministerial ranting of the Civil War, fin de siècle militarism celebrated blood sacrifice in combat, but with new and more secular emphases on sheer physical courage and the inherently revitalizing effects of conflict.

Popular misunderstandings of Darwinism equated evolution with inevitable progress, and assumed that progress could be achieved only through death-dealing struggle. "Antagonism," the *Popular Science Monthly* announced in 1888, is "a necessity of existence, and of the organism of the universe so far as we can understand it; [it is apparent] that motion and life cannot go on without it; that it is not a mere casual adjunct of nature, but that without it there would be no nature." A struggle for existence was at the heart of all life, among men as well as wolves, in commerce as in war, "as necessary to good as to evil." Without it life would be boring to the point of ennui, or nonbeing.

The specter of non-being sent men in search of testing grounds abroad, from the Klondike gold fields to the jungles of Africa to the frozen steppes of Siberia. How did George Kennan (intrepid traveler and father of the twentieth-century diplomat) develop the "bravery and coolness under danger" that he exhibited during his Siberian explorations? an interviewer wondered in 1897. Kennan told him that "the only unhappiness that boyhood had for me was a secret but deeply rooted suspicion that I was physically a coward." He was watching the amputation of a friend's arm through a window when a jet of blood sprayed the glass; "a sensation of nausea, faintness, and overwhelming fear" enveloped him and, he believed, revealed "the unsuspected weakness of my character." Finally at seventeen or eighteen, "morbid and miserable," he went to Cincinnati as a telegraph operator. "If I'm afraid of anything, I'll conquer my fear of it or die," he resolved. "If I'm a coward I might as well be dead, because I can never feel any self-respect or have any happiness in life: and I'd rather get killed trying to do something I'm afraid to do than to live in this way." So he took to carrying a revolver, walking the most dangerous streets at four a.m. and hanging around low dives and criminal haunts. He rescued a man knocked out with a slingshot by "highwaymen," saw a man's throat cut, and remained "under perfect self-control" as he faced certain death in a sinking boat at night. After three months he was satisfied "that while I did feel fear, I was not so much daunted by any undertaking but I could do it if I willed to do it." In the struggles of his first Siberian expedition he "lost the fear of being afraid."

Kennan's obsession with cultivating courage and overcoming fear stamped him of a piece with the upper-class men of his time. In the depths of the 1890s depression, while strikers clashed with militia and tramps trudged across the country in search of work, affluent young blades struck out to explore "the few territories still unknown to us," carrying the American flag into Africa "for fun"—as Richard Harding Davis observed in an admiring account of William Astor Chanler. According to Davis, the independently wealthy Chanler served as a model for "other young men who do not have to work," showing them that there are "more dangerous as well as more profitable sports than following hounds across country," demonstrating that "they may get much amusement, and may benefit the world and gain much experience and strength for themselves, not by following [Chanler's] footsteps, but by making their own footsteps mark the way into new countries and among strange peoples." Just how Chanler's exploits benefited "the world," Davis never made clear, but neither he nor his audience was ever in doubt that manly adventures abroad would redeem the "leadership class" from a life of aimless leisure.

The most redemptive adventures had a military purpose. By the mid-1890s, upper-class men's play was constantly being subordinated to an agenda of national greatness. "The time given to athletic contests," Lodge wrote in 1895, "and the injuries incurred on the playing field are part of the price which the English-speaking race has paid for being world conquerors." Physical courage became the universal antidote to the vices of overcivilization, and military service became the favored way—at least rhetorically—of demonstrating physical courage. "Are people less brave now, in these advanced times than formerly, or is civilization as a whole inimical to the warlike spirit?" a retired Union officer named S. R. Elliott wondered in 1893. There did seem to be some inverse relation between civilization and courage. "A Mexican or an Indian is more ready to risk his life than any of our folks. A contempt for human life or human suffering—their own or others'—is the chief virtue of the sincere among them, and the affectation of all others, and it may be that the people who have so little to lose may be readier for the risk." This was the strain of careful primitivism that came to characterize the fin de siècle martial ethos, leading Roosevelt and his ilk to urge the incorporation of the "barbarian virtues" to combat "over-softness" among the privileged. "Idleness and luxury have made men flabby," the *North American Review* complained in 1894, "and the man at the head of affairs is beginning to ask seriously if a great war might not help them to pull themselves together." In the safety of their book-lined studies, intellectuals imagined that "a great war" might not only lance the boil of overcivilization but also banish the specter of neurasthenia—restoring energy to a leadership class grown nerveless and flaccid. This was why writers like Elliott decided that "the courage of a soldier" demanded more than stoical indifference to death; it also required "merciless energy." Here was the germ of the worship of force, the secular religion that underlay the regeneration of masculine will.

The cult of courage challenged Christianity, though only a few Americans were willing to admit it. One was the physician-turned-journalist Woods Hutchinson, who declared courage "the chief virtue" in 1898, noting that the New Testament had "absolutely no place for courage, except in the passive forms of endurance, patience under persecutions, continuing 'steadfast to the end.'" Christianity served as "an excuse for ignorant and cowardly submission to injustice, or toleration of abuses"—such as the toleration of "boss" rule in cities by "the better classes." Indeed, Hutchinson said, "Christianity was an almost complete failure as a factor in the world's progress, until it was grafted upon races whose irresistible vigor and sturdy combativeness made a fighting religion of it, in spite of its doctrines." The key to human advance was the active courage of the soldier. "Willingness to risk the untried, to run the gauntlet of danger, for the sake of possible advantage, to imperil safety for the chance of improvement is . . . always presupposed in the accomplishment of any upward step." The gospel of love needed to be supplemented by the gospel of courage, as articulated by Kipling: "Whatever comes/Or does not come,/We must not be afraid." "It may not be much 'consolation,'" Hutchinson concluded, "but it is all there is, and it does remain as a living principle of action." This was the core of fin de siècle militarism—decisive action for its own sake, the recoil from stillness that animated Roosevelt's ideal of "the strenuous life." By the time Roosevelt coined the phrase, in 1900, the activist creed had already borne fruit.

IN 1898, AFTER years of bellicose posturing, American militarists finally got what they wanted: a "splendid little war" (in John Hay's phrase) with Spain. Imperialists could hardly have asked for a more propitious conflict. A war to free a Caribbean nation from the yoke of European colonialism left American motives looking pristine (at least to the Americans themselves). Concerns about markets and manhood could be subsumed in the rhetoric of humanitarian mission. "Shall Cuba Be Free?" Clarence King asked *Forum* readers in 1895; he recounted decades of anti-Spanish dissent, which had occasionally erupted into armed insurgency. When rebellion broke out again in 1896, the Spanish overlords moved brutally to suppress it, making themselves easy targets for American indignation. After the battleship *Maine* mysteriously exploded in Havana Harbor on February 15, 1898 (supposedly it was there "to protect American life and property"), the drumbeat for war became relentless, in the newspapers and Congress—even though no evidence was ever found to implicate the Spanish in the disaster, which recent historians have discovered was caused by an accidental coal fire in the engine room. The Spanish government struggled to avoid war, agreeing to American demands for an armistice with the insurgency and an end to the preventive detention of noncombatants. Ignoring these concessions, McKinley asked Congress to authorize "forcible intervention" by the United States in Cuba. On April 20, Congress declared the United States to be engaged in a war for Cuban independence, demanding that Spain withdraw from the island and disclaiming any U.S. intent to acquire Cuban territory.

War was a popular idea in 1898. Without question, there were strategic and economic advantages to be gained by expelling the Spanish from Cuba—coaling stations, agricultural investments in sugar and coffee and other cash crops. Militarists had been making these sorts of arguments for years. But what really captured the public imagination was the revivifying idea of alliance with the Cuban insurgency. It was irresistible to Americans of many social backgrounds, including tabloid newspapermen like Joseph Pulitzer and William Randolph Hearst (who stoked war fever to increase circulation), Social Christians like Bryan (who viewed their struggle as a just war against tyranny), and patrician cynics like Henry Adams (who opened his Lafayette Square, Washington, D.C., house to insurgent intrigues). No one was more enthusiastic than Roosevelt, who had been appointed assistant secretary of the navy and who had been spoiling for a fight for years. As soon as war was declared, he arranged for a commission as a lieutenant colonel and organized a cavalry regiment. Mingling Ivy League athletes and cowboys, Roosevelt's Rough Riders epitomized the male fantasy of revitalization through military action. They also became the vehicle Roosevelt used to charge up San Juan Hill, transform himself into a war hero, and ride to nomination as McKinley's running mate in 1900.

No wonder men like Roosevelt and Hay thought the war was splendid. It seemed morally just, it was short, and it was conveniently timed. Within days after the declaration, the war provided McKinley the opportunity to push legislation through Congress declaring the Hawaiian Islands a U.S. territory—the crux of the case being their strategic value as a naval base. Within four months, the U.S. Navy had destroyed the Spanish fleet in Santiago de Cuba and the U.S. Expeditionary Force (which included the Rough Riders) had seized the port city itself. All this was consistent with the intent of Congress. But what caught some Americans off guard was that Commodore George Dewey had meanwhile destroyed another Spanish fleet on the other side of the world in Manila Bay and laid siege to Manila itself. Reinforced by Filipino insurgents under Emilio Aguinaldo, Dewey assaulted the city and forced the Spanish garrison to surrender. Dewey was responding to a secret order sent to him by Roosevelt (then assistant secretary of the navy) on February 25, long before the declaration of war. Roosevelt instructed Dewey to keep his fleet intact and ready to attack the Spanish should war break out. Dewey's victory gave the United States an imperial presence in the Pacific—one that would provoke far more debate and bloodshed than the intervention in Cuba had done. Suing for peace, the Spanish signed a treaty that granted Cuba its independence, ceded the Philippines to the United States for $20 million, and threw in Puerto Rico and Guam for free.

Debate over the treaty raised fundamental questions in the Senate, which have haunted U.S. foreign policy down to the present. Like Hay and others who had backed the Cuban insurgents, Hay's friend Henry Adams wanted "a settlement that abandons the idea of conquest"—that is, true independence for Cuba and the Philippines, with access to coaling stations for American ships. The outcome was quite different. Cuba remained under U.S. military administration until the new Cuban government gave the United States a blank check to intervene militarily in the island's affairs—to preserve "law and order." The arrangement, which in effect made Cuba a U.S. protectorate, was formally ratified by the Congress in the Platt Amendment of 1901.

The Philippines, it turned out, were even more problematic. Despite McKinley's pious claim that "we seek no advantages in the Orient which are not common to all," the imperialist lobby viewed the Pacific archipelago as a prize new possession. Bryan, who led the Democrats in Congress, had supported the war for Cuban independence but opposed the imperial drive for overseas possessions. Still, he did not press opposition to the treaty, on the grounds that it would bring the war officially to a close and that the question of Philippine independence could be decided in the 1900 election. After weeks of debate, the treaty passed with two votes more than the necessary two-thirds, and the United States acquired an empire. The long-term consequences, Adams observed, were incalculable. It was the formal culmination of "the greatest revolution of all . . . that astounding economic upheaval which has turned America into the great financial and industrial center of the world, from being till now a mere colonial feeder of Europe." Emerging from the shadow of class war and depression, the United States was becoming not merely a world power, but—as Adams presciently saw—*the* world power.

The Filipinos had a different take on things. At first they had faith in Americans' professed ideals. "I have studied attentively the Constitution of the United States," Aguinaldo told the head of the U.S. occupying forces, "and find in it no authority for colonies, and I have no fear." But when he learned that the treaty gave the United States control over his country, Aguinaldo called on his people to declare their independence and, in February 1899, began a protracted armed revolt against U.S. rule.

In the Philippines as in the American West, native resistance provoked white rage. The army that struggled to suppress the Filipino independence movement had prepared for the task on the Dakota prairie and in the mountains of northern New Mexico. Terrorist tactics against indigenous populations could be exported to foreign settings. In a letter home, a soldier from Kingston, New York, told of a thousand Filipino men, women, and children killed in retaliation after "one of our boys was found shot and his stomach cut open." To this correspondent, the order to burn the town and kill every native in sight seemed a suitable response to such a crime. "I am growing hardhearted," the soldier reported, "for I am in my glory when I can sight my gun on some dark skin and pull the trigger."

The fight dragged on for years. The Filipinos' determination to resist domination pushed American commanders into desperate measures, such as General Jacob Smith's order to shoot anyone over ten. Many Americans, and certainly most policy-makers, shared the view of the *Philadelphia Ledger* with respect to the indiscriminate killing of civilians: "It is not civilized warfare, but we are not dealing with a civilized people. The only thing they know and fear is force, violence, and brutality, and we are giving it to them." A combat veteran of the war was more succinct: "The only good Filipino is a dead one," he said, neatly summarizing the connection between Geronimo and Aguinaldo.

Imperialists underscored the continuity between Indian wars and war for empire. As Lodge insisted, if the anti-imperialists were right, then "our whole past record of expansion is a crime." When McKinley reassured Americans after his decision to occupy the Philippines that "our priceless principles undergo no change under a tropical sun," he spoke more accurately than he knew. The westward march of Protestant Christianity and American capitalism could not be stopped at the water's edge. This was the core of the imperialist claim to historical legitimacy.

Still, war for overseas empire did indeed mark a departure from important republican traditions—the Founding Fathers' distrust of concentrated executive power, government centralization, and standing armies, not to mention their commitment to popular sovereignty and government by consent. With respect to the aboriginal inhabitants of North America, these ideals were more honored in propaganda than in practice; but it was harder to overlook them when dealing with movements explicitly for national independence, like the one led by Aguinaldo. So the imperialists did not get their way without some debate. Given the long-range significance of the policy issues involved, the arguments of both sides deserve some scrutiny.

What was most striking about imperialist claims was their vagueness, their detachment from any grounding in history or experience. To be sure, when confronted by their critics with their departure from republican tradition, imperialists could point to the unbroken saga of territorial expansion, as Roosevelt did when he said giving the Philippines back to the Filipinos would be like returning Arizona to the Apaches. But far more typically, imperialists deployed a mystical language of evolutionary progress and providential destiny: celebrating the renewal of masculine will and equating it with personal regeneration.

To apologists for empire, few tonics were more invigorating than the elixir of national unity produced by war. Overseas conflict banished the shadow of Appomattox by bringing the old warring sections together. It also gave immigrants an opportunity to demonstrate their Americanism by asserting their superiority to the nonwhite "savages" abroad. Most important, imperial adventure created a foreign alternative to class war at home; it disbanded the army of the discontented and regrouped its ragged recruits under the American flag. As Henry Watterson, editor of the *Louisville Courier-Journal*, summarized the situation: "We escape the menace and peril of socialism and agrarianism, as England has escaped them, by a policy of colonization and conquest."

But to its devotees, imperial war was far more than a convenient tool of social control. Its capacity to heal social divisions and counteract the vices of commerce made it an instrument of moral cleansing. As a Mississippi senator said in 1898, war "teaches us to rise above the petty, the unworthy, the selfish. . . . a wholesome war; like one for human liberty and human life, will have its purgatorial effect upon this nation." Only a man well insulated from battle could use a phrase like "a wholesome war," or celebrate its "purgatorial effects." Still, many civilians found the war wholesome. An *Atlantic* writer surveyed the impact of the war in 1899 and described it as "a wholesome stimulus to higher politics" as well as "the most wholesome exercise in constructive patriotism that this generation of Americans has had." The notion of war's wholesomeness reflected the intensity of popular longings for rebirth into primal harmony.

The emphasis on wholesomeness equated war with psychological healing—bringing fragmented selves together and making them strong again. This was not simply a matter of physical toughening but of emotional and moral revitalization. Though he later questioned the consequences of the war with Spain, at its outset Henry Adams thought the conflict "a Godsend to all the young men in America. Even the Bostonians have at last a chance to show that they have emotions." To people of privilege, the prospect of personal danger sharpened the outlines of military heroism, transforming it into a kind of ascetic sacrifice. "We think of war, nowadays, not so much as being a means of making others suffer as an occasion for giving ourselves up to suffering," the *Century* asserted in 1898. As always, the first-person plural collapsed crucial distinctions—between the elite and the larger society, between soldiers and civilians.

The insistent physicality of imperialist ideology made the empire into another testing ground—a place where an overcivilized bourgeoisie could return to its primitive roots and beat the barbarians at their own game, all the while remaining civilized by (tautological) definition, since the mission itself was a civilizing one. After the overseas victories of 1898, the *Washington Post* noticed "a new appetite" in the American public—"a desire to show our strength. . . . The taste of empire is in the mouth of the people even as the taste of blood in the jungle." Imperial adventure was a way to "show our strength," to demonstrate our revitalization. The recourse to bodily metaphors, the focus on appetite and blood, revealed a rationale for armed conflict that would have shocked previous generations—even the rabid ideologues of the Civil War era. By the end of the nineteenth century, the willingness to kill natives in foreign jungles was a sign of admirable physical vigor.

And if war was the health of the individual, it was also the health of the state. The link between personal and national regeneration became a commonplace in imperial rhetoric. Lodge, among many, made it explicit in his argument for the annexation of the Philippines: "The athlete does not win his race by sitting habitually in an armchair. The pioneer does not open up new regions to his fellow men by staying in warm shelter behind city walls," he asserted, sliding quickly from physical to moral conditioning. "If a man has the right qualities in him, responsibility sobers, strengthens, and develops him. The same is true of nations." Roosevelt was a master of this sort of mystification. He despised Bryan as a "small man" unwilling to take up the burdens of national greatness. "A man goes out to do a man's work, to confront the difficulties and overcome them, and to train up his children to do likewise," he announced. "So it is with the Nation." The portentous vacancy of this formula, its utter lack of evidence or argument, and its fundamental confusion of individual and national courage—all these qualities were characteristic of Roosevelt's imperial rhetoric, and none proved a barrier to his popularity. Indeed, the melding of moral into physical courage and the merging of nations with individuals proved enduring features of militarist posturing. This was the sort of thinking (or not thinking) that led Senator Chauncey Depew to dismiss the anti-imperialist critique of the Philippines War as a "scuttle and run" strategy. Similar category mistakes plague public discourse today.

If nations were like individuals, they were also like plants: they had to grow or die. The mystical language of empire included a heavy dose of organicist metaphor—rooted in the romantic nationalism of the Civil War but flowering more fully in the fetid hothouse of fin de siècle evolutionism. According to Joaquin Miller, one could no more blame Dole and the sugar planters for seizing Hawaii from its native population than one could hold "the persistent roots of the proud and glittering eucalyptus tree to blame for taking possession of your well, your sewer, your garden patch, and every other place in reach." Advocates of Hawaiian annexation declared it a result of "inevitable political evolution" and dismissed the native resistance led by Queen Liliuokalani. They charged that she "represented a weak, thriftless, dying race in its peaceful conflict with the stronger races, and she went down with it." Racism reinforced organicist metaphors, which made empire seem a force of nature and removed it altogether from the realm of politics. Old formulas like popular consent were simply irrelevant, said one apologist, asserting that "the development of nations cannot be limited nor predetermined by maxims, nor be confined within narrow limits; it is of a natural growth; and if there exist laws or institutions that hamper it or prevent the definite settlement of political issues, they will be shattered to pieces with the same power with which roots break the rock into which they descend." Mere principles could not withstand the force of nature. All this was a far cry from the distrust of unchecked power embodied in the Constitution and the Bill of Rights.

Brooks Adams put the organicist argument in a secular providential framework, with "natural" economic law replacing divine law and Darwinian struggle supplanting moral responsibility. "Everywhere society tends to become organized in greater and greater masses, the more vigorous and economical mass destroying the less active and more wasteful," Adams wrote in *America's Economic Supremacy* (1900). "It is in vain that men talk of keeping free from entanglements. Nature is omnipotent; and nations must float with the tide. Whither the exchanges flow, they must follow; and they will follow as long as their vitality endures." The key to national success, as to personal success, was the maintenance of vitality. Yet Adams's emphasis on national will coexisted with a contrary emphasis on the iron necessities of omnipotent nature. Like other social prophets before and since, Adams blurred the boundaries between free choice and evolutionary determinism: strong nations would choose to do what they had to do anyway—just as in the providentialist tradition, the Christian would freely choose the path that God had predestined him to take.

Most rhetoricians of empire preferred a Protestant idiom to Adams's vague Darwinism, though some blended scientific and religious language. Colonel A. K. McClure wrote in 1898 that a "new epoch" has been created by the war with a "new departure as inexorable as the law of gravitation." Our army and navy are "in every clime where a hostile flag is found . . . working out the new destiny no human agency has allotted us." God-talk still sanctified the quest for power, allowing imperialists to cleanse themselves of any taint of ambition. During the debate over Philippine annexation, a Methodist bishop named James Thoburn announced that "we ought to do our duty the best we can . . . in the field God has put us. We did not seek it." Providence created the justification for the mantra of reluctant empire.

But most advocates of empire decried any reluctance and urged a fervent embrace of God's plan for America. Senator Albert Beveridge of Indiana was among the most influential. He demanded annexation of the Philippines as part of a larger global strategy—a divinely ordained Anglo-Saxon mission to bring system and order to the world. "God has not been preparing our English-speaking and Teutonic peoples for a thousand years for nothing but vain self-contemplation and self-admiration," Beveridge shouted. "No! He has made us the master-organizers of the world to establish system where chaos reigns." The situation was urgent: "Were it not for such a force as this the world would relapse into barbarism and night." The Philippines are only the beginning, he said, "just beyond the Philippines are China's illimitable markets. We will not retreat from either. We will not repudiate our duty in the Orient. We will not renounce our part in the mission of our race, trustees under God of the civilization of the world. And we will move forward to our work, not howling out regrets like slaves whipped to their burdens, but with gratitude for a task worthy of our strength, and thanksgiving to Almighty God that he has marked us as his chosen people, henceforth to lead in the regeneration of the world." One could hardly find a more sweeping case for empire.

The election of 1900 ratified the U.S. grab for world power. The economic crisis had abated since 1896. Discovery of gold in the Klondike had loosened the money supply and the export-based recovery had lifted the burden of depression, while Morganization of railroads and other corporations had stabilized the chaos on Wall Street. The merger wave was well under way, enlarging the specter of monopoly power and generating renewed fear of its irresponsible use—but little in the way of specific policy debate. As economic issues receded, imperialism became the central focus of the campaign and McKinley, with the hero of San Juan Hill as his running mate, easily defeated Bryan. When McKinley was assassinated by an anarchist in 1901, Roosevelt became the youngest president in American history to that time. He was also the most prone to adolescent bellicosity.

The Filipinos continued to resist the "blessings of liberty and civilization" promised them by the Republican Party platform of 1900. And many prominent Americans sympathized with their struggle, using it as evidence in their critique of empire. Anti-imperialist arguments varied. Some shared the racist assumptions of their opponents but took them in the opposite direction, insisting that inferior races could never mix with American democracy. But more typically, what the anti-imperialists had in common was a style of thought grounded in concrete experience and specific actuality—in contrast to the imperialist invocation of vast, lumbering deterministic schemes powered by racial or providential destiny. In public discourse, to move from empire to anti-empire was to move from grandiose abstraction to plain speech, the language of the republican and liberal traditions, with its distrust of concentrated power, executive deceit, and the thwarting of popular sovereignty at home and abroad—and its distrust, as well, of the too-easy resort to force, combined with a painful awareness of war's consequences.

Anti-imperialism at its best was characterized by a particularity of vision, a refusal of euphemism, a realism tempered by ethical concerns about the corrupting effects of imperial power on both the rulers and the ruled. These concerns came straight from the framers of the Constitution, who were haunted by the historical pattern of republics trading their liberties for the false comforts of empire. Mahan caught the conflict in 1897, when he complained that "any project of extending the sphere of the United States, by annexation or otherwise, is met by the constitutional lion in the path." Acquisition of overseas empire was a departure from republican tradition.

Anti-imperialists drew strength from disparate sources. African-Americans were skeptical about the beneficence of white paternalism. "The white man's burden," wrote the black editor James Jefferson Roche, "is never so heavy that he cannot carry it out the door or window of the house he has just burglarized." The anti-imperialists also included prominent public figures, from Addams and Bryan and Andrew Carnegie to Mark Twain and William James. Carnegie's presence in this group suggests that even robber barons were not driven entirely by their economic interests. He, like the others, was appalled by the betrayal of the principles that had supposedly led us into war with Spain in the first place.

Unlike Roosevelt, the anti-imperialists knew the difference between a republic and an empire. Addams founded a grass-roots organization in Chicago that became one of the nodes of the American Anti-Imperialist League; and she helped to draft a resolution in 1899 that put the issues plainly: "We insist," wrote Addams and her colleagues, "that the forcible subjugation of a . . . people" was nothing less than "open disloyalty to the distinctive principles of our government . . . that all men are entitled to life, liberty, and the pursuit of happiness." Bryan was equally clear. "The fruits of imperialism, be they bitter or sweet, must be left to the subjects of a monarchy," he said in 1899. "This is one tree of which the citizens of a republic may not partake. It is the voice of the serpent, not the voice of God, that bids us eat." Despite his own commitment to evangelical Christianity, Bryan dismissed the missionary argument for empire as little more than euphemism. McKinley, he charged, was trying to convert the Filipinos by killing them. Accepting the nomination in 1900, Bryan merged Jesus and Jefferson in his critique of imperialism. How did the imperialists' claims of concern for the Filipinos differ from those of the British for the American colonists in 1776? How could the acquisition of empire not require the establishment of a standing army that would encourage more "wars of conquest"?

Carnegie shared Bryan's perspective on foreign affairs. What most outraged him was the imperialists' indifference to the Filipinos' own desires for self-determination. Advocates of empire, prating of freedom and democracy, were perfectly willing to crush the Filipino independence movement—even if it took years of guerrilla warfare (which it did). Unlike some other anti-imperialists, he did not dismiss the Filipinos as savages who should be allowed to stew in their own juices. On the contrary, he wrote in 1899, "They have just the same feelings as we have, not excluding love of country, for which, like ourselves, as we see, they are willing to die." One might well ask (as TR did) why Carnegie was unable to summon similar empathy for his own employees, and any answer would lead us into the mists of Carnegie's own self-deceptions, above all the faith that his workers viewed him as a benevolent father.

The example of Carnegie suggests the political complexity of the anti-imperialist movement. Many of the most active anti-imperialists were patrician intellectuals from the Northeast, most but not all Republicans who had long been dissatisfied with the crass compromises of party politics and had tried to create a more thoughtful alternative. This earned them the contempt of party regulars, including TR, and the epithet "mugwumps"—as the regulars' joke had it, they were fence-sitters, with their mug on one side and rump on the other. Historians have tended to dismiss them as ineffectual, though they included such figures as Senators Carl Schurz and George Hoar and Professor Charles Eliot Norton, who had outgrown his adolescent militarism and become a serious critic of empire. Ineffectual they may have been, but their critique was grounded in a stronger understanding of American tradition than Roosevelt, Lodge, or Beveridge displayed.

Still, the mugwumps' anti-imperialism was bounded by their provincialism. For a more capacious perspective, one has to look to Mark Twain and William James. They were the anti-imperialists whose views most clearly arose from a well-grounded way of looking at the world—a distrust of empty formulas and vague abstractions, a determination to be faithful to the facts of lived experience, as well as a capacious conception of both facts and experience. Sharing a common sensibility, they deployed different idioms and personae.

Twain's sharp awareness of vernacular social types, combined with his sense of the absurd, sometimes led him to adopt the pose of literalist buffoon—especially when he was being interviewed by the newspapers. An anecdote (perhaps apocryphal) captured the strategy, describing his response when a reporter asked if he believed in infant baptism: "Believe in it?" he supposedly said. "Hell! I've seen it done." Mocking the misunderstanding of the question, Twain also affirmed his own attachment to direct observation, and his distrust of formulaic theological debate. After centuries of bitter disputes over the efficacy of infant baptism, the only thing one could say with any certainty about the practice was that one had seen it done.

Twain's bitterest disdain focused on the American civil religion, especially its tendency to wrap the pointless slaughter of war in the robes of righteous heroism. As early as the 1880s, Mark Twain had already written against the grain of the emerging Civil War mythology in his contribution to the hagiographic "Battles and Leaders of the Civil War" series in the *Century* magazine. The antiheroic "Private History of a Campaign That Failed" evoked the terror, confusion, and wasted lives of young men at war. This was a long way from the sanitized version of events in the rest of the series.

Twain was primed for skepticism toward the pseudo-Christian arias of empire. So when the Republican platform of 1900 pledged to bring "the blessings of civilization" to the Filipinos, to spread the light of Protestant Christianity and American capitalism to one of the dark places of the earth—by force, if necessary—Twain penned a ferocious polemic, "To the Person Sitting in Darkness." He asked: "Shall we go on conferring our Civilization upon the peoples that sit in darkness, or shall we give those poor things a rest? Shall we bang right along in our old-time, loud, pious way, and commit the new century to the game; or shall we sober up and sit down and think it over first? Would it not be prudent to get our Civilization-tools together, and see how much stock is left on hand in the way of Glass Beads and Theology, and Maxim Guns and Hymn Books, and Trade Gin and Torches of Progress and Enlightenment (patent adjustable ones, good to fire villages with, on occasion), and balance the books, and arrive at the profit and loss, so that we may intelligently decide whether to continue the business or sell out the property and start a new Civilization Scheme on the proceeds?"

The chatter about Civilization, Twain believed, concealed fundamental departures from American tradition. After Dewey destroyed the Spanish fleet at Manila, "our traditions required that Dewey should now set up his warning sign [guaranteeing foreign lives and property against Filipino interference, and the insurgent Filipinos against foreign interference] and go away. But the master of the game [McKinley] happened to think of another plan—the European plan. He acted upon it. This was, to send out an army—ostensibly to help the native patriots put the finishing touch upon their long and plucky struggle for independence, but really to take their land away from them and keep it. That is, in the interest of Progress and Civilization." Twain's contrast between America and Europe was a little too neat; Americans, after all, as Roosevelt and Lodge insisted, had their own history of suppressing indigenous populations. But Twain's impulse to rip away the rhetoric of progress and reveal the actualities of empire led to a powerful polemical stance.

His hottest rage was directed at those pastors who claimed divine approval for the American cause. His fable "War Prayer" evoked a pastor of an affluent congregation, who beseeches "an ever-merciful and benignant Father" to protect our "noble young soldiers" and "bear them in his mighty Hand" forward to victory. Then a gaunt and aged stranger appears at the rear of the church, shocking the comfortable crowd with his assertion: "I come from the throne—bearing a message from Almighty God!" His message is to articulate to these Christians the true import of their importunings, the unspoken prayer-within-a-prayer. It is a prayer "to smite the foe. O Lord our God, help us to tear their soldiers to bloody shreds with our shells; help us to cover their smiling fields with the pale forms of their patriot dead; help us to drown the thunder of the guns with the shrieks of their wounded, writhing in pain; help us to lay waste their humble homes with a hurricane of fire; help us to wring the hearts of their unavailing widows with unavailing grief; help us to turn them out roofless with little children to wander unfriended the wastes of their desolated land in rags and hunger and thirst. . . ." Juxtaposing plain speech and hypocrisy, Mark Twain made clear that Christianity—if taken seriously—was a poor foundation for pro-war apologetics. When he circulated the manuscript in 1905, editors found it "unsuitable for publication."

Still, Twain was hardly alone in his rage. "God damn the United States for its vile conduct in the Philippine Islands," James confided to a correspondent. Some of his anger stemmed from the feeling that the United States had "puked up its ancient soul [its dream of serving as a moral example to mankind] . . . in five minutes without a hint of squeamishness." Whether that "ancient soul" was ever more than a self-righteous delusion, James left open to question. "We had supposed ourselves (with all our crudity and barbarity in certain ways) a better nation morally than the rest, safe at home, and without the old savage ambition, destined to exert great international influence by throwing in our 'moral weight,' etc.—dreams! Human nature is everywhere the same; and at the least temptation all the old military passions rise, and sweep everything before them." James sentimentalized the American past, assuming its freedom from "savage ambition" and overlooking the war of extermination required by westward expansion. But he at least realized that the creation of an overseas empire made mincemeat of the old faith in exceptional American virtue. The United States was a nation like any other: "In every national soul there lie potentialities of the most barefaced piracy and our American soul is no exception. . . . It is good to rid ourselves of cant and humbug, and know the truth about ourselves."

Even if he idealized the republican tradition, James grasped its fundamental significance—especially its resonance with his own style of thought, his distrust of grand abstractions, his devotion to the power of concrete experience. James's anti-imperialism stemmed from his political commitment to republicanism but also from his philosophical commitments to pluralism and radical empiricism. His empiricism was "radical" in its readiness to consider all sorts of evidence relevant to the empiricist project, its insistence on the importance of "wild facts" that fail to fit existing formulas, and its determination to get past the conventions of language to grasp the specific details of experience—to focus on Emilio Aguinaldo, say, rather than "the little brown brothers" or "the uncivilized Malay."

James's pluralistic openness to varieties of belief, which arose not out of mere tolerance but out of a passionate commitment to the possibility of multiple explanations, also had a political edge. In "On a Certain Blindness in Human Beings," he wrote of how difficult and important it was for people (including himself) to cultivate awareness of other people's inner lives—especially of that vital center of being that gave them meaning and purpose. A pluralistic foreign policy would sanction multiple vital centers, granting legitimacy to local aspirations even among "backward" peoples; an imperial foreign policy, by contrast, denied those aspirations in the name of progress. James's pluralism was a prescription for magnanimity and restraint—a far cry from regeneration through empire.

Yet despite James's contempt for imperial policy, he shared the longings for revitalization that produced it. The chapter on will and the heroism of effort is the peak moment in *Principles*: " 'Will you or won't you have it so?' is the most probing question we are ever asked," James wrote. His obsession with will, choice, and risk joined him with Roosevelt, Holmes, and other upper-class Victorian men who aimed to dispel doubt through action. But while James valued action, he did not flee doubt; he celebrated its capacity to deepen faith. His taste for "life's bitterer flavors," his awareness of the insoluble, tragic conflicts at the heart of existence, and his conviction that life must be "a real fight" for it to be worth living—all these qualities of mind kept him from embracing the conventional pacifist vision of a world without war. Like his contemporaries, James was obsessed with courage and he knew that war, for all its horrors, provided opportunities for cultivating it. But he wanted to redefine courage and redirect it to more humane ends. Unlike Roosevelt, James never confused individuals with nations, or physical with moral bravery. And ultimately his desire for regeneration led him beyond morality to a fascination with energy itself.

CHAPTER 6

Liberation and Limitation

✦

enry Adams was a brooder. He hadn't always been one, though he long had harbored some reservations about his countrymen's faith in progress. A historian of the early American republic and fourth-generation scion of a family that included two presidents, he felt there was no place for republican virtue in the corrupt politics of the Gilded Age. He took up the stance of skeptical observer, keeping an eye on the White House from his house across the street, on Lafayette Square. When his wife committed suicide in 1885, he plunged into a prolonged depression and eventually embraced a second career as a speculative artist of ideas. The Chicago World's Fair of 1893 marked a key moment in Adams's midlife transition. While his fellow patricians stood on the edge of the Court of Honor, rhapsodizing about the redemptive powers of art, he went inside Machinery Hall and contemplated the dynamos. Revisiting them repeatedly, he wondered why they fascinated him.

He decided that it was because "the dynamos were new, and they gave to history a new phase," as he recalled in his autobiography. They underwrote the new force—"capitalistic, centralizing, and mechanical"—of the corporations whose displays crowded Machinery Hall. The concentration of impersonal power carried personal weight for Adams. To him, the dynamo stood for "the whole mechanical consolidation of force, which ruthlessly stamped out the life of the class to which Adams was born, but created monopolies capable of controlling the new energies that Americans adored."

Adams's reverie was a blend of sense and nonsense. The "class to which he had been born" was not "ruthlessly stamped out" by the concentration of force in monopoly capital. On the contrary: during and after the crisis of the 1890s, established Anglo-Saxon elites embraced leadership roles in the megacorporations that were coming to dominate the economy—as well as in the Wall Street investment banks and law firms that were servicing corporate growth. To take just two of many possible examples, trivial but telling:

Adams's brother Charles was president of the Union Pacific Railroad, and his fellow Brahmin Henry Cabot Lodge was a charter stockholder in the General Electric Company. These people were hardly being left behind by corporate capitalism, and Adams was hardly an accurate guide to the political history of his own time.

Yet in fixating on the dynamo, Adams located an apt symbol for the transition from republic to empire. By transforming mechanical energy into the invisible force of electricity, and by placing that force in the service of concentrated capital, the dynamo epitomized the imperial reach of the new corporate economy. Adams recognized that the appeal of monopolies lay in their capacity to harness "the new energies that Americans adored," that sent locomotives speeding across the prairie and skyscrapers soaring heavenward. Which Americans actually "adored" those energies remained an open question, but some (including Adams) felt magnetically drawn to them. Like many of his contemporaries on both sides of the Atlantic, Adams was obsessed with "Force."

At the same historical moment when the educated classes felt enveloped by the languors of overcivilization, they also glimpsed new vistas of energy—Promethean, inexhaustible, perhaps even godlike. Some of the energy was economic: Wall Street bankers and brokers were amassing unprecedented concentrations of capital and corporations were using it to produce mountains of name-brand things. Some was psychological: seekers of personal regeneration were encountering, in high theory as well as popular self-help literature, a larger and more complex notion of the human psyche. And some was technological: the everyday impact of electricity, for example, was enormous; here was a force that was invisible, yet to its users apparently inexhaustible. Still, even electric power originated in such familiar sources as coal mines or waterfalls; what was more striking was the mysterious and perhaps even immeasurable energy released by radium, which Marie Curie had begun to explore.

Whatever its various sources, the broad preoccupation with "Force" implied a cosmic vision of power that could be tapped but must also be managed. Were human beings up to the job? Standing in Machinery Hall in Chicago in 1893, Adams began to wonder, implicitly anticipating the wasteland that would one day be made of Europe by the weapons of Westinghouse, Krupp, General Electric, and other corporate exhibitors in Machinery Hall. Such a vast display of force could hardly lack a dark side. In the dynamo, Adams found an icon to embody his ambivalence, one that focused both his distrust of modern hubris and his fascination with the engines that served it.

In 1900, at about the same time that the Republicans' imperial ticket was running roughshod over William Jennings Bryan, Henry Adams returned to another world's fair, the Paris Exposition, to contemplate the dynamos again. As he stared at them, he felt their significance deepen. To him they represented an end and a beginning: the shattering of the old positivist certainties and the start of new era characterized by profound uncertainty. "The period from 1870 to 1900 is closed," Adams wrote to Hay. "I see that much in the machine gallery of the Champs de Mars and sit by the hour over the great dynamos, watching them run noiselessly and smoothly as the planets, and asking them with infinite courtesy where in Hell they are going." The dynamos were the most palpable of many mystifying departures from the predictable, deterministic science of the nineteenth century. "The charm of the show, to me," he wrote, "is that no one pretends to understand even in a remote degree, what these weird things are that they call electricity, Roentgen rays, and what not." However mystifying Adams found the "weird things" unleashed by modern research, he was convinced that whoever controlled the new science would control international conflicts in the future.

Still, the dynamo was far more than an instrument of empire. By embodying unprecedented power, Adams wrote, it evoked a cosmic awe—a sense of "profound helplessness and dependence on an infinite force that is to us incomprehensible and omnipotent." His free-associating sensibility led him to fruitful speculation, far beyond the matter-of-fact perspective of his companion at the Paris Fair, the Smithsonian physicist Samuel Langley. To Langley, Adams wrote,

the dynamo itself was but an ingenious channel for conveying somewhere the heat latent in a few tons of poor coal hidden in a dirty engine-house kept carefully out of sight; but to Adams the dynamo became a symbol of infinity. As he grew accustomed to the great gallery of machines, he began to feel the forty-foot dynamos as a moral force, much as the early Christians felt the Cross. The planet itself seemed less impressive, in its old-fashioned, deliberate, annual or daily revolution, than this huge wheel, revolving within arm's-length at some vertiginous speed, and barely murmuring,—scarcely humming an audible warning to stand a hair's-breadth further for respect of power—while it would not wake the baby lying close against its frame. Before the end, one began to pray to it; inherited instinct taught the natural expression of man before silent and infinite force.

To Adams, the dynamo's value lay less in its practical application than in "its occult mechanism." It epitomized all the new, invisible forces converging to kill off the old scientific certainties—forces like X-rays, which were "occult, supersensual, irrational; they were a revelation of mysterious energy like that of the Cross; they were what, in terms of medieval science, were called immediate modes of the divine substance." Yet the X-ray and the dynamo had less in common with the Cross than with each other, as well as with other modern sources of occult energy—unconscious drives, hidden selves—that could not fit easily into the positivist conception of a completely measurable universe.

Adams's quest to make sense of a post-positivist universe stamped him as a man of his time. On both sides of the Atlantic, psychologists and physicists were redefining cosmos and self, departing from static Victorian certainties, en route to no one knew where. Avant-garde artists and writers rejected those certainties, too, as part of their broader dismissal of a bourgeois culture that seemed increasingly pinched and parochial. An atmosphere of experiment penetrated most academic disciplines, even philosophy, as William James, Henri Bergson, and other thinkers recast truth claims in more fluid and dynamic forms.

Nor was the fascination with force confined to the highly educated. A preoccupation with releasing energy from previously untapped sources (body, soul, psyche) pervaded popular culture. In *Good Housekeeping*, the *Saturday Evening Post*, and other mass-circulation magazines, self-help writers began turning the scarcity psychology of the nineteenth century into an abundance psychology more appropriate for the twentieth. Those who craved revitalization sought increasingly to spend rather than hoard psychic resources, assuming they could tap a continuous flow of psychic energy. The celebration of intense experience, of spontaneous "real life," pervaded the literature of self-help. As economists conceived an upward spiral of production and consumption powering endless economic growth, psychologists imagined a fluid, vital self pursuing a path of endless personal growth. Psyche and economy were twinned.

The new preoccupation with force promoted a complex reshuffling of norms that affected almost every area of Americans' lives, from their rhythms of work and play to their behavior in the bedroom. The changes were far too complex and varied to be characterized as either progress or decline, but they can be usefully simplified as a blend of liberation and limitation.

The breakout from positivist certainty, the mood of experiment in intellectual life and the arts—these developments encouraged the conviction that life contained more surprise and possibility than had previously been imagined. It is plausible to see a new sense of freedom among the educated middle and upper classes, and perhaps especially among women who were exploring fresh opportunities for work and play outside the domestic sphere. Despite occasional economic tremors, the persistence of prosperity after the depression of the 1890s meant that Americans of all classes had more time off and more money to spend on new forms of commercial fun. Amusement parks, dance halls, vaudeville shows, nickelodeons, and later movie theaters, all promised excitement to young men and women with a little loose change in their pockets. Intense experience could be purchased as well as pursued.

The mass marketing of fun was part of a broader culture of consumption, embodied in the brand-name goods that proliferated in people's parlors, kitchens, and (eventually) driveways. Yet in their very similarity, these goods suggested some of the limits on liberation. Behind their iconography of abundance lay the standardizing constraints of the scientifically managed corporation, which were felt by office workers as well as factory hands. As the working day shortened, for many people work itself became more tedious, repetitive, and demanding. Even as post-positivist science challenged familiar quantitative measurements of time and space, managerial strategies were subjecting everyday life to more rigorous quantitative control. Beyond the workplace lay other, more diffuse limits—new legal restraints on familiar leisure activities, especially the use of alcohol and drugs; new and more stringent definitions of sexual, psychological, and physical normality; and a new ethic of peak performance that enveloped work and leisure alike under the aegis of personal efficiency.

Modern visions of liberation cohabited with feelings of claustrophobia. Two visions grew in tandem: the self set free from all bonds, Promethean, triumphant, even airborne; and the self enchained in prisons that were sometimes more humane, but also more capacious and enduring than any before imagined. For every boundless self there was an iron cage in waiting: the

State, the Family, the Firm, even the invisible bonds of one's own commitment to peak performance. Dreams of freedom coexisted with nightmares of incarceration. The most palpable embodiment of those contradictions was Harry Houdini, the man whose stage name became synonymous with miraculous release from bondage.

ON A WARM Missouri afternoon in September 1915, five thousand people swarmed in the streets outside the offices of the *Kansas City Post*. For days the *Post* had been advertising a sensational event: Harry Houdini was going to release himself from a straitjacket while he hung upside down from a crane attached to the roof of the *Post* building, in full view of the throng below. The Kansas City Police Department supplied their "best and strongest straitjacket" and the detectives who fitted it on Houdini pulled the "straps to the very last ounce of their strength." One then turned to Houdini and said: "If you can get out of that you can get out of anything." As Houdini was hoisted aloft by his heels, the crowd looked up tensely. Reaching the top, he began to strain and flop about like a huge fish on a line. Within minutes he had worked the jacket loose, ripped it off, and tossed it into the sea of onlookers below. The street erupted with whistles and roars of amazement.

Houdini had been wriggling out of straitjackets for nearly twenty years, though the Kansas City event was the first time he had tried it in midair. He had also freed himself from handcuffs and shackles and manacles while sealed in coffins, milk cans, and a "Chinese Water Torture Cell." His apparently miraculous feats had mundane explanations. With long hours of physical conditioning, he combined resourcefulness, dexterity, and an extraordinary capacity to keep a secret (such as the keys and other tiny tools he somehow managed to conceal on his nearly nude body). He kept audiences guessing, and coming back.

Houdini was a contortionist, a muscle man, an acrobat, a magician. But above all he was an escape artist—an emblem of man alone, forever freeing himself from constraints that he had freely chosen. A society whose population (especially its male population) felt increasingly entrapped by institutional routine could make "escapism" an end in itself, a ceaseless quest for a feeling of freedom that seemed impossible to sustain. Houdini repeatedly reenacted triumphs over anxieties that were in some sense archetypal (the fear of premature burial, for example) but that resonated with particular force in the early twentieth century.

During the years before World War I, office work as well as factory work increasingly came under the sort of managerial discipline devised by Frederick Winslow Taylor, the "father" of scientific management. That meant less autonomy, more surveillance, more quantified timing and measurement of output. Taylor claimed that the new energies released by his system would accelerate productivity, increasing wages as well as profits and dissolving the futile wastes of class war in a harmonious new world of well-managed selves. Production became rationalized by scientific management, consumption by consumer credit. As the economist Simon Nelson Patten understood, good consumers made good producers, who stayed in harness year in and year out to meet the regular payments demanded by lending institutions. Patten implicitly allied himself with Taylor. "System" was the watchword of the nascent managerial society.

Not everyone was willing to suit up. Workers resisted the reign of scientific management: many were old-stock producers who clung to the shreds and tatters of republican tradition; others were immigrants hoping to preserve familiar customs against the ravages of modernization. The formulas of abundance psychology could hardly make much headway in the many working-class lives characterized by scarcity and ethnic or race-based constraints. And beyond class resistance there were subtler rebellions against the emerging system, sustained by idiosyncratic selves who bridled under managerial discipline. Many Americans, of all classes, distrusted the equation of corporate-sponsored progress and personal liberation. Sensing a subtle imprisonment, they harbored fantasies of escape. No doubt some of those seekers were in the crowd outside the *Kansas City Post* that September day in 1915, watching Houdini struggle to freedom in midair. No wonder he was the sensation of the age.

Houdini's career stretched from the 1890s to the 1920s, spanning the period when itinerant hoochie-koochie shows and patent-medicine fairs gave way to more sanitized forms of commercial entertainment: syndicated vaudeville acts, Hollywood films, eventually radio. Houdini was a product and beneficiary of this transformation, even as he resisted its standardizing impact through his idiosyncratic example.

His real name was Ehrich Weiss. Like many another vaudevillian, Houdini was a Jewish immigrant in ambivalent flight from his religious tradition—embodied in his father, Rabbi Mayer Samuel Weiss. Rabbi Weiss emigrated to the United States in 1876, when he was forty-seven years old. Within two years he found a Reform congregation in Appleton, Wisconsin, and sent for his wife, Cecelia, their four sons, and a fourteen-year-old son by a previous marriage. But it soon became apparent that Rabbi Weiss was too old or too Old World for an eagerly assimilating Jewish community in a bustling Midwestern town. The congregation let him go and he moved his family to Milwaukee, where he became a free-lance, offering a few services on the side, dragging his household from one address to another, increasingly dependent on charity.

Rabbi Weiss also had cause for concern in his middle boy, Ehrich, born Erik in Budapest in 1874. Ehrich's early adventures were innocent enough. At the age of nine, he was starring as a contortionist and trapeze artist in a 5-cent juvenile circus, calling himself "Ehrich, the Prince of the Air." Then he became an escape artist. When he was twelve, he ran away from home twice, to Kansas City and to Delavan, Wisconsin, where he stayed a whole summer with a couple who thought he was a homeless shoeshine boy. His career of self-invention had begun. The atmosphere of poverty and defeat in the tight-knit rabbinical household must have seemed claustrophobic to a prince of the air.

In 1887 the family moved to the Lower East Side of New York. Rabbi Weiss continued to struggle, eventually taking a job in a garment factory, where he cut neckties alongside his son Ehrich. Off the job, Ehrich set about becoming a champion swimmer, boxer, and runner. By the time he was seventeen, he was posing for a photograph with a chestful of medals, some real, some fake. The combination of bravery, skill, and fakery would become his formula for success. By the time he was nineteen, young Ehrich was performing at the World's Columbian Exposition in Chicago, as half of a magic act called "the Brothers Houdini." The transition from Ehrich Weiss to Harry Houdini was straightforward. Ehrich's nickname "Ehrie" easily metamorphosed into the manly and Anglo-Saxon "Harry." "Houdin" was homage to French conjurer Jean-Robert Houdin, who was widely known as "the founder of modern magic"; the concluding "i" was an Italianate embellishment common among magicians.

Houdini's relation to the magical tradition was complex. The modern-ization of magic had transformed its meaning—at least among more edu-cated and secular urban audiences—from evocation of supernatural forces to sleight of hand. But after the Civil War the rise of spiritualism restored a supernatural aura to the conjurer's art. Mediums provided Houdini with such inspirational examples of trickery as the Davenport Rope Tie, perfected by William and Ira Davenport. They managed to play pianos and other musical instruments while tightly lashed to chairs, all the while alleging that the real musicians were spirits they had summoned from the other side. Houdini hated spiritualism and later made a career out of exposing fraudulent mediums. Still he benefited from the atmosphere of mystery surrounding such performances.

After less than a year the Brothers Houdini broke up when Harry married a German Catholic girl named Bess Rahner, an elfin brunette from Brooklyn who became one half of "the Houdinis." They entered the world of commercial entertainment through its seamier side doors, playing in places like Huber's Palace Museum on East 14th Street, where they shared the bill with Count Orloff—the human windowpane—and Unthan, the armless wonder who could play the piano with his toes.

The Houdinis' specialty was the metamorphosis trick. Harry was tied in a sack, then locked in a trunk while Bess stood by; a curtain was placed in front of them; in three seconds, the curtain was removed and the two had changed places. Bess was bagged, tied, and locked in the trunk; Harry stood outside. The trick suggested Houdini's unwitting capacity to express masculine fears and concerns that might be abroad in his audience: Harry was the escape artist, not Bess; in the end he had bagged her and he was miraculously free. Harry and Bess bounced around on the fringes of vaudeville until 1899. Harry kept upping the ante from ropes to handcuffs to the "maniac cuff and belt," and Bess receded into the background as his assistant. In the spring of 1899 Houdini was seen and booked by Martin Beck, impresario of the Orpheum Circuit—top-of-the-line vaudeville that stretched from Chicago to the Pacific Coast. Houdini preferred the middle-class wholesomeness of the Orpheum to the seedy scams of the patent-medicine business. Eager to claim cultural respectability, he told the *Denver Times*: "I practice seven or eight hours a day, as conscientiously as Paderewski at the piano." He was neither a mountebank nor a medium, he claimed, just a gifted and hardworking artist. Houdini responded to his new situation with a creative burst that included a needle-swallowing trick, a straitjacket escape, and a jailbreak. In little more than a year he became a transatlantic sensation. Abandoning Beck, he booked his own European tour.

On the Orpheum circuit, Houdini learned that escapes were his biggest draw. In Europe he constantly raised the stakes by demanding more strenuous challenges. Their appeal sometimes seemed to rest less on magic than on struggle. The sweating, straining physicality of the effort fascinated audiences as much or more than being mystified by a conjurer's trick. Early on, he took to performing jailbreaks and handcuff escapes naked. It was out of the question in theaters, but police-station performances could demonstrate "nothing up my sleeve" and attract free newspaper coverage. Houdini had publicity photographs made of himself manacled and nude except for a loincloth the size of a jockstrap. A proper late Victorian, Houdini neutralized any hints of prurience by his direct and manly gaze. Theodore Roosevelt would have been proud. Houdini brought magic from spiritualism to strenuousness, an appropriate strategy for the Age of Roosevelt, when "overcivilized" office men sought regeneration through exertion more avidly than ever before.

Few figures focused such a range of longings for regeneration—from the fantasies of the desk-bound drudge to the ambitions of the immigrant striver. Though Houdini never hid his Jewishness, he sublimated it into a characteristically American form: a secular project of self-invention and self-promotion, a refusal to be imprisoned in origins or circumstances, a quest for success on his own terms, accompanied by a longing for acceptance among the Anglo-Saxon elites whose exclusivity he scorned. In later life, he awarded his father posthumous academic degrees and Americanized his own immigrant past, claiming that he had been born in Appleton and that his family had moved to New York City on the Fourth of July (it was the third). His moral stance yoked Victorian propriety to streetwise bravado. "Do others or they will do you," was his motto. The self-made man was also a confidence man.

No matter how often Houdini disavowed supernatural claims and celebrated his own ability, audiences were always ready to suspend disbelief when confronted with his powers. He did little to discourage this. Usually working behind a curtain, he concealed his struggles to escape handcuffs, straitjackets, chains, and padlocked containers. When he did allow himself to be seen—as in the aerial escape in Kansas City—he flailed about more than was necessary, to make the escape look harder than it was. The first approach preserved the possibility that unseen forces were at work; the second revealed the mystery as an awesome personal achievement. He was at once a Faustian hero for a claustrophobic age and a reluctant emblem of the supernatural in an age of religious doubt.

Houdini's performances epitomized popular longings for escape from the constraints of routine and normality but also from a subtler dis-ease, a feeling that one had somehow lost contact with "real life." In turn-of-the-century American culture, cravings for intense experience animated everything from the vogue of romantic adventure novels to the spreading popularity of wilderness recreation. Americans yearned to reconnect with some pulsating primal vitality—vicariously, reading on a couch in Hartford, or directly, hiking on a trail in Yosemite. Often the intense experience had no larger purpose beyond a renewed sense of well-being. The reverence for "life" as a value in itself could be traced to romantic origins, in the writings of Wordsworth, Emerson, and Thoreau. But never before had life-worship acquired such a wide following. Never before had so many people thought that reality was throbbing with vitality, pulsating with excitement, and always just out of reach.

THE SOURCES OF this emergent sensibility were, at bottom, religious. From the prophetic pronouncements of Martin Luther in the sixteenth century to the great revivals that swept across the young United States three hundred years later, Protestants insisted that the incandescent experience of God's grace was the only path to salvation. But by the later decades of the nineteenth century, especially among the more educated and affluent, emphasis on a soul-regenerating conversion experience receded. The emotional impact of this development was complex: feelings of liberation from fears of damnation were complicated by frustration with the blandness of liberal Protestantism—the sober self-congratulation, the calculating prudence, the equation of material with moral progress—all the cultural traits that provoked militarists to pine for the purgative of war. Yet the recoil from banality led beyond the battlefield, toward new directions in literature and the arts as well as in philosophical and religious thought. These explorations, disparate as they were, stemmed from a common longing—a desire to smash through the evasions of late-Victorian life and immerse oneself in a flood of unmediated, intense experience.

The religion of experience redefined reality, beginning in the realm of literary taste. The imitative aesthetic of Victorian realism could no longer satisfy the writers and artists who came of age in the 1890s. To them, Howells and his epigones were trapped in a stuffy parlor filled with knickknacks and furniture upholstered in floral patterns—they dealt, as the novelist

Frank Norris complained, with "the drama of a broken teacup, the tragedy of a walk down the block, the excitement of an afternoon call, the adventure of an invitation to dinner." Nietzsche's critique of bourgeois realism articulated views common on both sides of the Atlantic. He wrote that "the men of the seventies and eighties . . . were filled with a devouring hunger for reality, but they had the misfortune to confuse this with matter—which is but the hollow and deceptive wrapping of it. Thus they lived perpetually in a wretched, padded, puffed-out world of cotton-wool, cardboard, and tissue-paper."

To set their elders straight, the rising generation ripped the "hollow and deceptive wrapping" from reality, even if their reverence for the real was sometimes bound by romantic conventions. As early as the 1890s, surveyors of popular taste detected a spreading discontent with the tepid domestic dramas inspired by Howells—though Howells himself was far more probing in his treatment of social and personal conflict than his critics realized. A recoil from bourgeois realism led to a romance literature that was "as ephemeral as fireworks" and filled with "boisterous hilarity and animal spirits," as Charles Dudley Warner wrote. Throughout the first two decades of the twentieth century, longings to regenerate "boisterous hilarity and animal spirits" swept through the American middle and upper classes.

Yet often the recovery of the real was conducted more earnestly. In language, photography, architecture, and design, seekers of "real life" attacked the prettifying gesture, the useless ornament, the banal evasion. In part, their program was simply a matter of enacting Whitman's prophetic vision— closing the gap between ideals and actualities; admitting the cries of street vendors and starving children into the cotton-wool world of bourgeois culture. In their assaults on the genteel tradition, critics like George Santayana and Van Wyck Brooks spoke for dozens of disgruntled writers, from Norris and Theodore Dreiser to Sinclair Lewis, who felt that America's literary vitality was evaporating in an airless atmosphere of gentility.

Male anxiety energized those accusations. Santayana protested the influence of women teachers for helping "to establish that separation which is so characteristic of America between things intellectual, which remain wrapped in a feminine veil, and as it were, under glass, and the rough passions of life." Norris railed against Victorian literature as "a sort of velvet jacket affair, a studio hocus-pocus, a thing loved of women and aesthetes." Such outbursts bespoke men's fears of emasculating domesticity. The critique of bourgeois gentility was based on the belief that creative passion could exist only outside the domestic sphere. Feminists like Charlotte Perkins Gilman shared this assumption with misogynists like Norris.

The revolt against domesticity was part of a broader revolt against the modern fragmentation and mediation of direct experience. Modern forms of knowledge sliced experience into specialized disciplines. Modern industry removed work experience from primary processes of making and growing. Modern capitalism placed a premium on the manipulation of (often deceptive) appearances. And eventually, modern technology insulated the moderately affluent from much danger and discomfort. The idea of experience became an imagined holistic alternative to disenchanted, fragmented ways of being in the world. Whether seekers of experience located it on the banks of the River Wye or the white-hot floor of Death Valley, they imagined it to be full, rich, intense. It eluded quantification and resisted reductionism. It could not be explained in terms of something else. It was what it was, irreducible. Wholeness was all.

The agenda of wholeness defined regeneration as the recovery of lost energy. In particular, acolytes of experience thought that a return to nature might restore vigor to a depleted bourgeoisie—those "thousands of tired, nerve-shattered, over-civilized people [who have found] that going to the mountains is going home, that wildness is a necessity," as the naturalist John Muir observed in 1901. Yet alongside the quest for restored wholeness there developed a more ambitious vitalist agenda—making more force, not merely restoring it. This impulse revived romantic notions of the sublime, the mingling of pleasure and danger, the determination to press right to the edge of annihilation in search of peak experience.

An emerging wilderness cult revealed that the pursuit of life in extremis could be assimilated to agendas of manly strenuosity and empire-building. With the frontier officially closed, upper-class men constructed an ideal wild nature as a backdrop, a challenge, and a foil for masculine struggle. Arctic regions still beckoned to the intrepid, but more commonly, affluent men embraced the domesticated wilderness of Adirondack guides and camping with all the comforts of home. Theodore Roosevelt reduced this tendency to absurdity, embarking on an extended African safari after he left the presidency, posing for photographs among the corpses of the animals he had slaughtered, and declaring that East Africa was (and of right ought to be) "a white man's country" and "an ideal playground."

Yet other Americans pushed the wilderness ideal in more interesting directions. A few women writers—Sarah Orne Jewett, Gene Stratton-Porter—cast aside sublimity altogether, celebrating careful observation of nature near at hand rather than heroic conquest of wild places. A few male writers—Jack London, Frank Norris, Stephen Crane—redefined sublimity rather than rejecting it. Recalling the dark vision of Melville and Poe, they represented sublime nature as blank, meaningless, and potentially deadly. In their fictions, the manly self-tester was made vulnerable by his own hubris, pitting his puny strength and skills against the implacable indifference of nature and finding himself overwhelmed. Disdaining conventional assumptions of human centrality, these writers slipped into a pseudo-Darwinian worship of Force. But Muir himself showed that the movement beyond anthropocentrism need not lead to nihilism. Presaging contemporary ecological thinkers by emphasizing the interdependence of all living things, Muir redefined the sublime without losing his sense of awe before the "deep, brooding silence" of the wilderness.

John Muir was born in Scotland and moved to Wisconsin when he was ten. His father was a fire-breathing evangelical, committed to subduing the earth; young John soon found this creed distasteful. He was an ingenious tinkerer, but when he left home to study botany and geology at the state university in Madison, he began to glimpse a wider cosmos. He remained torn between two careers—inventor or naturalist—until 1867, when he was temporarily blinded in a shop-floor accident. He withdrew to a darkened room and emerged a month later with his sight restored, vowing to labor henceforth in "Nature's workshop." Eventually he found his way to the Sierra Nevada mountains, where he began the botanical and geological studies that would make his national reputation.

Like many nineteenth-century naturalists, Muir embraced aesthetic appreciation as well as scientific observation. As he melded the two realms, he developed a distinctive point of view. He was sympathetic to John Ruskin's romantic critique of industrial civilization but was bemused by the British critic's anthropocentrism. Ruskin, Muir wrote, "goes to the Alps and improves and superintends and reports on nature with the conceit and importance of a factor on a Duke's estate." Yet Muir also rejected "the dark chilly reasoning that chance and survival of the fittest accounted for all things." Nature was more playful, more purposeful—and perhaps more mysterious—than either Ruskinians or Darwinians imagined.

Muir envisioned an interdependent, animated natural world where "when we try to pick out anything by itself, we find it hitched to everything else in the universe." He found life in desolate places, and playfulness in dangerous situations. For Muir, even far above the timberline, on the highest peaks, "every rock seems to glow with life." In the midst of "one of the most-bracing wind-storms conceivable," Muir climbed a hundred-foot Douglas fir and clung to the tree as it swayed and swirled. "Nature was holding high festival," he recalled.

At its best, the religion of wilderness experience posed a fundamental challenge to the deep utilitarianism of the dominant culture, which was rooted in the anthropocentric conviction that nature was made for man. Santayana, a critic of utilitarianism who celebrated play as "whatever is done spontaneously and for its own sake, whether or not it have an ulterior utility," was also a critic of anthropocentrism. Discussing "The Genteel Tradition in American Philosophy" at Berkeley in 1911, Santayana argued that American thinkers had been crippled by the transcendentalist attitude toward nature. "Nature, for the transcendentalist, is precious because it is his own work, a mirror in which he looks at himself and says (like a poet relishing his own verses), 'What a genius I am! Who would have thought that there was such stuff in me?'" The way out of this solipsism, he thought, led through the California landscape itself. Amid its vastness, "you cannot feel that nature was made by you or for you. . . . You must feel, rather, that you are an offshoot of her life; one brave little force among her immense forces." The "primitive solitudes" of forest and sierra stirred the "subhuman depths and superhuman possibilities" of the human spirit, but they taught no "transcendental logic" or human morality. What they taught was "the vanity and superficiality of all logic, the needlessness of argument, the relativity of morals, the strength of time, the fertility of matter, the variety, the unspeakable variety, of possible life."

Few American thinkers could match Santayana's imaginative reach. Most, from Walter Lippmann and other mainstream liberals to such self-professed iconoclasts as Thorstein Veblen, confined their quest for "life" and "growth" within a pseudo-Darwinian framework of evolutionary progress. Much American thought in the early twentieth century combined the delusion that Darwinian theory underwrote linear human advance with a vague technological determinism. From this implicitly reformist view, social values as well as political and economic institutions had simply not "evolved" far enough to keep up with the realities of human experience.

Despite the prominence of progressive cliché, the vitalist celebration of spontaneity did lead to a new, more fluid style of thought—a distrust of static formulas and unchanging traditions, a fascination with energy, growth, and process; a willingness to lay "hands upon the sacred ark of absolute permanency," as John Dewey wrote in "The Influence of Darwinism on Philosophy" (1910), and recast truth-claims in more dynamic idioms. One can see this antiformalist tendency in everything from Holmes's influential slogan about "the life of the law" (it "has not been logic; it has been experience") to Dewey's ideal school, whose aim was "not learning, but first *living*," as a follower said in 1910, "and then learning through and in relation to this living." Antiformalist urges energized the pragmatic turn in American philosophy, the insistence that ideas be evaluated with respect to their actual consequences in everyday life. Pragmatism was conceived by Charles Peirce, nurtured to adulthood by William James, and applied to politics and society by Dewey. It was the most influential philosophical consequence of the quest for immediate experience. The long-term results were anticlimactic. Among Dewey's epigones, pragmatism never entirely escaped the utilitarian cast of mind; the pragmatic criterion of truth became "what works" and education for living became vocational training.

Yet the vitalist impulse itself had larger than utilitarian implications. Its significance, like its origin, was religious. It lay at the heart of a broad revolt against positivism, a rejection of a barren universe governed by inexorable laws, where everything was measurable and nothing mysterious. The real problem for many vitalists (and certainly for James) was the specter of a life (and death) without meaning. It is possible to see all the talk about "life" as a way of whistling past the graveyard of traditional Christianity. But the vitalist ferment was also a genuine attempt to explore new meanings for human existence amid the wreckage of collapsing dualities: body and soul, matter and spirit, this world and the next.

Educated Protestants, dissatisfied with desiccated theology, cast about for vital conceptions of cosmic meaning. Many explored medieval Catholic mysticism as an alternative to the banalities of the typical Sunday sermon, the sort of platitudes uttered by Henry Ward Beecher and other ministers who reduced the Protestant ethic to a mere prescription for worldly

38 REBIRTH OF A NATION

success. Buddhism and other Asian religions—discovered, imagined, and synthesized—also began to play a role in focusing popular longings. Vedanta, popularized at the Chicago World's Fair and after by Swami Vivekenanda, and theosophy, preached by Madame Blavatsky and Annie Besant, were both synthetic expressions of spiritual ferment. Paul Carus founded the magazine *Open Court* to carry forward the work of the World's Parliament of Religions, begun at the Chicago Fair, to create a common ground of ecumenical discussion, which might lead to a new synthesis—a "Religion of the Future" that might appeal to believer and skeptic alike.

The results were mixed. Contributors to *Open Court* asked questions like "What is Life?" and then stumbled about in a soupy haze of abstractions. "The truth is, there are, as there must be, original factors in the world . . . and life (or chemical activity and appetency) is like gravity, one of them," William Salter announced in 1901. "If we wish to account for *them*, we have to go back to the maker of all things (if there is a Maker) not to any of the things that are made." One thing was certain: "The only salvation for society as for the individual, is from within—it is more life." The reverence for "life" could overcome death itself. "Who knows but that that greater death which sooner or later overtakes us all . . . starts energies into play deeper than we had known before—that it is the death of the body, and freedom, new birth, to the soul?'

The desire for regeneration led to death's door and beyond. Yearnings for empirical proof of an afterlife and for communication with departed loved ones accelerated the appeal of spiritualism. Here was another example of fascination with invisible force, impossible to see but unmistakable (to believers) in its consequences—tables rising from the floor, sepulchral voices, mysterious music. Even William James was intrigued. While he remained skeptical of sweaty séances in darkened rooms, he joined the American Society for Psychical Research, providing legitimacy to the quest for connection with "discarnate spirits." His interest in spiritualism reflected his openness to all manner of evidence, no matter how bizarre or apparently inexplicable—his radical empiricism, as he called it.

Radical empiricism was the most profound intellectual consequence of the vitalist impulse. It animated James's attempt to imagine "a world of pure experience," a "blooming buzzing confusion" of perceptions from which we select and fashion our concepts. It validated his (and his contemporaries') probing of religious experiences and other extreme psychic states, explorations that underscored the revelatory power of the "unclassified residuum" in mental life and the tentative, provisional character of scientific claims about it. Here and elsewhere, James stood in the midst of the transatlantic maelstrom that became known as modernism—the reconstruction of fundamental concepts regarding cosmos, society, and self. Modernism was many things, but it was nothing if not a wide-ranging effort to comprehend and express the myriad new energies that seemed to be exploding all the old metaphysical certainties.

For James the most interesting energy was personal. In particular, he was drawn toward the unrealized force embodied in "second wind," toward mental and physical phenomena "beyond the very extremity of fatigue-distress, amounts of ease and power that we never dreamed ourselves to own, sources of strength habitually not taxed at all, because habitually we never push through the obstruction, never pass those early critical points." James was convinced that "as a rule men use only a small part of the powers which they actually possess and which they might use under appropriate conditions." The question was: how to get at those powers? James was not the only one asking it.

BY 1900, THE Victorian preoccupation with saving scarce psychic resources had come to seem inadequate, maybe even dangerous. Silas Weir Mitchell's rest cure, the therapeutic expression of scarcity psychology, had begun to fall out of favor, especially among women. Some suspected the rest cure was little more than a male strategy designed to reconcile women to a confining domestic sphere. Its most cogent critic was Charlotte Perkins Gilman, who suffered a nervous collapse soon after her marriage and who brilliantly described her own disastrous experience with Mitchell's therapy in her short story "The Yellow Wallpaper." Gilman revealed the rest cure to be a cruel fraud, and spent her career demanding more capacious definitions of human possibility, especially for women. Her life reveals how a psychology of abundance could be rooted in a revolt against domestic patriarchy.

In May 1884, at twenty-four, Charlotte Perkins had married the dashing artist Walter Stetson and quickly become pregnant. It was a miserable pregnancy; she was weak and exhausted most of the time, fretful, nervous, often hysterical. When her daughter Katharine was born, everyone thought Charlotte would rebound. The baby was "angelic," even "heavenly," but Charlotte soon fell apart again. Her depression was indeed a paradox: "Here was a charming home; a loving and devoted husband; an exquisite baby, healthy, intelligent, and good; a highly competent mother [her own] to run things; a wholly satisfactory servant—and I lay all day on the lounge and cried."

Surely this was some form of what we now call postpartum depression, but Charlotte's misery also stemmed from childhood sources. Her upbringing had not predisposed her to conventional family life. Her father abandoned his wife and their three daughters when the girls were babies. Her mother was a chilly disciplinarian, withholding affection even when she felt it. Charlotte grew up a solitary, bookish child, craving caresses she never received. She took refuge in a rich fantasy life, imagining "a Prince and a Princess of magical powers, who went about the world collecting unhappy children and taking them to a guarded Paradise in the South Seas." She told everyone about this "dream world," with guileless enthusiasm, until one day a friend of her mother's warned that the child's fantasies could have unhealthy consequences. Charlotte's mother demanded that she give up her childish illusions.

. . . This was a command. According to all the ethics I knew I must obey, and I did. . . .

Just thirteen. This had been my chief happiness for five years. It was by far the largest, most active part of my mind. I was called upon to close off the main building as it were and live in the "L." No one could tell if I did it or not, it was an inner fortress, open only to me. . . .

But obedience was Right, the thing had to be done, and I did it. Night after night to shut the door on happiness, and to keep it shut. Never, when dear, bright, glittering dreams pushed hard, to let them in. Just thirteen. . . .

That sacrifice set the course of her life. From adolescence on she embraced a stern agenda of self-improvement, cultivating habits of good posture and systematic study, remaining inwardly aloof from the goofy girlishness of her contemporaries. Occasionally her diary revealed her difference from her peers; at seventeen, she wrote: "Am going to try hard this winter to see if I cannot enjoy myself like other people." Her mother refused most of the social invitations that Charlotte received, especially the ones from boys. To reduce the pain of disappointment Charlotte denied her own desires and "became a genuine stoic." In dozens of small ways, she set about developing her will, her mind, and her body. She read William Blaikie's *How to Get Strong and Stay So*, took to exercising regularly, and developed a lifelong fondness for the "traveling rings," which hung from the ceiling of most gymnasiums—"that is as near flying as one gets, outside of a circus," she said. A girl forbidden flights of fancy could still fling her body through the air.

Then she met the Byronic Stetson, a typically passionate and tormented Victorian male who satisfied his sexual needs with many women, despising himself (and them) when he did. He became convinced that Charlotte was the One—the attractive, vigorous, and high-minded young woman who would redeem him from his lusts and elevate his passion to a higher plane. He pressed his suit: she resisted, then relented.

Trouble surfaced quickly. Charlotte recorded their first tiff in her diary: ". . . get a nice little dinner. I suggest he pay me for my services and he much dislikes the idea. I am grieved at offending him. Mutual misery. Bed and cry." A month later there is a hint of a more serious problem. "Am sad. Last night & this morning. Because I find myself too—affectionately expressive. I must keep more to myself and be asked—not borne with. Begin to make arrowpudding." Similar entries followed: "Get miserable over my old woe—conviction of being too outwardly expressive of affection." It is of course impossible to sort out the sources of domestic difficulty from such cryptic expressions, but as Gilman's biographer Ann Lane suggests, one suspects that Walter's ethereal ideals of womanhood could not accommodate Charlotte's emotional (and sexual) needs. Nor could he accommodate her need for independence.

Happiness flared briefly when she learned she was pregnant, but soon her depressions lengthened and deepened, "the not-wellness coming oftener and oftener." Walter was tender, devoted, and helpful, but nothing helped. And even holding baby Katharine brought no relief from pain. Charlotte felt weak, ineffectual, incompetent, and hopeless. Family and friends attempted to rally her with talk of willpower, to no avail.

Charlotte and Walter decided to seek professional help from Mitchell, the most prominent psychiatrist of the day. His rest cure required her to be closeted away in her bedroom, denied the possibility of writing or drawing or painting, and forbidden even to read for more than two hours a day. Soon she was reduced to infantile behavior. She made herself a rag doll and dangled it from a doorknob; she took to creeping about on her hands and knees, hiding in closets and under beds. After months of this nightmare, she and Walter agreed to divorce.

Charlotte experienced "the effects of nerve bankruptcy" throughout her life—periods of prolonged, inexplicable weakness and confusion, when even the ordinary language of books and letters became impossible to understand. Still, she summoned the effort to write, producing *Women and Economics* in 1898, and a number of feminist tracts as well as a utopian novel, *Herland* (1915), in the decades to follow. She married George Houghton Gilman, her first cousin, in 1900, and became known ever after as Charlotte Perkins Gilman. A pioneering feminist, she supported women's suffrage but insisted the emancipation of women required economic independence, not simply the right to vote. This was an important supplement to the suffragist argument, though Gilman's larger analysis was hampered by class and race blinders. She assumed all men were equally able to choose their own economic futures, and wrote as if gender were the only constraint on individual choice. Her outlook combined individualism and determinism, personal freedom and evolutionary necessity. She asserted that "the duty of human life is progress, development," arguing that "we are here, not merely to live, but to grow," as she wrote in *Women and Economics*. Like other pop-evolutionary thinkers of her time and ours, she merged fact and value: "It is time to change," she said, "because we are changing."

Ultimately she lived by a secular religion of evolutionary duty. Human beings were committed to "fulfillment of function," like all living things. "I figured it out that the business of mankind was to carry out the evolution of the human race, according to the laws of nature, adding the conscious direction, the relic force, proper to our kind—we are the only creatures that can assist evolution; that we could replenish our individual powers by application to the reservoir; and the best way to get more power was to use what one had. . . . Life, duty, purpose, these were clear to me, God was real, under and in and around everything, lifting, lifting. We, conscious of that limitless power, were to find our places, our special work in the world, and when found, do it, do it at all costs."

Gilman preserved Protestant habits of mind while she groped for new language to express them. Tapping into a divine "reservoir" of "limitless power," she aimed to harness that force to the regenerative regime of work. Work, she insisted throughout her career, was central to "growth." Seeking an enlargement of the self, she spent her career spurning scarcity psychology and the Victorian home that seemed its natural breeding ground. Gilman fled that supposed haven of privacy, and spent much of her life cooking up various schemes for professionalizing housework and making it more cooperative. And she kept taking flight on the traveling rings, well into her sixties.

Gilman's early "nerve bankruptcy" typified her class and gender. Respectable women had many reasons to feel suffocated in the Victorian home. The prescribed role of the "perfect wife" required demanding and contradictory performances: she was to be a pillar of strength in times of trouble, a submissive helpmate to her husband, and an exemplar of rectitude to her entire family and community. No wonder so many women took to their beds for days at a time, too weak to move. Neurasthenia was a sanctioned escape from the tedium of domestic responsibility, but the symptoms that accompanied it were a form of self-punishment for that escape. Headaches, eyestrain, and exhaustion were psychosomatic but real. And the pain of depression, however diffuse, was equally palpable.

Still, neurasthenia was far more than a female complaint. Its pervasiveness among both sexes provoked a broad rethinking of assumptions about the human psyche—a growing awareness of the interplay between mind and body, and of subconscious or unconscious mental powers that had been tapped by mystics and healers in the past but overlooked by mainstream medicine and religion in more recent times. The spate of psychosomatic illness embodied in neurasthenia coincided with the "discovery of the unconscious" pioneered by Freud and many other writers and artists at the turn of the century, a coincidence that created new possibilities for explaining apparently inexplicable behavior.

Religious changes also contributed to the ferment in conceptions of the self. Liberal Protestants lacked the firm theology of their Calvinist forebears but preserved old habits of inwardness. Without clear supernatural justification, self-scrutiny became "morbid introspection," the breeding ground for neurasthenia. No wonder some began to question the rigidities of orthodox Christian dualism, turning toward the possibilities of mental healing offered by Mary Baker Eddy, whose Christian Science teachings had (according to one *Good Housekeeping* writer) recalled the churches to a "forgotten truth—the message of the gospel of the body."

The irony was that Christian Science's "gospel of the body" denied physical existence altogether. Nevertheless, Mrs. Eddy's teachings were the first trickle of what became a powerful current in American Protestant thought—an outlook that considered the body's interaction with mental and spiritual life. Pastors of more educated and affluent flocks, especially in the urban Northeast, began to discover the healing powers of the subconscious mind, forces that could be released through hypnotism, psychoanalysis, or other forms of "autosuggestion." Ministers and therapists began to work along parallel paths.

For the neurasthenic, concerned observers agreed, "waste is going on in useless and unproductive channels." Tormented by sleeplessness and restlessness, "he never has any reserve energy but lives from hand to mouth on his capital." The task of renewing energy, as Mrs. Eddy understood, was blocked by "fear-thought." Fear was often the "first knot" healers needed to unravel, and as Charles Tuckey pointed out in *Good Housekeeping*, "Fear is largely the outcome of morbid self-suggestion and must be overcome by healthy suggestion applied from without but acting from within." It was only a short step from a focus on unraveling the knot of fear to the idea that one could actually increase psychic energy by releasing pent-up emotions— by emulating the healthy baby who "lets himself go" with unconscious ease, as the popular therapist Annie Payson Call advised in *Power Through Repose* (1891, 1913). "The most intense sufferers from nervous excitement," Call wrote, "are those who suppress any sign of their feeling." Pastors and psychologists alike began to think that, amid unprecedented abundance and opportunity, perfectly healthy people were leading pinched and fearful lives for no good reason.

This was no time for the church to urge a reduction of energies for the sake of greater spirituality, the *Outlook* observed soon after the turn of the century. Rather, "the work of the church today is not to preach poverty, but a more vigorous and commanding spiritual life; men cannot be helped by being made poor; they can only be saved by being made strong." The search for strength energized new Protestant efforts at "mind-cure," among them the Emmanuel Movement in Boston, spearheaded by the Rev. Elwood Worcester. The remedy for American nervousness, Worcester believed, was "increasing the strength of the individual and the race"—lightening the burdens of modernity would involve reversing progress, which was unthinkable. "Following upon the introduction of steam came electricity, with its incredible marvels; the next step is the unlocking of untold spiritual forces," Worcester said. "We seem to be on the verge of vast discoveries in this direction."

The discoveries, however vast, often seemed pat and reassuring. As Worcester and his coauthors Samuel McComb and Isador Coriat announced in *Religion and Medicine* (1908), "The subconscious mind is a normal part of our spiritual nature . . . [and] what we observe in hypnosis is an elevation of the moral faculties, greater refinement of feeling, a higher sense of truth and honor, often a delicacy of mind, which the waking subject does not possess. In my opinion the reason for this is that the subconscious mind, which is the most active in suggestion, is purer and freer from evil than our waking consciousness." Unlike James (or Freud), who recognized the darker dimensions of the human psyche, Worcester and his contemporaries believed that the subconscious mind was a reservoir of benign energy. If properly tapped, this psychic force would heal the body and soothe the soul. This was positive thinking with a new psychological pedigree.

The desire to draw on hitherto undreamt-of psychic resources led many Americans (including James and his brother Henry) to embrace such fads as "Fletcherism"—Horace Fletcher's method of slowly and thoroughly chewing one's food, savoring every bite, and never eating more than one's appetite demands. This system brought Fletcher "back from death's door to a richer and intenser life," he claimed. The economist Irving Fisher advocated Fletcherism on grounds of national efficiency—national health equals national wealth, he reasoned. "In brief," Frances Bjorkman summarized in *Good Housekeeping*, "Fletcherism is one of the many forms under which one of the most dynamic ideas of our time finds expression: the faith in the power of man to make himself what he will through the use of powers which, up to the present time, have lain dormant within him." Other self-help regimes suggested it was possible "to become beautiful by thought." Mental and physical revitalization were joined.

After 1900, amid new models of mind-body cooperation and psychological abundance, old prescriptions for neurasthenia continued to lose legitimacy. The rest cure, as Gilman had testified, could be a positive danger. Richard Cabot concurred in *Good Housekeeping* in 1909. If nervous prostration were due to overwork, rest might be indicated, but "the vast majority of cases" were due not to overwork but to "overemotionalism, distraction, worry, and fear. Many neurasthenics were born tired and have been getting more tired the more they rest. Nothing will ever rest them but work." So Cabot preached "The Healing Power of Work," insisting that "soul and body alike, we are creatures made and meant *to react to a need*, to answer to a stimulus from without. We do not carry our energy like a storage battery. We run on a trolley responding to currents of energy supplied from without, by our fellow-men, by nature and by God," each of us responding in his individual way.

Whether energy came from within or without, it was as limitless as electricity apparently was. The obstacles to access were not material—class barriers or economic deprivation were never mentioned by devotees of abundance psychology—they were mental and emotional. The most debilitating emotion was fear, which cropped up constantly as the core problem in diagnoses of neurasthenia. The preoccupation with freeing oneself from internal constraints undermined the older, static ideal of economic self-control at its psychological base. As one observer noted in 1902: "The root cause of thrift, which we all admire and preach because it is so convenient to the community, is fear, fear of future want; and that fear, we are convinced, when indulged overmuch by pessimist minds is the most frequent cause of miserliness. . . ." Freedom from fear meant freedom to consume.

And consumption began at the dinner table. Woods Hutchinson claimed in 1913 that the new enthusiasm for calories was entirely appropriate to a mobile, democratic society. The old "stagnation" theory of diet merely sought to maintain the level of health and vigor; it was a diet for slaves or serfs, for people who were not supposed to rise above their station. "The new diet theory is based on the idea of progress, of continuous improvement, of never resting satisfied with things as they are," Hutchinson wrote. "No diet is too liberal or expensive that will . . . yield good returns on the investment." Economic metaphors for health began to focus on growth and process rather than stability, on consumption and investment rather than savings.

As abundance psychology spread, a new atmosphere of dynamism enveloped old prescriptions for success. After the turn of the century, money was less often seen as an inert commodity, to be gradually accumulated and tended to steady growth; and more often seen as a fluid and dynamic force. To Americans enraptured by the strenuous life, energy became an end itself—and money was a kind of energy. Success mythology reflected this subtle change. In the magazine hagiographies of business titans—as well as in the fiction of writers like Dreiser and Norris—the key to success frequently became a mastery of Force (as those novelists always capitalized it), of raw power. Norris's *The Pit* (1903) was a paean to the furious economic energies concentrated in Chicago. "It was Empire, the restless subjugation of all this central world of the lakes and prairies. Here, midmost in the land, beat the Heart of the nation, whence inevitably must come its immeasurable power, its infinite, inexhaustible vitality. Here of all her cities, throbbed the true life—the true power and spirit of America: gigantic, crude, with the crudity of youth, disdaining rivalry; sane and healthy and vigorous; brutal in its ambition, arrogant in the new-found knowledge of its giant strength, prodigal of its wealth, infinite in its desires." This was the vitalist vision at its most breathless and jejune, the literary equivalent of Theodore Roosevelt's adolescent antics.

The new emphasis on capital as Force translated the psychology of abundance into economic terms. The economist who did the most to popularize this translation was Simon Nelson Patten, whose *The New Basis of Civilization* (1907) argued that the United States had passed from an "era of scarcity" to an "era of abundance" characterized by the unprecedented availability of mass-produced goods. His argument was based on the confident assumption that human beings had learned to control the weather. "The Secretary of Agriculture recently declared that serious crop failures will occur no more," Patten wrote. "Stable, progressive farming controls the terror, disorder, and devastation of earlier times. A new agriculture means a new civilization." Visions of perpetual growth were in the air, promising both stability and dynamism.

The economist Edward Atkinson pointed the way to a new synthesis with a hymn to "mental energy" in the *Popular Science Monthly*. Like other forms of energy, it was limitless. "If . . . there is no conceivable limit to the power of mind over matter or to the number of conversions of force that can be developed," he wrote, "it follows that pauperism is due to want of mental energy, not of material resources." Redistribution of wealth was not on the agenda; positive thinking was. "When it becomes plain that every man has his place in the progress of continuous creation, and is a factor; that nothing is constant but change; that there is no such thing as fixed capital; all the doubts and fears regarding the future of humanity vanish in the light of sure progress," Atkinson concluded.

The vision of limitless prospects drew strength from technological marvels—moving pictures, automobiles, and above all airplanes, which epitomized the conquest of nature by fulfilling the ancient dream of flight. Wilbur and Orville Wright had first set the flying machine aloft over Kitty

Hawk, North Carolina, in 1903, but for five years few people had actually seen the strange device and most dismissed it as a hoax. In September 1908, the Army Signal Corps arranged for Orville Wright to conduct two weeks of test flights at Fort Myer, Virginia. Word got around; crowds grew. By Labor Day, September 7, five thousand people had gathered at the parade grounds. When the Wright Flyer ascended from the ground, the crowd uttered "a sound of complete surprise," recalled Theodore Roosevelt Jr., a roaring exhalation he would "never forget." At every subsequent air demonstration, spectators marveled at the "miracle" of human flight. In Los Angeles in 1910, one observer described the moment of liftoff: "Thirty thousand eyes are on those rubber-tired wheels, waiting for the miraculous moment—historical for him who has not experienced it. Suddenly something happens to those whirling wheels—they slacken their speed, yet the vehicle advances more rapidly. It is the moment of miracle." The first time a plane flew over Chicago, later that same year, a million people jammed the streets below to watch. "Never," said a minister who was among the crowd, "have I seen such wonder in the faces of the multitude. From the gray-haired man to the child, everyone seemed to feel that it was a new day in their lives." Here was a palpable embodiment of regenerative force, more concrete and compelling than even the dynamo, more charged with the promise of realizing archetypal desires. Yet it was only the most visible example of the new energies abroad in the land, energies that promised to empower ordinary folk with a new sense of possibility in their lives—down to and including new ways to buy fun.

THE RISE OF an entertainment industry stemmed from changing economic conditions. Between 1870 and 1900, despite managers' efforts to minimize labor costs, average real wages for nonfarm workers increased by more than 50 percent: blue-collar workers shared unequally in this growth but nevertheless benefited from it. And between 1900 and 1920, manufacturing wages rose another 25 percent. Meanwhile the nonfarm workweek dropped 10 percent in the first decade of the twentieth century, from 55.9 to 50.3 hours. Some employers, at least, were yielding to workers' demands for an eight-hour day and a half-holiday on Saturday. Whatever the color of their collars, workers had a little more time on their hands.

Many, especially in sedentary occupations, felt a new fascination with the body and what it could do. Charlotte Perkins's flight on the traveling rings was a foretaste of things to come. After the turn of the century, more American men and women than ever took to flinging themselves about in gymnasia, flexing their muscles, leaping on bicycles and pedaling off on adventures together, leaving the sex-segregated world of the Victorian parlor behind. The centrifugal force of commercial amusement spun people in search of pleasure from the home into the world.

New venues beckoned, promising escape into a realm of intense experience. Men and women huddled together on Ferris wheels and roller coasters, screeching at the sublime mix of pleasure and danger as the machine hurtled them out into the air and then down, down on a seemingly endless slide. They danced to the syncopated rhythms of ragtime and laughed at more aggressively physical forms of comedy—the New Humor that first appeared in the 1890s was a departure from elaborate narratives, a brazenly burlesque style dominated by fat women in evening gowns and skinny men in baggy pants, full of pratfalls and double entendres. The carnival celebration of bodily excess had been present in the capillaries of nineteenth-century market culture, in the myriad encounters between peddlers of magic elixirs and tired businessmen or bored housewives, in the voluptuous nudes that were included with every pack of Bull Durham cigarettes or that hung behind the counter of the corner bar. But now the carnival was being marketed to a mass, mixed-sex audience.

Fun was not hard to find, even for the economically strapped. Neighborhood movie theaters proliferated, inviting patrons to "Stay As Long As You Like" for a nickel. These "nickelodeons" were often little more than rat-infested shacks nestled into grimy industrial districts, but inside they were a swarm of sociability. The aromas of garlic and sweat mingled as the crowd gave itself over to eating, drinking, sleeping, and talking, as well as cheering the heroes and jeering the villains while the silent film unfolded on the screen to the tinkling accompaniment of an upright piano. Mothers nursed babies and gossiped in Italian, German, Yiddish, even English. Children scurried shrieking up and down the aisles. Young couples fondled each other in the darker back rows. And workingmen, even if they were exhausted after a twelve-hour day at the steel works, stopped in for a smoke and some conversation on the way home.

What was on screen varied. In the early years movie patrons were likely to see cinematic attractions that called attention to visual tricks one could play with the medium, but as film became more established, its makers turned increasingly to narrative. In 1912, for example, the Edison Company collaborated with *Ladies World* magazine to produce twelve twenty-minute episodes of *What Happened to Mary*. Its heroine was an intrepid orphan of humble means, who rises to a responsible white-collar position by foiling embezzlers and repelling seducers. Later she takes a job as a chorus girl and—true to formula—when asked to fill in for the lead, becomes the hit of the show. As Mary's popularity suggests, the nickelodeon played to women's as well as men's fantasies of escape from dreary lives.

So did the dance hall, another new urban institution that appeared af-ter the turn of the century. Various folk traditions of dance survived in the twentieth-century city, as immigrants hired halls for weddings and other communal celebrations; so did the haute bourgeois tradition of the costume ball. But the dance halls of the early twentieth century were public spaces where anyone could come to play, provided he or she had the price of ad-mission. They included the back rooms of saloons but also brilliantly lit pa-vilions at Coney Island and other amusement parks, as well as opulent dance palaces run by the liquor interests in large cities. Their male clientele ranged from upper-class blades looking for prostitutes to shipping clerks and fac-tory hands treating girls to food, drinks, and a good time on the dance floor, in exchange (they hoped) for sexual favors. To young, unescorted working-class women, the dance hall offered a sublime mix of pleasure and danger, of sheer physical exuberance and unpredictable erotic possibility.

The "dance madness" that swept metropolitan America after 1900 was rooted in sexual excitement. The new dances themselves suggested as much. A style known as "tough dancing" migrated from the whorehouses of San Francisco to the dance halls of major cities, animating the shimmy, slow rag, bunny hug, turkey trot, and grizzly bear. While the band played the latest ragtime tunes, couples clung to each other, cheek to cheek and sometimes hip to hip, gyrating in more or less explicit imitation of sexual intercourse or animal movements. Once they learned the basic steps, one vice inves-tigator noted, "the participants can, at will, instantly decrease or increase the obscenity of the movements, lowering the hands from the shoulders to the hips and dancing closer and closer until the bodies touch." During the 1910s, Irene and Vernon Castle led the way in sanitizing these dance styles for respectable folk, but more explicitly erotic versions survived.

Public dancing was, among other things, a social performance—one of many expressions of a new commercial culture of spectacle. This was a more democratic version of the "conspicuous consumption" anathematized by Veblen. By the early twentieth century, more people, especially women, had access to spectacular rituals of display. Department stores pioneered this cultural form, in such events as John Wanamaker's lush *tableau vivant* from *The Garden of Allah*, a steamy sentimental novel of 1904. Interior and shop-window designers deployed color, light, and glass in imaginative ways, enchanting customers, persuading them to hope that they could be as fashionable as any society dame. During the two decades after 1900, respectable women (and would-be respectable women) took to wearing cosmetics—a practice previously confined to actresses and prostitutes. Glamour was becoming a mass-marketed commodity.

Theater and eventually film provided new opportunities for imaginative identification with compelling characters and disparate experiences. This was a mass-market version of the psychology of abundance, the creation of a larger, more fluid self. The prototype of a psychologically abundant self was Sarah Bernhardt, whose name became synonymous with emotional volatility and over-the-top theatricality. Between 1880 and 1910, Bernhardt played a series of femmes fatales torn between aggression and subservience, openly expressing the erotic tension that energized their inner struggle. She played classic roles like Camille with a combination of romantic intensity, Parisian charm, aristocratic grandeur, and "serpentine undulations." She somehow arranged her agile body into a "spiral." And she smiled. Everybody loved it. This was powerful stuff, new sorts of energy to explore, vicariously or directly—emotional and erotic force. Bernhardt blurred the boundaries between good women and bad women, between modern New Women and traditional True Women. At various times, she both affirmed and denied her "Hebrew blood," creating differing life stories as she pleased. She embodied a startling range of possibilities.

So did the female comics who dominated vaudeville during the first decade after the turn of the century. Fat and funny, they flouted old and new ideals of femininity, the shrinking Victorian violet and the slender Gibson girl. They were strong, athletic, and outspoken. Marie Dressler engaged in "whole-body comedy"—pratfalls, contortions, somersaults, extraordinary caperings about the stage. Eva Tanguay played with social conventions and ultimately debunked them in her anthem "I Don't Care." Trixie Friganza flaunted her appetites for sensuous enjoyment in the face of official injunctions to self-control. A carnival spirit of subversion was the female comics' stock-in-trade. Like Bernhardt, they took the psychology of abundance onstage (and on the road), recasting carnival forms for a multiethnic, multi-class audience.

The relation of African-Americans to that audience was complex and problematic. In many ways, the new forms of entertainment ratified the re-alities of Jim Crow. Deprived of their rights and often their physical safety as well, African-Americans were the butt of humor in "coon songs" and other racist artifacts of popular culture, such as the "Dunk the Jig" booths common at amusement parks. The common American idiom that united disparate ethnic groups in a mass culture depended for its coherence on the exclusion of African-Americans, or on their ritual humiliation if they ap-peared in public at all. Yet there was another dimension to this black-white pas de deux. Like the nineteenth-century tradition of black minstrelsy, "coon songs" revealed attraction as well as derision—at bottom a faint sus-picion that the "coon" enjoyed an ease and freedom simply unavailable to the buttoned-up white bourgeoisie. The comedienne May Irwin appropri-ated "coon songs" and perfected a "black voice" crooning to white admir-ers, evoking forbidden fantasies of interracial sex. After 1900, the emergence of ragtime and jazz combined with the increased notoriety of certain black athletes (notably the heavyweight boxing champion Jack Johnson) to raise the profile of African-Americans in popular culture. And in 1909, seven-year-old Nehemiah "Skip" James heard some local blues musicians playing at a juke joint in his hometown of Bentonia, Mississippi. He got so excited he persuaded his mother to buy him a guitar. By 1917 he had developed what became known as the Bentonia sound, the combination of a complex picking pattern on the upper strings with somber bass patterns and minor-key tunings. He made that eerie sound his own.

Decades later, Skip James would be celebrated by white tastemakers as a master of the Delta blues—a symbol of intense musical experience, unme-diated by the cheesy formulas of white pop. But even in the early 1900s, to some among the white middle class, African-American culture had begun to embody the palpitating spontaneity of the primitive Other. To be sure, rac-ist hostility did not dissipate—in some ways it intensified, especially among white men against sexual threats like Johnson, who flaunted his affairs with white women. But African-Americans had begun to play a contrapuntal role in American cultural life, one that would expand throughout the twentieth century.

The new leisure industry sold escape to an emerging mass audience of working- and middle-class Caucasians, segregated by race but not by sex or age or religion or national origin—boys and girls, parents and children, Italian Catholics and Russian Jews, all mingling together. The existence of new venues for fun transformed the rhythms of daily life and the experience of growing up, but perhaps nothing more dramatically than courtship.

Sadie Frowne's story provides an example. She was a Jewish girl from Poland, whose family had been economically secure until her father died, when she was ten. After struggling for some time, her mother decided to accept her sister Fanny's invitation to come to New York. Mother and daughter came over in steerage, "a very dark place that smells dreadfully." Hundreds of people, many of them sick, were packed into that airless space; "We thought we should die," Sadie recalled. At last they saw "the beautiful bay and the big woman with spikes on her head and the lamp that is lighted at night in her hand." A greenhorn of thirteen, Sadie took a job as a domestic and began to save some money. But three years later her mother came down with "hasty consumption" and died. The sickness and funeral expenses wiped Sadie out; she had to start over, which she did in an Allen Street sweatshop making skirts, receiving $4 for a six-day week with Saturdays off.

The work was hard but at sixteen, Sadie could resist fatigue: "The machines are all run by foot power, and at the end of the day one feels so weak that there is a great temptation to lie right down and go to sleep. But you must go out and get air, and have some pleasure. So instead of lying down I go out, generally with Henry." He was a young man who worked at the factory but was plotting his escape. Tall and dark-haired with big brown eyes and a small mustache, he was "pale and much educated, having been to school." He also knew "a great many things" and had $400 saved. He had his eye on Sadie from the day she started work. She and the daughter of her landlady were the only women among the fourteen machine operators. "At first a few of the young men were rude," Sadie said. "When they passed me they would touch my hair and talk about my eyes and my red cheeks, and make jokes." She cried and threatened to leave and the boss told the boys to knock it off. Henry stuck up for her, too, offering to punch out his unchivalrous comrades. He was smitten but Sadie was cautious.

Still, she let him walk her home every night and take her out in the evenings. "I am very fond of dancing, and in fact, all sorts of pleasure," said

Sadie. "I go to the theater often, and like those plays that make you cry a great deal"—*The Two Orphans*, for example, which made her cry all night because of "the hard times the children had in the play." She also bought pretty clothes to wear on those outings, in spite of the older women's disapproval. "Those who blame me are the old-country people who have old-fashioned notions, but the people who have been here a long time know better. A girl who does not dress well is stuck in a corner, even if she is pretty, and Aunt Fanny says that I do just right to put on plenty of style." Aunt Fanny gave good advice. For new arrivals in the city from whatever origin, the new leisure industry offered a bewildering variety of amusements and fun, even for humble machine operators. It also placed a new premium on appearance and display. Even a pretty girl needed "to put on plenty of style," if she was going to play in the new venues of commercial entertainment.

For young people like Sadie and Henry, the cheap amusements of metropolitan life promised new possibilities, beyond "the old-fashioned notions" of "old-country people." But the very intensity of the packaged experience depended on the sense of futility and fatigue surrounding it. Vendors of the new fun defined it against everyday routine. Most Americans purchased intensity as an escape from what they had to do for a living, even if they only had to do it for eight hours a day. After 1900, the scientific management of the workplace might (or might not) reduce the length of the workday, but it guaranteed that the work itself would be tedious, demanding, and frequently mindless. No wonder vicarious escape became a commodity on the mass market. Taylorism and the leisure industry shaped a new dialectic of work and play.

AMID ALL THE clamor about abundance, industrial workers' lives remained enmeshed in market discipline. The dynamic pace of life celebrated by the middle and upper classes was an inescapable feature of working-class routine. Factory managers perfected the speedup and the stretch-out, and kept employees in line with the constant threat of layoffs. For the workers themselves, migration was often the only alternative to stagnation or starvation. Many migrants moved reluctantly, while others picked up and went willingly, from the country to the city or the Old World to the New. Employers' demands for cheap labor kept a huge population on the move.

Saverio Rizzo left Cimigliano in the Catanzaro province of Italy in 1903. He was a sixteen-year-old with no prospects in that bleak agricultural district. His neighbor Tomasso had been to the United States and come back flaunting several hundred dollars in cash, an unimaginable sum. Tomasso asked Saverio to return to the States with him and Saverio's parents agreed to let the boy go, entrusting him to Tomasso's care. After an eight-mile walk in the rain to Naples, they booked passage on an "insect laden and decrepit Spanish merchant ship" to Ellis Island. On landing they rushed through Grand Central and caught a train to Albany, and another from there to the mining town of Talcumville. The miners were covered with white dust, the water was polluted, and everyone had to trade with the conniving Uncle Gabriel at the company store.

For the next few years Saverio bounced back and forth between blacksmith's jobs in various upstate mining towns (he was judged too young and puny to be a miner) and factory or construction work in New York City. Tomasso stuck by him and they endured cheating employers, collapsing shanties, and the enmity of other ethnic groups—especially the Anglo-Saxon miners, who tried to dynamite the Italians' houses in the mining town of Witherbee. Yet the two men also encountered neighbors and kin from Cimigliano; from time to time they helped each other out. Within a few years of the dynamiting episode, peace had come to Witherbee and the Italians had made the town their own.

But many migrants' odysseys did not turn out so well. "Rose Fortune," as *Frank Leslie's Popular Monthly* called her in 1903, was "an unskilled, friendless, almost penniless" country girl, "utterly alone in the world," seeking work in New York City. "Having taught two winters in the village school," she nurtured "a hope born of youth and inexperience" and decided to seek what she deemed "ladylike" employment. After renting a room from a landlady recommended by the YWCA, Rose began writing replies to the scores of newspaper ads requesting ladies' companions, readers to invalids and the blind, assistants in doctors' offices and galleries. Most turned out to be confidence games. Invited to an interview, she covered miles by "trolley, el, ferry and foot power in freezing slushy streets" only "to reach my destination, cold and hungry, and be interviewed by a seedy man with a patent stove lifter, a shirt-waist belt, a contrivance for holding up a lady's train—or a new-fangled mop—anything, everything that a persistent agent might sell to the spendthrift wife of an American workingman." Pressed to economize, Rose took a cheaper room from a drunken, maudlin landlady who decorated her parlor with flowers left over from the undertaker downstairs. After a month, still unemployed, Rose had only $2 left to her name and felt a "growing fear of hunger."

She decided to look for industrial work, and finally took a job in a bonnet-box factory—$3 a week to learn, with the eventual possibility of $7–8 a week on piecework "if you hustle." Rose was thrilled. But the factory was not as liberating as she had expected. The work involved pasting "slippery, sticky strips of muslin" over the corners of boxes piled high to the ceiling, "ceaseless shoving and shifting and lifting," carrying "tottering piles" every few minutes back to the machines for the next step. It was hot, noisy, and tedious. The place stank of glue. And her mentor, Phoebe, warned her: "Always do as the other girls do, or you'll never get along in a factory. If you don't they'll get down on you, and they'll make it mighty hot, with complaining to the forelady . . . well, it's just this, a girl mustn't be odd." Everyone had to fit in. Metropolitan life was often more characterized by conformity than restless rural folk imagined.

Rose's difficulties typified those of young women who had to fend for themselves. Often the coils of money constraint fell around women who were orphaned, widowed, or abandoned by men (as Charlotte Perkins Gilman's mother was) and then forced to find employment. Girls who could converse in French and bang out the "Moonlight Sonata" at a moment's notice suddenly found themselves scraping by, sewing pants linings and taking in washing. As Gilman argued in *Women and Economics*, female suffrage was not enough; women would never have a shot at a secure footing in society without major steps toward economic equality.

Neither would African-Americans, as a "Negro peon" made clear to a Northern journalist in 1904. Born during the Civil War in Elbert County, Georgia, he was orphaned soon after and raised by an uncle who hired him out as a farm laborer on a local plantation when the boy was ten. The plantation owner, whom everyone called "the Captain," was a benevolent despot who kept his workers on the premises by force or fraud. When the narrator was eighteen, he tried to hire himself out to a neighboring plantation and the Captain ordered him whipped. When he was twenty-one, the Captain told him he was free to leave but persuaded him to stay for $3.50 a week.

He married a house servant named Mandy and the Captain gave them $25 worth of furniture and a two-room shanty. "I thought I was the biggest man in Georgia," the narrator remembered.

But the Captain soon died and his son, "the Senator," leased a shedful of convicts from the state. Eventually the Senator reduced all his workers to convict status. He tricked his illiterate free laborers into signing ten-year contracts that allowed their employer to chain them or lock them up at will and hunt them down with bloodhounds if they tried to escape. "In other words, we had sold ourselves into slavery—and what could we do about it?" the narrator asked. "The white folks had all the courts, all the guns, all the hounds, all the railroads, all the telegraph wires, all the newspapers, all the money, and nearly all the land—and we had only our ignorance, our poverty, and our empty hands. We decided that the best thing to do was shut our mouths, say nothing, and go back to work." Locked in a stockade, sleeping in stalls like draft horses, they were separated from their families and forced to watch while white foremen took their wives as mistresses. When the ten-year sentence was finally served, the men who tried to leave were told they first had to work off their debts to the company store. The narrator's was $165.

Three years later, one of the foremen (who was living with the narrator's wife) told him his time was up, gave him a 75-cent pair of overalls, and drove him across the river to South Carolina. As the narrator recalled, he "set me down and told me to 'git.'" Penniless and light-headed from hunger, he somehow managed to beg his way to Columbia, where he found work with a man recruiting laborers and ended up in North Alabama. "I have been here in the Birmingham district since they released me, and I reckon I'll die either in a coal mine or an iron furnace. It don't make much difference which. Either is better than a Georgia peon camp. And a Georgia peon camp is hell itself."

Not all economic restrictions were as confining as peonage, but still they were palpably physical. Women workers at the General Electric lightbulb works in Toledo had to put wet cloths over their eyes at night to stop the aching and get some sleep; handling electric filaments, they said, was like "threading a very fine cambric needle" three thousand times a day. A thirty-four-year-old "mill girl" (who looked forty-five) from Fall River, Massachusetts, admitted, "Lots of us is deaf—weavers," which was the reason she couldn't get hired as a domestic servant: "The lady said I couldn't hear the doorbell if it would ring." You get used to the noise in the mill, she said, but there was a problem: "When the bobbin flies out and a girl gets hurt, you can't hear her shout—not if she just screams, you can't. She's got to wait till you see her. I saw a man hit once with his mouth open. His teeth got knocked out and all the roof of his mouth tore. You can't never tell when you will get hit—in the eye some time, most likely!" Most working-class jobs involved damage to the body—slow, steady, and long-term or sudden and violent.

These difficulties were exacerbated by managerial strategies that extended the inherent dynamic of capitalism: the drive for an ever higher return on investment through ever greater productivity. Speedups were nothing new; nor was the effort to replace skilled workers with machines run by unskilled operatives. Carnegie and Frick, among others, had been pursuing this plan for decades. But after 1900, managers developed new theoretical rationales for deskilling work and reinforcing hierarchy. The manager's brains would no longer be under the worker's cap, but distributed throughout the planning department to men with white collars and academic credentials. Workers themselves would lose all control over the pace and process of their work.

A key figure in this transformation was Frederick Winslow Taylor, a neurotic obsessed with control, whose compulsions became the common currency of managerial thought. He was born in 1856 to a wealthy Quaker family on Philadelphia's Main Line. His father was a nonpracticing attorney who lived on his investments; his mother was a moralist with a sense of mission. Young Fred was accustomed to the perquisites of leisure-class life, but impatient with its aimlessness. He yearned for a more disciplined and purposeful existence. His yearnings became obsessions as he relentlessly organized and measured the particulars of his life, down to and including the length of his stride when walking and the exact dimensions of the fields where he and his friends played rounders. He feared any situation in which he was not in control, including sleep. Tormented by recurring nightmares, he devised a sleeping cage that prodded him awake whenever he lay on his back, the position that left him most vulnerable to those horrific dreams.

By the time he went to Phillips Exeter Academy, Taylor's inner demons were driving him to study far into the night, in a barely successful effort to stand at the head of his class. Clinging by his fingernails to his class rank, he complained to his parents of headaches, insomnia, and eyestrain. In March of his junior year (1873), the eye problems forced him to leave school. Eighteen months later, he swerved away from his parents' upper-class expectations, taking a job as an apprentice patternmaker in a family friend's factory, the Ferrell & Jones pump works.

It could not have been an easy choice. Taylor had never shown any interest in or aptitude for manual labor. Making wooden patterns for iron molds was a difficult and demanding task, one that took skilled craftsmen years to master. Yet for Taylor the work was satisfying. What he learned of materials and techniques seemed to him a secret knowledge, unavailable to his foppish friends back on the Main Line. Commuting between two worlds, he must have been a mystery to the men at the pump works. Unlike Roosevelt, who never pretended he was anything but an Eastern dude out West, Taylor wanted to be one of the boys. He took up extravagant swearing, but so ineptly that the results were often comic. His awkwardness captured the anomalies of a rebellion against gentility constrained by privilege. Young Fred was not looking at a life's work as a patternmaker, and everyone knew it. After a few months, he was off to another apprenticeship, as a machinist, running drill presses, lathes, and planers—the master tools that made the parts for the locomotives, printing presses, textile mills, and all the other behemoths that powered the second industrial revolution. Finally in 1878 he completed his apprenticeship and took a machinist's job at Midvale Steel Company in Philadelphia.

Within a few years Taylor was promoted to foreman of a machine shop at Midvale. Like many other skilled workers, machinists were caught in the contradictions of the piece rate. The more they produced, the more money they made—but only up to a point. Then the boss cut the rate per piece to save labor costs. To the workers the solution was obvious: cool down the pace, have a smoke, shoot the breeze. Restrict output to maintain the going rate, and in the process maintain a companionable atmosphere in the workplace. Taylor was infuriated by these tactics. He cursed, he bullied, he ran the lathe himself to show how productively it could be done. Nothing worked.

Gradually he began to formulate a more effective strategy. Part of it was technological: new grinding machines, thicker belts, high-speed steel that could withstand the temperatures produced by continuous use. Part of it was motivational: a differential piece rate, which paid more to workers who produced more. But the core of the new strategy was the method Taylor devised for fixing the higher rate: disassembling each job into segments, timing the swiftest possible performance of each, and reassembling them to demonstrate "the one best way" to machine a locomotive wheel or overhaul a boiler. Taylor wrote up each task as a series of steps on an instruction card, which he mounted at the job site. Workers were rewarded with the highest rate if they followed instructions—if they did things Taylor's way, not their way.

What drove Taylor was a hatred of waste, rooted in an inner necessity. As productivity at Midvale increased, Taylor's reputation spread. In 1890 he left the plant to take up freelance work as the first practitioner in what became known as "management consulting." Under Taylor's influence, employers found a new rationale for lowering labor costs by reducing the number of skilled workers, demanding continuous productivity from those who were left, and above all, shifting control over the details of the labor process from workers to managers. Scientific management provided new ways to eliminate the practice of "soldiering"—slowing down the pace by taking little breaks.

Taylor spent his career looking for scientific law in the workplace, but it is an open question how much he found there and how much he put there. The more closely one examines his "science," the more spurious it seems. Consider the most famous application of scientific management, the one that Taylor cited repeatedly in subsequent years to support his claims for his system. He had been hired by Bethlehem Steel to bring efficiency to the common labors of the plant, such as loading pig iron onto railroad cars. To show just how productively it could be done, Taylor had first to find the right man. He picked Henry Noll, who was wiry, energetic, and ambitious, but not too bright. And that last trait was the most significant one, Taylor explained in his later accounts. He wanted a man "so stupid and phlegmatic that he more nearly resembles in his mental make-up the ox than any other type." In the promotional lore of scientific management, Noll became the cloddish "Schmidt," who quadrupled his output and raised his pay from $1.15 to $1.70 a day, merely by following Taylor's instructions.

There are two things to notice about this story. The first is that Noll's raise came nowhere near to matching his increase in output. The second is that the actual events were more complicated than Taylor let on. He picked ten of the best men in the yard gang (Noll was one) to see how fast they could load one car. Flat-out, they loaded 16.5 tons in fourteen minutes. On that basis, Taylor calculated each man could load 71 tons a day, which he rounded up to 75. Then he lopped off 40 percent for rest and other delays, to come up with a final figure of 45 tons a day. The 40 percent figure was as arbitrary as the 75-ton baseline, yet this was standard procedure for scientific management. Calculations were based on figures chosen virtually at random. The appearance of precision counted more than the actuality. (One of Taylor's assistants routinely recorded three seconds as ".00083 hours.") Scientific management was often more about simulating efficiency than delivering it.

From the outset, the results at Bethlehem were mixed. Workers bitterly resented the new standards. Few were willing to endure the oppressive toil required to become a "high-priced man." After several days, only Noll was left from the original ten. In recalling his stint at Bethlehem to rapt industrialists, Taylor put a triumphant façade on what was actually a disaster. He had wrecked morale, had promoted conflict, and had eventually been fired. Yet he turned his tale into a parable of progress, a key moment in the inexorable movement toward utopian harmony between workers and managers. Submission to the impartial arbitration of science, he insisted, would render old conflicts obsolete.

For more than a decade, Taylor preached his gospel to industrialists and engineers, at professional meetings and at fireside gatherings at his Philadelphia estate. In 1910, he became a national celebrity when Louis D. Brandeis, "the People's Lawyer," used the Taylor system as the linchpin of his argument before the Interstate Commerce Commission. The big Eastern railroads had proposed a rate hike; Brandeis argued that the public was being asked to subsidize the railroads' inefficiency. The next day, the *New York Times* headline read: "ROADS COULD SAVE $1,000,000 A DAY—BRANDEIS SAYS SCIENTIFIC MANAGEMENT COULD DO IT." Almost overnight, Taylorism became a panacea, the science that would solve social conflict without challenging the unequal distribution of wealth. Suddenly Taylor was everywhere, granting interviews to obsequious reporters, serializing *Principles of Scientific Management* in the *American* magazine. The *American* advertised his articles as the answer to the question posed by William James in "The Powers of Men" (which had appeared in the magazine a few years earlier): "The problem is, then, how can men be trained up to their most useful pitch of efficiency?"

The Taylor system seemed a way of harnessing the excess energy that everyone knew was out there, of putting random force to productive use. Anything that smacked of scientific method and also promised harmony between capital and labor was bound to attract support among the anxious middle and upper classes. Decades of bitter strife lay behind Brandeis's reassuring remark: "Under scientific management, men are led, not driven."

But labor did not want to be led, at least not in Taylor's direction. Wherever scientific management was introduced, workers had trouble seeing how it served their interests. At the Watertown Arsenal in Massachusetts and the Rock Island Arsenal in Illinois, they resisted, as they had at Midvale and Bethlehem. Since those were government facilities, the House Labor Committee held hearings to allow workers to express their grievances. Congressmen heard angry testimony from union leaders, including the machinists' head James O'Connell. "The whole scheme of the system is to remove the head of the workmen," he charged. "Taylor and his assistants declare: 'Give us big physical men and we will do the thinking for them.' The scheme tends to wipe out all the manhood and genius of the American workman and make him a mere machine, to be driven at high speed until he breaks down, and then to be thrown on the scrap heap."

This was the voice of nineteenth-century labor republicanism, the old emphasis on the manly dignity of the producers. That creed fell into eclipse in the early twentieth century. Workers dug in against Taylorism at every turn, sometimes with success. But scientific management, in Taylorite or other forms, advanced inexorably. Where unions did not exist, workers had no leverage against it. Where unions did exist, their leaders increasingly struck a bargain with management, ceding control over the labor process in exchange for shorter hours and higher pay. The bargain implicitly acknowledged that workers would seek satisfaction off the job, in the pleasures and comforts that money could buy.

The same trade-off characterized the other major managerial strategy of the early twentieth century, the development of the assembly line. In itself, the line was nothing new. But never before had it been combined with Taylorite scientific management, as it was in the automobile plants organized by Henry Ford. Like other managers, Ford reduced the number of skilled workers and converted the remainder into foremen or toolmakers, assigning production to untrained operatives doing minutely subdivided tasks under tight supervision. He carried this process further than anyone else had before, due to the unique mass demand for his product, the Model T. He hired machine-tenders who had "nothing to unlearn"—i.e., who knew nothing about metal finishing and who would "simply do what they are told to do, over and over again, from bell time to bell time."

Ford has often been hailed as a prophet of a new consumer culture, on the strength of his $5-a-day wage and profit-sharing plan, which he announced with great fanfare in January 1914. But the $5 day was not as simple as it sounded. Workers still had to work their way there from a starting point of $2.50 a day; and to be eligible for the top wage they had to be judged "acceptable" by Ford's "sociology department"—the snoops who made sure the employees were leading respectable lives. That meant conformity to Ford's definition of American values. Four days after Ford announced the $5 day, the company fired nine hundred men for observing the Eastern Orthodox Christmas. "If these men are to make their home in America," a Ford official said, "they should observe American holidays." Americanization combined with labor discipline and scientific management in a comprehensive agenda of control. The long arm of the job would extend beyond the workplace into workers' "free time" and family life.

That, at least, was the management plan. Workers did not take to it too well. As the vogue of scientific management spread after 1910, employers began to complain of a "turnover crisis" and an "epidemic of strikes." In or out of the automobile business, quitting and striking were two modes of resistance to management's demands for productivity. In 1913 a newspaper in Elwood, Indiana, observed of a strike at a local tin-plate company: "The men do not seem to value their jobs as they should." They stayed home to plant gardens, help with the spring cleaning, or go fishing. This was the kind of behavior that simply baffled the Frederick Taylors and Henry Fords of the world. Still, Taylor and Ford had seen the future. Scientific management would develop more sophisticated strategies, while employers would join hands with creditors and moralists to seek new forms of social discipline for an increasingly heterogeneous and unruly working class.

White-collar employees, too, would come under more systematic direction. In the pre-corporate office of the 1880s and 1890s, work was task-oriented, almost artisanal in its varying rhythms. A former clerk at Aetna Life Insurance recalled that era: "If . . . somebody wanted to go to a ballgame, he would hustle and get all his work done as far he could go and then ask his desk companion if he would take over if anything unexpected came in. . . . next week it would be another fellow who wanted to go fishing—or something. The work was always kept up, and no complaints were heard." Interdependence and improvisation were the order of the day. But after 1900, management journals led by *System* and *World's Work* advocated Taylorizing office work, especially at the lower end—typing, filing, sorting, mailing—introducing a quota and bonus system, decreasing time spent socializing or disappearing to go to ball games. Executives heeded this advice. In corporate offices, standards of productivity stiffened; improvisational task-orientation gave way to systematic time-orientation. Punch-in time clocks, gongs, and bells began to regulate the comings and goings of employees. And while executives, too, faced new performance demands, they could structure their own schedules. Their time-freedom, as well as their access to their own private space, underscored their distance from the underlings in the increasingly hierarchical corporate office.

Yet, like factory work, office work could never be completely rationalized. Human needs and idiosyncrasies kept getting in the way. What especially complicated the picture in the office was the proliferation of women on the premises. Beginning in the 1880s and 1890s, young, literate, native-born white women began to take jobs as "typewriters." Often they came from respectable families fallen on hard times. Typewriting paid better than giving piano lessons. The presence of single, often attractive women dismantled the all-male preserve of the pre-corporate office, introducing new and sometimes erotically charged forms of sociability. Skyscrapers like the Metropolitan Life building in Manhattan became social scenes comparable to dance halls and amusement parks, places to find a mate or have a fling. By the early 1900s, the pretty secretary on the boss's knee had become a stock image in popular culture, epitomized in the popular postcard with the caption "I Love My Wife But OH! You Kid." Sex undermined the rationalization of the office.

Employers adjusted to the presence of women in several ways. They kept most female employees segregated at the bottom of the pecking order, a practice that allowed male middle managers to reaffirm their precarious place in the status hierarchy. By the 1910s, many corporations also embraced revisionist theories that softened Taylorism into "personnel management," promoting both "efficiency and happiness" (as Metropolitan Life claimed to do) for employees, underwriting their well-being with diet and exercise programs. The recognition that workers were not mere machines for making money advanced most rapidly in insurance and other financial-service companies, which pioneered the feminization of the clerical workforce, as well as in the people-oriented practices of advertising and public relations. From the public relations point of view, the presence of women in the office could sweeten the corporate image, endow it with soul, domesticate it by associating it with family ties. The cloak of sentiment concealed the persistence of utilitarian aims. This became a recurring rhetorical pattern throughout the twentieth century.

Despite the varieties of corporate rhetoric, by the 1910s it was possible to see the contours of an emerging managerial consensus. Energized by the dream of a self-regulating system, managerial thinkers envisioned a society engineered by expert technicians and operated by obedient functionaries. For most people, working hours would be shorter but work itself more routine. Everyday tedium would be compensated by intensity purchased off the job. At work, employees faced new and more enveloping constraints; at play, they could contemplate the freedom of mass-marketed "stars" like Douglas Fairbanks and Mary Pickford. "We are our own sculptors," Pickford said, summarizing the fantasy of celebrity self-fashioning.

But the gap between plodding work and spontaneous play did not have to be so wide, especially for upwardly mobile strivers. Old dualities dissolved in a new regenerative ideal. According to the success ideologues and advertising copywriters who helped make the managerial ethos, longings for revitalization could be channeled into peak performance, on or off the job. A more sophisticated Taylorism could be part of the answer to William James's question about how to train the powers of men. The pattern of success presented in self-help literature and corporate advertising after 1900 recalled the classic pattern of conversion; the proof that rebirth had occurred lay in the conduct of the reborn self. Anyone who had truly tapped into hidden reserves of vitality would lead a more dynamic, efficient life. But of course it was not that simple. The ideal of system still provoked fears of suffocation. Vitalist impulses—including James's—continued to animate alternative visions, even while the managerial consensus acquired unprecedented power.

SCIENTIFIC MANAGEMENT AND vitalist life-worship shared an antiformalist style of thought. Taylor & Company claimed to be unleashing workers' "reserve powers" from the constraints of habit, just as abundance psychologists urged the release of "suppressed feelings" in the service of a larger self. Yet the language of liberation concealed new forms of limitation. The rhetoric of sexual freedom offered a prime example. Havelock Ellis, Margaret Sanger, and other advocates of freer sex created new categories of normality and abnormality, notably heterosexuality and homosexuality. Their common idiom of clinical frankness robbed sexual intimacy of its romantic aura and placed it on the agenda of peak performance. Similar changes occurred in the language of play: it became "recreation," a means of returning more efficient workers to factory or office on Monday morning. The rise of a more fluid ideal of self was less a liberation than a shift from moral to managerial idioms of control, an upping of the ante in the game of success. How much people's behavior actually changed, especially in the bedroom, is an open question. What is certain is that norms of achievement became more capacious and more subtly coercive.

The turn toward dynamism in the language of the self paralleled trends in economic thought. Professional economists focused increasingly on the generative powers of consumption, arguing that twentieth-century capital was not the result of savings but of reinvested or surplus earnings. The Standard Oil publicist George Gunton and other proto-Keynesians insisted that spending was more effective than saving in raising the standard of working-class life. As *Gunton's* magazine observed in 1902, once workers have carpets they don't return to bare floors. The developing self demanded an escalating standard of living.

But this was hardly a prescription for hedonism, as Patten understood. Departing from generations of moralists' warnings, he predicted that workers' desires for things would reinforce rather than undermine their capacity for disciplined achievement. The multiplication of wants would become part of the civilizing process, as workingmen and their wives would broaden their horizons and take pride in their accumulating possessions. "In the course of consumption expanding by orderly processes the new wants become complex, oppose each other, project themselves into the future, and demand forethought in their balances," Patten wrote. "The worker steadily and cheerfully chooses the deprivations of this week in order to secure the gratifications of a coming holiday." Status-striving, from this view, was not a threat to the work ethic but a new and secular way of reinforcing it. Install-ment buying, far from demoralizing the worker, kept him on the path of steady ascent.

What Patten called an "economy of abundance" was more plausibly described as a hamster cage of earning and spending. Continuous produc-tion and consumption demanded new standards of sobriety and rationality, epitomized in a war on alcohol as well as a war on drugs. The war on alcohol was a mass movement for moral revival, which spread after 1900 as local temperance groups coalesced into a national drive for Prohibition. The war on drugs was a more focused effort to raise safety standards in the food and patent-medicine industries. Commercial nostrums and soft drinks, including the aptly named Coca-Cola, often contained liberal doses of cocaine or other addictive drugs as well as alcohol. Reformers were determined to expose and regulate those ingredients. Still, the question remained: how much of such reform was meant to protect public health, and how much to reinforce new rationales for self-control? Purity crusades against alcohol, drugs, gambling, and illicit sex involved a rationalization of regeneration. Beginning in the 1890s, the United States began jailing more people, for more different kinds of crimes, than ever before. The early-twentieth-century United States was turning into a place where previously private matters were becoming the business of the state (or the corporation, in the case of Ford's sociology department) on an unprecedented scale.

For centuries, alcohol had been a staple of everyday leisure—especially male leisure. The new challenge to it was bold and striking, justified on both moral and managerial grounds. Some Prohibitionists denounced al-cohol with Old Testament zeal. Carry Nation of Kiowa, Kansas, was the most notorious. Her first husband was a hopeless drunk who left just before the birth of their daughter and died soon after. She married a teetotaling preacher and started a local branch of the WCTU in Medicine Lodge, Kan-sas. Dissatisfied with her progress, she prayed for inspiration. Like Frances Willard, she heard a call from God.

> On the 6th of June, before retiring, as I often did, I threw myself face downward at the foot of my bed and told the Lord to use me any way to suppress the dreadful curse of liquor. . . . The next morning before I awoke, I heard these words very distinctly: "Go to Kiowa, and" (as

in a vision and here my hands were lifted and cast down suddenly) "I'll stand by you." I did not hear these words as other words; there was no voice, but they seemed to be spoken in my heart. I sprang from my bed, as if electrified, and knew this was directions given me for I understood that it was God's will for me to go to Kiowa to break, or smash the saloon. I was so glad, that I hardly looked in the face of any-one that day, for fear they would read my thoughts, and do something to prevent me. I told no one of my plans, for I felt that no one would understand, if I should.

Nation took to staging "hatchetations," which involved wrecking local sa-loons, smashing the liquor bottles and beveled glass mirrors, and ripping gashes in the paintings of fleshy nudes that typically hung above the bar.

Nation was atypical in her violence, but many other women felt as com-mitted as she was to Prohibition. They wanted to protect women who were otherwise at the mercy of drunken husbands, men who might be deadbeats or wife-beaters unless required to stay sober. The movement to ban alco-hol overlapped with the movement to win women the vote. Prohibition was appealing to women for practical reasons. Given the dependence of most women (especially women with children) on a male breadwinner, separation from a drunken husband was no solution to an abused wife's woes. Apart from a few pioneering feminists like Gilman, few people were talking about economic independence or equality for women; for most, the way to secu-rity was a man they could depend on. Small wonder, then, that many women viewed a dry America as a consummation devoutly to be wished.

The Prohibitionist rhetoric of regeneration blended moral and manage-rial themes. Textile-mill and factory owners were intrigued by the possibility of a sober workforce. As the Prohibition movement gathered force, even Northern states with large immigrant populations fell into line, influenced by ministers and managers. Sometimes the latter claimed pride of place. The vice president of the Detroit Executives' Club, Boyd Fisher, announced proudly in 1917, "It wasn't Billy Sunday, it was the employers of Michigan that put the state in the prohibition column. They wanted to remove the saloon on the route between home and factory."

Fisher exaggerated the employers' role, but he put his finger on an important issue. Sobriety would be an integral part of the interdependent managerial system, which would require freedom from confusion as well as from corruption. Old habits of heavy drinking simply could not survive the pace of life in the developing managerial society. Or so the new corporate-sponsored advertising suggested. Even the most banal products were enveloped in a rhetoric of youth, speed, dynamism. An ad for Shredded Wheat in 1902 promised "BOUNCE!": "If you want to be rid of that stomach heaviness after eating breakfast and in its place have that 'feeling of bounce'—an elastic step—a bright eye—an alert mind and the spirit to dare and do—try this simple yet satisfying dish for breakfast." By 1916 the copywriter for Quaker Oats had picked up the stress on dynamism, pronouncing the product "The Foe of the Easy Chair."

> Folks who love the chimney corner don't love Quaker Oats. Mark the lovers of Quaker Oats. They are the wide-awakes, active and ambitious, whether they are seven or seventy. They believe in keeping young. For oats create vitality. They feed the fires of youth. They are vim-producing, spirit-giving. Light and laughter seem to bubble from them. They make folks "feel their oats." Quaker Oats are luscious, fragrant, flavory—But it's their tonic effect—the life-force that's in them—that makes them the staple of millions. Lovers of life eat them liberally. Lovers of languor don't.

Patent medicines had promised rejuvenation, but had usually defined it in more sensual terms: the restoration of the capacity for intense taste, smell, or sexual arousal, as well as the revitalization of energy. The newer advertising after 1900 more explicitly linked regenerative products with "wide-awake" consciousness, dynamic movement, and urban modernity; it dismissed the chimney corner as a relic of sleepy rural conditions. Corporate advertising was less hedonistic and more hectic than the earlier advertisements, heralding a world where "languor" was deemed the opposite of "life." The new corporate advertising was nearly devoid of primitive sensuality and exotic decadence, which had pervaded the symbolic universe of nineteenth-century advertising. It was set amid the everyday lives of the striving middle and upper classes.

Even leisure scenes provided backdrops for peak performance, usually within conventional gender roles. Swimming, golf, and tennis offered healthy outdoor settings for displaying the streamlined, athletic bodies that had displaced the heavyset man and voluptuous woman as icons of success.

In the new symbolic universe of corporate advertising, women were often Gibson girls with tans—new, healthier ornaments for their men; and the men themselves were trim, efficient go-getters.

Despite much talk of play, and more opportunities to pay for it, the emerging managerial system offered few opportunities for more than fitful spontaneity. Sports revealed a new focus on discipline and teamwork. Spokesmen for male regeneration from Roosevelt to Luther Gulick (who founded the Campfire Girls) and G. Stanley Hall (who created the concept of adolescence) all shackled play to utilitarian values, insisting that sport could be a form of character-building—socializing children to adult roles; revitalizing adults for more efficient labor. Truly this was the embourgeoisement of leisure: play, formerly an end in itself, was becoming something useful.

Nowhere was this clearer than in the vogue of bodybuilding. Beginning in the 1890s, Eugen Sandow and other bodybuilders became national celebrities, posing in skintight leopard-skin leotards and "making muscles" for ladies and men to feel. (Houdini played variations on this theme.) As the historian John Kasson observes, Sandow and his fellow musclemen "adroitly tapped antimodern sentiments and fears of an emasculating civilization. Yet ultimately [they] raised a new, potentially more punishing 'scientific' standard against which to measure one's inadequacy. The concept of a perfect body, ostensibly devised in opposition to modern industrial society, in fact capitulated to the presumption that perfection lay in materially defined, standardized, and repeatable processes and products."

In popular theater after 1910, fat and funny females were gradually displaced by squads of well-drilled "chorus girls," who were slimmer, younger, and more conventionally attractive. The development paralleled the shift in advertising imagery away from voluptuous women, exuding mature sexuality, toward sweet young things less threatening to men. Deprived of the power that characterized female stars like Bernhardt or Dressler, chorus girls were dependent, vulnerable, and easily disciplined into mass demonstrations of male mastery. Certainly that was the goal of Ned Wayburn, "the chorus king" and the Frederick Winslow Taylor of Broadway. Wayburn specialized in dance routines of geometric precision. "It is system, system, system with me," said the busy choreographer in 1913. "I believe in numbers and straight lines." Along with Florenz Ziegfeld and other promoters, Wayburn created a new entertainment form, the revue, which presented standardized images of "all-American" beauty in dance "numbers" that resembled close-order military drill. On the Broadway stage as well as in more conventional workplaces, managers captured energy and put it to corporate use. The well-managed self became the new social ideal of the middle and upper classes.

Still, longings for regeneration kept leading elsewhere. During the early 1910s, bohemian enclaves appeared in places like Davenport, Iowa, encouraging young Floyd Dell, Max Eastman, and other aspiring Midwestern writers to head for New York City, below 14th Street. In Greenwich Village, they found more bracing alternatives to middle-class convention, more exotic outsiders to emulate. Referring to the Russian Jews in a novel by Anna Strunsky Walling, Eastman wrote: "They burn with hot fire. Their being is self-justified. They live and are sources of life. . . . As for me, I loaf, and smoulder, and dodge life, and tinker with trivialities." Like Jane Addams several decades before, Eastman sought relief from an aimless existence by identifying with the "real life" of the working class. He became a socialist. Other young rebels were less politically inclined, like the myriad "extra girls" who flocked to the new film studios in Hollywood, hoping to catch the eye of a producer in search of prospects. Broadway may have succumbed to rationalization but Hollywood was generating new icons of female sexuality and power—such as Theda Bara, the slinky "Vamp," star of steamy silent films who had started out as Theodosia Goodman from Cincinnati.

Bohemia blurred the boundaries between culture and politics. Occasionally the consequences were substantial: Max Eastman's writings sought seriously to meld political and cultural radicalism; he and other contributors to *The Masses* made the magazine a fresh voice for labor rights, outside the emerging managerial ethos. But more often the blurring of boundaries led to a politics of style that sometimes verged on self-parody. Even Theda Bara styled herself a "feministe." In the writings and speeches of Greenwich Village radicals, the pursuit of private needs and desires—especially sexual needs and desires—became part of a broader public agenda. Eager to infuse politics with personal drama, the rebel socialite Mabel Dodge conducted a salon where young radicals could flock to feel the energy exuded by Big Bill Haywood, head of the Industrial Workers of the World and an embodiment of labor authenticity. The bohemian cult of experience laid the foundations of radical chic.

But the public figure who best embodied the politics of regeneration remained Theodore Roosevelt, the vitalist who was also a moralist, who defined "real life" as strenuous life. His version of vitalism pointed the way toward a politics of experience that would regenerate established elites by combining Progressive reform at home with imperial adventures abroad. Domestic and foreign policies cohered as empire became a way of life.

Serious thinkers stayed outside the imperial consensus, taking the vitalist impulse in more profound directions. William James and Henry Adams were both well acquainted with life's darker dimensions, and both knew that the powers unleashed in the new century could be demonic as well as divine. Their fascination with new sources of energy coexisted with a distrust of hubris. Resisting the empty ideal of strenuous efficiency, they embodied two extraordinary expressions of American modernist thought.

JAMES'S FASCINATION WITH vital energy was rooted in his desire to rescue the self (including his own) from ennui and paralysis of the will. Like other Americans, James viewed the unconscious mind as a potential fount of creative energy, applauding "mind-cure" and other emergent psychotherapies for making "unprecedented use of our subconscious mental life" and reconnecting neurasthenic patients with hidden psychic sources of health and strength. Perhaps mind influenced body as well as the other way around, and belief in an idea could help to make it so—at least for the believer. James knew this from his own experience, his decision to believe in free will as a young man paralyzed by depression.

Still, James could never be merely a positive thinker. Unlike the advocates of mind-cure, he realized that the resources of the unconscious were neither always benign nor easily explicable. That became apparent in *The Varieties of Religious Experience* (1902), which contrasted "the religion of healthy-mindedness" with the travails of "the twice-born sick soul"—among whom James included himself (disguised). Healthy-minded believers felt at home in the universe; sick souls felt that they were living on a frozen lake surrounded by cliffs, knowing that the ice was melting. Their sense of dread could be cured only through some kind of conversion experience. Yet even this could not heal their inner wounds. This was autobiography. As James's student John Jay Chapman recalled, "There was, in spite of his playfulness, a deep sadness about James. You felt that he had just stepped out of this sadness in order to meet you, and was to go back into it the moment you left him."

In *Varieties*, James focused on the foundational texts of Protestant regeneration, conversion narratives. This made it easier to locate his goal: the "hot place in a man's consciousness" that constituted *"the habitual center of his personal energy."* Sometimes the experiences in *Varieties* resonated with James's own "hot places." This was especially true of the ineffable but noetic experience of mysticism, the feeling that one's individual identity was somehow merging with a larger cosmic or perhaps even divine identity.

From Jonathan Edwards to Emerson and Whitman, an American mystical tradition celebrated such experiences as orgasmic congress with Nature (if not with God). James had experienced something like this one July night in the Adirondacks in 1898, not long after he had been invited to give the Gifford Lectures at the University of Edinburgh. He described that strange event as a *Walpurgisnacht*: "The streaming moonlight lit up all things in a magical checkered play, and it seemed as if all the gods of all the nature-mythologies were holding an indescribable meeting in my breast with the moral gods of the inner life." This was the experience that triggered *Varieties*, and unlike much of the rest of the mysticism recounted in that volume, it was pluralistic rather than monistic. It was not a matter of merging with the One, but of mingling with the many.

James's pluralism in religious matters was a polite name for polytheism—the paradoxically antimodern impulse animating many forms of modernist thought. More democratic and inclusive in his sympathies than Henry Adams, T. S. Eliot, or other antimodern modernists, James nevertheless shared their desire to escape the metaphysical dead end of positivist certainty. At the apex of monotheism and secularism, in the confident Anglophone culture of the turn of the century, antimodern modernists imagined a return of repressed gods that might be more than a heap of broken images.

Adams was more pessimistic and desperate than James, and also more paradoxical. He combined a hatred of modernity and a fascination with the engines that generated its force. Descendant of presidents, he loved proximity to power, and described his consultation with Secretary of State John Hay as "probably . . . the moment of highest knowledge that a scholar could reach." His obsession with the dynamo sometimes reached Faustian heights, as when he announced that the twentieth-century American, "the child of incalculable coal power, chemical power, electrical power, and radiating energy, must be a sort of God compared with any former creation of nature."

But ultimately he turned from technological power toward a different sort of regenerative force.

In 1901, the year after he stood brooding over the dynamos at the Paris Exposition, Adams penned a poem that foreshadowed the great themes of his late work. His "Prayer to the Virgin of Chartres" posed the dynamo against the virgin, masculine world mastery against "the mystery of Maternity." He begged the Virgin Mother's pardon for abandoning her, for joining other men in their struggle for knowledge, wealth, and power. The quest for mastery was strongest among Americans.

> Crossing the hostile sea, our greedy band
> Saw rising hills and forests in the blue;
> Our father's kingdom in the promised land!
> —We seized it, and dethroned the father too.
>
> And now we are the father, with our brood,
> Ruling the Infinite, not Three but One;
> We made our world and saw that it was good;
> Ourselves we worship, and we have no Son.

This was the ultimate consequence of praying to the dynamo—self-absorption and sterility. The worship of technological force ended in a solipsistic blind alley, a worship of ourselves. Recoiling from his bleak, disenchanted vision of modern America, Adams turned from Father to Mother.

> Waiting I feel the energy of faith
> Not in the future science, but in you!

To the heterodox Adams, the Virgin embodied the force of maternal fecundity—"the greatest and most mysterious of all energies," as the childless widower called it. In his dualistic formulation, the male will to mastery could not acknowledge "the mystery of Maternity," could not even bend a knee to it, but only rush by, producing dynamos and steam engines. Yet somehow the machines' power failed to match the Virgin's, especially in the art they inspired. Factories were not cathedrals. As Adams wrote, "All the steam in the world could not, like the Virgin, build Chartres." What built

Chartres, he believed, was the power of faith, the power he would explore in his most profound work, *Mont-Saint-Michel and Chartres* (1904).

Adams's contrapuntal play with the Virgin and the dynamo, like James's polytheistic vision, reminds us that longings for regeneration could have idiosyncratic consequences. The rise of imperial ambitions, the redirection of social conflict, the renewal of ruling-class rule, the incorporation of vitalist impulses—these developments were essential to the making of modern America. But they were not the whole story, and they should not obscure the myriad private struggles to regenerate larger meaning amid the triumphalist inanities of empire.

CHAPTER 7

Empire as a Way of Life

✦

For the last thirty years of his life, Louis Sullivan was the angriest architect in America. The reasons for his rage could be traced to the Columbian Exposition. By the early 1890s, Sullivan had designed some of the most innovative structures in the United States, pioneering in the skeleton construction that sent skyscrapers soaring, recasting ornament to reflect his conviction that form must follow function. Having made a name for himself in Chicago, he was invited to join the team of architects planning the World's Fair. But apart from his own Transportation Building, the architecture of the White City sickened him. He viewed it as a virus that in subsequent decades became a contagion, the vogue for "the bogus antique" that left banks looking like Greek temples and insurance companies like Florentine palaces.

The fair destroyed Sullivan's hopes for an architecture that was both uniquely modern and uniquely American. Inhaling deep drafts of Whitman, he dreamed of buildings that merged the pulsating power of Nature and Democracy. There was nothing hostile to commerce in his inclusive vision; his most famous buildings included the Carson Pirie Scott department store and the Stock Exchange in Chicago, as well as the Union Trust bank in St. Louis. Those structures embodied the new energies and attractions of corporate modernity, but Sullivan's approach to their design was highly idiosyncratic. His organic style of ornament was rooted in his attachment to an older rural America; it was less suggestive of power than of play—as in, for example, the terra-cotta griffins and porthole windows of the Union Trust building. In the years after the Chicago Fair, as his Chicago firm failed and he faded into comparative obscurity, Sullivan designed a number of small banks and commercial buildings—still standing and celebrated as "jewel boxes"— in towns throughout the Midwest. The locale was somehow appropriate. Sullivan had always been a pragmatic student of vernacular forms, whose functionalist creed owed more to American folk tradition than to the European avant-garde.

Sullivan's vernacular attachments energized his assault on the Classical and Renaissance revival, which in his view exuded pseudo-scholarship, evoked social hierarchy, and withdrew from the most vital currents of American life. "By the time the market had been saturated" with domed Pantheons and Doric columns, Sullivan wrote, "all sense of reality was gone." The cultural consequences were catastrophic. "Thus architecture died in the land of the free and the home of the brave,—in a land declaring its fervid democracy, its inventiveness, its resourcefulness, its unique daring, enterprise, and progress. Thus did the virus of a culture, snobbish and alien to the land, perform its work of disintegration; and thus ever works the pallid academic mind, denying the real, exalting the fictitious and false, incapable of adjusting itself to the flow of living things," he wrote. Sullivan's lament became a canonical text in the history of modernism, a seer's indictment of the "pallid academic mind" that insulated American architects from their time and place.

But the historical styles derided by Sullivan were more appropriate to their time and place, and more consistent with a revitalizing agenda, than he imagined. When the New York Stock Exchange moved to a brand-new Greek temple on Broad Street in 1903, its Corinthian columns supported a triangular pediment inscribed with the words "Business Integrity Protecting the Industries of Man" beneath an allegorical female figure (Integrity), whose open arms sheltered figures embodying Agriculture, Mining, Science, Industry, and Invention. Classical style provided legitimacy for Wall Street as it emerged from decades of disrepute into what the historian Steve Fraser calls its "imperial age" of power and respectability as the major source of capital for corporate expansion. When Metropolitan Life completed its Italian Renaissance tower in 1909, the building combined skyscraper technology with design details that alluded to civic ideals and familial tradition as well as aristocratic elegance. Here as elsewhere in early-twentieth-century America, corporate innovators clothed themselves in the garments of tradition.

The most appealing traditions were those of Old World elites with imperial aspirations. Corporation executives, university presidents, and other leaders of the patronage establishment found themselves attracted to

symbols that affirmed the new role of America among the powerful nations of the world. European references, far from embodying a flight from
American reality, reaffirmed its new contours—the decisive departure of
elite foreign policy-makers from all but the rhetorical vestiges of republican
tradition, the determination to create a place for the United States at the
trough of imperial spoils. The early twentieth century was no time for Sullivan's playful and idiosyncratic architecture of democracy. What was far
more appropriate, in retrospect, was what was actually built: an architecture
of empire.

The building of an imperial architecture involved a redefinition of neoclassical tradition, a subtle cultural shift that reflected the broader transition
from republic to empire. Since Jefferson's time, imitation Greek (and sometimes Roman) public buildings had embodied America's claim to classical
republican virtue. The chaste marble city of Washington, D.C., was itself a
monument to this sense of identification with ancient ideals. But as fortunes
accumulated during and after the Civil War, trends in neoclassical architecture began to shift from republican simplicity to imperial grandeur. Buildings became bigger and more ornate as banks and other corporate offices
sought legitimacy through style. Neoclassical associations could metaphori-
cally cleanse concentrated wealth of moral taint and at the same time assert
the legitimacy of America's imperial aspirations, its right to a place at the
table set by Europeans. The White City and the New York Stock Exchange
enshrined neoclassicism as a core feature of the architecture of empire.

Few Americans, even imperialists, would have openly referred to an
architecture of empire. Those who advocated imperial policies denied any
connection with European precedents, claiming instead that they were
exporting American democracy and morality. Those who inhabited imperial structures did not take allegorical friezes seriously or historical allu-
sions literally, or indeed pay much attention to them at all. And many less
affluent Americans remained faithful to republican tradition, deploying it
as a weapon in their continuing battle against plutocracy. Most Americans
would have been put off by the very notion of an architecture of empire. Yet
the phrase has value. It suggests how imperial influences were becoming
interwoven with everyday life, were creating a culture of empire.

The American empire would indeed be different from the older European model—but only in its form, not in its essence. Rather than acquiring
territory overtly, United States policy-makers sought access to foreign re-

sources, investment opportunities, and markets in less direct ways: installation of client regimes, intimidation of critics when client regimes failed, periodic military interventions, and occasionally prolonged occupations. What committed Americans to imperial policies, whether they were aware of it or not, was their dependence on empire for their prosperity, for their racial, social, and even moral identity as a people, and for the power that undergirded their dreams of personal and national regeneration.

To be sure, those dreams led toward domestic as well as foreign policy goals. Progressive reformers, led by Bryan and other persistent populists, sought regeneration by building a kingdom of God on Earth—a cooperative commonwealth to counter the rapacious force of monopoly capital. While they succeeded in laying the foundation of a welfare state, in the end they were shunted aside by men with more power, or swept up in the broad imperial enthusiasm for regenerating the world in America's image. Even Bryan, for all his distrust of military intervention, could not always resist imperialism when it came wrapped in idealism—as it did in U.S. policy toward Latin America and the Caribbean. In the end, despite populist suspicions of overseas adventure, one conclusion is inescapable: the American empire was not simply an imposition by old elites eager to preserve and extend their power. It was also a new way of life.

DURING THE EARLY 1900s, when Cuba still roiled in the aftermath of war and revolution, U.S. troops remained on the premises. According to the official justifications, they were there to promote stability—which meant only that capital could be safely invested in agriculture and other enterprises on the island. This narrow definition of stability lay at the core of the culture of empire. It allowed the U.S. government to pass up major territorial claims, to be satisfied with comparatively small and scattered parcels of land that could serve as bases to protect commercial penetration.

All the talk about maintaining stability was profoundly misleading. U.S. imperial policy was based on a search for economic opportunities that destabilized existing governments and promoted social disorder. Theodore Roosevelt himself was no conservative; he stirred up disorder at every turn. In Latin America especially, Roosevelt's policies worsened conditions that triggered upheaval. Driven by a myopic nationalism and tendentious reading of world history, Roosevelt "played a role in creating a revolutionary, war-wracked world, instead of creating a balance of power complex that maintained a healthy, gradually evolving international system," as the historian Walter LaFeber observes.

Roosevelt's actions in Panama typified his disruptive interventionism. For years, Mahan had been instructing him on the need for an isthmian canal. The question was whether to build it through Nicaragua, where there were few engineering problems, or through Panama, where the difficulties were greater and where a French effort led by Ferdinand de Lesseps had failed in the 1880s. The matter was decided by the lobbying efforts of the French businessman Philippe Bunau-Varilla and the Wall Street lawyer William Cromwell, who controlled the French company that had taken over de Lesseps's operation. In 1902, they persuaded Congress to empower the president to pay $40 million to their Panama Canal Company and purchase canal rights from Colombia, which claimed Panama as a province. Secretary of State Hay then negotiated the Hay-Herran Treaty, which authorized the United States to buy the rights from Colombia for $10 million plus $250,000 annually for a canal zone six miles wide.

When the skeptical Colombians rejected the treaty, Roosevelt raged: "I do not think that the Bogota lot of jackrabbits should be allowed permanently to bar one of the future highways of civilization." He contemplated seizing the land by force but was saved from that indignity by Cromwell and Bunau-Varilla. Keeping the state department informed of their plans, they fomented a Panamanian uprising against the Colombians in November 1903. An American warship happened to be anchored off the coast at the time, poised to protect U.S. interests. The uprising succeeded and Hay signed a new treaty with Bunau-Varilla (not the Panamanians) granting the U.S. sovereignty over a ten-mile strip of land slicing through the center of the isthmus.

Less than a year after the seizure of the Panama Canal Zone, Roosevelt faced another opportunity. In Santo Domingo (the Dominican Republic), a sugar elite backed by North American capital had been expanding its landholdings since the early 1890s. The spread of big plantations drove peasants off the land and created food shortages by replacing subsistence farming with cash-crop agriculture—the classic colonial pattern of social upheaval. German and French investors, alarmed by the spread of U.S. influence, began looking for their own opportunities on the island. Competition among foreign capitalists provoked revolutionary stirrings among the Dominicans. By early 1904 Roosevelt was determined to "do what a policeman has to

do in Santo Domingo" because "the attitude of the Santo Domingans has
become one of half-chaotic war towards us." Roosevelt's vague threats provoked a positive response. The chief North American sugar investors, the
San Domingo Improvement Company of New York, joined U.S. diplomats
and a compliant Dominican government to request the U.S. government to
run the country's customhouses. Roosevelt sent several ships to protect the
regime from its own citizens, who were outraged by their government's subservience to Yankee capital. He then tried to push a treaty through the Senate to ratify the customhouse deal. When the Senate rejected it, TR made his
own unconstitutional executive agreement with the Dominican government.
He stationed several ships offshore to keep the lid on any revolutionary outbreak and exclude foreigners. By 1907, the Senate bowed to Roosevelt's fait
accompli and gave the intervention its official approval.

In the Caribbean and Central America, the consequences of TR's policies were not peace and security but conflict and poverty. Backed by Washington, foreign investors and the small Dominican elite profited from the
burgeoning sugar trade, but the vast majority of the population remained
dirt-poor and landless, excluded from the export economy and increasingly
willing to risk resistance. Elsewhere in the region, the Roosevelt administration supported war and revolution whenever it seemed to be in U.S. elites'
interest. In particular, TR backed revolutionary movements, coalitions, and
nations that aimed to undermine the influence of José Santos Zelaya, the
dictator of Nicaragua, who envisioned a united Central America under his
control. Roosevelt was willing to make common cause with the Mexican
dictator Porfirio Díaz to contain Zelaya's power.

These policies were not about stability and still less about morality; they
were about sustaining the penetration of North American capital into new
fields of possibility. After William Howard Taft succeeded Roosevelt in
1909, the same pattern spread to Mexico, where the United States shifted
its stance in accordance with the needs of U.S. landowners in Mexico, sup-
porting first Díaz, then his opponent Francisco Madero, then *his* opponent Victoriano Huerta. It was, according to the German ambassador in
Washington, Count von Bernstorff, "the usual American policy of replacing
hostile regimes with pliable ones through revolution without taking official
responsibility for it."

In the Far East, where TR could not throw his weight around so easily, he could more persuasively impersonate a man on a civilizing mission.

That meant siding with the Japanese against the Russians. Russia's own imperial ambitions portended a clash with Japan in Manchuria or Korea. When Japan struck the czar's Pacific fleet in 1904, Roosevelt was elated. "The Japs will win out," he wrote to Hay. "The Japs have played our game because they have played the game of civilized mankind." Compared to the Russians, they had. Word of anti-Semitic pogroms and the Siberian exile of political dissidents reached the U.S., intensifying popular sentiment against the czar. On "Bloody Sunday," January 9, 1905, revolution broke out in St. Petersburg, distracting the Russian army from mobilizing a full counterattack on the Japanese, who could not have survived a war of attrition. Soon both sides were ready for peace, which Roosevelt mediated at Portsmouth, New Hampshire, in summer 1905. He won the Nobel Prize, but failed to get what he had hopefully anticipated from the Japanese—an open door to U.S. economic expansion in the Far East. TR's inability to acknowledge that Japan might have a legitimate claim on commercial preeminence in East Asia epitomized the imperial double standard that characterized U.S. foreign policy for much of the twentieth century.

TR's policies were primarily designed to protect American corporations' access to raw materials, investment opportunities, and sometimes markets. The timing was appropriate. In the wake of the merger wave of 1897–1903, Wall Street generated new pools of capital, while Washington provided new places to invest it. Speculative excitement seized many among the middle and upper classes who began buying stocks for the first time. Prosperity spread even among the working classes, leading Simon Nelson Patten to detect a seismic shift from an era of scarcity to an era of abundance. For him, a well-paid working population committed to ever-expanding consumption would create what he called *The New Basis of Civilization* (1907).

Patten understood that the mountains of newly available goods were in part the spoils of empire, but he dissolved imperial power relations in a rhetoric of technological determinism. The new abundance, he argued, depended not only on the conquest of weather but also on the annihilation of time and space—a fast, efficient distribution system that provided Americans with the most varied diet in the world, transforming what had once been luxuries into staples of even the working man's diet. "Rapid distribution of food carries civilization with it, and the prosperity that gives us a Panama canal with which to reach untouched tropic riches is a distinctive laborer's resource, ranking with refrigerated express and quick freight carriage." The specific moves that led to the seizure of the Canal Zone evaporated in the abstract "prosperity that gives us a Panama Canal," which in turn became as much a boon to the workingman as innovative transportation. Empire was everywhere, in Patten's formulation, and yet nowhere in sight.

What Patten implied (rather than stated overtly) was that imperialism underwrote expanding mass consumption, raising standards of living for ordinary folk. "Tropic riches" became cheap foods for the masses. The once-exotic banana was now sold from pushcarts for 6 cents a dozen, "a permanent addition to the laborer's fund of goods." The same was true of "sugar, which years ago was too expensive to be lavishly consumed by the well-to-do," but "now freely gives its heat to the workingman," as Patten wrote. "The demand that will follow the developing taste for it can be met by the vast quantities latent in Porto Rico and Cuba, and beyond them by the teeming lands of South America, and beyond them by the virgin tropics of another hemisphere." From this view, the relation between empire and consumption was reciprocal: if imperial policies helped stimulate consumer demand, consumer demand in turn promoted imperial expansion. A society committed to ever-higher levels of mass-produced abundance required empire to be a way of life.

Through the nineteenth century, American elites had depended on the westward advance of white settlement to diffuse class consciousness by creating a sense of abundant possibility, if not always actual abundance. But after 1900, as attention shifted from the settlers' empire to an overseas empire, advocates of commercial expansion envisioned a system of economic growth untethered to possession of territory. At home it depended on rising wages, rationalized credit, and consumer demand; abroad it depended on the entrepreneurial exploitation of opportunity. As early as the 1870s, American firms had begun establishing European subsidiaries, to lower freight and labor costs, circumvent tariff barriers, and take on European competitors on their home turf. The merger wave accelerated this process: between 1897 and 1914, U.S. overseas investments quadrupled from $634 million to $2.6 billion. During the years around the turn of the century, General Electric, Westinghouse, the National Cash Register Company, and the Singer Sewing Machine Company all set up plants abroad, to be closer to foreign markets. In 1900, Frank D. Lewis took his Waterman fountain pens to the Paris Exposition, where the ultra-large #20 won a gold medal. A year earlier, the

J. Walter Thompson advertising agency had set up a London office. In 1904 the company claimed that it would "annex the entire British domain to the advertising realm of the ambitious American manufacturer who sighs for more worlds to conquer."

The British were not amused. In 1902, the London journalist W. T. Stead published *The Americanization of the World; or, the Trend of the Twentieth Century*. He urged his countrymen to face the new reality of economic life. American products had already penetrated every area of British life. Quoting another journalist's account of *The American Invaders*, Stead described a typical Englishman beginning his day.

> In the domestic life we have got to this: The Average man rises in the morning from his New England sheets, he shaves with Williams' soap and a Yankee safety razor, pulls on his Boston boots over his socks from North Carolina, fastens his Connecticut braces, slips his Waltham or Waterbury watch in his pocket, and sits down to breakfast. There he congratulates his wife on how her Illinois straightfront corset sets off her Massachusetts blouse, and he tackles his breakfast, where he eats bread made from prairie flour (possibly doctored at the special establishments on the lakes), tinned oysters from Baltimore and a little Kansas City bacon, while his wife plays with a slice of Chicago ox-tongue. The children are given "Quaker" oats. At the same time he reads his morning paper printed by American machines, on American paper, with American ink, and possibly edited by a smart journalist from New York.

Unlike Latin America, Great Britain and Western Europe provided an affluent market rather than a source of raw materials. Stead's catalogue included agricultural as well as manufactured goods, suggesting that American farmers' post-1900 prosperity was also related to overseas economic expansion. At the same time, the Americanization of the world was cultural as well as economic. Stead's use of "Americanization" instead of "Americanisation" suggested that, even in matters of orthography, the American influence was spreading inexorably. As early as the 1880s, Buffalo Bill had toured the capitals of Europe, exciting audiences from Vatican City to Paris with his star-spangled simulation of Wild West adventure. But after the turn of the century, the ersatz cowboys had company. That "smart journalist from New York" embodied the looming pervasiveness of a wise-ass American style.

The Yanks were coming, accompanied by their things. The proliferation of American products abroad was reflected in the positive trade balances that reappeared every year and rooted in the productivity increases promoted by mechanized farming and assembly-line manufacturing. Productivity rose as stretch-outs and speedups continued—with or without a Taylorite rationale. Absent imperial expansion, overproduction would have been a problem. There had to be someplace for all those things to go.

Yet the American empire was about more than material interests. Imperial adventures and the rhetoric that justified them were fundamental to the maintenance of a manly national self-image, framed by a triumphalist creed of moral revitalization. Martial exploits abroad were heroic counterpoints to the corruptions of commerce, the banality of lives ruled by rational self-interest, the blandness of a society dedicated to little more than physical comfort. After 1900, imperial ambitions still possessed a redemptive thrust.

Roosevelt deployed the rhetoric of regeneration, winning wide popular approval for his tactics in Latin America. A master of public relations, Roosevelt sanctified his Panamanian strategy—a mix of crony capitalism and military intimidation—by sounding the moral chord of regenerative democracy. He claimed that Colombia had so "misgoverned and misruled" Panama that when the Colombian government ("the Bogota lot of jackrabbits") turned down the Hay-Herran treaty, "the people of Panama rose literally as one man." This was the sort of reassuring narrative that would justify many a foreign intervention in the future.

In 1904, he came up with a more capacious rationale for his work by announcing what became known as the "Roosevelt Corollary" to the Monroe Doctrine. The United States, he insisted, had no ambitions in the Western Hemisphere, and only wanted its nations to be "stable, orderly, and prosperous"—"If a nation shows that it knows how to act with reasonable efficiency and decency in social and political matters, if it keeps order and pays its obligations, it need fear no interference from the United States." But if it failed to meet this standard, U.S. intervention would be required. Far from extending the Monroe Doctrine, the Roosevelt Corollary subverted it. The original policy of 1823 had been meant to protect Latin American revolution from European intervention; TR's revision was designed to protect U.S. intervention from Latin American revolution.

The peroration that justified the corollary clothed the narrow interests of North American capital in universal values. "Chronic wrongdoing, or an impotence which results in a general loosening of the ties of civilized society, may in America, as elsewhere, ultimately require intervention by some civilized nation, and in the Western hemisphere the adherence of the United States to the Monroe Doctrine may force the United States, however reluctantly, in flagrant cases of such wrongdoing or impotence, to the exercise of an international police power." The statement was a classic text in the genre of regeneration through empire. U.S. "police power" would come to the aid of "civilized society," combating not only "chronic wrongdoing" but also social chaos and political "impotence." This was not old-style, corrupt European imperialism but a new, morally invigorating American version.

Roosevelt's phrase "however reluctantly" was a masterstroke that would shape foreign policy debate down to the present. Generations of politicians, historians, and journalists have embraced the preposterous assumption that imperialists like Roosevelt were somehow reluctant to exercise power. In a PBS documentary aired in the 1990s, for example, David McCullough praised TR for recognizing that "America, like it or not, would have to play a large part in the world." The mythic image of a peace-loving, gun-toting nation—slow to anger but deadly when it rises to the defense of righteousness—has sanitized American ambitions for decades. The actuality has been less ennobling: TR, like his ideological descendants, was salivating for opportunities to extend U.S. power overseas, in the name of "civilized society."

The coherence of the civilizing mission depended on racial and ethnic hierarchies. Doctrines of Anglo-Saxon superiority reshaped relationships with nonwhite others in various ways, depending on the (actual or imagined) threat they posed to existing structures of power. Aboriginal North Americans, having nearly "vanished," acquired a new nobility as objets d'art. "To perpetuate the Indians' picturesque physiognomy Uncle Sam is having made photographs and life-masks of as many braves as will submit to the camera and the modeler," the *Ladies' Home Journal* reported in 1907. "Washington is the mecca of all red men having grievances against the government" and "every aborigine having business with the 'Great White Father' puts up" at a hotel reserved for Indians, "where one of the first bits of news imparted to him is that Uncle Sam has a portrait gallery where Poor Lo can have his picture taken free." The consequences were reassuring, at

least to this writer: "After the Indian has become extinct, as such, his picturesque features and graceful form will thus be preserved as art."

Immigrants were more problematic. As they swarmed into cities in record numbers, hostility to them hardened. Restrictionist sentiment, which
began as a vague Anglo-Saxon prejudice, by the 1910s became part of a
comprehensive eugenic program. Henry James was not the only upper-class
observer who viewed "the inconceivable alien" as a different breed of humankind, unable to be reborn as an American. And for those less privileged
than James, economic anxieties intensified ethnocentric mistrust. To the labor economist John R. Commons, the sheer numbers of immigrants combined with their degraded habits and values to depress wages and widen
the gap between managers and workers. By undermining workers' purchasing power, immigration threatened to reinstate the very problem that the
American empire was designed to solve: overproduction. Anti-immigration
sentiments among the working class might have preserved a more radical
edge, had they been turned against employers who happily exploited immigrants. But instead those sentiments were turned against the immigrants
themselves. For Commons and other advocates of American labor, immigration restriction became another means of maintaining a prosperous, imperial way of life. Yet despite the rising tide of restrictionist sentiment, it
was at least possible for European immigrants to become "honorary Anglo-
Saxons" by embracing the culture of empire.

That option was not available to African-Americans, even the ones who
fought in Cuba and the Philippines. Of all ethnic or racial minorities, black
people stood in the most fraught relationship to the emerging American
empire. For white Americans in the early twentieth century, Jim Crow at
home complemented imperialism abroad. Both policies depended on the
same racial hierarchy. But the situation was by no means peculiarly American. No one saw more clearly that "the color line belts the world" than
W. E. B. DuBois, who observed in 1906 that "the tendency of the great nations of the day is territorial, political and economic expansion, but in every
case this has brought them in conflict with darker people. . . . The question
enters European imperial politics and floods our continents from Alaska to
Patagonia."

The flood even seeped into new forms of fun. Race and empire converged in the emergent culture of spectacle created by mass entertainment.
In part this involved the persistence of "coon songs" and Sambo stereotypes

in leisure-industry advertising, such as Ringling Brothers' promotional pamphlet *The Plantation Darkey at the Circus*. But the melding of race and empire was more apparent in the exhibit of imperial subjects themselves. The St. Louis Exposition of 1904 continued the practice begun with Dahomeans and Inuits at Chicago in 1893—exhibiting the dark-skinned Other as a focus of popular fascination. But in St. Louis, the Igorot people from the Philippines, who were on display, were more than curiosities. They were advertisements for imperial policy, evidence (as one observer saw it) for the triumph of "civilization" over "natural wilderness and . . . savage men."

Popular amusements did more than represent the racial ideology of empire; they also pioneered its characteristic cultural form, the imperial spectacle. As the British critic J. A. Hobson observed in 1902, "Jingoism is merely the lust of the spectator," and the spectacle of empire could be enjoyed in many genres. World fairs were among the more solemn and self-consciously educative, though even they contained carnival zones. Travel accounts could combine enlightenment with attempts at humor, as in Richard Harding Davis's account of Zanzibar as a "comic-opera capital" out of Gilbert and Sullivan. "You feel sure . . . that the chorus of boatmen who hail you will reappear immediately as the Sultan's bodyguard, that women bearing water-jars will come on in the next scene as slaves of the harem, and the national anthem will prove to be Sousa's Typical Tune of Zanzibar." On the whole it was "a most difficult city to take seriously," Davis concluded. The imperial gaze could establish the observer's superiority to the natives (at least in the observer's mind) through distanced derision, as Davis did, or sometimes simply through the kind of unashamed gaping that itself constituted a form of consumption and possession. Often the gapers concluded that behind the amusing surfaces of Africa or the Orient there was a desperate debasement that justified, indeed demanded imperial control. As TR reported from Africa, there were many "out of the way regions where the English flag stands for all that makes life worth living."

That sort of self-conscious superiority was not always so easy to maintain. Many Americans revealed a more complex view of the alleged barbarians whose ways of life were unveiled by imperial policies. They evoked contempt and pity but also exerted a magnetic attraction. After the turn of the century, in spite of efforts to simplify Victorian taste, a persistent appetite for the exotic kept Americans incorporating Orientalist motifs into their household furnishings. Imperial domesticity sanctioned sensuous display for comfortable Americans who were eager to escape inherited Protestant scruples. But for those who felt overcivilized and who yearned for regeneration through intense experience, acquisition of exotic goods was insufficient. They looked beyond the exotic toward the primitive. The physical and sensual vitality that marked peoples as backward proved profoundly appealing to people who had marked themselves as "overcivilized." A stream of imperial primitivism flowed through the culture of empire.

Imperial primitivism embodied the widespread suspicion that dark-skinned people might have characteristics worth knowing, enjoying, and even appropriating. By the early twentieth century, patent medicines had been making such claims for several decades—especially with respect to the secret tribal lore supposedly behind remedies for dyspepsia, neurasthenia, or impotence. After 1900, the imperial primitivism in advertising converged with a corporate rhetoric of rationality. In 1906, for example, the United Fruit Company evoked but also contained primitivist longings for revitalization in a pamphlet titled *A Short History of the Banana and a Few Recipes for Its Use*. The cover deployed a giant phallic banana as its centerpiece. A blond woman in flowing robes leans against the banana while she writes with a quill pen in a huge folio volume. Despite her vague erotic potential she is entrusted with the tools of literacy and supposed North American supremacy. On the other side of the banana stands a barefoot black woman. While the white woman smiles demurely, the black woman grins salaciously. She doesn't need to know how to write, the image implies; she has other powers. Inside, the introductory text mentions a revealing "fancy": "Until within the last 25 years the fruit of the so-called banana *tree* had been looked upon by people of northern climes with something akin to reverence and awe. The feeling arose, perhaps, from the almost universal fancy that this was the forbidden fruit of the garden of Eden. The specific name *M. paradisaca*, and the habitat of the fruit in tropical countries, helped foster this idea." After conjuring up mythic associations, the text explained them away by invoking the idiom of expertise. The Edenic aura, dismissed as the "fancy" of a more credulous generation, nevertheless was allowed to linger and add luster to rejuvenative fantasies. Even the humble banana, selling for 6 cents a dozen, could be part of the spectacle of empire.

In a culture more and more attuned to the importance of seeing and being seen, romantic primitivist quests could be staged as spectacular events. The Arctic explorer Robert Peary praised the "Esquimaux" for their toughness and resiliency and echoed TR in describing the U.S. failure to reach the North Pole as "a reproach to our civilization and our manhood." Disdaining the motorized airships used by his rival Frederick Cook, Peary stuck to dogs and heavy sledges but did deploy the good ship *Roosevelt*, an emblem of manliness as it thrust northward through the ice. The primitive could overlap with the theatrical.

Much of the theater was a matter of boys performing for girls, as the psychologist G. Stanley Hall recommended adolescents should do. But it was also a matter of boys imagining they were performing for girls by identifying with fictional heroes. The agenda of male revitalization continued to pervade popular literature. The novelist Jack London, among others, produced a series of Anglo-Saxon *Übermenschen*. The merger between savage vitality and Anglo-Saxon gentility was in the making for years, but found its fullest expression in Edgar Rice Burroughs's *Tarzan of the Apes* (1914), which detailed the exploits of a man as deft as a chimpanzee at swinging from tree to tree, who also happened to be an English lord.

Imperial spectacle promised feminine as well as masculine revitalization. Alongside the careful primitivism of Tarzan there was the soft Orientalism of Salome. The Biblical femme fatale had been a staple of 1890s exoticism in Europe; she starred in Oscar Wilde's play of 1894 and Gustav Klimt's paintings from about the same time, as well as a Strauss opera of 1905. Her European avatars embodied misogynist fears as well as a decadent fascination with the mingling of sex and violence. But in the United States she became a vehicle of female self-assertiveness as well as of male fears and fantasies. By 1908, a show-business newspaper announced that "the country is Salome mad." She appeared in various guises, from the over-the-top version of Eva Tanguay to the more refined (and black) one of Aida Overton Walker. But everywhere she embodied female sexuality and power. This combination was at the core of many female figures in the culture of empire—most memorably, perhaps, the striking Congo woman in Joseph Conrad's *Heart of Darkness*, who is the renegade Kurtz's dominatrix and queen.

Kurtz's queen personified the sexually charged ambivalence at the heart of the culture of empire. But this tangle of motives and longings rarely revealed itself directly. Much more common among the imperialists, as Hobson wrote, was a more acceptable kind of excitement—that of the spectator who ejaculates "over the perils, pains, and slaughter of fellow-men whom he does not know, but whose destruction he desires in a blind and artificially stimulated passion of hatred and revenge. In the Jingo all is concentrated on the hazard and blind fury of the fray." One cultural casualty of long-range war against a dark-skinned foe, Hobson thought, was that in the mind of the imperialist warrior, "respect for the personality of enemies whose courage he must admit and whom he comes to realize as fellow-beings" was destroyed. In this passage, Hobson sentimentalized combat and overlooked the recent development of total war, which had already gone far toward robbing enemies of their humanity. Yet he had a point: the remnants of an older chivalric code, of fair play among equals, disappeared amid the race wars of empire. Roosevelt never noticed. True to his patrician upbringing, he continued to take the moral high ground, abroad or at home. Where that stance served him best was at home. The aristocratic disdain for mere trade that sustained Roosevelt's militarism also animated his effort to contain the power of irresponsible wealth.

AFTER THE DEFEAT of Bryan, relieved investors poured huge sums into the New York Stock Exchange, financing an unprecedented surge in corporate mergers and enshrining Wall Street as the primary source of investment capital. Under the aegis of Morganization, speculative risk-taking—or at least the kind sponsored by the white-shoe firms—began to seem rational and respectable. Popular participation in the stock market doubled from four to eight million individual investors. This was hardly a mass movement but it did suggest that, despite occasional doubts about irresponsible speculation, investing was becoming domesticated among the white-collar classes.

Still, the vast majority of Americans remained suspicious of big money and its power. The new dominion of Wall Street underwrote the triumph of the trusts—the monopolistic corporations that came to dominate most industries. Within a few years after 1900, U.S. Steel, International Harvester, Quaker Oats, American Tobacco, Standard Oil, Diamond Match, Kodak cameras, Carnation milk, and DuPont gunpowder (to mention just a few) all became household names. These behemoths bumped about the economic landscape at will, dominating legislatures and local businesses alike, ignoring all the old laissez-faire pieties as they swallowed or squeezed out competitors. Rockefeller, Morgan, and other trust-builders aimed for domination, not competition. Left to their own devices, they transformed free markets into unfree monopolies.

Among the broader populace, they provoked anxiety and awe. After Morgan had financed the creation of the U.S. Steel corporation in 1902, the humorist Finley Peter Dunne captured some of the popular sense of Morgan's power. According to Dunne's fictional Irish saloonkeeper, Mr. Dooley, "Pierpont Morgan calls in wan of his office boys, the' president of a nationl bank, an' says he, 'James,' he says, 'take some change out iv the damper and r-run out an' buy Europe f'r me,' he says, 'I intend to re-organize it an' put it on a paying basis,' he says." Such apparently unlimited power provoked old republican fears. A broad swath of Americans—white-collar professionals as well as skilled workers, farmers, and small proprietors—felt their whole way of life threatened by new, unprecedented concentrations of economic power.

What made matters worse was that ordinary people seemed to have little legal recourse. Since its passage in 1890, the Sherman Antitrust Act had been construed narrowly by the Supreme Court as a prohibition of price-fixing and cartels but not of large-scale consolidations. In fact the courts had turned it into an antilabor weapon, declaring unions that interfered with interstate commerce to be combinations in restraint of trade. But then Roosevelt decided to revive the Sherman Act as an antitrust instrument. On February 19, 1902, Attorney General Philander Knox shook the financial markets by announcing that at the president's request the justice department would bring an antitrust suit to break up the Northern Securities Company, a huge holding company for three northwestern railroads whose capital was controlled by the best-known plutocrats in the country—not only the railroad men James J. Hill and E. H. Harriman but also Morgan and Rockefeller. Northern Securities epitomized bloated monopoly. Its capital stock of $400 million was about 30 percent pure water, and this overcapitalization meant that its organizers would need to overcharge the public in order to maintain their "unwarranted profit" (Knox's term) for themselves and their other shareholders. TR could not have chosen a target more freighted with symbolic significance.

By arguing that Northern Securities was a combination in restraint of trade, the Roosevelt administration challenged the Wall Street equation of white-shoe investors' interests with those of the entire country. TR came up with the novel idea (novel, at least, in the White House) that Wall Street and Washington represented different constituencies. He recognized that Morgan represented "the Wall Street point of view," from which the president of the United States appeared "a big rival operator, who either intended to ruin all his interests or could be induced to come to an agreement to ruin none." Roosevelt refused that role, insisting on his own paternalistic obligation to serve the public good, and correctly inferring that most Americans believed monopoly capital needed to be brought under some kind of government control.

Even the Supreme Court began to agree. In 1904, the court ruled that the Northern Securities Company was a combination in restraint of trade and would have to be dissolved. TR's own court appointee, Oliver Wendell Holmes Jr., dissented, arguing that mere bigness was not the same as badness and that the key question was the effect of the corporation on commerce. This would become the "rule of reason" that would guide later court decisions in antitrust cases. But for the moment the legal challenge to consolidation seemed straightforward. Emboldened by his reelection in 1904, in combination with the outcome of the Northern Securities case, Roosevelt brought antitrust suits against Standard Oil, American Tobacco, the DuPont corporation, and the New Haven Railroad. This was the legal history that built his reputation as a "trust-buster."

The label was never all that accurate. TR was too much the patrician to ally himself with populists—men who wore wool hats, overalls, or leather aprons, men whose hatred of monopoly was incandescent. Unlike them, he was not a victim but a beneficiary of big corporations. A man who lived on his investments, who indeed had never needed to earn a nickel in his life, Roosevelt could hardly be expected to identify with the "producing classes." Yet his economic and social distance from the plain folk also allowed him to cultivate a larger self. A patrician rentier capitalist, Roosevelt refused the life of "ignoble ease" he might have led, committing himself instead to a paternalistic sense of responsibility for the commonweal—as he, of course, defined it.

This was the ruling-class blend of narrowness and largeness that shaped TR's attitude toward trusts, mixing self-interested assumptions with more generous moods. Like many among the comfortable, Roosevelt held a vague, pop-evolutionary belief that historical developments benefiting himself and his class were not only benign but somehow natural and inevitable. That included the concentration of industry. We could no more reverse that trend than we could stop the spring floods on the Mississippi, he said—though we could "regulate and control them by levees." And this was where the

paternalist sense of public responsibility came in. From the outset, TR believed in regulating trusts, not busting them. But regulation was not on the
congressional agenda in 1902. (Not until 1906 did TR sign the Meat Inspection Act, the Pure Food and Drug Act, and the Hepburn Act—the last of
which gave the Interstate Commerce Commission the power to set railroad
rates and put interstate oil pipelines under its domain.) So in his first full
year in office, Roosevelt turned to antitrust as the only way to reassert public
authority against what he believed was "of all the forms of tyranny the least
attractive and the most vulgar . . . the tyranny of mere wealth, the tyranny of
a plutocracy." Suffused with the pride of old money, he refused to let Morgan, a fellow patrician, treat him as merely "a big rival operator."

In the end, though, Roosevelt and Morgan had more in common than
either at first acknowledged. Both moved in similar ruling-class circles,
and both inherited a sense that privilege bestowed responsibilities as well
as entitlements. In 1902, soon after he had brought suit against Northern
Securities, TR turned to Morgan to help end a coal strike that threatened
to cripple the industry. The anthracite miners in northeastern Pennsylvania
had walked out in May, demanding an eight-hour day, a 20 percent increase
in pay, and recognition of their union. The mine operators dug in and refused to arbitrate. One of them, George F. Baer, even claimed that he and
his colleagues had been granted their property rights by God himself. The
arrogance of the operators contrasted with labor's willingness to arbitrate.
Public sentiment turned against the mine owners. Even the Republican governor of Pennsylvania called for compulsory arbitration, and by September,
with cold weather on the way, the nation's fuel supply was threatened. Some
in the press proposed government ownership of the mines, to protect access
to a necessary resource. Roosevelt brought John Mitchell of the UMWA to
the White House to meet with Baer and the other operators. Negotiations
quickly collapsed when Baer and his friends huffed out. Roosevelt fumed
and began to make threatening noises about federal seizure of the mines,
even as he also sought out Morgan to put pressure on the operators to arbitrate. They submitted; the miners went back to work and awaited the decision of an expert commission, which recommended a 10 percent raise for
the miners, a 10 percent increase in coal prices for the operators, reduction
of hours to nine (in a few cases, eight), and nonrecognition of the UMWA.
This was Roosevelt's leading example of a "square deal" between capital
and labor, when he coined the phrase in the 1904 presidential campaign.

It was the sort of square deal that Morgan could tolerate. Indeed, he backed TR in 1904 and remained a major Republican contributor. Roosevelt had kept lines of communication open to Morgan even at the height of the Northern Securities case, when he encouraged Morgan to organize a trust to dominate the shipping industry. This, presumably, was to be a "good" trust rather than a "bad" trust—an elusive distinction TR began to make during his second term. The rapprochement between Roosevelt and Morgan was wary but real. It was rooted in their common ethos of paternalism. Both men were involved, in varying ways, in what the historian Christopher Lasch once called "the moral and intellectual rehabilitation of the ruling class." Both helped to transform a plutocracy into a socially conscious imperial elite.

Morgan's key role in this process was to create a new tone on Wall Street, a new dignity. While good times lasted, that was not too hard to do. But by the late summer of 1907, the U.S. banking system faced a liquidity crisis. Bankers blamed Roosevelt's antitrust and regulatory policies for undermining business confidence; Roosevelt blamed "malefactors of great wealth" who wanted to discredit him. In fact, as Morgan understood, the main problem lay in the money supply, or lack of it. Foreign banks had been failing and credit had been tightening worldwide. The stock market had been falling for months; on October 22 it tumbled sharply as word spread that the Knickerbocker Trust Company had closed its doors while a crowd of depositors clamored to get in. Worried brokers serviced a panicky stock sell-off. Then the big shots stepped in. Rockefeller announced he would give half his securities to stabilize the nation's credit—"and I have cords of them, gentlemen," he told reporters, "cords of them." He put up $10 million. Morgan convened a series of meetings with bankers, whom he persuaded to lend nearly $50 million to failing banks and brokerage firms. Treasury Secretary George Cortelyou pledged a $25 million government loan, too, but this was a sideshow compared to the dramatic role played by Morgan. As the credit markets slowly emerged from the crisis, pedestrians on Fifth Avenue cheered Morgan while he drove downtown to his office. "There goes the Old Man!" they shouted. "There goes the Big Chief!" Roosevelt, who had been on the sidelines, sent Cortelyou a public letter congratulating him as well as "those conservative and substantial business men who in this crisis have acted with such wisdom and public spirit." And in a further bid to reassure investors, Roosevelt privately informed the Morgan interests that he would allow U.S. Steel to acquire the Tennessee Coal and Iron Company, withdrawing any threat of antitrust action. Despite tensions, Morgan and Roosevelt pulled together to serve what they deemed the public good.

The panic of 1907 mostly affected people who had something to lose, like the young couple who told *Ladies' Home Journal* readers how they managed to survive a drop in income "From $3500 a Year to $1200." More commonly, newspaper commentators focused on the supposed sufferings of the rich. Dunne's Mr. Dooley countered sympathy for the well-heeled by creating the character of Mr. Plumkins, president of the Eighth Incredible Trust. He had tried to save the bank, Plumkins said. "I surrendered me inthrest in the Gum Dhrop Thrust, me participation in underwritin' th' syndicate f'r th' mannyfacthern iv bath-tubs f'r canary-burrds, me option on th' railroad in th' moon, me bonds on the Consolydated Noodle an' Macaroni Comp'ny, me inthrest in th' Sahara Improvement Comp'ny, me contrl iv th' equities in Fountainblow-on-th'-Mud, a beautiful home f'r a few in th' Okyfinokee swamp, within five minyits walk iv an alligator lair." But still "F'r hours our senseless depositors surged against our window. I niver before knew there were so many bank officers among our depositors." He planned to leave "th' ongrateful city" and seek seclusion on "a little farm at Newport." For Dunne as for other critics, the bankers brought the crisis on themselves, through their irresponsible use of other people's money. From country clubs to grange halls, Americans of varying social backgrounds drew a common lesson from the panic: the country's money supply was too important to be dependent on a handful of private individuals, let alone one man. The Populists had argued this point in the 1890s, but now the bankers and brokers were on board too. Nearly everyone agreed that there had to be some government agency involved in managing monetary policy. The question was: whose interest would it serve? This was the debate that would lead to the fashioning of the Federal Reserve Board, itself a compromise between the interests of the investing classes and those of the rest of the population. Meanwhile, Morgan had saved the nation, in the opinion of the financial papers, by saving Wall Street.

The episode underscored the key role played by Wall Street investment banks in the transition from family to finance capitalism, and from hundreds of small competing firms to handfuls of corporations. At the same time, Morgan's intervention helped redefine the old republican vision of the public good in corporate and technocratic terms. A new ideal of neutral expertise began to displace older notions of civic virtue, especially among the educated professionals who worked in corporations, government agencies, and universities—including the managerial thinkers who constituted one wing of Progressive reform.

The "incorporation of America," as Alan Trachtenberg has called it, necessitated a broad reorientation of ruling-class values. Idioms of self-justification shifted from moralism to meritocracy. Advocates of expertise endowed universities with new prestige in the business world, creating institutions and academic disciplines designed to train expert managers. The Harvard Business School led the way, opening its doors in 1907. In many ways it was a fulfillment of Charles William Eliot's vision for the university. Eliot had become president of Harvard in 1869 and spent forty years transforming a provincial college into a national university. A utilitarian modernizer, Eliot disdained literary aesthetes and celebrated a masculine ethos of practicality. His curricular reforms were meant to assure the triumph of the fittest. In Eliot's view, the historian Kim Townsend writes, "the young men who could wean themselves from a predigested, prescribed curriculum and face the challenge of the elective system were America's elect." In 1902, Eliot described "American democracy" as "the democracy [that] preserves and uses sound old families" but "also utilizes strong blood from foreign sources." In seeking ethnic diversity, he implied, established elites would revitalize themselves, defining a new standard of excellence while maintaining their old hold on power and creating a meritocratic ruling class. That is what Eliot, Roosevelt, and other privileged men told each other at the turn of the century. Their desires for class renewal did more than transform higher education; they also spawned a host of preparatory schools, from Groton to Andover and Lawrenceville, designed to discipline gilded youth into an apprentice meritocracy. Older emphases on character melded with a newer stress on expertise. Established elites were determined to show that they deserved to run the emerging managerial society.

Still, merit was not always self-evident. As they came into public disfavor, business leaders began to seek out ways to reshape their presentation of self. After the Roosevelt administration brought suit against Standard Oil, Rockefeller hired Joseph Clarke of the *New York Herald* to generate favorable publicity and locate sympathetic interviewers. One was William Hoster of the *New York American*, who was intrigued by Rockefeller's simple tastes and pleasures, his fascination with the common folk and his distrust of the highfalutin. This pseudo-populist persona would become a favorite of rich men in the later twentieth century. Rockefeller showed exceptional shrewdness in adapting it to his own uses. Eventually he hired Ivy Lee, who, along with Edward Bernays, was one of the earliest masters of the art of public relations, and who convinced many newsmen (according to the humorist Robert Benchley) that "the present capitalist system is really a branch of the Quaker Church, carrying on the work begun by St. Francis of Assisi." With extraordinary prescience, Benchley's mordant observation anticipated what would become a major problem in political discourse—the gullibility of journalists in the presence of skilled public relations.

Nevertheless, Rockefeller had more to offer than PR. By the early twentieth century he had retired from business and become a full-time philanthropist. Like Andrew Carnegie, Rockefeller endowed major universities and other cultural institutions. He also made specialties of backing medical research and Negro education in the South. It soon became impossible to deny the importance of his generosity. Rockefeller embraced a doctrine of stewardship, which meant that God had entrusted him with his money for disbursal in accordance with the divine will; while Carnegie preached a secular "gospel of wealth," which insisted that it was a disgrace for a man to die rich and that only great munificence could justify great wealth.

Rockefeller and Carnegie were the most conspicuous among the philanthropists, but they were hardly alone. By the early twentieth century, urban ruling elites had begun to display a newfound civic consciousness. In New York City they were especially visible, sustaining such new cultural institutions as the American Museum of Natural History and the Metropolitan Museum of Art. Morgan was active in both; he and TR both sat on the board of the Museum of Natural History. These were places where elites could affirm their legitimacy and their leadership. Yet a perceptive observer could quickly grasp what gave life to the common enterprise. "There was money in the air, ever so much money," Henry James wrote after a visit to the Metropolitan Museum in 1905, "and the money was to be for all the most exquisite things—for *all* the most exquisite except creation, which was to be off the scene altogether, for art, selection, criticism, for knowledge, piety, taste." As James understood, this was a culture of acquisition and display, not creation. Canonical objets d'art, certified by such experts as Morgan's friend and advisor Bernard Berenson, would become sacred emblems of social authority. To be sure, Morgan and other manic collectors could let the whole thing get out of hand: Berenson, astonished by the accumulation of stuff in Morgan's Manhattan home, described it as a "pawnbroker's shop for Croesuses." Still, the new cult of expertise endowed hierarchies of taste with professional legitimation.

Women could assist in this process, though at first they ceded leadership to men. But after 1900 they pushed to the front of the museum world, led by Isabella Stewart Gardner and later Gertrude Whitney and Abigail Aldrich Rockefeller (John Sr.'s daughter-in-law). Such women as Whitney, Rockefeller, and the sugar heiress Louisine Havemeyer played an increasingly critical role in accommodating the American ruling class to cultural modernity, assembling huge collections of avant-garde paintings and arranging for them to be housed in major museums. Within a few decades, the Whitney Museum and the Museum of Modern Art would reinforce a growing alliance between modern art and established privilege. At the same time, upper-class women also managed the many private spectacles that more and more took place in public places—weddings and coming-out parties that received reverential treatment on the "society" pages of newspapers, coverage that ratified the social authority of the participants.

In the early twentieth century, these developments were just getting under way. The process of ruling-class revitalization was proceeding by fits and starts. One of the major obstacles to it was the challenge posed by the persistence of populism in new institutional and ideological forms. The Populist Party may have been dead, and Tom Watson reduced to a sodden shadow of his former self, but the populist principle survived: man over money. A stubborn distrust of concentrated wealth played havoc with the moral pretensions of the rich.

Antimonopoly sentiments spread from the countryside to the cities and suburbs, creating new bonds between agrarian radicals and white-collar professionals. What began as a movement of angry Populists in the 1890s became, within two decades, a broad consensus of Progressives demanding social and moral regeneration. But the Progressives' shared rhetoric tended to conceal important differences among them, especially between those who distrusted the cult of expertise and those who began to accept it. The first group demanded statutory regulation of corporations, laws forbidding bad business behavior; the second group was willing to leave the regulation up to the discretion of bureaucratic administrators. While there were pragmatic reasons for picking one version of regulation over another (the courts were pro-business and reformers might well want to circumvent them), in fact the division over regulatory strategies reflected broader divisions in worldview—between local and cosmopolitan, egalitarian and paternalist perspectives. Presidents Roosevelt and Wilson belonged in the cosmopolitan camp; both deployed the rhetoric of regeneration primarily for foreign rather than domestic policy; both distrusted rabble-rousers. Presidential leadership moderated egalitarian demands from the agrarian periphery; so did the egalitarians' need for congressional support. In the crucible of the legislative process, as deals were made and coalitions built, populist principles were diluted and sometimes disappeared altogether. Policies animated by egalitarian sentiment often made crucial compromises with corporate hierarchy. Yet the overall result was undoubtedly a service to the commonweal, a vast advance beyond the galloping conscienceless capitalism of the Gilded Age. The Progressives, for all their compromises and confusions, created the foundation for an American version of the welfare state. That was their most humane accomplishment.

THE ELECTION OF 1896 killed Populism and left farmers demoralized. But cotton prices finally bottomed out, and in 1902 began an upturn. In Rains County, Texas, Newt Gresham felt a quickening of hope and decided it was time to get his neighbors organized again. Gresham was a former Alliance man and Populist who became a Bryan Democrat. He persuaded five Democrats, one Socialist, one independent, and three Populists to show up at his house, and they became the ten charter members of the Farmers' Union, which was dedicated to helping farmers get better prices for their crops, and breaking down their isolation through fraternal and cooperative activities. Rains was a dirt-poor county dominated by tenant farmers; when word of the new organization spread among them, they flooded the local post office at Point, Texas, with inquiries. The Farmers' Union grew with astonishing speed, especially in the Southeast and Southwest. Like the Farmers' Alliance it was racially segregated, but black farmers formed their own parallel organization. Within five years, the Farmers' Union claimed a membership of nearly a million—comparable to the Knights of Labor at its height in the mid-1880s.

Like the Knights, the Farmers' Union cast a wide net, aiming to represent a capacious version of the "producing classes." Besides farmers, its members included schoolteachers, mechanics, ministers, and doctors, and excluded bankers, merchants, lawyers, and speculators. Its ideology melded producerist distrust of money manipulators with republican suspicion of concentrated power and egalitarian demands for direct elections and a democratically managed currency. The Farmers' Union advocated enforcement of antitrust laws, regulation of railroads, public control of banking and currency, government-backed credit for farmers, lower tariffs, aid for agricultural and industrial education, popular election of senators as well as the president (by abolishing the electoral college) and the Supreme Court, and legal prohibition of commodity speculation. Apart from the last few proposals, nearly all of these became part of the Progressive agenda.

The domination of the Farmers' Union by Southerners meant that most of its membership would look to be represented by the lily-white Democratic Party that had recently purged itself of Populists. But part of the white supremacist crusade to purify politics was the effort to wrest control of nominations from party bosses through the institution of the direct primary, which was introduced in the South Carolina state constitution of 1896. Throughout the old Confederacy, where Democrats had secured one-party rule, the primary broke the hold of Bourbon elites and allowed poor white men access to the vote—at least anywhere that local officials might wink at the literacy and other requirements written into the new state constitutions. The Southern brand of populism for whites only led to the popularity of figures like Senator James K. Vardaman of Mississippi, a race-baiting demagogue who advocated regulating the railroads and abolishing the convict-lease system, as well as much of the rest of what became the Progressive program.

Yet Vardaman and his ilk were by no means the whole story. Populist sentiments survived in many forms, in various sections of the rural periphery. The trick for agrarian rebels was broadening their appeal beyond the countryside, creating the kind of rural-urban, cross-class coalition that could pose an effective challenge to monopoly capitalism. One of the leaders in that effort was Eugene Debs, who headed the Socialist Party throughout the early twentieth century. In the years before World War I, Socialism was an important part of American public discourse, a complement and a goad to reformist impulses. What was most striking about this peculiarly American Socialism was that it was always stronger in the heartland than in the industrial Northeast. The leading Socialist newspaper, the *Appeal to Reason*, was published in Girard, Kansas, and circulated among thousands of farmers and small-town folk throughout the Midwest and mid-South. And Socialists maintained their greatest electoral strength in such states as Oklahoma, Arkansas, and Texas, as well as Wisconsin and Minnesota. Nothing more palpably embodied the homegrown character of American Socialism than Debs's own life.

Debs was the son of Alsatian immigrants in Terre Haute, Indiana. His parents' grocery store began to prosper soon after the boy was born in 1855. Local public schools immersed him in the pieties of the civil religion, heated by war fervor. Outwardly deferential to conventional authority, Eugene was restless. At fourteen he quit school, with no skills, and through a family friend (and fellow Alsatian) secured a job as a locomotive paint-scraper for the Vandalia Railroad. Fired by dreams of upward mobility, young Debs took business courses at night and imagined he might make the jump from labor to management. His plans were upset by the Panic of 1873 and subsequent business downturn, which led to his layoff and forced him to go "on the tramp," homesick and frightened, to East St. Louis. Eventually he returned home and landed on his feet, securing a job as an accounting clerk for Hulman's wholesale grocery in Terre Haute.

Still emotionally attached to railroad work, he joined the Terre Haute lodge of the Brotherhood of Locomotive Firemen. It was less a union than a fraternal society. The brotherhood's motto was "Benevolence, Sobriety and Industry," and the young men who signed on identified strongly with their employers' success. It was, they believed, the platform for their own rise in the world. Memories of this egalitarian harmony led Debs later to recall Terre Haute as "that sacred little spot" of small-town democracy. Yet already class lines were hardening, beginning at the top. The business elite had become more self-conscious about their own authority and perquisites, had taken to calling themselves "the best people." The railroad strike of 1877 exposed the developing class fissures in Terre Haute. When workers occupied the local depot to protest the wage cuts inaugurated by the Pennsylvania Railroad, the president of the Vandalia Railroad requested federal troops "to restore order." The strike disbanded peacefully, but the limits of social harmony had been revealed. Strikers believed they had been defending the local community against the disruptive forces of outside capital (the Pennsylvania), but they soon learned that the local elite could be as ruthless as any outsiders.

Radicalized by the strike, Debs ran as a Democrat for city clerk in 1879, and won by building a cross-class alliance based on common concerns about autocratic and corrupt Republican rule. This was a portent. By the mid-1880s, Debs had become a rising star in regional Democratic Party politics and had begun to demand justice for "the producing classes." The laboring people of America, he announced, "create all the wealth" and "make all the money" for the rest of society. The inference was clear: "simple justice demands that the laws of the land . . . shall not operate to their detriment." Like other critics of laissez-faire and "natural law" economics, Debs now realized that poverty was not a natural result of population outstripping food supply (as the British economist Thomas Malthus had argued) but rather the consequence of unfair distribution.

And the root of that unfairness, thought Debs, was monopoly power. In 1886, the Pennsylvania Railroad opened its own relief agency for workers, intending to undercut union organizers by providing an alternative. When the workers refused it, Debs applauded them in the producerist language of manliness: "It is only in 'the direction of one's own affairs without interference' that absolute independence can be secured, and it is this independence and this *absolute right* that the employees of the Pennsylvania railroad demanded, nothing more; and by demonstrating that they were manly men, not 'squaw men,' and the fact should elevate them in the estimation of their employers." Condemning the Haymarket anarchists for their lack of faith in American democracy, he endorsed the Knights of Labor, because the organization "is modern—and it is American. It sounded a key-note. It recognized certain great fundamental facts—the independence and sovereignty of the American citizen." Debs remained committed to whatever policy program would restore independence to the American worker. His Socialism would always contain a strain of labor republicanism.

It would also contain a strain of Christianity. After the disastrous railroad strike of 1894, when he had been jailed for organizing the American Railway Union's boycott of roads using Pullman equipment, Debs reflected: "The crime of the American Railway Union was the practical exhibition of sympathy for the Pullman employees. Humanity and Christianity, undebauched and unperverted, are forever pleading for sympathy for the poor and oppressed." After the Pullman debacle, he renounced strikes as a tactic, substituting a naïve faith in the ballot box. He also gravitated decisively toward Socialism.

This was not a sharp break with either Christianity or American democracy. Debs was fond of quoting the Christian Socialist Rev. George

Herron, who asserted that "Cain was the author of the competitive theory" and "the cross of Jesus is its eternal denial." Inspired by Jefferson, Lincoln, and Jesus rather than orthodox Marxian texts, Debs envisioned a cooperative commonwealth rather than a dictatorship of the proletariat. During the late 1890s, he became involved with the Social Democracy Party, which was headed by Victor Berger, who later became a socialist congressman from Milwaukee. Berger was cautious and bureaucratic and too devoted, in Debs's view, to immediate aims without regard for larger ideals. In 1901, Debs helped found the Socialist Party of America with a view toward promoting those ideals. With Julius Wayland, the editor of the *Appeal to Reason*, Debs believed that "the revolutionary red, white, and blue of our forefathers is good enough" to symbolize Socialism. No foreign coloration was necessary. When Debs ran as the Socialist candidate for president in 1904, his party platform declared that "Socialism makes its appeal to the American people as the idea of liberty and self-government, in which the nation was born." There was no conflict, in Debs's view, between Socialism and American individualism; indeed, collective ownership of the means of production could lead to a rebirth of a more genuine, a more democratic commitment to liberty. Corporate organization provided the platform for the collective ownership of the means of production, which would return the instruments of wealth-creation to the people who actually created it. This was what Herron meant when he called Socialism "the real and ransomed individualism." For him and Debs and their followers, Socialism was as American as cherry pie.

When the Panic of 1907 provoked an economic downturn, Debs stood poised to take advantage of workers' discontent in the election of 1908. But the Socialist Party realized only slight gains over the 1904 election. It was true that the transient unemployed were not a strong electoral base; many tramps could not fulfill the stringent residency requirements imposed by local party officials. But Debs knew the problems ran deeper. The people were not ready for Socialism, he kept saying. That included the unions and the Democratic Party. Indeed in 1908, the leading union man in America, Samuel Gompers, had only just come around to endorsing the candidate he had deliberately overlooked in 1896: William Jennings Bryan.

As he deflected the Populist Party challenge in 1896, Bryan also absorbed populist principle. Smarting from his defeat by big money, he became a true champion of the plain people—but mainly the white plain people. Like nearly every white politician of his time (except Debs), Bryan was blinkered by race. Though he was no race-baiter, he accepted white supremacy to win the South, and Chinese exclusion to win labor. These expedient moves reinforced his enormous power within the party; in three of the four elections between 1900 and 1912, he exercised de facto control over the Democratic presidential nomination. He personified the populism of the agrarian periphery. His electoral defeats did not prevent him from moving the party decisively to the left on policy, making it less hospitable to Wall Street, and cultivating the common sentiments of farmers, small-business people, and industrial workers. (Gompers's endorsement in 1908 was the culmination of a decade-long courtship.) Bryan, in short, played a pivotal role in negotiating the transition from Populism to Progressivism.

Part of the reason was his own indefatigable energy. Though he had been driven from the field twice by McKinley, Bryan never called retreat. Throughout the first two decades of the new century, he maintained a killing pace of stump speaking on the Chautauqua lecture circuit. Under big tents pitched in places like Chillicothe, Ohio, and Davenport, Iowa, he sweated, he waved his arms, he mesmerized audiences for hours with his booming, mellifluous, yet oddly conversational voice, his plainspoken anecdotes and biblical cadences.

After his defeat in 1900, Bryan created *The Commoner* as a vehicle for developing his vision of social democracy, which gradually merged with the widening Progressive mainstream. What made the merger work was a common current of Social Gospel Protestantism. Reverent readers applauded *The Commoner*'s effort to apply "the teachings of Jesus to everyday life and public affairs." Neither Bryan nor his audiences bothered with theological niceties. They displayed a typical American trait, as William James characterized it, disbelieving "facts and theories for which we have no use." Bryan had no use for the doctrines of original sin or hell; with respect to humanity's ultimate fate he was a liberal optimist. Between runs for the presidency, his ceaseless speechmaking was a way of "doing God's work by defending the interests of suffering humanity." So his biographer Michael Kazin observes, and so Bryan and his audiences believed.

Doing God's work was not merely a matter of obligatory plodding. Bryan went about it with unending gusto well into his sixties, his paunch hanging over his belt, his pants bagging at the knees, his morning-coat tails flapping in the prairie wind. What gave a special energy to his Social Gospel was its emotional core—a yearning for regeneration at once personal and

social, moral and spiritual. That common chord of longing resonated between Bryan and his audiences, recalling the excitement generated by the
Populists' regenerative vision of the 1890s.

There were serious limitations on the Social Gospel program. The most
obvious was race: African-Americans were largely ignored by the reformers,
some of whom were white supremacists who viewed racial segregation as
another form of social purification. More subtle were the cultural anxieties
aroused by the Social Gospel. Not everyone was ready to be regenerated
in quite the same way. The immigrant working class remained somewhat
suspicious of this Protestant crusade, especially when the crusaders closed
their saloons and poured their beer down storm drains. There was also
good reason to suspect that the self-transformative promise of Prohibition
was a convenient cover for employers' drive to intensify labor discipline.
Rockefeller and his son were only the most prominent of Prohibition's big
business supporters.

For all the limitations of the Social Gospel, though, Bryan's mobilization
of it was a significant achievement. He caught the Populist fire and carried
it into the Democratic Party, joining Jefferson and Jesus. Like his idol Tol-
stoy, Bryan was convinced that the spirit of Jesus could regenerate an entire
society, not only saving individual souls but also suffusing social relations
with democratic fellow-feeling. Social Christianity would be the cement that
held the cooperative commonwealth together. In the meantime, it would
perform the humbler task of holding the Progressive coalition together.

By the time Bryan and his wife, Mary, returned from a world tour in
1906, the middle-class public had caught Progressive fever, fed by such
investigative journalists as Ida Tarbell, who revealed the corruption of entire legislatures by Standard Oil, and David Graham Phillips, who exposed
what his book called *The Treason of the Senate* in the service of big business. These writers played a crucial role in refashioning public morality for a
managerial age; they clarified personal moral responsibility, indeed kept the
very idea of it alive, amid the mystifyingly complex interdependence of the
modern corporation—which had been constituted an "artificial person,"
with all a person's civil rights, by the Supreme Court decisions of the Gilded
Age. "This giant race of artificial persons," the sociologist Edward A. Ross
observed in 1907, was engaged in "sinning by syndicate"—exploiting workers, poisoning consumers, fleecing investors—but the apparent imperson-
ality of their organizations diffused responsibility for decision-making and

made the actual sinners hard to pin down. Rockefeller and Carnegie were notoriously adept at distancing themselves from subordinates' execution of their orders. Ross urged reformers to "follow the maxim, 'Blame not the tool, but the hand that moves the tool'" in assessing responsibility. The trick was to find the "men who give orders but do not take them." In a corporation they were the directors, who enjoyed economic freedom. The directors' suite, wrote Ross, "is the moral laboratory where the lust of an additional quarter of a per cent of a dividend, on the part of men already comfortable in goods, is mysteriously transmuted into deeds of wrong and lawlessness by remote, obscure employees in terror of losing their livelihood." The appropriate strategy was clear, Ross thought: *"The anonymity of the corporation can be met only by fixing on directors the responsibility of corporate sinning."*

While Roosevelt criticized the investigative journalists as "muckrakers" who could only see the sordid side of American life, Bryan saw a political opportunity in the atmosphere of moral outrage. He bundled an attractive package of Progressive reforms, sidled up to urban labor, and won the 1908 nomination. But in that Progressive atmosphere, where even the Republican Roosevelt was being hailed as a trust-buster, Bryan and the Democrats failed to formulate a compelling alternative perspective. His party's platform thundered against money, advocating vigorous enforcement of the Sherman Act and a federal mandate that national banks guarantee deposits, but otherwise it differed little from the Republicans'.

Bryan's opponent William Howard Taft, speaking for the embryonic regulatory state that began to emerge under Roosevelt, identified the source of the Democrats' timidity as their small-government tradition. He claimed that the Democrats wanted "to reduce the government to a mere town meeting, by whom the laws should be enforced against the rich, but should be weakened against the poor." Taft put his finger on the fundamental conflict in the Populist tradition, between distrust of government as an agent of concentrated wealth and desire to use it as an agent of the dispossessed. Bryan's successor Wilson would address that conflict directly, but in 1908, Taft won easily. Temporary heir apparent to the popular Roosevelt, Taft turned out to be a standpatter in the White House—a president who would be brought down by the spreading, bipartisan Progressive insurgency.

Amid the ruling-class effort to consolidate power, political controversy boiled. Old Populist outrage against irresponsible wealth resurfaced in the intensifying critique of the "money trust." Even while participation in the market broadened after 1900, the gap widened between ordinary share-holders and the Wall Street insiders who manipulated securities for gain. The "money trust" was the web of interlocking directorates and gentlemen's agreements that inflated security prices and protected insider profit-taking. It epitomized everything the producing classes disdained and feared: privi-leged parasites secretly fashioning fictitious values out of thin air, diverting money from necessary capital improvements to satisfy private greed. For all the talk of their titanic accomplishments, monopoly capitalists themselves were often little more than beneficiaries of the money trust. As James J. Hill admitted, a trust was not meant to manufacture any particular commodity except "sheaves of printed securities which represent nothing more than good will and prospective profits to promoters." On Wall Street, the myste-rious power of money prevailed over more palpable considerations, such as the quality of the product manufactured—let alone the public good.

Muckrakers and reformist critics encouraged popular suspicions of money manipulators. In 1904, *Everybody's Magazine* serialized Thomas Lawson's "Frenzied Finance," an exposé of Wall Street by a former insider determined to rip away the robes of respectability that the Morganizers had fashioned for themselves. The legal scholar Louis Brandeis developed a more systematic critique in more measured tones in *Other People's Money* (1906). The developing assault on finance capital represented a maturing—perhaps an embourgeoisement—of Populist tradition. No wonder Pro-gressive reform flourished among rural Democrats from the South and the Midwest.

But it also flourished among insurgent Republicans, mostly from the Midwest—men like Senators Robert M. LaFollette of Wisconsin and George Norris of Nebraska. They shared the antimonopoly, anticorruption, and anti-imperial convictions of the populist Democrats. Unable to stom-ach the party of the old Confederacy, they were equally repelled by their own party's rapprochement with big business. Hamlet-like, they hesitated. In 1908, they had let Theodore Roosevelt persuade them that the Repub-lican Party could still be the home for Progressive reform—but they were impatient with Taft, and they were getting restless.

So were the representatives of organized labor, and the industrial work-ing class they were trying to represent. Employers' continuing efforts to increase productivity and lower labor costs meant more speedups, stretch-outs, and wage cuts. Workers walked out, demanded fair wages and an

eight-hour day, occasionally won and usually lost. Debs's homegrown Socialism won more respectful attention as class structure hardened in such
cities as Reading, Pennsylvania, and Schenectady, New York (both of which
elected Socialist mayors), as it had in Terre Haute. In contrast to the careful craft orientation of the AFL, Debs invoked the spirit of the Knights of
Labor by insisting that "industrial unionism is the structural work of the
co-operative commonwealth, the working-class republic." Still, people who
warmed to that traditional rhetoric could also make common cause with
Bryan's program. That indeed was what the Democrats hoped as they enlisted urban workers into their ranks.

Discontent with monopoly capitalism took many forms, and Progressive reform proved the most capacious way of translating a vague sense of
injustice into specific policy proposals. The Progressive movement sheltered uneasy alliances in a big tent. But most Progressives spoke a common
populist idiom that animated their initial impulses toward policy-making.
Egalitarian ideas pervaded Progressive discourse, energizing the initiative,
the referendum, the recall, and other electoral reforms meant to promote
direct democracy; they also sustained the drive for women's suffrage, the
most successful movement to enlarge the electorate in U.S. history.

The preoccupation with direct democracy flowered most fully at the local level. Progressive mayors were often the best at revitalizing democracy—
partly through the innovation of "home rule," which freed city governments
from conservative and often corrupt state legislatures, and partly through
the encouragement of citizens' engagement in policy-making. This was how
Tom Johnson, the Democratic mayor of Cleveland, operated: he created
his version of a classical republic by bringing agrarian populist traditions to
an industrial city. Chief among these was the tent meeting, which Johnson
extolled as the arena of true democratic debate. "In a tent there is a freedom from restraint that is seldom present in halls," he wrote. "The audience
seems to feel that it has been invited there for the purpose of finding out the
position of various speakers. There is a greater freedom in asking questions,
too, and this heckling is the most valuable form of political education. Tent
meetings can be held in all parts of the city—in short the meetings are literally taken to the people." John Dewey, too, understood the importance of
locally grounded debate, and recommended that public schools be used as
centers for evening meetings. Innocuous as the idea sounds, it could create a vital setting for cross-class debate. The city of Rochester, New York,

put Dewey's ideas into practice, establishing a network of Social Centers in schools where citizens could debate questions of local or larger public concern. On a frigid evening in February 1907, the suffragist Harriet Childs reported one such discussion: "The topic being the commission form of government, a Polish washerwoman and the president of the WCTU were opposed by a day cleaner and a college professor." So the populist tradition flowed into urban scenes, fostering democratic speech, widening and enlivening the public sphere.

But at the national level, Progressive reformers increasingly spoke in varying idioms. The Progressive worldview was torn by tensions—populism vs. expertise, producerism vs. consumerism, statutory vs. administrative regulation. Ultimately, populist Progressives were forced to compromise their principles to get legislation they wanted. In federal policy, the managerial vision would supersede the democratic one. Some Progressive leaders, like Brandeis, held both ideals simultaneously. Others—including Wilson himself, after he became president—drifted toward management.

The National Civic Federation, a private nonprofit organization founded in 1901, typified the emerging vision of managerial Progressivism. Composed of corporation executives, university presidents, public officials, and one labor union representative (Samuel Gompers), the NCF provided an ideological common ground for various interest groups to come together and transcend their narrow concerns to serve the national interest—as defined by the authority of experts. This was the sort of partnership between private and public elites that excited paternalists like TR and J. P. Morgan, and it was also the sort of organization that has led historians to accuse Progressives of selling out to the ruling class, by embracing "the corporate ideal in the liberal state." There is a lot to this critique, but it tends to read unintended consequences back into the intentions of the reformers. It also overlooks the persistence and spread of agrarian populism as an animating force behind Progressive legislation.

The focus on the managerial accommodations of leading Progressives also neglects the larger meanings of the reformers' vision. Progressive reform was never merely a matter of policy; it was always dedicated to a broader agenda of moral regeneration. Women played a central role in shifting reformers' attention from personal to social renewal—or combining the two, as prohibition of alcohol did. Women remained in the front rank—and the front pew—of the Prohibition movement. When Bryan came out for national Prohibition in 1909 he won praise from female correspondents. "Men should be redeemers and benefactors—noble clay in the hands of the Almighty. This will bring success and reform always," a woman from Little Rock, Arkansas, wrote. The key to this morality was its assumption of malleability. People and politics were corrupt but could be purified through the alteration of circumstances. Regeneration was not simply a matter of personal will. Transforming the environment played a crucial role.

Environmental explanations for the causes of social ills did more than absolve the worthy poor of blame and promote public solutions for their misery. A focus on the corrupting power of circumstance also bred crusades for social purification—which in turn was believed to breed personal purification. Prohibition was only the most obvious example of these assumptions at work. Women's suffrage, too, was promoted as a purification of politics, a way to expand the influence of the home into the machinery of power. This was not mere sentimentality. In Chicago as elsewhere, women could claim a decisive influence in refocusing municipal government from the priorities of business to those of ordinary families and communities. Addressing a crucial public health concern that had somehow escaped men's notice, Jane Addams's hands-on effort to secure efficient garbage collection in Chicago was only one example of the "municipal housekeeping" she practiced at Hull House—which included taking care of the elderly and ill as well as setting up a kindergarten, a day nursery for working women's children, a public kitchen, a coffeehouse, cooperative dinners, a playground, a public bathhouse, a cooperative boardinghouse, a library, social clubs, and dances. As Frances Willard had urged, settlement-house workers were trying to "make the world more Home-like." Domestic ideals could sponsor social renewal.

Women's concerns reinforced the consumerist basis of many purification campaigns. Cleansing politics was of a piece with cleansing medicine, meat, and milk—and even with preserving wilderness. Indeed, the creation of a federal commitment to conservation, which was TR's greatest and most lasting achievement, acquired its main strength from popular longings for revitalization through wilderness experience. All of these Progressive campaigns promised invigorating effects on the wider population. Ideals of physical and social regeneration merged, unifying managers and moralists, efficiency and uplift. Yet while a common rhetoric masked policy differences, fundamental disagreements still had to be sorted out. This was the situation that confronted Woodrow Wilson as he began his meteoric political rise, from president of Princeton University to governor of New Jersey in 1910 to nominee of his party for president in 1912.

Wilson was born in Staunton, Virginia, in 1856, the son of a Presbyterian minister. Young Woodrow was devout and serious. He believed that life was to be lived according to God's purpose, but he was true enough to traditional Christianity to acknowledge that he could not always discern that purpose. He pondered and brooded, but when he finally embraced a moral position he was apt to maintain it rigidly. He was a complex blend of self-questioning and self-righteousness. After graduating from Princeton in 1879, he studied law at the University of Virginia and politics at Johns Hopkins, where he wrote the dissertation that became *Congressional Government* (1885), an influential critique of legislative gridlock and a call for a stronger executive. Quickly making a name for himself, he secured an appointment as professor of jurisprudence and political economy at Princeton in 1890. In 1902 he was named the school's first nonclerical president, winning fame second only to Charles Eliot's as a national educator but eventually antagonizing old-guard alumni with his meritocratic agenda. In 1910, he was elected governor of New Jersey, where he quickly won national acclaim as a successful sponsor of Progressive reform.

Yet Wilson moved only gradually toward the Progressive cause. As a rising academic, he held conventional political views. In 1899 he applauded the "young men who prefer dying in the ditches of the Philippines to spending their lives behind the counters of a dry-goods store in our eastern cities. I think I should prefer that myself." These were the complacent assumptions of a privileged professor, as insulated from Philippine ditches as he was from most other forms of physical danger. Wilson's racial views, too, were a predictable product of his moment and milieu. His *History of the American People* (1901) was pervaded by defensiveness about slavery and disdain for Reconstruction; his speech "The Ideals of America" defended the imperial transformation wrought by the Spanish-American War and urged Anglo-Saxons to take up the white man's burden.

In foreign and domestic affairs alike, Wilson was in tune with the culture of empire. During the years leading up to the 1908 election he was a leading spokesman for anti-Bryan Democrats. "We cannot abolish the trusts," he announced in 1905. "We must moralize them." Nor, in Wilson's view, could we avoid backing our businessmen's effort to locate investment opportunities abroad. "Since . . . the manufacturer insists on having the world as a market . . . the flag of his nation must follow him, and the doors of nations which are closed against him must be battered down," he announced in 1907. "Concessions obtained by financiers must be safeguarded by ministers of state even if the sovereignty of unwilling nations be outraged in the process." Though Wilson would later prefer an "imperialism of the spirit," he was unquestionably aware of empire's economic basis.

The outlook captured Wilson's characteristic melding of principle and expediency. "Because you steer by the North Star," he said in 1909, "when you have lost the bearings of your compass, you nevertheless steer a pathway on the sea—you are not bound for the North Star." Toward the end of his time at Princeton he moved away from the North Star of limited government and toward a greater acceptance of government intervention in the economy. He believed this was consistent with his own Burkean conservatism—"The only thing that is conservative is growth," he said. He backed government regulation primarily "to release the energies of our time," which included generosity as well as ambition. As he edged toward the outlook of the Bryan Democrats, Wilson began to demand that finance capital serve the needs of the entire population, and not just Wall Street insiders. He challenged financiers to back creative entrepreneurs. "Are you seeing to it that the energy of this country is renewed from generation to generation—is refreshed with those bold individuals here and there who venture upon novel enterprises, who show courage and initiative in novel fields?" he asked an assemblage of bankers in 1910.

By that time, Wilson had resigned his position at Princeton and entered New Jersey politics. Ill at ease among party regulars, he remained a solitary man at the barbecues and beer parties he was required to attend. Yet as the journalist John Reed later wrote, Wilson possessed "a principle, a religion, a something, on which his whole life rests." He imagined that social transformation could be effected by "some great orator who could go about and make men drunk with his spirit of self-sacrifice," and he bent his own oratory toward that end. This appealed to the Democratic Party elite, who preferred the rhetoric of reform to the realities of redistributive justice.

But once Wilson was elected he realized that his success as governor as well as his future ambitions required the support of the party's Progressive majority. Repudiating the party bosses, he supported the Progressive Democrats' candidate for U.S. Senate as well as their entire agenda—a statewide corrupt-practices law to prevent business-government connivance, a Public Service Commission to set utility rates, a workmen's compensation law, and the empowerment of municipalities to use the initiative, referendum, and recall. "I regard myself as pledged to the regeneration of the Democratic Party," Wilson said soon after he was elected. Within a few months, to the bosses' consternation, he had defined regeneration as Progressive reform.

As his ambitions ascended toward the presidency, Wilson embraced a new role as "champion of the common people." More and more he insisted on the importance of renewal from below. "The foundation of our lives, of our spiritual lives included, is economics," he said. The pursuit of self-interest was inescapable and needed only to be fair and to be encouraged toward ends that improved society.

This material emphasis gradually won the respect of the Bryan Democrats, ambitious Southerners and Midwesterners who felt excluded from opportunity and wanted a fair crack at it. As for Bryan himself, Wilson at first recoiled from the Great Commoner's crudity but gradually warmed up to him. Bryan's support, after all, was crucial to Wilson's campaign to grasp the ring of power. That became clear at the 1912 convention, where Bryan played a commanding role despite his physical decline. "The fine, strong features that made him so handsome sixteen years ago have hardened and grown coarse," a Texas congressman's wife observed. "His neck is thick and his jaw has an iron rigidity." Still, Bryan recalled the crowd to their populist heritage with a grandstanding gesture, demanding the withdrawal from the convention of any delegates beholden to J. P. Morgan. At a crucial point in the balloting Bryan shifted his support from Champ Clark of Missouri to Wilson, claiming that the Missourian was in bed with Wall Street interests while the Virginian opposed them. Wilson, once nominated, did not disappoint. Influenced by Brandeis and other populist Progressives, Wilson attacked the money trust and pledged himself to a New Freedom—Brandeis's term for a set of policies designed to help "the men who are on the make and not the men who already made."

Roosevelt, an "already made" man if ever there was one, did not share Wilson's desire to promote upward mobility, and dismissed Democratic proposals as hopelessly anachronistic. But what really repelled him was Wilson's character, which he came to feel embodied a certain academic type, epitomized by the dour Social Darwinist William Graham Sumner—"a college professor, a cold-blooded creature of a good deal of intellect, but lacking the fighting virtues and all wide patriotism." In TR's view, Wilson would never provide the leadership that America needed. Neither, Roosevelt decided, would Taft. Many insurgent Republicans had come to the same conclusion. They persuaded Roosevelt to try to regain the party nomination; when party regulars successfully resisted the insurgency and renominated Taft, the Progressives formed a third party and convinced Roosevelt that he was the man to head the ticket.

It could not have been too hard. Roosevelt had been champing at the bit to get back into the White House ever since he left. Constantly comparing himself to Lincoln, TR brooded on the absence of great events in his presidency, a circumstance he believed had prevented him from assuming the heroic stature he craved. What was antitrust litigation, he wondered, compared to a Civil War? He was obsessed with proving his own capacity for disinterested service by creating opportunities for heroism. The Taft administration, in Roosevelt's view, was contemptibly unheroic. Taft's "dollar diplomacy" was too openly beholden to Wall Street investors, too bereft of the moralizing rhetoric and military adventure that Roosevelt adored. When Taft signed a mandatory arbitration treaty with Great Britain in 1911, Roosevelt denounced it as a "sham" that ignored national honor, and urged his countrymen to pursue "righteousness" instead of peace. "The truth is," Taft observed of TR, "he believes in war and wishes to be a Napoleon and to die on the battle field. He has the spirit of the old berserkers." Deploring the influence of "mugwumps, ultra-peace advocates, and maudlin, hysterical sentimentalists, plus Bryanites" on American foreign policy, Roosevelt desperately cast about for kindred souls with similar yearnings for national greatness.

He found an important one in Herbert Croly, whose book *The Promise of American Life* (1909) provided some ideological and emotional coherence for TR's resurgent ambition. He loved the book, because it was full of talk about subordinating individual interests to national purpose, as well as examples of the sort of heroism needed to revitalize civic life. In Croly's view, imperialism and Progressive reform could be merged in a common campaign of moral regeneration. Abroad, "the Christian warrior must accompany the evangelist," Croly wrote; at home, a powerful administrative state could partner with the corporate behemoths created by the second industrial revolution, curbing their excesses but also serving their needs to expand investment opportunities abroad. One could hardly write a more straightforward prescription for empire as a way of life.

Roosevelt incorporated Croly's views into a speech he gave at Osawatomie, Kansas, in 1910, "The New Nationalism." Besides preaching the doctrines of inevitable monopoly and administrative regulation by experts, TR called for civil life to be lived in the same spirit that animated the Union Army during the Civil War—"heroic struggle." Progressive intellectuals loved this sort of talk. William Allen White, the editor of the *Emporia* (Kansas) *Gazette*, was one. So was Croly himself, as well as his friends Walter Lippmann and Walter Weyl (later founders of *The New Republic*). All embraced the New Nationalism. Yearning for release from sedentary, cerebral lives, eager for practical engagement with "real life," they hailed the invigorating effects of ideological change. TR sensed he was on the brink of another heroic struggle. There was no way he would turn down the Progressive Party when its leaders came calling. Not to run, he said, "would be cowardice, a case of il gran rifiuto." At the party convention in Chicago he accepted the nomination, announcing to the cheering delegates that "We stand at Armageddon and we battle for the Lord." And while Roosevelt was standing at Armageddon, Taft was playing golf.

Yet TR's Social Gospel rhetoric was misleading. He adapted it for pro-business purposes. His emphasis on expert commissions placated Progressives while protecting large corporations. In his New Nationalist program, statutory regulation yielded to administrative regulation, and executive discretion was embodied in vague distinctions like the one he had made between good trusts and bad trusts. Wilson and the Democrats were suspicious. In accepting the party nomination, Wilson had acknowledged that economic concentration was inevitable, but later in the campaign he made a sharp distinction between himself and his opponents: "Ours is a program of liberty, and theirs is a program of regulation." Bureaucratic discretion was no protection against crony capitalism and business-government connivance. "What I fear," said Wilson, "is a government of experts." The Democrats were shrewder about power than the Progressive Republicans (except for LaFollette, who quickly became disillusioned with the Roosevelt campaign), and truer to the populist heritage. The question for the campaign was: how would the plain people respond?

Labor was up for grabs. Debs and the Socialists avidly courted the unions. Circumstances appeared to favor the Socialists' cause, but in the end they fell to fighting among themselves. In January 1912, unannounced wage cuts provoked Polish women textile workers to walk out of the mills in Lawrence, Massachusetts. They were followed by the Italians, who damaged some equipment on the way out. Ethnic differences divided the workers; most could not speak English. In the classic pattern, the governor called in the state militia to keep order. Local police attacked striking families who had assembled peacefully at the train station. Yet the textile workers resisted violence and stayed united, eventually winning their major demands in mid-March. The Socialists had been on the premises, seeking to present their own united front of support for the workers. Their main spokesmen were Debs, Berger, and Big Bill Haywood, the charismatic leader of the revolutionary syndicalist faction that called itself the Industrial Workers of the World. When news of their victory reached the workers, Haywood struck a stance that was meant to contain multitudes: spreading his arms wide, he announced to the milling crowd: "We are a united working class."

But it was not to be. Haywood himself had made incendiary remarks, debunking trade unionism as a bourgeois tool, demanding "direct action" (his euphemism for violent class struggle) instead of traditional labor organizing. He broke openly with the Socialist Party at their 1912 convention, which picked Debs and voted to expel anyone who advocated violence—a thinly veiled allusion to the IWW. To Debs, the IWW were no more than anarchists who played into the employers' hands. Yet his dispute with them underscored a key strategic problem for the Socialists: how to position themselves to the left of the Progressives without romanticizing violence or assuming that workers were more revolutionary than they actually were. Meanwhile, in the absence of any convincing alternatives, the Northern urban working class was beginning to turn toward the Democrats.

In the election of 1912, TR stood at Armageddon, Taft stood pat, and Wilson easily defeated his divided opponents. Debs received 6 percent of the vote, his highest percentage ever and an indication of just how far the electorate had swung to the view that monopoly capitalism must somehow be tamed. In his inaugural address, Wilson claimed that the election indicated a bipartisan commitment "to cleanse, to reconsider, to restore, to correct the evil without impairing the good, to purify and humanize every process of our common life without weakening or sentimentalizing it." The cleansing election signaled the triumph of a Progressive coalition, bringing regions and classes together after the conflicts of the previous half-century, creating a white consensus based on exclusion of blacks. The results were made clear at the fiftieth reunion at Gettysburg. Wilson addressed the crowd of Union and Confederate veterans, now gray and stooped. He celebrated their bravery and their sacrifice in the apolitical terms that had become the norm on such occasions, never once mentioning slavery or even the presence of African-Americans in the conflict. The previous year, the black intellectual W. E. B. DuBois had published "A Mild Suggestion" in his journal *The Crisis*, commemorating the fiftieth anniversary of the Emancipation Proclamation. Recalling Jonathan Swift's "A Modest Proposal" (to serve up Irish babies for dinner) and sustaining a tone of calm rationality throughout his essay, DuBois proposed a bold solution to "the Negro Problem"—mass extermination by poisoning . The Wilson administration, which made Jim Crow the official policy of federal offices in Washington, marked the post–Civil War nadir of African-American participation in United States public life.

Still, the Wilson administration did bring a mixed bag of Progressive policies to fruition. Nearly all were promoted by the rural coalition of Southern and Midwestern Democrats, with the support of insurgent Republicans. With Wilson in the White House, farm-state congressmen finally pushed through some key provisions in the agrarian agenda—lower tariffs, an expansion of Sherman Antitrust Act, and public control of currency. In every case, the need for compromise to get the legislation passed led to a dilution of populist demands.

Pressure for tariff revision reflected traditional agrarian needs but also the growing importance of foreign markets. Advocates of freer trade argued that protective tariffs were awkward baggage to carry into the international arena. Still, Republicans remained skeptical. Their opposition to lower tariffs was rooted in habit, in continued dependence on the domestic market (despite the growing importance of exports), and in the fear that tariff revenues would be replaced by those from an income tax, which would fall most heavily on affluent Northeasterners. (They need hardly have worried: by the time income tax legislation passed Congress, the highest rates were 7 percent for individuals, 1 percent for corporations.) Still, compromise was in the air. Tariff rates had already been reduced from 57 to 38 percent in the Payne Aldrich Tariff of 1909, and enough Republicans peeled off from the old guard in 1913 to pass the Underwood Tariff, which reduced rates to 30 percent and put iron, steel, raw wool, and later sugar on the free list.

Far more important than low tariffs, to farmers, was the attempt to wrest control of the money supply from private bankers—the "sound-money men" who had made debtors miserable for decades. Here, too, the agrarian Democrats had to compromise with entrenched power for pragmatic purposes. Since the panic of 1907, financiers had been as eager as ordinary folk to stabilize capital markets; the difference was that the bankers wanted to combine the appearance of public oversight with the preservation of Wall Street prerogatives. In November 1910, at the remote resort of Jekyll Island, Georgia, they convened an extraordinary meeting disguised as a duck-hunting expedition. Several Wall Street investment bankers—Frank Vanderlip of Rockefeller's First National City Bank, Henry Davison of Morgan, and Paul Warburg of Kuhn, Loeb met with Senator Nelson Aldrich and A. Piatt Andrew, a Harvard economist. There they drafted the legislation that would become the Federal Reserve Act. But they did not have carte blanche when they came back to Washington. They had to accommodate the agrarian Democrats, just as the Democrats had to come to terms with them.

In many ways, the creation of the Federal Reserve System in 1913 seemed to fulfill the farmers' dream of a democratic monetary policy. Its structure was decentralized; its leaders were publicly appointed; it was empowered to rediscount agricultural paper and to authorize national bank loans on farmlands. The *Commercial and Financial Chronicle* found reason to fret: "No one doubts that the President will appoint high-minded men to the Federal Reserve board," its editors said, "but what intelligent people fear is that these men may be responsible to the popular clamor and be more anxious to carry out Mr. Bryan's and Mr. Wilson's ideas of how credit facilities should be dispensed than to act in absolute fidelity to correct banking principles." Ultimately the white-shoe boys had no cause for alarm. The "high-minded men" that Wilson appointed would faithfully reflect the views of the New York investment banking community, above all the conviction that what was good for Wall Street was also good for Main Street. This outcome, which would become even more pronounced under Wilson's Republican successors, confirmed the populist fear that regulatory agencies would ultimately be staffed by representatives of the industries they were supposed to regulate. Arising from agrarian discontent, the Federal Reserve eventually epitomized the managerial ideal of a partnership between private and public elites, directing the flow of capital toward new investment opportunities at home and abroad.

A similar pattern can be seen in the fate of antitrust policy under Wilson—populist origins, managerial conclusions. The Clayton Antitrust Act emerged from the House of Representatives in the spring of 1914 as a model of statutory regulation: it prohibited many monopolists' methods outright—price discrimination, interlocking directorates, and intercorporate stockholding for banks and corporations above a specified size; it made corporate directors personally liable for their companies' antitrust violations; and it authorized injured individuals to sue for triple damages in federal courts. It also exempted labor unions from antitrust prosecution, declaring that "the labor of a human being is not a commodity or an article of commerce" and that unions could therefore not be viewed as combinations in restraint of trade. To custodians of corporate privilege, the Clayton Act was nothing less than a revival of the radical specter. The *New York Times* accused agrarian Democrats of "pandering to what they still suppose to be the prevailing sentiment of the country, hatred of corporations." Martin Madden, a Republican representative from Chicago, denounced the Clayton Act as a measure that unleashed "the dogs of war . . . to tear and cripple the fabric of business life," which was already slipping into a recession.

Wilson began to fret. Maybe the Clayton Act was too bitter a pill for business to swallow. Besides, there was another antitrust measure on the table, one that signaled a shift toward administrative regulation under bureaucratic discretion: the proposal to establish a Federal Trade Commission to monitor unfair business practices. Opponents of the Clayton Act viewed the FTC as a substitute. But Brandeis, perhaps the most prominent policy intellectual associated with the Wilson administration, backed both measures. Both finally passed, the Clayton Act with some of its provisions softened by the Senate, the FTC strengthened into a body that could evaluate business practices in accordance with its own definition of the national interest. This was a decisive moment in the shift from statutory to administrative regulation. In the fall of 1914, as the European "dogs of war" began to snarl in earnest, the New Freedom had come to look suspiciously like the New Nationalism.

That change was not fortuitous. Farmers and their allies had always been both more antibusiness and more anti-imperial than Wilson. The longer he stayed in office, the more he realized his distance from the agrarian Democrats who had elected him. Nowhere was this clearer than in foreign policy, where Wilson continued the imperial interventions of his predecessors even as he wrapped them in a more capacious rhetoric of regeneration.

WILSON UNDERSTOOD THE fusion at the core of the culture of empire—the interdependence of rising mass consumption and overseas imperial expansion. This enabled him to promote "the rise of a great imperium with the outlook of a great emporium," in the historian Victoria DeGrazia's phrase. He formulated what became a key rationale for foreign intervention, a rationale that would be invoked repeatedly down to the present. Since American entrepreneurs had blessed the nation with a uniquely high standard of living, we now had the duty as well as the opportunity to promote the universal spread of our prosperous way of life. This approach not only would prove beneficial to American trade; it would also promote political democracy and world order. It was a softer, less bellicose version of what Beveridge had in mind when he called for "the regeneration of the world" in 1900.

Hard and soft imperialists shared a common commitment to global commercial supremacy, but differed in their tone and tactics. While Beveridge and Roosevelt thrilled to military conquest, Wilson preached a gospel of cultural uplift through consumption. It was altogether appropriate that when the Woolworth Tower opened in 1913 (upstaging the Metropolitan Life Tower as the tallest building in Manhattan), Wilson turned on the lights by flicking a switch in the White House. Frank Woolworth's department store chain epitomized the democracy and accessibility of consumer goods in America, as well as his company's efforts to export them abroad (Woolworth opened his first overseas branch in Liverpool in 1909). The five-and-dime store was an advertisement for the American standard of living; from Wilson's view, it was well worth official government support.

Salesmanship could assist statesmanship; the values embodied in American consumer culture could become the common language of the world. "The great barrier in the world, I have sometimes thought, is not the barrier of principle, but the barrier of taste," Wilson told an audience of salesmen in Detroit in 1916. "Certain classes of society" found "certain other classes of society distasteful" because of poor dress, uncleanliness, or unpleasant habits. (By the 1910s, respectable Americans had learned to wrinkle up their noses at body odor.) But the merger of hygiene and fashion in American advertising suggested a new, universal standard of taste—the American standard. Wilson urged the salesmen to "go out and sell goods that will make the world more comfortable and happy, and convert them to the principles of America." These were not moral or political principles, in this case, but matters of taste, of comfort and happiness.

Wilson also eagerly backed the export of American cultural products, especially movies. He was reported to be a huge fan of D. W. Griffith's racist epic *Birth of a Nation*. He recognized the propaganda power of cinema at precisely the moment when entrepreneurs like Griffith, along with Carl Laemmle, Samuel Goldwyn, and other enterprising Jewish immigrants, were beginning to incorporate film into the Hollywood studio system. Fordist standardization would expand from durable goods to mass entertainment. Wilson believed that the power of film was virtually unlimited. It was, he said, "the very highest medium for the dissemination of public intelligence, and since it speaks a universal language, it lends itself importantly to the presentation of America's plans and purposes." Wilson had more than mere propaganda in mind; he wanted to use American film to capture the imagination of the world.

That seemed to be happening in Paris as early as 1916. The surrealist Philippe Soupault remembered that "one day we saw hanging on the walls great posters as long as serpents. At every street corner a man, his face covered with a red handkerchief, leveled a revolver at the peaceful passersby. . . . We rushed into the cinemas and realized immediately that everything had changed." The "almost ferocious smile" of the actress Pearl White announced "the revolution, the beginning of a new world." This may not have been the regeneration of the world foreseen by Beveridge, but it signified the unprecedented "soft power" of the American empire.

Soft imperialist that he was, Wilson nevertheless found himself resorting to familiar military methods, especially in the Western Hemisphere. Like Roosevelt, Wilson enveloped the interests of North American capital in reassertions of righteousness. He claimed he wanted "to teach the South American republics to elect good men," and the good men turned out always (if Wilson could manage it) to be men who opposed the redistribution of wealth and supported American oil, railroad, financial, mining, timber, rubber, and agricultural interests. The fusion of money and morality posed no problem for Croly and other New Nationalist Progressives, but it provoked ambivalence and even anger among the Bryan Democrats.

This was especially awkward for Wilson, since he had appointed Bryan his secretary of state—a quid pro quo for the Nebraskan's support at the convention. It was not as crass a political move as it may have seemed. Bryan was by no means as provincial as his detractors assumed: he had traveled widely, observing the operations of empire in India and Malaysia, the modernization of tradition in Japan; he had informally adopted a Japanese "son." More important, he and Wilson shared key sensibilities. Both were Presbyterians with a fondness for the messianic gesture; both abhorred the pro-business priorities of "dollar diplomacy." Wilson was sterner, Bryan sunnier, but both men were given to grandiose visions of America's role in the world—even as they tried to define that role in language outside the familiar idioms of military adventure and imperial power. As early as 1900, Bryan had envisioned the United States as "the supreme moral factor in the world's progress and the accepted arbiter of the world's disputes—a republic whose history, like the path of the just, 'is as the shining light that shineth more and more unto the perfect day.'" A City on a Hill that would lead by example rather than try to force its ways on the rest of the world—that was Bryan's alternative to the imperial vision. But he had a hard time keeping it on Wilson's interventionist agenda.

While leading by example rather than conquest was a tricky business, Bryan was not bereft of ideas. By the time Wilson asked him to serve as secretary of state, Bryan had conceived an ambitious plan to reduce the likelihood of American involvement in war. He proposed that the United States sign a series of bilateral treaties in which each signatory would agree to submit any quarrel to an investigative tribunal and begin no conflict for a year afterward. One of the conditions of his accepting the appointment was that Wilson allow him to pursue this plan. (The other was that there be no liquor served at his and Mary's table on state occasions.) Wilson agreed, and Bryan entered the period that marked the decisive downturn in his career. Bryan's unhappy tenure at the state department was characterized by blundering interventions in Latin America that violated his own reluctance to use force except as a last resort, and by the coming of World War I—a cataclysm that made Bryan's beloved bilateral treaties seem obsolete overnight.

Yet for a while, Bryan and Wilson were on the same page. From the outset, Wilson's Latin American foreign policy was more than half Bryanite. Both men rejected any desire to take colonies or seek material plunder; both wanted to guide Latin America to a peaceful democratic future. This idealistic imperialism created disaster at every turn. Intoxicated by their own good intentions, Wilson and Bryan overlooked local politics, to say nothing of local cultural attitudes, in the name of promoting democracy. Moralism always seemed to bring militarism in its wake.

Interventions in Mexico, beginning in 1913, set the prevailing pattern. Wilson, disdaining diplomacy with the dictator Victoriano Huerta, praised the insurgency led by Venustiano Carranza and sought to set up an election that would exclude Huerta. When Huerta refused, Wilson declared a strict arms embargo but resisted American businessmen's pressure to intervene. The United States, he told a crowd in Mobile, Alabama, in October 1913, "will never again seek one additional foot of territory by conquest." Several months later he lifted the arms embargo to allow munitions to reach the Mexican insurgency and stationed U.S. warships offshore to block European shipments of arms to Huerta. The new empire was once again facing off against the old. On April 22, 1914, Congress granted Wilson the right to use force to secure U.S. rights and redress grievances. But like Roosevelt, Wilson and Bryan had already taken matters into their own hands, without congressional authorization. Having heard that a German ship was en route to the port of Vera Cruz with munitions, Bryan advised Wilson to use the navy to prevent delivery. On April 21, Wilson ordered his local commander to bombard Vera Cruz and send in the marines. Nineteen Americans were killed. Argentina, Brazil, and Chile offered to arbitrate and Wilson accepted. The upshot was that Huerta left office, Carranza became the de facto president, the U.S. occupying forces departed, and Mexican politics descended into chaos.

The United States had hardly covered itself with glory in this intervention, and Wilson sensed it. For all his imperial sentiments he was not a mystic militarist like Roosevelt. Indeed, Wilson was shaken by the pointless loss of life at Vera Cruz. When one of his foreign policy advisors, Lindley Garrison, urged that the United States should restore order by marching on Mexico City and installing a government, Wilson announced "very solemnly that this is no affair of ours." Still, he continued to intervene, seeking to shore up Carranza's rule by sending General John J. Pershing in vain pursuit of the insurgent (and alleged bandit) Pancho Villa.

Caribbean adventures revealed a comparable blend of moralism and military intervention. As a Haitian journalist observed after the United

States established a military regime there in 1915—supposedly to protect the Haitians from exploitation as well as the Americans from expropriation: "The Americans are enemies of despotism, and to prevent its return, they invaded the country." Naïveté could be as destructive as realpolitik. In the fall of 1913, Bryan was fooled by Joseph Sullivan, the U.S. envoy to Santo Domingo who was heavily involved in its biggest bank. Sullivan persuaded Bryan (and through him Wilson) to back the Dominican president, José Bordas Valdez, who was trying to extend his term beyond its one-year limit. Bryan in turn cajoled Wilson into sending U.S. naval vessels to Santo Domingo harbor "for moral effect." Bryan lurched from one Dominican leader to another, each of whom kept promising to hold free elections. Finally in 1916, Wilson sent in the U.S. marines to run the country as a military police state, which they did for twenty years. In the Caribbean as in Mexico, the consequences of idealistic imperialism included botched invasions and needlessly lost lives, as well as lingering Latin distrust of the pious bully to the north.

The blunderings of Bryan and Wilson in Latin America were a comic opera by comparison to what was happening in Europe, where men were murdering each other en masse. If Wilson and Bryan bungled together in Latin America, when it came to the Great War they pulled quickly apart. Like most Anglo-Americans, Wilson was instinctively pro-British—as was the established press, which derived most of its news from British sources and depicted the Germans as marauding savages. Bryan's insistent neutrality isolated him from the rest of the Wilson administration.

The key issue involved German submarine warfare against civilian belligerent vessels, which the Germans charged were carrying ammunition and other war materiel to their enemies. The problem was that these same ships were also carrying civilian passengers, including some from the officially neutral United States. When a German U-boat sank the British liner *Lusitania* in May 1915, 128 Americans were among the 1,195 people who perished. Bryan wondered if the ship had been carrying munitions, and in fact, later investigation revealed that six million rounds of ammunition in the ship's hold had increased the death toll dramatically. But at the time of the sinking, American policy-makers were in no mood for anti-British muckraking. Bryan wanted to warn Americans against riding belligerent vessels; Wilson rejected the idea and insisted on a harsh note demanding that the Germans ensure the safety of neutrals or abandon submarine warfare altogether. Bryan soon afterward resigned, to be replaced by the far more hawkish Robert Lansing.

Wilson had now cut himself off from the agrarian Democrats who had elected him. He was freer than ever to associate with a different crowd, one more suited to his upper-class education and Anglophile tastes. Still, he remained a solitary man, morally serious, prone to self-questioning as well as self-doubt. He was no pacifist, but he hated war and sought to prevent it by imagining a League of Nations that would replace realpolitik with international law. Ultimately, Wilson decided that the only way to end war as an instrument of international policy was to enter the war that was raging in Europe. In the three years leading up to that decision, he stood poised on the brink of policies that would transform the world order even as they eventually led to his own destruction. It would be an "irony of fate," he once said, if his administration—which had been elected to enact a Progressive domestic agenda—would find itself enveloped in foreign policy concerns. Wilson was right. It was indeed an irony. But it was also a tragedy.

✦

B y the time world war broke out in 1914, longings for regeneration had taken a myriad of private and public forms. On both sides of the Atlantic, the very success of bourgeois culture bred among its beneficiaries a subtle sense of failure—a feeling that everyday life had been drained of spontaneity and vitality, that material progress contained a hollowness at its core. Yearnings to reconnect with "real life" inspired innumerable idiosyncratic explorations of religious and artistic experience but they also led into the civic arena. In Western Europe, Great Britain, and the United States, Progressives and Social Democrats imagined a cooperative commonwealth purged of corruption and committed to social justice, a vision of political renewal that included personal revitalization as well.

The religious charge of that vision was especially strong in the United States, where Social Christians embraced Progressive causes as the path to the Kingdom of God on Earth. Through the pull and tug of legislative compromise, utopian dreams were brought down to earth and translated into policies that laid the foundations of the modern welfare state. The taming of capitalism was the most desirable—indeed, necessary—public consequence of popular longings for renewal. But crusades for regeneration led in less benign directions as well. The meanings of social rebirth shifted and evolved under pressures of power and circumstance. Utopian visions could be rooted in moral absolutism, and could enforce conformity to a particular, provincial morality. This was clearest in the Prohibition movement. Progressive reform was at its most humane when empowering the previously powerless—women, workers, children—rather than reinforcing majority values.

The most dangerous regenerative crusades stemmed from the assumption that creation could only come through destruction. Though Joseph Schumpeter had not yet coined the term "creative destruction," Frank Norris, Theodore Dreiser, and other worshippers of capitalist Force were attracted by its destructive as well as its productive capacities. But this was more a literary stance than a business ideology. Whatever their actual practices, investment bankers and other business apologists preferred to focus on their firms' stability and reliability rather than their transformative potential. A more influential idea of creative destruction focused on the revitalizing impact of war.

Dreams of martial renewal combined tradition and innovation. Nationalists and militarists on both sides of the Atlantic continued to insist that the corrupting softness at the core of bourgeois civilization could be excised only by the sword. Roosevelt remained the most prominent American advocate of this view, merging Civil War memories of heroic struggle with Victorian ideals of manhood and nationhood. But Wilson cultivated a more capacious vision. He would fight a war, he finally decided, in the service of all humanity—a war that would lead to the regeneration not merely of the individual and the nation, but of the world.

Wilson had started political life as a conventional imperialist. But after 1914, events converged to wean him from the childish equation of war with manly moral vigor that was embraced by so many of his contemporaries. Troubled by the needless loss of life at Vera Cruz, he was also appalled by the carnage in Europe. Yet Wilson's horror at war was complicated by his developing vision of international cooperation—a concert of nations that could manage conflict and perhaps even move, however incrementally, toward a world without war. This would require that the slaughter in the trenches be concluded in a just peace, one that could come only, Wilson decided, through his own leadership. The United States would have to enter the war on the side of the Allies, help assure their victory, then take the lead in fashioning a "Peace Without Victory." The loss of American lives could be justified only in a war to end war.

There were several questionable assumptions behind this reasoning, but the most problematic was Wilson's belief that he had to enter the war in order to influence the peace. In fact one could argue just the reverse: that Wilson's role as impartial arbitrator would have been strengthened by maintaining his policy of armed neutrality. Indeed, noninterventionists had long warned that a convincing victory by either side would upset the balance of power in Europe, creating a dangerous disequilibrium. Yet Wilson finally yielded to his own messianic impulses. Unwilling to go to war solely for the abstract principle of neutral rights, he had to embrace a more exalted rationale for intervention. Troubled by an endless war, eager for a lasting peace, Wilson still failed to transcend the militarist conventions of his own moment and milieu—above all the faith that war could lead to moral rebirth. He alone, he believed, could redeem the blood sacrifice by creating a new postwar world order.

By the time the Armistice was signed in November 1918, Wilson was an international hero who inspired democratic hopes in Cairo and Delhi as well as Paris and Berlin. But the treaty that emerged from months of negotiations was so punitive toward Germany and so full of territorial concessions to existing empires that it could hardly be considered a "Peace Without Victory," still less a step toward democracy. Indeed, Lloyd George of Great Britain and Georges Clemenceau of France (and even Wilson himself, in some moods) were ultimately more concerned with containing the threat of world revolution, already raging through Russia, than with securing the "self-determination of peoples" that inspired anticolonial nationalists. Still, the treaty contained the League of Nations Covenant, the charter for the international organization Wilson hoped would change the world. But he could not persuade his own countrymen to approve it. He isolated himself from contrary voices, failed to mend fences with his political enemies, and retreated into moral rigidity.

A fitting coda to the age of regeneration, Wilson's crusade was more grandiose in its aims and more catastrophic in its conclusions than many of the imperial adventures that preceded it. Wilson wanted to transcend adolescent faith in the revitalizing effects of combat and recast regenerative longings toward peaceful, democratic aims. Without question this was a worthy aspiration, but it was undone by the violent means used to achieve it. In the end Wilson faced some fundamental truths, whether he acknowledged them or not. War was still war, no matter how noble the sentiments surrounding it. Bloodshed could not be redeemed by rhetoric alone. The dead and the maimed could still call their leaders to account.

WILSON'S CRUSADE CULMINATED two decades of militarist fantasy. By 1910, the beneficent effects of war had become a staple theme of public discourse. Even the most thoughtful dissenters acknowledged its power. William James said we had no right to "sow our ideals, plant our order, impose our God" on foreign populations. Yet he also thought that "militarism is the great preserver of our ideals of hardihood, and human life with no use for hardihood would be contemptible." James's "Moral Equivalent to War" revealed him to be a man of his historical moment. His argument idealized war's revitalizing force, but he aimed to integrate his longings into a moral universe more humane than the one inhabited by Roosevelt or Beveridge.

James's outlook was idiosyncratic, while the notion of regeneration through empire was conventional wisdom—especially among Republicans. But some Democrats had a weakness for militarist imaginings too. Colonel Edward House, an urbane Texan who attached himself to Wilson's rising star in 1911, was one. House, whose military rank was fictitious and honorific, soon became what Wilson called "my second personality . . . my independent self." In 1912 House published *Philip Dru*, a Progressive fantasy of utopian social transformation through military violence and temporary dictatorship. One can only speculate what effect it might have had on Wilson's views. House claimed in 1913 that Wilson considered war "as an economic proposition, ruinous, but he thought there was no more glorious way to die than in battle." But that was before he had actually ordered men into battle, at Vera Cruz. After that he sobered. *Philip Dru* is less illustrative of Wilson's views than of House's—as well as those of other Progressive intellectuals who came to advocate entry into World War I.

Dru is a young military officer graduating from West Point in 1920, when the country is on the brink of civil war between haves and have-nots. His classmate Jack Strawn has a sister named Gloria, who with her characteristic bluntness poses a question to Dru: "I am wondering, Mr. Dru, why you came to West Point and why it is you like the thought of being a soldier? . . . An American soldier has to fight so seldom that I have heard that the insurance companies regard them as the best of risks, so what attraction, Mr. Dru, can a military career have for you?" Dru is taken aback by her candor but answers earnestly: " 'As far back as I can remember,' he said, 'I have wanted to be a soldier. I have no desire to destroy and kill, and yet there is within me the lust for action and battle. It is the primitive man in me, I suppose, but sobered and enlightened by civilization.' "

Dru envisions a role for himself in a coming Armageddon between privilege and the people. "And from the blood and travail of an enlightened people, there will be born a spirit of love and brotherhood which will transform the world; and the star of Bethlehem, seen but darkly for two thousand years, will shine again with a steady and effulgent glow." In the face of such outbursts, Gloria can only murmur admiringly: "You belong to the world of real life, not the [peacetime] army." Ultimately Dru leads the Progressive army against the monopolists and their political lackeys, crushes them in a murderous battle with hundreds of thousands of casualties on both sides, appoints himself dictator to oversee the return to a constitutional and efficiently administered democracy, subdues "the revolutionaries and bandits" in Mexico, extends the United States throughout North America from the equator to the pole, and finally abdicates power to sail away with Gloria.

The key psychological moment in this narrative occurs at the height of the climactic battle. "In that hell storm of lead and steel Dru sat upon his horse unmoved. With bared head and eyes aflame, with face flushed and exultant, he looked the embodiment of the terrible God of war. His presence and his disregard of danger incited his soldiers to deeds of valor that would forever be 'an inspiration and a benediction' to the race from which they sprang." Fantasies of invulnerability underwrote dreams of imperial rebirth, the reveries of old clubmen nodding off in their Morris chairs and of middle-aged intellectuals sitting poised at their Smith-Coronas. But the fantasy of *Philip Dru* has a different aim; the book puts "the terrible God of war" in the service of democracy, not nationalism or empire. Wilson, with House at his side, would seek this same sublimity.

That goal proved easier imagined than achieved, especially once the war broke out on August 4, 1914. At first only a few observers foresaw the full significance of the catastrophe to come. "The plunge of civilization into this abyss of blood and darkness," Henry James wrote the day after the British declared war on the Central Powers, "is a thing that so gives away the whole long age during which we have supposed the world to be, with whatever abatement, gradually bettering, that to have to take it all now for what the treacherous years were all the while really making for and *meaning* is too tragic for any words." But most journalists and intellectuals clung to the militarist formulas of the age, celebrating the outbreak of war as an opportunity for "the moral regeneration of Europe." With the realization that their nation was at war, the German novelist Thomas Mann recalled, "a great wave of moral feeling" swept over him and his countrymen. In every combatant country, ideologues agreed that war brought people together, encouraging them to transcend petty personal and social conflicts by immersing themselves in the sacred unity of nationhood. A British journalist exulted that "one beautiful result of the war is the union of hearts." Each nation had its narrative of national destiny, nurtured by intellectuals. "Among the elite of each country," the French novelist Romain Rolland observed dryly, "there is not one who does not proclaim and is not convinced that the cause of his people is the cause of God, the cause of liberty, and of human progress." But the European faith in progress, as Henry James realized, was about to be repealed.

Within weeks after the war declaration, armies were hurling themselves at each other as they had not done since the American Civil War, in frontal assaults on fortified positions, at a fearful price. In September 1914, when the British and French struggled and finally succeeded in stopping the German advance on Paris at the River Marne, the casualties were half a million on both sides. As the British army died in droves, officials frantically lowered height standards for recruits. By the end of the year, since neither side had been able to outflank the other, both had settled into an extraordinary network of trenches stretching from the Belgian coast to the Swiss border—the Western Front. For four years, each side tried to pound a large enough hole in the other's trench line to push through a force that could overwhelm its opponent. British officers were especially attached to the dream of a cavalry breakthrough—a remnant of chivalric fantasy, ever more anomalous among men mowed down by machine guns. The most appalling consequence of this strategy was the British assault on the German fortifications at the Somme on July 1, 1916, when 60,000 out of the 110,000 British troops who attacked were killed or wounded as they marched forward in plain view of the German machine gunners who had been nestled safely underground during the pre-attack bombardment. The cries of the wounded in no-man's-land could be heard for days. Not since Grant's Wilderness campaign had the world seen comparable carnage.

Still, there was a question of how much the rest of the world could see. Photographs from the front were forbidden, and newspaper publishers cooperated enthusiastically with government censorship. Lord Northcliffe's *Times* perfected a cheery euphemistic style—later easily and bitterly parodied—that presented the war as jolly good sport. This was hard to sustain amid the staggering casualty reports, and by the end of 1915, even the British poet laureate Robert Bridges acknowledged a collective "grief that is intolerable constantly to face, nay impossible to face without that trust in God which makes all things possible." It became more and more and more necessary to assert that "man is a spiritual being," as Bridges did, while the corpses multiplied into meaninglessness.

Numbers alone, however huge, were insufficient to convey the enormity of the horror. As Paul Fussell has brilliantly shown, a basic theme of soldiers' diaries, fiction, letters, and memoirs was the widening gap between men who had seen combat and "the Rest." Americans, safe across the water, were surely among the Rest. Still, they were gradually made aware of the magnitude of the slaughter. The statistics were undeniable, and the Grim Reaper soon became a standard figure in U.S. political cartoons depicting the impact of the war. A cartoon is not a corpse, but enough information was available for Americans to feel confirmed in their fundamental impulse—to stay the hell out.

The arguments for nonintervention were various and powerful. LaFollette and other antiwar Progressives correctly perceived the war as a struggle over imperial spoils. Neither side had any political, still less moral claim on the United States, and no U.S. interests would be served by involvement. This argument was only strengthened by the mad logic of mass slaughter. The higher the piles of corpses mounted, the more committed each side became to annihilating its enemy. Nothing less than total victory, propagandists proclaimed, would ensure that the dead should not have died "in vain"—a phrase that became a staple of public discourse during this war. Nothing less could transform the pointless death of millions into a sacred blood sacrifice. Yet total victory by either side would upset the balance of power, leaving resentments that might lead to renewed conflict. The longer the war wore on, the weaker was the argument for American involvement. One did not have to be a sentimental pacifist to see this. Indeed, there was a pragmatic argument for pacifism—or at least nonintervention—that the broader population instinctively grasped.

At first national leaders were equally suspicious of involvement. Wilson urged neutrality, despite his own Anglophilia. Even TR said in September, after the German invasion of Belgium: "We have not the slightest responsibility for what has befallen her." But by November, references to blood sacrifice began to reappear. *The New Republic* denounced pacifists for failing to realize that "treaties will never acquire sanctity until nations are ready to seal them with their blood." Roosevelt demanded that the United States condemn Germany, and privately grumbled at Wilson's timidity. As always, TR confused moral with physical courage. "Wilson is, I think, a timid man physically," Roosevelt wrote to the British diplomat Cecil Spring-Rice in November 1914. And to the imperial bard Rudyard Kipling the former president said that Wilson "comes of a family none of whose members fought on either side in the Civil War"—a false assertion that revealed Roosevelt's own shame over his father's avoidance of that conflict.

Even while the casualties multiplied, the idea of revitalization through battle was resurfacing in American minds. Some openly abandoned what the novelist Robert Herrick called "that vague pacifism which I, like so many others, voiced under the first shock of the European war." Now that outlook seemed to signify "a sickliness in our national spirit." Having just returned from France in 1915, Herrick announced that "There is not a Frenchman who will not tell you of the immense good that has already come to his people, that will come increasingly from the bloody sacrifice. It has united all classes, swept aside the trivial and the base, revealed the nation to itself. . . . A new, a larger, a more vital life has already begun for invaded and unconquered France."

Mystical nationalism resurfaced in public debate about the war, intensified by outrage at the German use of submarine warfare. Roosevelt led the charge, but Wilson was not ready to join up. When the *Lusitania* went down, Roosevelt railed at "piracy" and "murder," while Wilson took higher ground: "There is such a thing as a man being too proud to fight," he said. "There is such a thing as a nation being so right that it does not need to convince others by force that it is right." Believing that talking was better than fighting, Wilson sought through diplomacy to persuade Germany to give up submarine warfare—an unreasonable expectation since the submarine was Germany's only weapon against Great Britain's naval blockade. Eventually Germany offered an apology and an indemnity for the *Lusitania* sinking. Wilson and Secretary of State Robert Lansing were relieved, but the problem of submarine attacks on merchant shipping was not going away. Clinging to the pre–Civil War credo that war has rules, Wilson tried to persuade the Allies to stop arming merchant ships, a practice that in his view invited U-boat attack. Roosevelt raged, telling Owen Wister that Wilson personified "the demagogue, adroit, tricky, false, without one spark of loftiness in him, without a touch of the heroic in his cold, selfish, and timid soul." Cut off from power, the former president was becoming unhinged.

But Roosevelt was the least of Wilson's problems. Britain refused to disarm its merchantmen, or to alter its economic warfare against the German population. On March 24, 1916, a German submarine sank the French steamer *Sussex*. Wilson again demanded cessation of submarine warfare, while Lansing threatened to sever diplomatic ties to Germany. Under pressure, Germany made what became known as the *Sussex* pledge, agreeing to abide by rules of visit-and-search before attacking merchantmen, but also demanding that the United States compel the Allies (especially the blockading British) to obey international law as well. Wilson was elated: his diplomacy had apparently vindicated "the force of moral principle." Actually he had boxed himself in by making clear that German violation of the pledge would be a casus belli; he had cut off all other diplomatic options.

Meanwhile his humanitarian agenda grew more specific. On May 27, 1916, in a speech to Taft's League to Enforce Peace, Wilson evoked for the first time his vision of a postwar international organization—promoting cooperation among sovereign states based on "the consent of the governed" within them and equality among them. "We believe that every people has a right to choose the sovereignty under which they shall live," Wilson said, and that "the small states of the world shall enjoy the same respect for their sovereignty and their territorial integrity" as the great powers did. This was a far cry from the politics of empire, as anticolonial nationalists soon began to recognize.

In the election year of 1916, Wilson had to cover his right flank by deploying a new rhetoric of "Americanism" and increasing military spending to satisfy the demands of Roosevelt and the Republicans for "preparedness." But these were not the themes that resonated with his Democratic constituency. At the 1916 Democratic convention, midway through his keynote address, Representative Martin Glynn of New York said he would not bother with a "dull recital" of Wilson's diplomatic notes. "No, no, go on!" the delegates shouted. So Glynn recounted the major events in the saga of the president's diplomacy, and after each one asked the crowd: "What did we do? What did we do?" And the crowd boomed back: "We didn't go to war!" "We didn't go to war!" Wilson's campaign ran with the slogan "He kept us out of war," fusing Progressivism and peace. As he pulled out a narrow victory over the Republican Charles Evans Hughes, Wilson continued to evoke his vision of a concert of nations, keeping peace after this war was over.

For a while it looked as if his hopes might be realized without American entry into the war. On December 12, 1916, the Germans offered to negotiate peace. Wilson's relief was palpable. He had watched the death toll mount with shock and disbelief. He had no more illusions about the revitalizing effects of modern combat. "Deprived of glory, war loses all its charm," he wrote, "the mechanical slaughter of today has not the same fascination as the zest of intimate conduct of former days, and trench warfare and poisonous gases are elements which detract alike from the excitement and the tolerance of modern conflict. With maneuver almost a thing of the past, any given point can be carried by the sacrifice of enough men and ammunition. Where is any longer the glory commensurate with the sacrifice of the millions of men required in modern warfare to carry and defend Verdun?" The question answered itself. In a war of attrition, as Ernest Hemingway later wrote, "the things that were glorious had no glory and the sacrifices were like the stockyards at Chicago if nothing was done with the meat except to bury it." Even Wilson the idealist shared Hemingway's awareness of the waste behind "the words sacred, glorious, and sacrifice, and the expression in vain."

But in the wake of his election victory and the German offer to negotiate, Wilson's hopes soared. On January 22, 1917, speaking for "the silent mass of mankind everywhere," he announced his plans for a "Peace Without Victory." It was based, he later said, on his faith in "the single supreme plan of peace, the revelation of our Lord and savior"—the belief that "wars will never have any ending until men cease to hate."

The speech was more than pious wish; it embodied a critique of imperialism, more far-reaching than Wilson could have intended or implemented. "No peace can last, or ought to last, which does not recognize and accept the principle that governments derive all their just powers from the consent of the governed, and that no right anywhere exists to hand peoples about from sovereignty to sovereignty as if they were property," Wilson announced. The means for implementing this critique was to be a League of Nations that would allow the "community of nations" to prosper by exercising restraint—reducing armaments to agreed-upon minimums, creating procedures for peaceful arbitration of disputes, ensuring the collective maintenance of security if arbitration broke down.

In some ways the League of Nations epitomized the Progressive mentality at its most ambitious—or quixotic. The League was a managerial scheme designed to create a cooperative commonwealth of nations. Efficiency and uplift, science and morality, merged in its complex harmony of bureaucratic system. Yet the League was more than a monument to Progressive hubris. It also contained some important departures from conventional foreign policy assumptions. Wilson was convinced that the League should have the authority to abridge national sovereignty, the sacred center of the romantic state-worship that emerged from the cult of the union during the Civil War. In the campaign of 1916, Wilson had dared to approach the subject directly: "There is coming a time, unless I am very much mistaken . . . when nation shall agree with nation that the rights of humanity are greater than the rights of sovereignty." This was little short of treason to nationalists like Roosevelt, who declared after the "Peace Without Victory" speech that "President Wilson has earned for the nation the curse of Meroz, for he has not dared to stand for the Lord against the wrongdoings of the mighty." Few politicians on either side of the Atlantic could transcend their parochial views and respond with courage to Wilson's challenge.

The cult of total victory held. On January 31, 1917, the Germans announced their negotiating terms, which were so expansive as to assure rejection by the Allies. The next day they announced their decision to conduct unrestricted submarine warfare. The day after that, *The New Republic* was already bursting with brisk war plans: "Without any delay diplomatic relations must be broken. The German ships in American harbors should be seized at once and held as hostages. The navy should be mobilized. An antisubmarine fleet should be assembled. Steps should be taken to arm all merchant ships. Plans for financial and economic assistance to the Allies should be set in motion." This was the viewpoint of Croly, Lippmann, and other nationalist Progressives, who were sick of feeling impotent on the sidelines and eager to immerse themselves in the realities of international conflict. Of course that immersion was entirely vicarious.

Wilson, stuck in the box he had created for himself, broke off diplomatic relations with Germany and pondered a decision to declare war. On February 25, he learned of a coded message sent by the German foreign minister Alfred Zimmerman to the German minister in Mexico, outlining a plan to bring Mexico into the war on the side of Germany if war broke out between the Germans and the Americans; the Mexicans, said the note, would have the opportunity to win back all the territory they had lost in the Mexican-American War of 1846–48. The Zimmerman note had been decoded by British intelligence and delivered to Wilson by his Anglophile ambassador to the Court of St. James, Walter Hines Page. But despite its suspicious source, it was taken at face value by the press and intensified the clamor for war among Roosevelt and the Republicans. While Wilson hesitated, TR ranted. "He is a very cold and selfish man, and a timid man when it comes to physical danger," Roosevelt wrote to Senator Hiram Johnson. "As for shame, he has none, and if anyone kicks him, he brushes his clothes, and utters some lofty sentence."

For weeks Wilson deliberated, still trying to imagine alternatives to war, still promoting his postwar vision to skeptical Europeans. The obligation to submit disputes to arbitration, he told the French ambassador, would be introduced incrementally: "There would thus be created, little by little, precedents that would break the habit of having recourse to arms." This recalled Bryan's prewar dream of bilateral agreements. Wilson still wanted to be a man of peace.

Yet ultimately Wilson uttered the only lofty sentences that would satisfy Roosevelt. Having consulted repeatedly with his hawkish cabinet and advisors, he finally decided that war was the only means to lasting peace. The continuation of armed neutrality, he thought, would bring the destruction of war without the ability to influence its conduct and aims. This logic arose from Wilson's messianic streak; he was convinced that if the United States joined the Allies he could influence them to accept a negotiated settlement and a just peace. But why did the messiah have to become a warrior? The idea that a noncombatant could serve as an impartial arbiter remained more plausible than the idea that only a combatant could redeem the Allies from resentment and redirect their war aims toward humanitarian ends. In the end Wilson was swept up in his own version of regeneration, carried off to the activist conclusion that doing something was always better than doing nothing, and that doing something meant military engagement.

The decision to go to war was more than a matter of Wilson's psychological needs. Complicated national interests were involved, especially the safety of American merchant shipping. Though Wilson was addicted to absolute ideals like "freedom of the seas" and the sanctity of neutrality, his response to the submarine threat was not simply guided by messianic idealism. He was following the logic of empire as a way of life. Few people needed to be told that American prosperity was dependent on foreign trade, especially with the Allies. But the questions remained: How equally was this prosperity to be shared? Were business elites its main beneficiaries? And even if the economic benefits were more broadly dispersed, were they worth risking mass death to achieve? Wouldn't we, in the end, be sacrificing more young lives on imperial altars?

LaFollette and a handful of antiwar Progressives in the Senate raised those questions, resisting Wilson's reluctant march to war every step of the way. After the German resumption of submarine warfare, shipping interests pressured Wilson to arm U.S. merchantmen. Wilson pushed Congress for authorization but his efforts were filibustered to death by LaFollette and a handful of antiwar Progressives. "A little group of willful men, representing no opinion but their own, have rendered the great government of the United States helpless and contemptible," the president fumed. Ignoring Congress, he armed merchantmen by executive order on March 9; within ten days three of them were sunk by German submarines. The push to war seemed inevitable, but not because the people demanded it. Wilson's claim that LaFollette and his antiwar allies represented "no opinion but their own" was sheer bravado. Available evidence indicates that a clear majority of Americans opposed their nation's entry into the war. LaFollette sensed this and demanded a popular referendum. "The poor, sir, who are the ones called upon to rot in the trenches, have no organized power, but oh, Mr. President, at some time they will be heard," he told the Senate.

But the die was cast. There would be no popular referendum. The representatives of "organized power" in Washington had decided that war was necessary. Even most Progressives, eager for engagement with "real life" and swept up in their own humanitarian hopes, had embraced what they believed was the inevitable logic of events. When Wilson announced that he would address Congress on April 2, everyone knew that he would ask Congress for a declaration of war against Germany. He spoke solemnly, authoritatively. "The world must be made safe for democracy," he said. "Its peace must be planted on the firm foundations of political liberty." Congress burst into applause; men rushed forward to congratulate him. Wilson's face was ashen as he made his way through the crowd. "My message today was a message of death for our young men," he told his aide, Joseph Tumulty. "How strange it seems to applaud that."

Wilson was full of forebodings. The night before his war speech, he unburdened himself to Frank Cobb, a friendly reporter from the *New York World*. Cobb recalled the conversation in his memoirs. " 'Once lead this people into war,' [Wilson] said, 'and they'll forget there ever was such a thing as tolerance. To fight you must be brutal and ruthless, and the spirit of ruthless brutality will enter into the very fibre of our national life, infecting

Congress, the courts, the policeman on the beat, the man in the street. . . . If there is any alternative, for God's sake, let's take it,' he exclaimed."

But Wilson had already decided there was no alternative. His worried words were prescience, or self-fulfilling prophecy. The war was a distant intervention for abstract ends. Despite congressional enthusiasm, it never won spontaneous public support, especially west of the Alleghenies and outside elite Anglo-American circles. From the outset Wilson knew he would have to mobilize public opinion as well as men and guns. That was why he appointed the newsman George Creel as the head of his Committee on Public Information, more aptly called a propaganda ministry, to whip up public support. One innovation was the "four-minute man," who commandeered captive audiences in theaters with brief rants against the enemy. Professional propagandists were equally important. Creel hired advertising executives to serve as "cheer leaders of the nation," deploying their arts to demonize the Hun, sanitize war bonds as "Liberty Bonds," and shame the citizenry into embracing the war effort.

Still, popular resistance flourished—among German-Americans and Irish-Americans, among socialists and pacifists, among agrarian Democrats in the South and Midwest, and among ordinary citizens everywhere. The imposition of a draft was especially outrageous. "In the estimation of Missourians," Champ Clark announced, "there is precious little difference between a conscript and a convict." This opinion was pervasive. Hundreds of thousands evaded the draft. The provost marshal general recorded in 1919 that 337,649 men had either refused to report when inducted or deserted after arriving in boot camp. Other opponents of war took more direct action. In summer 1917, five hundred tenant farmers in eastern Oklahoma organized the Green Corn Rebellion; in the tradition of Coxey's Army, they meant to march on Washington to protest the war, but they were quickly surrounded and arrested by a sheriff's posse. Clearly persuasion alone would not be sufficient to mobilize Wilson's crusade.

Popular hostility to the war provoked reprisals, official and unofficial. "Pro-German sympathizers" were liable to terrorist intimidation, even lynching, by local vigilantes. In the propaganda war, words were weapons. Antiwar statements were nothing short of treason. As Nicholas Murray Butler, president of Columbia University, said of LaFollette, "you might just as well put poison in the food of every American boy that goes to his transport as to permit that man to talk as he does." Congress made that point of view official by passing the Espionage Act of 1917 and the Sedition Act of 1918. Together these measures made blind obedience the law of the land. They sanctioned the suppression of written or spoken opposition to the war, including any statement judged "disloyal, profane, scurrilous, or abusive" toward the American flag, government, or uniform. More than fifteen hundred persons were arrested under these laws, among them Eugene Debs, who was jailed as a traitor in 1918. During the German offensive that summer, as manpower needs accelerated and draft evasion persisted, Attorney General Thomas Gregory sent federal and local law enforcement officers on a series of "slacker raids" in a dozen cities. Hundreds of thousands of young men were stopped randomly on the street and interrogated. If the interrogators suspected them of draft evasion they were detained without warrants or formal charges. Later it was learned that only 5 percent of the detainees were draft evaders.

One would think that Progressive reformers and intellectuals would protest the suppression of civil liberties. LaFollette, Jane Addams, and a few others did. But many others embraced the war as a regenerative crusade. Even Dewey was swept up in Wilson's humanitarian mission, along with the nationalist Progressives who clustered around Croly and Lippmann at *The New Republic*. The war, they thought, would be a great laboratory for social engineering; it was the ultimate marriage of management and morality. It was also the ultimate fantasy of creative destruction, the belief that creation of a new world would result from destruction of the old.

War promised the realization of the managerial dream: an administrative state that would supervise but also cooperate with big business. Wilson's appointment of the investment banker Bernard Baruch to head the War Industries Board, which oversaw the production and distribution of war materiel, epitomized the wartime marriages between labor and capital, Wall Street and Washington. Despite occasional talk of trust-busting, Roosevelt and other nationalist Progressives had been promoting those unions for years.

But Progressive hopes for wartime regeneration went far beyond the managerial vision of efficient social engineering. The war, many felt, would be an opportunity for remaking both the polity and the self—erasing class differences, elevating women, eliminating selfishness, disciplining indolence and pleasure. In early 1917, the muckraker Ray Stannard Baker expressed a prevalent Progressive mood when he recoiled in disgust from the

"unutterable hogsheads of sickly sweet drinks" accompanied by "decorated ice cream" that he observed among the young people of Minneapolis at play. "All overdressed! All overeating! All overspending!" The war,
like others before it, seemed to moralists to be a chance to lance the boil
of luxury and rededicate a self-indulgent population to spartan purpose.
The opportunity was especially appealing to young men of breeding on
Wall Street, who joined the "millionaires' unit" of naval aviators training
at Henry Davison's Long Island estate, or enlisted in the "Silk Stocking
Regiment," the 107th Infantry. War provided Anglo-American elites with
a shot at sacrifice, physical courage, loyalty, magnanimity—all the virtues a
"leadership class" needed to counter the debilitating effects of commerce.
The old republican contrast between luxury and virtue still echoed faintly
among the well-to-do.

The restriction of consumer appetites and the war on waste could have
moral as well as economic benefits. Prohibitionists embraced the war as an
opportunity to complete their agenda of national purification. The wartime
emergency demanded we conserve our grain supply, they said, not pour it
down drunkards' throats. "We can no longer contemplate the waste of human food in order to secure alcohol in any form for beverage purposes,"
Harvey Wiley, director of the Pure Food and Drug Administration, told
Good Housekeeping readers in 1917. Now that scientific investigation had
exposed the fallacy that "men were more brilliant mentally and more efficient physically if slightly intoxicated," we could recognize that Prohibition
enhanced the efficiency of our fighting men. Victory in the war would mean
that "two great blessings would be conferred upon humanity, namely political freedom, implying world-wide democracy, and the establishment of prohibition through all the nations of the world." The world would be made
safe for sobriety. Yet Social Christianity transcended the reform of personal
habits. Many Social Christians agreed with Secretary of War Newton Baker,
a former pacifist, who said that the war was "a high and holy mission" that
might usher in the Kingdom of God on Earth.

Visions of revitalization also came in secular, psychological forms. Positive thinking enveloped the violence of war and made it an empowering
experience. Lieutenant W. R. Gayner of the Royal Air Force told *American
Magazine* readers that the war had revealed hitherto undreamt-of resources
of energy and stamina. As men who had been injured and could have hon-
orably quit returned to fighting, they came to realize "that there is almost no

limit to human endurance and human achievement, if the will to endure and achieve is strong enough." Gayner had nearly been killed by an explosion at Ypres in 1915. It "shot my nerves to pieces," he said. Convalescing, he decided to become a flyer; a crash landing "shot my nerves to pieces again." Still he wouldn't ask for a discharge. "The will really does command the body," he said. Assigned to "light duty," he insisted on flying. Even the routine testing of planes left him a "nervous wreck." "At day's end, I would fall into bed, bury my head in the pillow and cry. Cry like a hysterical woman. I was a nervous wreck and I wouldn't quit." Claiming fitness for duty, he managed to get reassigned to France. But there he broke down, finding himself unable to complete his bombing missions, dropping his bombs early or returning without dropping them at all. When his major asked, "Have you got wind up?" [i.e., "Are you afraid?"] he "ran amuck" and was hospitalized. Declared unfit for duty, he still wanted to fly—"the will, the determination to fly was persisted in so long that it is still there in spite of everything." If the will to "carry on became a fixed idea," one could persevere. If this was true for the "hard business of war," Gayner concluded, then it should be true too for the "business of living and working under normal conditions."

American Magazine presented Gayner's tale of repeated breakdowns as a life lesson in "Doing More Than You Ever Dreamed You Could Do." But not even Americans could stretch positive thinking this far. In Gayner's narrative, the tension between the ideology of will and the experience of war reached the snapping point. Victorian ideals of manliness were dissolving in the muck of "no-man's-land." Meanwhile the neurologist W. H. R. Rivers was working on a different project of regeneration, searching for an end run around sheer willpower, seeking through talk therapy to release shell-shock victims from their nightmares and reintegrate them with their own shattered selves—as well as with some sort of community, however provisional. This was a chastened and humane alternative to older militarist aims—though the ultimate irony was that if Rivers succeeded, his patients would be returned to the trenches. Rivers's work was conducted behind closed doors, at the remote Craiglockhart hospital in Scotland. Most people, on either side of the Atlantic, heard little besides the familiar jargon of heroism and cowardice.

The most interesting critic of war-thinking was the brilliant Randolph Bourne, who before he had turned thirty had developed a reputation as an enemy of slogans and a champion of ambiguity. Indeed, for Bourne and his bohemian cohort, ambiguity was a principle of liberation, the fountainhead of their hopes for a new cultural space where old racial and sexual boundaries were blurred, a "Trans-National America," in Bourne's phrase. But war fever brought the death of ambiguity, and the person best positioned to write its obituary was Bourne—an intense romantic idealist, a passionate believer in the regenerative power of friendship, youth, and life. For several years Bourne had been writing cultural criticism that blended Progressive and bohemian dreams of liberation. No one could exceed the articulacy of his disdain for the stuffy gentility of the fading Victorian order, or of his devotion to the new creed of "education for living" that "Professor Dewey" was preaching at Columbia. As a student there, Bourne had nurtured his vitalist enthusiasms and declared himself a pragmatist. But as he watched Dewey and his colleagues at *The New Republic* unfold their rationale for war, he rethought his worldview in public. Eventually he realized the futility and danger of a politics that promised reconnection with "real life"— especially in wartime, when the pursuit of intense experience led inexorably to the battlefield. For Bourne, the Western Front was the graveyard of the politics of regeneration.

After college, Bourne made his way as a freelancer, trying with only limited success to sustain working relationships with the *Atlantic Monthly* and *The New Republic*, finding a home eventually at the upstart *Seven Arts*. There he developed his critique of war-thinking. When Dewey defended America's entry into the war, Bourne deplored what he believed was a betrayal of pragmatism. The man whose philosophy was supposed to provide us unprecedented power to intervene intelligently in the course of history was instead preaching "adjustment" to "the logic of events." Bourne traced this reversal to a key weakness in the pragmatic celebration of experience. "If your ideal is to be adjustment to the situation, in radiant co-operation with reality, then your success is liable to be just that and no more," he declared. "You never transcend anything."

Dewey's acquiescence in the war was only a symptom of its impact on "responsible" intellectuals. Though "the academic mind" was appalled by militarism in 1914, Bourne observed, "two years later would find it creating its own cleanly [sic] reasons for imposing military service on the country and for talking of the rough rude currents of health and regeneration that war would send through the body politic." Liberal intellectuals, he observed, were "not content with confirming our belligerent gesture. They are now complacently asserting that it was they who effectively willed it, against the hesitation and dim perceptions of the American masses." As intellectuals abandoned their critical role, "their thought becomes little more than a description and justification of what is going on," said Bourne. They had all embraced "realism." "This realistic boast is so loud and sonorous that one wonders whether realism is always a stern and intelligent grappling with realities. May it not sometimes be a mere surrender to the actual, an abdication of the ideal through a sheer fatigue from intellectual suspense?" he asked. The quest for contact with "real life" had become the nationalist Progressives' capitulation to the realities of the war.

Bourne was damned if he was going to surrender to the actual or abdicate the ideal. His antiwar writings made him a target of the newly created FBI. Even on summer outings to the Connecticut shore he was followed by government agents, whom he believed to have been put on his trail by Dewey. Penniless, isolated, he died a victim of the influenza epidemic in 1918. Even in his desperate last months, he still wore his trademark black cape, while he worked on a manuscript dissecting the new lineaments of power emerging in the modern state. Its most famous sentence became a slogan among dissenters for decades: "War is the health of the state." Bourne had put his finger on a crucial feature of modern politics.

But Wilson wanted far more from the war than a healthy national state. Indeed, that was the least of his concerns. He remained largely oblivious to the abuses of police power and the suppression of civil liberties at home, while he became ever more deeply absorbed in "playing for a hundred years hence" (as he told an aide), laying the foundation for long-term epochal change in the postwar world. In January 1918, he presented his plans for a just peace in his "Fourteen Points" speech. The first point was an end to secret agreements in favor of "open covenants of peace, openly arrived at." This was Wilson's attempt to move the Protestant ideals of plain speech and social transparency into that most opaque and indirect of speech arenas, international diplomacy. It is tempting to dismiss as a sentimental relic of the Victorian cult of sincerity, but important to remember how many secret treaties were woven together to form the fuse of World War I. Among the other "points" were freedom of the seas, the reduction of armaments, an end to tariff barriers, and an impartial adjustment of colonial claims—all compatible with nineteenth-century traditions of great-power diplomacy. The departure was the fourteenth point: "a general association of nations must be formed under specific covenants for the purpose of affording mutual guarantees of political independence and territorial integrity to great and small states alike."

This capacious international vision helped fitfully to widen Wilson's perspective on his own country. After years of silence on the subject, in July 1918 he denounced the lynching of African-Americans (as well as "German sympathizers"). "How shall we commend democracy to the acceptance of other peoples, if we disgrace our own by proving that it is, after all, no protection to the weak?" he asked. Wilson also switched his position on female suffrage, which he had opposed before the war. His utopian vision of democracy demanded women's inclusion, and besides, he said in September 1918, equal suffrage would help win the trust of the plain people of the world, who "think, in their logical simplicity, that democracy means that women shall play their part in affairs alongside men." The reference to "simplicity" was a vestige of paternalism but Wilson was clearly groping toward a larger vision of democracy.

For more than a year after American entry into the war, things looked bleak for the Allies. As the U.S. war department scrambled to mobilize and dispatch an army overseas, the Germans made a separate peace with the Russian Bolsheviks and began transferring forces from the Eastern to the Western Front. Through the spring and early summer of 1918, the Germans advanced across the Western Front, retaking contested villages, plundering wine cellars, celebrating what they thought was imminent triumph. But the celebration was premature. Victorious but exhausted, the Germans settled into sodden complacency and finally fell back before an Allied counterattack on August 8, which Count von Ludendorff called "The Black Day of the German Army." The Allies broke into the clear and discovered they could maneuver forces for the first time in four years. By this time the Yanks had arrived. They hastened the German retreat by attacking at St. Mihiel and in the Argonne Forest. Suddenly the end seemed near, and Wilson's dream less distant.

During the congressional campaign of 1918, Wilson ignored domestic politics, remaining obsessed with securing conditions for a just peace. TR was disgusted by Wilson's "limited liability" war; he wanted nothing less than unconditional surrender. When Germany opened negotiations for an armistice in October 1918 on the basis of the fourteen points, Roosevelt sneered: "Let us dictate peace by the hammering guns and not chat about peace to the accompaniment of the clicking of typewriters." Though few voters (if any) joined Roosevelt in genuflecting to the gods of war, many were swept up in fitful bursts of war fever, even as they felt increasingly fatigued by the relative discomforts and deprivations of life on the home front. With the Democrats divided and Wilson distracted, the Republicans swept to majorities in both houses.

At the same time, the German government was collapsing. On November 9, 1918, the kaiser fled and Germany declared itself a republic. Two days later, in the Forest of Compiegne, German representatives signed an armistice that halted the fighting. When the guns finally stopped, the silence was deafening. The Central Powers had lost 3.5 million men, the Allies over 5 million. American casualties, after only six months of actual fighting, were 112,000 dead and 230,000 wounded. It was unthinkable, especially to Wilson, that they could have died in vain.

Increasingly isolated even within his own party, Wilson announced soon after the armistice that he would attend the Paris Peace Conference to negotiate the details of the settlement himself. Roosevelt continued to grumble, warning against the influence of "professional internationalists"—a "sorry crew" who appealed to "weaklings, illusionists, materialists, lukewarm Americans and faddists of all the types that vitiate sound nationalism." The appeal to "sound nationalism" would ultimately doom the League of Nations.

Wilson did not take sufficient pains to anticipate Republican hostility. In putting together his Paris delegation, he passed over Elihu Root, William Howard Taft, and other Republicans who would have helped to persuade the opposition. Instead he chose Lansing and House and two low-profile public servants, General Tasker H. Bliss and Henry White, a quiet career diplomat. The stage was set for a partisan confrontation on Wilson's return.

Flawed as Wilson's tactics seem in retrospect, by the time of the armistice he had acquired a nearly godlike stature in the eyes of the world. The six months in the winter and spring of 1919, when the peace treaty was being negotiated at Versailles, were truly "the Wilsonian Moment," as the historian Erez Manela has said. "For a brief interval, Wilson stood alone for mankind," H. G. Wells recalled. "And in that brief interval there was a very extraordinary and significant wave of response to him throughout the earth. So eager was the situation that all humanity leapt to accept and glorify Wilson—for a phrase, for a gesture. It seized upon him as its symbol. He was transfigured in the eyes of men. He ceased to be a common statesman; he became a Messiah." If Wells was right about world opinion (and Manela's research suggests he was), then Wilson might be pardoned an occasional lapse into narcissistic grandiosity.

From the outset, Wilson was forced to accede to eviscerating compromises. First he abandoned the dream of transparency: negotiations were conducted the old-fashioned way, in secret and only among the victors—himself, Clemenceau, and George. Germany and Austria were excluded. There was no way this would be a peace without victory. Nationalist commitments, intensified by years of killing, prevented any cooperation on economic matters. The Americans bowed to French and British demands for harsh reparations from Germany, and insisted themselves that the British repay their wartime loans to the last cent. Economic nationalism prevented agreements on tariff reduction, and import duties soared. Rather than creating a new world order, imperial nation-states were intent on re-creating the old. Their efforts were made more urgent by the specter of revolution in Russia. The Allies' panic became apparent in June 1919, when they sent troops to Russia in support of Admiral Kolchak's inept last-ditch effort to restore ruling-class power. Wilson contributed five thousand American soldiers to that botched counterrevolution. Meanwhile, to many observers, the results of the treaty were beginning to seem like little more than a reshuffling of existing empires.

Still there was the League, Wilson's sole remaining hope for genuine transformation. Eventually he won clear approval for the crucial Article X, which bound signatories "to respect and preserve as against external aggression the territorial integrity and . . . political independence of all . . . members of the League." For Wilson, this acknowledgment that war and the threat of war were everybody's responsibility was the core of the new doctrine of collective security. But for the League to work, the dream of democratic plain speech would have to envelop the entire world. "We are depending primarily . . . upon one great force," said Wilson, "the moral force of the public opinion of the world—the cleansing and clarifying and compelling influences of publicity—so that intrigues can no longer have their coverts, so that designs that are sinister can . . . be drawn into the open, so that those things . . . may be properly destroyed by the overwhelming light of the condemnation of the world." Such a blinding vision of enlightenment was bound to darken.

When Wilson came home, he confronted a phalanx of opposition to the treaty. It included Progressives at *The Nation* and *The New Republic*, whose editor Croly concluded that "the League is not powerful enough to redeem the treaty." Lippmann was more vehement, denouncing demands for punitive reparations as "the most drastic kind of interference in the internal life of Germany," and dismissing the League as an excuse for imperial delusions. In the Senate, Wilson faced opposition from Progressive noninterventionists, led by LaFollette, and conservative nationalists, led by Lodge. Opponents were especially perturbed by Article X of the League. Its concept of collective security, in their view, abridged Congress's power to declare war.

Lodge and his allies proposed a series of reservations designed to preserve U.S. sovereignty. Wilson insisted that Article X imposed no legal restraints on Congress, but only a moral obligation on the nation to do its share in promoting the peace of the world. Yet the distinction between legality and morality was elusive. Indeed, Wilson never really clarified the relationship between the League Covenant and the U.S. Constitution, or the ambiguity at the core of the concept of collective security. One did not have to be an "isolationist" to worry that the United States might be dragged into a war—with the highest of humanitarian purposes—against the wishes of its citizens. And one did not have to be a militarist to worry about the abridgement of U.S. sovereignty. Conflicts between abstractions like "the national interest" and "the interests of humanity" were not easy to sort out, unless they were grounded in specific cases. The League ran aground on its managerial ideals of system—above all, the faith that a well-designed organization could overcome deep-rooted human attachments and resentments.

Wilson could not grasp the intractability of these conflicts. Nor could he acknowledge the legitimacy of his opponents' objections. Still, he tried to confront the problem of sovereignty. Wilson acknowledged that membership in the League would entail "some sacrifice" from every nation, but he insisted that the United States "would willingly relinquish some of its sovereignty . . . for the good of the world." Such vast abstractions could hardly reassure his Senate critics, who wondered just who was to decide what was "for the good of the world." Even Wilson could see that the prospects for passage without major compromises were dim. So he decided to take his case over the heads of Congress, directly to the people. It was his final act of hubris.

In late summer 1919, Wilson's train headed west, toward the part of the country where he thought pro-League sentiment was strongest. He appealed to what he hoped was the people's generosity of spirit, admitting that membership in the League—under certain circumstances—could impose restrictions on U.S. policy. "The only way in which you can have impartial determinations in this world is by consenting to something you do not want to do," Wilson told an audience in Butte, Montana. Plagued by the persistent ambiguity of collective security, he also faced increasing suspicions. In the West as elsewhere, generosity of spirit was beginning to flag amid domestic and foreign anxieties. Race and class conflict had flared throughout the war years. In July 1917, a white mob had raged through the African-American sections of East St. Louis, accusing blacks of strikebreaking, killing dozens of people, and reducing their neighborhoods to ashes. This was a straw in the wind. As black migrants streamed into border and Northern cities in search of work, class and race tensions intertwined.

The radicalization of the working class was rooted in their rising expectations. With European immigration cut off by the war, industrial workers had a new power in the labor market. Flexing their muscles, they struck more often than ever before, especially in the mining towns and lumber camps of the West, where the IWW was strong and support for the war contested. But after the armistice, power began to shift back to employers. As orders for war materiel declined, manufacturers cut production, laid off workers, and reduced the wages of the rest.

As in previous decades, the workers fought back. In summer 1919, a fresh wave of strikes swept through steel, coal, and other basic industries, bringing much of the economy to a standstill. In Chicago, white hostility to black migrants erupted in another race riot, which only the National Guard could effectively end. Fears of social upheaval were intensified by revolution abroad. After the Bolshevik seizure of power in October 1917, the Wilsonian vision of universal peace was shadowed by the specter of Communism. Certainly this was true for A. Mitchell Palmer, who had succeeded Thomas Gregory as attorney general. For several months in late 1919 and early 1920, Palmer sustained the wartime mood of hysteria by conducting raids on suspected radicals, deporting many without trial, and helping to orchestrate a nationwide Red Scare. Amid roiling discontent at home and abroad, Wilson's vision of peace began to look less attainable.

Exhausted and sick, Wilson continued his Western tour, committed to making sure that the boys who had died in the war to end war had not died in vain. His rhetoric verged on the apocalyptic as he placed himself at the crossroads of history. "The world did not realize [in 1914] that it had come to the final grapple of principle," he announced. Now that America had been granted "the infinite privilege of fulfilling her destiny and saving the world," we could not retreat, especially from Article X. It aimed at "the taproot of war," which was "still sunk deep in the fertile soil of the human family." At Helena, Montana, on September 11, he posed the question that animated his mission: "Shall the great sacrifice that we made in this war be in vain, or shall it not?" The climax came two weeks later at Pueblo, Colorado. The day was warm, the crowd attentive as Wilson ascended to his conclusion. "There is one thing that the American people always rise to and extend their hand to," he said, "and that is the truth of justice and of liberty and of peace. We have accepted that truth, and we are going to be led by it, and it is going to lead us, and through us the world, out into pastures of quietness and peace such as the world never dreamed of before." Rarely had the religious longings behind Wilson's dream of regeneration been so apparent.

The Pueblo speech was Wilson's last. For weeks he had been suffering from severe headaches and insomnia. His doctor, alarmed by his condition, finally ordered him to cut the tour short. Tossing in his berth, Wilson tried to rest as the train headed home. Soon after he returned to the White House, on October 2, he collapsed with a cerebral thrombosis. Though he eventually regained some speech and movement, he spent the few years left to him a shadowy invalid, closeted in darkened rooms. Like many a wounded veteran, Wilson was a lingering victim of the crusade to remake the world. While Colonel House and Edith Wilson took over most presidential duties, the president himself became more inflexible and irascible than ever, seldom exposed to public view but steadfastly disdaining any compromise with his opponents. What motivated many of them, though Wilson refused to see it, was not head-in-the-sand "isolationism" but a healthy skepticism toward humanitarian arguments for military intervention abroad. In the end, Wilson's rigidity doomed his dream. When the Senate rejected the treaty, he shuffled off the stage a ruined man. The age of regeneration was over.

LONGINGS FOR REGENERATION would not disappear from American public life, but seldom if ever would they again animate such a wide variety of political crusades, with such ambitious goals. The Progressives' dream of a Kingdom of God on Earth inspired a host of reform efforts, many of which led to improvements in American life. Antitrust suits and regulatory commissions, while not altogether consistent with each other, did begin a serious effort to tame capitalism in the name of the public good. Workmen's compensation, child-labor legislation, and eight-hour laws did begin to lay the foundations for the welfare state. Both regulatory and welfare impulses remained on the margins of public discourse during the 1920s, and when they returned to the mainstream in the Great Depression they were expressed in more secular language, as pragmatic responses to a national emergency. For most liberal policy-makers, longings for a cooperative commonwealth had been relegated to the realm of utopian delusion. Indeed, the Prohibition movement, the most immediately successful of Progressive movements for moral renewal, was in little more than a decade declared an abject failure—an emblem of the cultural blinders worn by many seekers of social rebirth.

The Kingdom of God on Earth, like the cooperative commonwealth, was undoubtedly unattainable. American society was too pluralistic to submit to Protestant visions of revitalization, too entrepreneurial to subordinate private ambition to public good. But without those visions of the commonweal, one wonders whether even a limited welfare state would have ever had a chance. The Social Gospel agenda, despite its provincial moralism, was in most respects benign and necessary. Rejecting the rule of mere money, Social Christians set an important precedent for later policies meant to counteract the catastrophic impact of "creative destruction" on everyday life.

While the war brought a temporary end to Progressive reform, it also had salutary unintended consequences. The wartime suppression of civil liberties helped provoke a new language of liberal jurisprudence, more solicitous of minority rights (though it would be nearly fifty years before they included racial minorities' rights), more concerned with privacy and personal freedom. This was part of a broader turn from a politics of regeneration to what one might call a politics of restraint, a politics its proponents characterized more often as liberalism than as Progressivism. When Progressive ideas resurfaced in response to the economic collapse of the 1930s, they were chastened and secular, incrementalist rather than transformative.

The retreat from regenerative dreams was even more apparent in military and foreign policy. The idea of regeneration through war, which inspired dozens of ill-advised interventions and cost millions of lives, finally fell into disgrace in the trenches of the Western Front. After such knowledge, what forgiveness? To postwar ears, Victorian militarists began to sound like posturing fools. Roosevelt's rants and the Creel Committee's chauvinism were the last gasp of a discredited dogma, at least for quite some time. Except among Fascists, the idea that manhood and nationhood could be revitalized through blood sacrifice on the battlefield fell into disuse for decades. This was as true of Wilson's vision as it was of Roosevelt's. Even in World War II, surely a justifiable war, Americans avoided rhetorical exaltation, focusing instead on getting the dirty business done and getting home. The Cold War revived moralistic militarism, which fostered the suicidal grandiosity of the nuclear arms race and wasted thousands of lives in Vietnam and other battlegrounds of counterinsurgency. The U.S. defeat in Vietnam launched a temporary wave of national self-questioning, but the election of Ronald Reagan returned militarist posturing to a central place in American foreign policy. It also coincided with a resurgent cult of Theodore Roosevelt among the makers of mainstream opinion.

The end of the Cold War and the long bull market of the 1990s revived familiar militarist fears of peace, evoking the false comfort and complacency, the "ignoble ease" that had enraged TR. But the terrorist attacks of September 11, 2001, brought militarism back with a vengeance, providing the idea of regenerative war with a luster it had not enjoyed (outside Fascist circles) for nearly a century. Recalling the nationalist Progressives of the 1910s, Paul Berman, Christopher Hitchens, and other "liberal hawks" sang the praises of war from the safety of their studies. The ghost of Roosevelt returned to haunt the corridors of power. So did the ghost of Wilson, though pundits missed the mark when they called the preemptive unilateralist George W. Bush a "Wilsonian." Despite Wilson's failings, his reputation deserved a better fate. He hated war, and was even willing to abridge national sovereignty to avoid it. TR, not Wilson, was Bush's ideological ancestor.

Wilson's fatal error lay in persuading himself that he could achieve peace only through war. Seduced by what James Joyce called "those big words . . .

which make us so unhappy"—justice and liberty, freedom and democracy—
Wilson lost his way in a fog of humanitarian intentions. Many Progressives
followed him, abandoning the logic of nonintervention to obey something
deeper than logic—"an unanalyzable feeling," as Randolph Bourne called
it, "that this was a war in which we had to be." Safely ensconced at their
desks, they longed to immerse themselves vicariously in the regeneration of
the world. High-sounding words were a comforting refuge.

What language was adequate to characterize the enormity of modern
war? The question haunted peacemakers after World War II as well. The
United Nations Charter of 1945 recalled Wilson's rhetoric, but in a chastened spirit. Henry Cabot Lodge Jr. noted with pride that the charter included all his father's reservations. An international organization could be
tolerated, it appeared, only so long as it could be subordinated to national
sovereignty. Still, the Geneva Conventions, as revised and extended in 1949,
persisted in pursuing the dream that nations could be held to a common
set of ethical standards. The Conventions' intent to avoid the murkiness of
subjectivity could lead to an abstract universalism that overlooked idiosyncratic situations and context-dependent decisions. International law could
unintentionally legitimate war by accepting the rhetoric of "clean, smart
bombs" or "appropriate" levels of casualties. Violence, as always, could be
legitimated by bland, universalist language.

Yet the language of the Conventions continues to exert a salutary restraint, a reminder that certain kinds of behavior are simply unacceptable.
Even contemporary apologists for torture contort themselves to claim that
they are not in violation of international law. So we are left with the modest
insight that the Wilsonian language of universal rights, however flawed, is
the best alternative we have to unspeakable slaughter. Talking really is better than fighting.

This is a humane and sensible conclusion, but it leaves something out.
There are more languages of war than were dreamt of in Wilson's philosophical universe. To hear them we need finally to turn to literature. In *The
Ghost Road*, Pat Barker's great novel of World War I, the protagonist Billy
Prior echoes Hemingway's Frederick Henry in asserting that after years of
mass death, only the names of places had any meaning left: "Mons, Loos,
the Somme, Arras, Verdun, Ypres." But then he looks around at the "linked
shadows" of himself and his men and remembers "another group of words
that still mean something. Little words that rip through sentences unre-

garded: us, them, we, they, here, there. These are the words of power, and long after we're gone, they'll lie about in the language, like the unexploded grenades in these fields, and any one of them'll take your hand off."

Prior dies in the last week of the Great War, but Barker has one unexploded grenade left. From the memoirs of the neurologist W. H. R. Rivers she fashions a scene of a soldier dying at Craiglockhart hospital, an idealistic young officer named Hallett.

> The whole left side of his face drooped. The exposed eye was sunk deep in his skull, open, though he didn't seem to be fully conscious. His hair had been shaved off, preparatory to whatever operation had left the horseshoe-shaped scar, now healing ironically well, above the suppurating wound left by the rifle bullet. The hernia cerebri pulsated, looking like some strange submarine form of life, the mouth of a sea anemone perhaps. The whole of the left side of the body was useless. Even when he was conscious enough to speak, the drooping of the mouth and the damage to the lower jaw made his speech impossible to follow. This, more than anything else, horrified his family. You saw them straining to understand, but they couldn't grasp a word he said. His voice came in a whisper because he lacked the strength to project it. He seemed to be whispering now.

"Shotvarfet," Hallett seems to say. "Shotvarfet." Finally Rivers realizes what he is saying: "It's not worth it." The cry spreads across the ward. "A buzz of protest not against the cry, but in support of it, a wordless murmur from damaged brains and drooping mouths. *'Shotvarfet. Shotvarfet.'*" The cry goes on and on, until in the end the mangled words fade into silence, and Hallett dies.

This is another language of war, a language closer to ritual incantation than to reasoned discourse, not the sort of language you could use in political debate. Yet it has a political point. Amid the official language of war, then and now, it is worth recalling that darkened ward of broken men and their dark, insistent truth. They remind us that sometimes a pacifist stance is the least sentimental of all, the most thoroughly embedded in the viscera of experience.

ACKNOWLEDGMENTS

EVERYONE MENTIONED HERE contributed substantially to this book; none of them, of course, is responsible for its shortcomings. Those are my responsibility. I am grateful, first of all, to Sean Wilentz for proposing that I write the book, for reading the manuscript with sustained critical attention, and for helping me clarify some crucial matters of fact and interpretation. I also owe a debt of gratitude to Tim Duggan, my editor at HarperCollins, who has provided essential criticism and advice in seeing the book through to publication. Leon Wieseltier and Adam Shatz gave me generous space to think about people and ideas in print. Bill Taylor reminded me why this work matters.

The generosity of friends and colleagues has been extraordinary. Gregory Conti, Rochelle Gurstein, Alison Isenberg, and Jean-Christophe Agnew read the manuscript with uncommon care and made many valuable suggestions. Rutgers University has once again provided a superb setting for scholarship. The Rutgers Center for Historical Analysis seminar on "The Question of the West," which I led with Ann Fabian for two years, created a continuing ferment of ideas and possibilities. Many of those ideas came from Ann herself, who influenced my thinking at a number of crucial junctures. Lloyd Gardner offered his expertise in foreign policy history. Hilary Hallett and Chris Brown also provided well-timed advice and encouragement. So did Robert Johnston. Eric Barry and Kelly Enright contributed valuable research assistance. Stephanie Volmer and Donna Green created a wonderfully congenial work environment at *Raritan*, sustaining the magazine with good cheer and fine style despite its editor's preoccupations with his manuscript.

Virginia Gilmartin deserves a paragraph unto herself. She not only performed all the usual research assistant's tasks with thoroughness and precision—checking facts and footnotes, tracking down sources—she also summarized and quoted from various kinds of evidence with judgment, tact, and taste, and unearthed many of the characters and stories that helped to make this more than a history of the prominent and powerful. Without her, this book could not have been written.

Nor could it have been written without the scholars whose work I cited, summarized, paraphrased, and synthesized. I have tried to acknowledge my dependence on them in my end notes and bibliographic note. Undoubtedly I have left some out, but I am reminded again of the truthful old chestnut that (however solitary the experience of writing) scholarship is a collaborative enterprise.

My largest and least calculable debt is to Karen Parker Lears, who lived this book with me and who contributed immeasurably to whatever value it might possess. She took essential time from her own artistic work to read the manuscript with a patient and perceptive editor's eye, promoting its nuances, grounding its abstractions, widening its reach. She stirred my imagination at every turn, challenging me to engage the most important intellectual issues raised by the story I was trying to tell, even while she reminded me that the story was about human beings rather than scholarly concepts. And she gave me my epigraph. In my work and in my life, she has been an emissary of grace.

I dedicate this book to my dear daughters, Rachel and Adin, who both embody and inspire radical hope. I borrow the phrase from Jonathan Lear, and extend its meaning. Lear's great book on the Crow Indians, *Radical Hope: Ethics in the Face of Cultural Devastation*, explores how the Crow were able to go forward when there was no way even to conceive of going forward, when their way of making meaning had collapsed into nothingness: by cultivating *poesis*, poetry in the largest sense of artistic making, they somehow regenerated hope when the familiar ground for hope was gone. To compare contemporary Americans to the Crow Indians may seem preposterous; surely this privileged society has not descended to such a hopeless condition. Yet the point about the Crow, as Lear makes clear, is not that they suffered physically (they made peace with the U.S. government and survived more successfully than their enemies, the Sioux) but that they suffered metaphysically—they lost their reference points for moving into the future. Most Americans would deny that we have come to such a catastrophic pass. But there are times when our public challenges seem so complex and overwhelming that it is hard to imagine a future without some version of radical hope. That is one reason my daughters—along with the rest of the rising generations—are so precious to me. They want and need a future. I want to help provide them with one.

Furman's Corner, New Jersey
August 2008

NOTES

INTRODUCTION: DREAMING OF REBIRTH

2   "The color . . . world": W. E. B. DuBois, "The Color Line Belts the World," *Collier's*, 28 (October 20, 1906), 30.

2   "creative destruction": Joseph Schumpeter, *Capitalism, Socialism, and Democracy* [1942] (Harper and Row: New York, 1975), 82–85; "marked us . . . the world": Albert Beveridge, "Our Philippine Policy," in Daniel Schirmer and Stephen Rosskamm Shalom, eds., *The Philippines Reader: A History of Colonialism, Neocolonialism, Dictatorship, and Resistance* (South End Press: Boston, 1987), 23; "Peace Without Victory": Woodrow Wilson, Speech to U.S. Senate, January 22, 1917, in Arthur Link et al., eds. *Papers of Woodrow Wilson*, 69 vols. (Princeton University Press: Princeton, 1966–1990), 40, 533–539.

3   "Vengeance . . . Lord": Romans 12:19.

6   "a machine . . . itself": James Russell Lowell quoted in Michael Kammen, *A Machine That Would Go of Itself: The Constitution in American Culture* [1986] (Transaction Books: Edison, N.J., 2006), 18.

7   "neurasthenia . . . hopelessness": George Miller Beard, *American Nervousness: Its Causes and Consequences* (New York, 1881), vi, 5, 7, 8; "Every . . . spirit": Ralph Waldo Emerson, "Fate" [1851], reprinted in Joel Porte, ed., *Emerson: Essays and Lectures* (Library of America: New York, 1983), 946.

8   "it will . . . weightless": Friedrich Nietzsche quoted in Karl Jaspers, *Nietzsche and Christianity*, trans. E. B. Ashton (J. Regnery: Chicago, 1963), 14.

CHAPTER ONE: THE LONG SHADOW OF APPOMATTOX

14   "The ditch . . . touching ground": George A. Mercer Diary, July 21, 1863, Southern Historical Collection, University of North Carolina, Chapel Hill, quoted in Charles Royster, *The Destructive War: William Tecumseh Sherman, Stonewall Jackson, and the Americans* (Knopf: New York, 1991), 275.

14   "Multiply . . . this war": Walt Whitman, *Specimen Days* [1882], Louise Pound, ed. (Doubleday, Doran: New York, 1935), 69.

15   "savage. . . . military necessity": Lieber's Code, reprinted in Leon Friedman, *The Law of War: A Documentary History*, 2 vols. (Random House: New York, 1972), I, 158–86; "turn the Shenandoah Valley . . . carry their provender with

them": Grant quoted in Harry S. Stout, *Upon the Altar of the Nation: A Moral History of the Civil War* (Viking: New York, 2006), 380.

17   "pass . . . blood": *Richmond Examiner*, February 4, 1862, reprinted in Frank Moore, ed., *The Rebellion Record: A Diary of American Events,* 11 vols. (D. Von Nostrand: New York, 1861–68), 4, 22; "I rejoice. . . . John Brown": Henry Wise, in ibid., 1, 324.

18   "smite . . . the world is won": "A National Fast Day Hymn," *Banner of the Covenant*, September 21, 1861, quoted in Stout, *Upon the Altar of the Nation*, 76; "both a prayer . . . ages": Rev. Alexander Vinton, *A Sermon Preached on the National Thanksgiving Day* (New York, 1863), 8; "let it be . . . burned": O. T. Lanphear, *Peace by Power: A Discourse* (New Haven, Conn., 1864), 13, quoted in Royster, *Destructive War*, 363.

19   "religious war. . . . the battlefield": Charles Eliot Norton, "The Advantages of Defeat," *Atlantic Monthly*, 8 (1861), 361–62; "a vigorous war. . . had passed": *Albany Argus*, quoted in Royster, *Destructive War*, 265; "I have felt . . . for the nation": Benson Lossing to Sue Wallace, Lew Wallace Papers, Indiana Historical Society, Indianapolis, Ind., quoted in ibid., 258.

20   "My old friend . . . free' ": Frederick Douglass, *Life and Times of Frederick Douglass* [1893], *Autobiographies: Frederick Douglass* (Library of America: New York, 1994), 791–92.

21   "that races develop . . . self-government": Josiah Strong, quoted in Stephen J. Gould, *The Mismeasure of Man* (Norton: New York, 1981), 118–19.

22   "*feels* like a real fight": William James, "Is Life Worth Living?" [1895] in his *The Will to Believe and Other Essays* (Harvard University Press: Cambridge, Mass., and London, 1979), 55.

24   "What a moment . . . for words": Frederick Douglass, *My Bondage and My Freedom* [1855] (Dover: New York, 1969), 336–37.

25   "Men talk. . . . against it": Douglass quoted in William S. McFeely, *Frederick Douglass* (Norton: New York, 1991), 371.

26–27   "birth of constitutional liberty": John Cochrane quoted in David W. Blight, *Race and Reunion: The Civil War and American Memory* (Harvard University Press: Cambridge, Mass., and London, 2001), 87; "the War. . . . determination": John C. Ropes, "The War as We See It Now," *Scribner's*, 9 (1891), 778, 785.

27   "Whether just. . . . our sons": General M. M. Trumbull, "The Dilemma of a Double Allegiance," *Open Court*, 3 (1889), 1511–13; "survival of the fittest": Herbert Spencer, *Principles of Biology*, 2 vols. [1864] (D. Appleton: New York, 1898), 1, 530.

28   "A hundred. . . . enduring": William Blaikie, "Is American Stamina Declining?" *Harper's Monthly*, 79 (1889), 241–44.

30–31   "Through our great. . . . come after us": Oliver Wendell Holmes, "Memorial Day" [1884], in Mark DeWolfe Howe, comp. *The Occasional Speeches of Justice Oliver Wendell Holmes* (Harvard University Press: Cambridge, Mass., 1962), 15; "a race fit . . . for command": Oliver Wendell Holmes, "The Soldier's Faith" [1895], in Howe, *Speeches*, 81; "we fight . . . for the joy of it":

Holmes quoted in George Frederickson, *The Inner Civil War: Northern Intellectuals and the Crisis of the Union* (Harper and Row: New York, 1967), 219.

31 "temptations . . . all its forms": in Holmes, "Soldier's Faith," 81; "the faith . . . the use": Holmes, ibid., 76.

32 "*the creating . . . wants*": Josiah Strong, *Our Country* [1885] (Baker and Taylor: New York, 1891), 15.

33 "During the War. . . . were there?": Philip Sheridan quoted in Stout, *Upon the Altar of the Nation*, 460.

33–34 "We must act . . . the case": William Tecumseh Sherman to U. S. Grant, quoted in Evan S. Connell, *Son of the Morning Star: Custer and the Little Big Horn* (North Point Press: San Francisco, 1984), 132; "race ruled . . . be known": Henry Adams, *The Education of Henry Adams* [1907] (Modern Library: New York, 1931), 411.

34–35 "the world . . . on earth": Josiah Strong, *The New Era, or The Coming Kingdom* (Baker and Taylor: New York, 1893), 81; "swarthy . . . sunlight": Charles Dudley Warner, *In the Levant* (J. R. Osgood: Boston, 1877), 16.

35 "I am . . . salmon": Frederick Benteen quoted in Connell, *Morning Star*, 12.

36 "make . . . body": TR quoted in Kim Townsend, *Manhood at Harvard: William James and Others* (Harvard University Press: Cambridge, Mass., and London, 1996), 258; "As I rose . . . senseless": Theodore Roosevelt, *An Autobiography* [1913] (Library of America: New York, 2004), 378.

36–37 "During . . . effects and importance": Theodore Roosevelt, *The Winning of the West*, 3 vols. (G. P. Putnam: New York, 1889–96), 1, 1; "on the whole . . . the frontier": Roosevelt, *Thomas Hart Benton* [1887] (Houghton Mifflin: Boston, 1890), 211; "but a few . . . joint ownership": Roosevelt, *Winning*, 3, 43; "I don't go . . . of the tenth": Roosevelt, quoted in Walter LaFeber, *The American Search for Opportunity, 1865–1913* (New York, 1993), 189.

37–38 "Over-sentimentality . . . little avail": Roosevelt quoted in Matthew Frye Jacobson, *Barbarian Virtues: The United States Encounters Foreign Peoples at Home and Abroad, 1876–1917* (Hill and Wang: New York, 2000), 3; "huge drops. . . . down": Nelson Miles, *Personal Recollections* (Werner: Chicago, 1896), 317.

38 "What shall be done. . . . let others do it": *Yankton Press & Dakotan*, quoted in Connell, *Morning Star*, 238; "One does not . . . walk": Crazy Horse quoted in ibid., 73.

39 "noble savage. . . . pleasure": Mrs. Frank Leslie, *California: A Pleasure Trip from Gotham to the Golden Gate* [1877] (B. de Graaf: Nieuwkoop, Netherlands, 1972), 106, 107.

40–41 "This perennial . . . character.": Frederick Jackson Turner, "The Significance of the Frontier in American History" [1893] reprinted in his *The Frontier in American History* (Henry Holt: New York, 1920), 2.

41 "The first scalp for Custer!": William Cody quoted in Robert W. Rydell and Rob Kroes, *Buffalo Bill in Bologna: The Americanization of the World, 1869–1922* (University of Chicago Press: Chicago and London, 2005), 29.

42–43 "the Northern Pacific . . . his men had died": Elizabeth Custer quoted in John B. Kennedy, "A Soldier's Widow," *Collier's*, 79 (January 29, 1927), 10; "I think . . . for a week": John Hay to Whitelaw Reid, January 27, 1880, quoted in Richard Drinnon, *Facing West: The Metaphysics of Indian-hating and Empire Building* (University of Minnesota Press: Minneapolis, 1980), 261.

43   "The North alone . . . the Saxon race": *Richmond Whig*, quoted in Connell, *Morning Star*, 331.

43   "Frank, brave. . . . his ability": "Mrs. Custer's Army Life," *Atlantic Monthly*, 62 (1888), 426.

44   "President Roosevelt. . . . think it": Elizabeth Custer quoted in Kennedy, "Soldier's Widow," 41; "Far better . . . defeat": Roosevelt quoted in Connell, *Morning Star*, 277.

45   "I never . . . a thrill": Louise Knight, *Citizen: Jane Addams and the Struggle for Democracy* (University of Chicago Press: Chicago and London, 2005), 57; "the greatest man in the world": ibid., 62; "We felt . . . surrounded us": ibid., 58; "I always . . . happen": ibid., 66; "career . . . heroism": ibid., 88.

45–46   "You do not know. . . . the morning": Jane Addams, *Twenty Years at Hull House* (Macmillan: New York, 1910), 32; "The great cry . . . militant": ibid., 30; "self-absorbed and priggish": Knight, *Citizen*, 161.

46   "One . . . interdependence": ibid., 141; "keen . . . fiber": ibid., 213.

47   "The thought. . . . marrow": Mark Twain, "The Private History of a Campaign That Failed," [1885] in his *Tales, Speeches, Essays, and Sketches,* Thomas Quirk, ed. (Penguin: New York, 1994), 180; "seemed . . . needed it": ibid., 181.

48   "My words . . . men": William James, "Is Life Worth Living?" in his *The Will to Believe and Other Essays* (Longmans, Green: New York, 1897), 39; "The existence . . . explained": ibid., 48; "not . . . maybe": ibid., 53; "If this . . . redeem": ibid., 55.

CHAPTER TWO: THE MYSTERIOUS POWER OF MONEY

51   "Money. . . . quicker": Benjamin Franklin, "Advice to a Young Tradesman, Written By an Old One," in *The American Instructor, or Young Man's Best Companion* [1748], reprinted in *The Papers of Benjamin Franklin*, Leonard Labaree, ed., 38 vols. (Yale University Press: New Haven, 1961), 3, 306.

53   "The Colonel's tongue . . . riches": Mark Twain and Charles Dudley Warner, *The Gilded Age* [1873] (Penguin: New York, 2001), 59.

53   "Universal Distrust": Charles Dickens, *American Notes for General Circulation* [1842] (St. Martin's: New York, 1985), 224; "No Trust": Herman Melville, *The Confidence Man* [1857] (Northwestern University Press: Evanston and Chicago, 1994), 5; "Beautiful credit! . . . promises?": Twain and Warner, *Gilded Age*, 189; "a distinguished speculator . . . dollars": ibid., 189.

55   "from this . . . to understand": 1891 guidebook quoted in William Cronon, *Nature's Metropolis: Chicago and the Great West* (Norton: New York, 1992), 264.

55   "the icy waters . . . calculation": Karl Marx and Friedrich Engels, "Manifesto of the Communist League" [1844], reprinted in Robert C. Tucker, ed., *The Marx-Engels Reader* (Norton: New York, 1978), 475.

56 "the patient. . . . their sorrows": T. P. Childs & Co., *Childs Catarrh Remedy* (T. P. Childs: Troy, Ohio, 1877), n.p., Warshaw Collection of Business Americana, National Museum of American History, Smithsonian Institution, Washington, DC, Patent Medicines, Box 5.

58 "the community": Andrew Carnegie, "The Gospel of Wealth II" in his *The "Gospel of Wealth" Essays and Other Writings*, David Nasaw, ed. (Penguin: New York, 2006), 61.

58–59 "I considered . . . capital": Andrew Carnegie, "From Bobbin Boy to Millionaire," *The Golden Penny*, 23 (1899), 87, quoted in David Nasaw, *Andrew Carnegie* (Penguin: New York, 2006), 55; "tied himself . . . never let go": ibid., 58; "I shall remember . . . eggs' ": Andrew Carnegie, *Autobiography of Andrew Carnegie* [1920] (Northeastern University Press: Boston, 1986), 76; "How money . . . a 'capitalist' ": Andrew Carnegie, "How I Served My Apprenticeship," in Joseph Wall, ed., *The Andrew Carnegie Reader* (Pittsburgh, 1992), 37.

60 "the poor man's light": Ron Chernow, *Titan: The Life of John D. Rockefeller, Sr.* (Random House: New York, 1998), 257.

61 "God gave me my money": 1905 interview, quoted in Peter Collier and David Horowitz, *The Rockefellers: An American Dynasty* (Holt, Rinehart, and Winston: New York, 1976), 48.

61 "God's bounty . . . life's cares": Chernow, *Titan*, 24; "I was. . . . at the note": Allan Nevins, *John D. Rockefeller*, 2 vols. (Scribner: New York, 1940), 1, 105; "The impression . . . money": Ida Tarbell, *History of the Standard Oil Company*, 2 vols. (Macmillan: New York, 1914), 1, 40.

62 "Something . . . schedule": Inglis quoted in Chernow, *Titan*, 502; "Do unto . . . first": David Leon Chandler, *Henry Flagler* (Macmillan: New York, 1986), 82.

62 "the world . . . freedom": John D. Rockefeller to Laura S. Rockefeller, January 30, 1872, quoted in Chernow, *Titan*, 138. Emphasis in original.

63 "keep cool. . . . happy": Jerome Bates, *The Imperial Highway: Essays on Business and Home Life with Biographies of Self-made Men* (National Library Association: Chicago, 1888), 228.

64 " 'civilized' . . . morality": Sigmund Freud, " 'Civilized' Sexual Morality and Modern Nervous Illness," [1908] in James Strachey, ed., *The Standard Edition of the Complete Psychological Works of Sigmund Freud*, 24 vols. (Hogarth Press: London, 1959), 9, 177–204.

64 "a man. . . . poverty": Junius Henri Browne, "Pecuniary Independence," *Harper's Monthly*, 88 (1894), 903–06.

66 "a Speculator. . . . a hundred others": Henry Ward Beecher, *Lectures to Young Men on Various Important Subjects* (J. C. Derby: New York, 1856), 76–77; "unhealthy . . . shiftlessness": Thomas McIntyre Cooley, "Federal Taxation of Lotteries," *Atlantic Monthly*, 69 (1892), 523–35.

66 "pecuniary emulation": Thorstein Veblen, *The Theory of the Leisure Class* [1899] (Macmillan: New York, 1912), 21–22 *et passim*.

67   "American girl": Rudyard Kipling, "The American Girl," *Ladies' Home Journal*, 16 (1899), 5.

67   "to arrive. . . . too much": C. S. Messinger, "Family Expenses," *Good Housekeeping*, 3 (1886), 73–74.

68   "the chief . . . modern civilization": George Miller Beard, *American Nervousness: Its Causes and Consequences* (G. P. Putnam's: New York, 1881), vi.

68–69   "Louisa lived. . . . we could": Frances Dyer, "Economize Your Strength. A Reserve Force," *Good Housekeeping*, 1 (1885), 5–6; "has not kept . . . could": Anna C. Brackett, "The Technique of Rest," *Harper's Monthly*, 83 (1891), 46.

69   "Pierpont . . . the sun": Letter, Henry Adams to Elizabeth Cameron, February 11, 1901, in *The Letters of Henry Adams*, 6 vols., J. C. Levenson et al., eds. (Harvard University Press: Cambridge, Mass., and London, 1982), 5, 199.

70   "The invalid. . . . this fashion": A. B. Ward, "Invalidism as a Fine Art," *Harper's Monthly*, 77 (1888), 926–27.

71   "relapsing fever . . . ever had": Edward Crapsey, "The Nether Side of New York, VII—Tenement Life," *Galaxy*, 12 (1872), 177.

71   "The Pensioner's. . . . a hero!": ibid., 172–73.

72   "in a year. . . . hard work": "Three Typical Workmen," *Atlantic Monthly*, 42 (1878), 717–27.

74   "be . . . a misfortune": Karl Marx, *Capital: A Critique of Political Economy*, 3 vols. (Charles H. Kerr: Chicago, 1906), 1, 558.

74   "unselfish brotherhood": David Montgomery, *The Fall of the House of Labor* (Cambridge University Press: New York, 1987), 17; "Oh, they . . . slow": ibid., 90.

75   "You keel . . . long time": Whiting Williams, *What's on the Worker's Mind, By One Who Put On Overalls to Find Out* (Scribner: New York, 1920), 15.

75   "as roving . . . their locations": Montgomery, *House of Labor*, 134.

76   "benastied. . . . trick": Emily French, *Emily: The Diary of a Hard-Worked Woman* [1890], Janet Lecompte, ed. (University of Nebraska Press: Lincoln, 1987), 23, 32, 35, 40, 108, 124.

78   "anxiety and suffering. . . . their notes": "Workingmen's Wives," *Atlantic Monthly*, 43 (1879), 59, 64, 70.

80–81   "Since last week. . . . the simple truth": Letter, John Hay to Amasa Stone, in William Roscoe Thayer, *John Hay*, 2 vols. [1915] (Kraus Reprints: New York, 1969), 1, 1–2; "regular army . . . emergencies": *New York Tribune*, July 19, 1877, quoted in Richard Slotkin, *The Fatal Environment: The Myth of the Frontier in the Age of Industrialization* (Atheneum: New York, 1985), 485.

81   "the strike. . . . that is all": Henry Ward Beecher, "Plymouth Pulpit. The Strike and Its Lessons," *Christian Union*, 16 (August 8, 1877), 112–14.

83   "no pride . . . no craft": Montgomery, *Fall of the House of Labor*, 161.

83   "The Eight-Hour Song": quoted in Roy Rosenzweig, *Eight Hours for What We Will: Workers and Leisure in an Industrial City, 1870–1920* (Cambridge University Press: New York and London, 1983), 1.

84   "this republic . . . opinions": Howells quoted in James Green, *Death in the Haymarket* (Pantheon: New York, 2006), 272; "frantic opinions": ibid., 257.

84   "The enemy . . . the Rhine": John Higham, *Strangers in the Land: Patterns of American Nativism* (Atheneum: New York, 1963), 42.

86   "Kind Master . . . for you": Nasaw, *Carnegie*, 468–69.

87   "If it was right. . . . those laws": Henry C. Adams quoted in Daniel T. Rodgers, *Atlantic Crossings: Social Politics in a Progressive Age* (Harvard University Press: Cambridge, Mass., and London, 1998), 96–97.

87   "in restraint of trade": *Encyclopedia of American History*, Richard B. Morris, ed. (Harper: New York, 1953), 261.

90   "chromo-civilization": [E. L. Godkin] "Chromo-civilization," *The Nation*, 24 (September 1874), 201–02.

CHAPTER THREE: THE RISING SIGNIFICANCE OF RACE

92   "The smoking car . . . camp-meeting": Harold W. Mann, *Atticus Greene Haygood: Methodist Bishop, Editor, and Educator* (University of Georgia Press: Athens, 1965), 123–24.

92   "With the tubes. . . . immobile": Mell Marshall Barrett, "Recollections of My Boyhood: The Picnic at Pitman's Mill," typescript in Georgia Department of Archives and History, Atlanta, Ga., 49–50, quoted in Edward L. Ayers, *The Promise of the New South: Life After Reconstruction* (Oxford University Press: New York and Oxford, 1992), 159.

96   "a step. . . . prosperity": Thomas Wentworth Higginson, "Some War Scenes Revisited," *Atlantic Monthly*, 42 (1878), 3, 5, 7, 8.

97   "the savage . . . border": quoted in Matthew Frye Jacobsen, *Whiteness of a Different Color: European Immigrants and the Alchemy of Race* (Harvard University Press: Cambridge, Mass., and London, 1998), 156.

98   "ostentation . . . incivility": quoted in ibid., 161.

98–99   "There were. . . . Puddlers' Jubilee": Michael McGovern, *Labor Lyrics, and Other Poems* (Youngstown, Ohio, 1899), 27–28, cited in David Roediger, *The Wages of Whiteness: Race and the Making of the American Working Class*, rev. ed. (Verso: London and New York, 1998), 179; "drive . . . California": Jacobson, *Whiteness*, 160.

101   "too much . . . manhood": *Dallas News* [1886], quoted in Lawrence Goodwyn, *The Populist Moment: A Short History of the Agrarian Revolt in America* (Oxford University Press: New York, 1978), 53; "It would. . . . politically": John Boyle O'Reilly quoted in Rebecca Edwards, *Angels in the Machinery: Gender in American Party Politics from the Civil War to the Progressive Era* (Oxford University Press: New York, 1997), 4.

101   "His long hair . . . on the farm": Booker T. Washington, "Incidents of Indian Life at Hampton: Bears Heart Returns to the West," *Southern Workman*, 10 (1881), 55. Emphasis in original.

102   "body, mind, spirit": Clifford Putney, *Muscular Christianity: Manhood and Sports in Protestant America, 1880–1920* (Harvard University Press: Cambridge, Mass., and London, 2001), 70; "The world . . . respect": "The Young Men's Christian Association," *Harper's Monthly*, 64 (1882), 261.

103–104 "'a person . . . kind'": quoted in James Cook, *The Arts of Deception* (Harvard University Press: Cambridge, Mass., and London, 2001), 134; "there . . . conditions": Nathaniel Southgate Shaler, "The Negro Problem," *Atlantic Monthly*, 54 (1884), 703.

104   "original . . . type": Phillip Alexander Bruce, *The Plantation Negro as a Freeman* (G. P. Putnam's: New York, 1889), 129.

105   "Prof. Shaler . . . retrograde": *The Caucasian*, September 26, 1889, quoted in Joel Williamson, *The Crucible of Race: Black-White Relations in the American South Since Reconstruction* (Oxford University Press: New York, 1984), 184; "justified. . . . years": *The Caucasian*, September 10, 1891, quoted in ibid.

106   "public. . . . interests": W. E. B. DuBois, *Black Reconstruction in America, 1860–1880* [1935] (Atheneum: New York, 1963), 700; "There is . . . obstacle": Bruce, *Plantation Negro*, 83.

106   "and not . . . animals": ibid., 84.

107   "the conquest. . . . white people": John Fiske, " 'Manifest Destiny,' " *Harper's Monthly*, 70 (1885), 583, 584, 588.

108   " 'What is . . . mankind' ": Josiah Strong, *Our Country: Its Possible Future and Its Present Crisis* [1885] (Baker and Taylor: New York, 1891), 14–15; "more vigorous. . . . any other": Strong, *The New Era; or The Coming Kingdom* (Baker and Taylor: New York, 1893), 54–55; "Is there any . . . mankind": Strong, *Our Country*, 178; "the impression . . . prey": E. L. Godkin, quoted in Walter LaFeber, *The American Search for Opportunity, 1865–1913* (Cambridge University Press: New York and London, 1993), 101.

108   "then will . . . fittest": Strong, *Our Country*, 175.

109   "man . . . life": Frank Norris, quoted in Thomas F. Gossett, *Race: The History of an Idea in America*, new ed. (Oxford University Press: New York, 1997), 203; "We whites. . . . from it": Jack London, *Adventure* (Macmillan: New York, 1911), 106.

110   "There is . . . year": Strong, *New Era*, 77.

110   "walking slowly. . . . the same thing": Louis Bagger, "A Day in Castle Garden," *Harper's Monthly*, 42 (1871), 547, 548, 554.

111   "Dear Brother. . . . beer": William I. Thomas and Florian Znaniecki, *The Polish Peasant in Europe and America* [1918–20], Eli Zaretsky, ed. (University of Illinois Press: Urbana, 1984), 133.

112   "the two movements. . . . largely recruited": Franklin Sanborn, "The Tramp—His Cause and Cure," *The Independent*, 30 (1878), 1.

113   "I am. . . . humbugs of the day": "H.D.B.," "Disappointment in Swedes and Germans as Laborers," *Southern Planter and Farmer*, 3 (1869), 406–07.

114   "abnormally increased. . . . all races": "Chinese Immigration and Political Economy," *New Englander*, 36 (1877), 3–5, 6, 9–10.

115   "like a feverish dream. . . . glazed and lifeless": Mrs. Frank Leslie, *California: A Pleasure Trip from Gotham to the Golden Gate* [1877] (B. de Graaf: Nieuwkoop, Netherlands, 1972), 157, 144, 160ff.

115 "the Irish . . . labor": "The Chinese in California," *Scribner's Monthly*, 13 (1877), 414–15; "The Declaration. . . . of man": "Current memoranda: Our Chinese Cousins," *Potter's American Monthly*, 8 (1877), 62.

116 "Either . . . possess it": James G. Blaine, quoted in Gossett, *Race*, 291.

117 "most ominous. . . . from the Church": "Will New England Become Catholic?" *Independent*, 29 (September 13, 1877), 16.

117 "whole expression. . . . snaky venomousness": John Hay, *The Bread-winners: A Social Study* (Harper: New York, 1884), 74–75.

118 "sturdy stock . . . intelligence": Woodrow Wilson, *A History of the American People*, 5 vols. (Harper: New York, 1902), 5, 212; "droves . . . suffrage": James Bryce, *The American Commonwealth*, 2nd ed., 2 vols. (Macmillan: London and New York, 1891), 2, 95.

118 "decent and sober. . . . got a beau!": H. C. Bunner, "Shantytown," *Scribner's Monthly*, 20 (1880), 867.

119 "a cleanly . . . the next berth": William Rideing, "The Immigrant's Progress," *Scribner's Monthly*, 14 (1877), 580.

119 "our own rattlesnakes . . . as they": *New York Times*, March 15, 1891, 1.

120 "It was a beautiful spring morning. . . . the power of fact": Jacob Riis, *The Making of an American* (New York, 1901), 35–36, 39, 42, 75, 99.

122 "huddled . . . free": Emma Lazarus, "The New Colossus" [1882–3], available at www.libertystatepark.com/emma.htm; "fusion . . . energy": Emma Lazarus, *An Epistle to the Hebrews* [1887] (Jewish Historical Society: New York, 1987), 20.

123 "a sort of dumb awe. . . . visions of starvation": "A Year of the Exodus in Kansas," *Scribner's Monthly*, 20 (1880), 211, 216, 215, 213.

124 "sort of foreman. . . . bad whiskey": Nat Love, *The Life and Adventures of Nat Love* [1907] (Arno Press: New York, 1968), 6, 11, 19, 21, 37, 107.

127 "The nihilism . . . progress": C. Vann Woodward, *Origins of the New South, 1877–1913* (Louisiana State University Press: Baton Rouge, 1951), 105–06; "the great arm. . . . the mule": quoted in Steven Hahn, *A Nation Under Our Feet: Black Political Struggles in the Rural South from Slavery to the Great Migration* (Harvard University Press: Cambridge, Mass., and London, 2003), 353.

127 "the colored people . . . together": quoted in ibid., 354; "idle negroes . . . peace and order": quoted in ibid., 421.

128 "to *force ladies* from the pavement": quoted in ibid., 403. Emphasis in original.

129 "the old men. . . . white supremacy lies": quoted in Ayers, *Promise of the New South*, 147.

130 "I refused. . . . the winepress alone": Ida B. Wells-Barnett, *Crusade for Justice: The Autobiography of Ida B. Wells*, Alfreda M. Duster, ed. (University of Chicago Press: Chicago and London, 1970), 19, 21.

131 "strong . . . physique": Booker T. Washington quoted in Louis R. Harlan, *Booker T. Washington: The Making of a Black Leader, 1856–1901* (Oxford University Press: New York, 1972), 60.

131 "straight as an Indian chief," *New York World*, September 19, 1895, quoted in ibid., 217; "cast down your bucket. . . . mutual progress": Booker T. Washington, "The Atlanta Exposition Address," chapter 14 in his *Up from Slavery* (Doubleday, Page: New York, 1901), 218–25.

CHAPTER FOUR: THE COUNTRY AND THE CITY

133 "It is a revelation. . . . as any battle would": Henry W. Grady, "The Glitter of Gold," *Atlanta Constitution*, March 24, 1880, 1; "gone. . . . are real": Joel Chandler Harris, *Henry W. Grady: His Life, Writings, and Speeches* (Cassell Publishing: New York, 1890), 19–20.

133 "It takes. . . . 'blue milk' ": Tom Watson, Manuscript Journal, 2, 403, in Watson Papers, Southern Historical Collection, University of North Carolina, Chapel Hill, quoted in C. Vann Woodward, *Tom Watson: Agrarian Rebel* [1938] (Oxford University Press: New York, 1969), 127.

136 "Those who . . . . ambition": Thomas Jefferson, *Notes on the State of Virginia* [1785] (J. W. Randolph: Richmond, Va., 1853), 176; "The mobs . . . body": ibid., 177.

137 "What developed . . . land values": Richard Hofstadter, *The Age of Reform* (New York, 1955), 41; "Oh, it sets . . . shock": James Whitcomb Riley, "When the Frost Is on the Punkin" [1883], st. 3, in John Hollander, ed., *American Poetry, the Nineteenth Century*, 2 vols. (Library of America: New York, 1993), 2, 473; "soft . . . landscape": Mark Twain, *A Connecticut Yankee in King Arthur's Court* [1889] (Signet Classics: New York, 1963), 19; "that fireless . . . the door": Sarah Orne Jewett, *Deephaven* [1877] (Library of America: New York, 1994), 124.

138 "Once let . . . is certain": Woods Hutchinson, MD, "The Physical Basis of Brain-Work," *North American Review*, 146 (1888), 189–90, 522–31; "was not by nature. . . . a strange land?": Hamlin Garland, *A Son of the Middle Border* [1914] (Macmillan: New York, 1930), 43, 58, 82–83, 238.

139 "ten years. . . . to buy land": "Sentenced to the Prairie: Mary Larrabee," in Carol Fairbanks and Bergine Haakenson, eds., *Writings of Farm Women: An Anthology* (Garland: New York, 1990), 127–33.

140 "tended to warp. . . . far away": Garland, *Middle Border*, 205; "hardly more than a high school": ibid., 197.

140 "Chicago. . . . herself": Charles Dudley Warner, "Stories of the Great West: III.—Chicago," *Harper's Monthly*, 76 (1888), 869, 877–78.

141 "I was lost. . . . at that time": Theodore Dreiser, *Dawn: An Autobiography of Early Youth* [1931], T. D. Nostwich, ed. (Black Sparrow Press: Santa Rosa, Calif., 1998), 159, 573.

143 "used . . . squeal": William Cronon, *Nature's Metropolis: Chicago and the Great West* (Norton: New York, 1991), 249.

144 "Most of us. . . . square miles": quoted in Hofstadter, *Age of Reform*, 57.

145 "panic-stricken . . . bond": *Raleigh Observer*, August 8, 1877, quoted in C. Vann Woodward, *Origins of the New South, 1877–1913* (Louisiana State University Press: Baton Rouge, 1951), 113.

146 "The absorbing thought . . . three dollars a week": Ella Gertrude Clanton Thomas, *The Secret Eye: The Journal of Ella Gertrude Clanton Thomas, 1848–1889*, Virginia Ingraham Burr, ed. (University of North Carolina Press: Chapel Hill and London, 1990), 377, 382, 391–92.

147 "Brisk men . . . religion": Mark Twain, *Life on the Mississippi* [1883] (Dover: Mineola, N.Y., 2000), 182.

148 "BELK'S . . . NO BULL": Legette Blythe, *William Henry Belk: Merchant of the South* (University of North Carolina Press: Chapel Hill, 1950), 73; "we will take. . . . along": advertisement for New York Cash Store in Greenville, Alabama, *Advocate*, February 2, 1897, quoted in Edward Ayers, *The Promise of the New South: Life After Reconstruction* (Oxford University Press: New York, 1992), 99.

148 "They loved. . . . to chop": Harry Crews, *A Childhood, the Biography of a Place* (Harper and Row: New York, 1978), 128–29.

148–149 "It was not . . . his little nightgown": Etta Bundrick Oberseider, *So Fair a Home: An Eastern Shore Childhood* (n.p., 1986), 12, quoted in Ayers, *Promise*, 99; "is considered . . . fire": Henry Grady, Address to New England Club, 1886, in Harris, *Grady*, 87.

149 "We have. . . . Vermont": Harris, *Grady*, 88.

150 "In a declining. . . . decaying countries": Lewis Harvie Blair, *A Southern Prophecy: The Prosperity of the South Dependent Upon the Elevation of the Negro*, C. Vann Woodward, ed. (Little, Brown: Boston, 1964), 42.

153 "the people's . . . country": *Workingman's Advocate* (Chicago), April 21, 1866, quoted in Laurence Goodwyn, *Democratic Promise: The Populist Moment in America* (Oxford University Press: New York, 1976), 14.

153–154 "The bloody . . . Vinces!": *New York Tribune*, January 4, 1879, quoted in Woodward, *Origins*, 49; "We would. . . . the jury?": quoted in Ayers, *Promise*, 36.

155 "movement culture": Goodwyn, *Democratic Promise*, 51.

156 "we extend . . . oppression": Evan Jones, quoted in ibid., 66.

157 "call . . . office": S. O. Daws, quoted in ibid., 67.

158 "it is useless . . . so should we": *Augusta Chronicle*, September 14, 1888, quoted in Woodward, *Watson*, 141.

159 "a pentecost . . . a crusade": Goodwyn, *Democratic Promise*, 194; "the extortions. . . . twine": quoted in ibid., 105.

160 "Upon my knees. . . . illustration": Frances E. Willard, *Glimpses of Fifty Years* (Women's Temperance Publication Association: Chicago, 1889), 351; "Hundreds . . . children": quoted in Ayers, *Promise*, 173.

161 "Not the war . . . revolution": L. L. Polk quoted in Goodwyn, *Democratic Promise*, 259.

162 "Here is a tenant. . . . old lady's ear": *People's Party Paper*, October 14, 1892, quoted in Woodward, *Watson*, 131–32; "the accident . . . laborers": ibid., 221; "burning corn . . . for food": quoted in Goodwyn, *Democratic Promise*, 183.

163 "decline . . . caucus": quoted in Woodward, *Watson*, 186–87.

164 "about fifty . . . studious man": Hamlin Garland, "The Alliance Wedge in Congress," *Arena*, 5 (1892), 451, 452; "iniquitous . . . people": Woodward, *Watson*, 194–95.

164 "He speaks. . . . liberty": Garland, "Wedge," 449, 450.

165 "You are kept . . . beggars both": Tom Watson, "The Negro Question in the South," *Arena*, 6 (1892), 548.

165 "The time . . . people": Polk quoted in Goodwyn, *Democratic Promise*, 264–65.

165 "We meet. . . . liberty": Ignatius Donnelly, "Preamble" to Populist Party platform, St. Louis, 1892, reprinted in George B. Tindall, ed., *A Populist Reader* (Harper and Row: New York, 1966), 90–91.

CHAPTER FIVE: CRISIS AND REGENERATION

167 "Not Matter . . . Men": Daniel Burnham quoted in Alan Trachtenberg, *The Incorporation of America: Culture and Society in the Gilded Age* (Hill and Wang: New York, 1982), 213; " 'Look here . . . century?' ": Augustus Saint-Gaudens, quoted in ibid., 217.

168 "no distinct. . . . Fair": Burnham quoted in ibid., 213.

169 "the floor . . . Bedlam": *New York Times*, May 6, 1893, 5.

169–170 "an honest . . . pocket": "The Rev. Dr. Peck's Sacrifice," ibid., November 12, 1893, 3; "I found . . . notes": Henry Adams to John Hay, August 12, 1893, in *The Letters of Henry Adams*, 6 vols. (Harvard University Press: Cambridge, Mass., and London, 1982–88), 5, 119.

170 "I suppose . . . as here": Blanche Butler Ames, *Chronicles from the Nineteenth Century: Family Letters of Blanche Butler and Adelbert Ames Married July 21st 1870,* vol. 2 (Privately printed: Clinton, Mass., 1957), 601.

170–171 "rabid pessimists": *New York Times*, January 12, 1894, 9; "An advertisement . . . discarded": ibid., December 24, 1893, 18.

171 "a perfectly . . . help": "Comfort for the Farmer," *Ohio Farmer*, 84 (November 16, 1893), 377; " 'Yes, sir'. . . . saucers": *New York Times*, January 22, 1894, 5.

172 "having . . . Poormaster": ibid., August 25, 1893, 6; "the city. . . . again": Marie Hall Ets, *Rosa, the Life of an Italian Immigrant* (University of Minnesota Press: Minneapolis, 1970), 211.

173 "Dear Sir. . . . yours_____": *New York Times*, December 31, 1893, 2.

174 "The distress . . . a crime": Assistant District Attorney O'Hare, quoted in ibid., August 7, 1894, 8.

175 "the lack of confidence. . . . away": "Gold Shipments—the Responsibility Rests with Congress," *Commercial and Financial Chronicle*, 15 (December 17, 1892), 1013.

176 "little talks": Michael Kazin, *A Godly Hero: The Life of William Jennings Bryan* (Knopf: New York, 2006), 10; "caught a vision . . . a new country": Bryan quoted in ibid., 17–18.

176 "Last night . . . wisely": ibid., 25.

177 "can you cure. . . . his use": Bryan quoted in ibid., 39.

180 "We . . . U.S.": Morgan quoted in Jean Strouse, *Morgan: American Financier* (Random House: New York, 1999), 341.

180 "I take. . . . 3 o'clock": letter to Governor L. D. Lewelling, quoted in Lawrence Goodwyn, *The Populist Moment: A Short History of the Agrarian Revolt in America* (Oxford University Press: New York, 1978), 209.

181 "A rustic. . . . wash them down": "A Rustic in New York," *Atlantic Monthly*, 73 (1894), 858.

182 "have . . . as anybody": "C.B.S.," "The Coxey Army at Washington," *Outlook*, 49 (May 12, 1894), 823.

182 "when the divine . . . vagabonds": Rev. George Herron, *The Christian State* (Thomas Y. Crowell: New York, 1895), 98.

183 "all that. . . . recognition": quoted in Christopher Lasch, ed., *The Social Thought of Jane Addams* (Bobb-Merrill: Indianapolis, 1965), 106; "a civilized relic. . . . dying here": Rev. William Carwardine, *The Pullman Strike*, 4th ed. (Charles H. Kerr: Chicago, 1894), 25.

183 "The theater. . . . his men": Jane Addams, "A Modern Lear" [1912], reprinted in Lasch, ed., *Social Thought*, 112.

183 "that conception . . . never seen": ibid., 115.

184 "The inhuman . . . civilization": *Churchman,* July 7, 1894, 7, quoted in Henry May, *Protestant Churches and Industrial America* [1949] (Harper and Row: New York, 1967), 109.

185 "Populist-negro . . . ticket": quoted in Goodwyn, *Populist Moment*, 194; "inferentially approved": *New Orleans Daily States*, quoted in ibid., 195; "There is . . . exchanged": Stephen McCallin, quoted in ibid., 211.

186–187 "not only . . . anti-American": "Platform of the Chicago Convention," *New York Times*, July 10, 1896, 7; "Having behind . . . gold": William Jennings Bryan, speech at Democratic Party National Convention, Chicago, 1896, in his *The First Battle: A Story of the Campaign of 1896* (W. N. Conkey: Chicago, 1896), 190–200, 203–06; quoted in Kazin, *Godly Hero*, 61.

187 "everybody . . . women": *New York World*, quoted in ibid.

187–188 "A WILD . . . MOB": *New York Times*, July 10, 1896, 1; "It was . . . oppressed": William Allen White, *The Autobiography of William Allen White* [1946], Sally Foreman Griffiths, ed. (University of Kansas Press: Lawrence, 1990), 142; "two . . . government": Bryan, speech at 1896 Convention, quoted in Kazin, *Godly Hero*, 65.

188 "And then. . . . injuring us": Bryan, *First Battle*, 378, quoted in ibid., 69; "as if . . . medicine": Roosevelt, quoted in ibid., 68.

190 "Besides the lesson. . . . poorer": "The Political Menace of the Discontented," *Atlantic Monthly*, 78 (1896), 447–51.

192 "NEGRO. . . . with them": Furnifold M. Simmons, quoted in Steven A. Hahn, *A Nation Under Our Feet: Black Political Struggles in the Rural South from Slavery to the Great Migration* (Harvard University Press: Cambridge, Mass., and London, 2008), 437.

193 "We will. . . . carcasses": Alfred Waddell, quoted in Timothy B. Tyson and David S. Cecelski, "Introduction" to *Democracy Betrayed: The Wilmington*

Race Riot of 1898 and Its Legacy, Tyson and Cecelski, eds. (University of North Carolina Press: Chapel Hill and London, 1998), 4.

193   "put . . . necessary": Rebecca Latimer Felton, quoted in Williamson, *Crucible of Race*, 128.

194   "were not. . . . colored woman": Alex Manly, quoted in LeeAnn Whites, "Love, Hate, Rape, Lynching: Rebecca Latimer Felton and the Gender Politics of Racial Violence," in *Democracy Betrayed*, 158–59.

194   "Go to . . . kill him": Waddell quoted in Tyson and Cecelski, "Introduction" to ibid., 4.

196   "the priests . . . their brothers": Rev. George Herron, *The New Redemption* (Thomas Y. Crowell: New York, 1893), 60; "enlightened self-interest. . . . humanity": Herron, *The Christian Society* (Fleming H. Revell: Chicago, 1894), 108–10; "any wealth . . . fictitious": Herron, *New Redemption*, 23.

196   "the people. . . . labor": Herron, *Christian State*, 86–87.

196   "I see . . . social practice": ibid., 183; "It was only . . . the great grace": Frances Willard, quoted in May, *Protestant Churches*, 128.

197   "that in holding . . . view of life": Jane Addams, "The Subtle Problems of Charity," *Atlantic Monthly*, 83 (1899), 169–70.

198   "To make the world more Homelike": Frances Willard quoted in Michael McGerr, *A Fierce Discontent: The Rise and Fall of the Progressive Movement in America, 1870–1920* (Oxford University Press: New York, 2003), 53.

198   "the essential similarity. . . . a dowry": Albion Small, "Private Business Is a Public Trust," *American Journal of Sociology*, 1 (1895), 276, 282, 280, 285, 287.

200   "the entire life . . . social": Methodist minister quoted in McGerr, *Discontent*, 70; "A great . . . to be done": Washington Gladden quoted in ibid., 70.

201   "the march . . . prosperous": Hernando Money quoted in LaFeber, *Opportunity*, 25.

201   "We must . . . been lacking": Henry Cabot Lodge quoted in ibid., 158.

201   "In China. . . . a market!": Charles S. Campbell Jr., *Special Business Interests and the Open Door Policy* [1951] (Archon Books: Hamden, Conn., 1968), 12.

202   "The Central Americans. . . . nor its use": Richard Harding Davis, *Three Gringos in Venezuela and Central America* (Harper: New York, 1896), 147; "When money . . . reached": Leonard Wood quoted in Lloyd Gardner, "A Progressive Foreign Policy, 1900–1921," in William Appleman Williams, ed., *From Colony to Empire: Essays in the History of American Foreign Relations* (Wiley: New York, 1972), 217; "in the savage. . . . with dollars!": Merrill Gates quoted in Robert Berkhofer, *The White Man's Indian: Images of the American Indian from Columbus to the Present* (Knopf: New York, 1978), 173.

203   "A brief . . . for rich": Sanford Dole, "Evolution of Hawaiian Land Tenures," *Overland Monthly*, 25 (1895), 579; "A revenue producing property": Peter C. Jones, "Will It Pay the United States to Annex Hawaii?" ibid., 580; "Some day . . . islands": Joaquin Miller, "Kamehameha the Great," ibid., 632.

203 "the jackfools. . . . town meeting": TR to Rudyard Kipling, November 1, 1904, in Elting E. Morison, ed., *The Letters of Theodore Roosevelt*, 8 vols. (Harvard University Press: Cambridge, Mass., 1951–54), 4, 107.

203 "There must be . . . from without": TR quoted in Jacobson, *Barbarian Virtues*, 226.

203 "Strong masculine impulse . . . peace prophets of to-day": Alfred T. Mahan, *The Interest of America in Sea Power, Present and Future* (Little, Brown: Boston, 1898), 121.

204 "Antagonism . . . evil": Sir William Grove, F.R.S., "Antagonism," *Popular Science Monthly*, 33 (1888), 608, 618.

204 "bravery and coolness. . . . being afraid": Kenyon West, "Mr. Kennan's Apprenticeship in Courage," *Atlantic Monthly*, 79 (1897), 717–19.

205 "the few territories . . . . strange peoples": Richard Harding Davis, "An American in Africa," *Harper's Monthly*, 86 (1893), 632–33.

205–206 "The time . . . conquerors": Henry Cabot Lodge quoted in Kim Townsend, *Manhood at Harvard: William James and Others* (Harvard University Press: Cambridge, Mass., and London, 1996), 103; "Are people. . . . the risk": S. R. Elliott, "The Courage of a Soldier," *Atlantic Monthly*, 71 (1893), 237, 239; "Idleness and luxury . . . together": Sarah Grand, "The Man of the Moment," *North American Review*, 158 (1894), 626.

206 "courage . . . energy": Elliott, "Courage," 244.

206 "the chief virtue. . . . principle of action": Woods Hutchinson, "Courage the Chief Virtue," *Open Court*, 12 (1898), 193–99.

207 "splendid little war": John Hay to Roosevelt, quoted in Hugh Thomas, *Cuba, or the Pursuit of Freedom*, rev. ed. (Da Capo Press: New York, 1998), 404; "Shall Cuba Be Free?": Clarence King, *Forum*, 20 (1895), 50–65; "to protect American life and property": Richard B. Morris, ed., *Encyclopedia of American History* (Harper: New York, 1953), 287; "forcible intervention": McKinley quoted in Morris, ed., ibid., 288.

209 "a settlement . . . conquest": Henry Adams to John Hay, May 26, 1898, in *Letters*, 4, 594; "we seek . . . to all": McKinley quoted in Henry F. Graff, *The Presidents: A Reference History* (Scribner: New York, 2002), 320.

209 "The greatest revolution . . . Europe": Henry Adams to Worthington Chauncey Ford, November 26, 1898, in *Letters*, 4, 624; "I have studied attentively . . . no fear": Emilio Aguinaldo quoted in Stuart Creighton Miller, *"Benevolent Assimilation": The American Conquest of the Philippines, 1899–1903* (Yale University Press: New Haven and London, 1982), 42.

210 "One of our boys . . . the trigger": *Kingston* [New York] *Evening Post*, May 8, 1899, quoted in ibid., 88.

210 "It is not. . . . to them": *Philadelphia Ledger*, November 19, 1900, quoted in ibid., 211; "the only good . . . dead one": *Kansas City Times*, n.d., quoted in ibid., 180; "our whole . . . a crime": Henry Cabot Lodge, quoted in Walter Williams, "United States Indian Policy and the Debate Over Philippine Annexation: Implications for the Origins of American Imperialism," *Journal of*

American History, 66 (1980), 820; "our priceless principles . . . tropical sun":
McKinley quoted in Morris Swift, *Imperialism and Liberty* (Ronbroke Press:
Los Angeles, 1899), 54.

211   "We escape . . . conquest": Henry Watterson quoted in Leon Wolff, *Little
Brown Brother* (Doubleday: Garden City, N.Y., 1961), 269.

211–212 "teaches us . . . this nation": Hernando Money quoted in Kristin Ho-
ganson, *Fighting for American Manhood: How Gender Politics Provoked the
Spanish-American and Philippine-American Wars* (Yale University Press: New
Haven and London, 1998), 73; "a wholesome . . . has had": "A Wholesome
Stimulus to Higher Politics," *Atlantic Monthly*, 83 (1899), 289, 291; "a God-
send . . . emotions": Henry Adams to Elizabeth Cameron, May 9, 1898, in
Letters, 4, 589; "We think . . . suffering": "The Nobler Side of War," *Century*,
56 (1898), 794.

212   "a desire . . . jungle": *Washington Post*, quoted in John Judis, *The Folly of Empire: What George W. Bush Could Learn from Theodore Roosevelt and Woodrow Wilson* (New York, 2004), 37; "The athlete . . . nations": Lodge quoted
in ibid., 41; "small man": Roosevelt to Lodge, October 14, 1900, in Morison,
Letters, 2, 1408; "A man. . . . Nation": Roosevelt quoted in Kazin, *Godly Hero*,
106.

213   "scuttle and run": Chauncey Depew quoted in David Nasaw, *Andrew Carnegie* (Penguin: New York, 2006), 545; "the persistent roots . . . reach":
Joaquin Miller, "Kamehameha the Great," *Overland Monthly*, 25 (1895), 629;
"inevitable. . . . down with it": W. N. Armstrong, "Kalakaua's Trip Around the
World," ibid., 644, 652.

213   "the development . . . they descend": "Americanism and Expansion," *Open
Court*, 13 (1899), 218.

213   "Everywhere . . . endures": Brooks Adams, *America's Economic Supremacy*
[1900] (New York, 1947), 84, 80–81.

214   "new epoch. . . . allotted us": Col. A. K. McClure, "Our Flag in Foreign
Lands," *Frank Leslie's Popular Monthly*, 47 (1898), 4.

214   "we ought. . . . seek it": Rev. James Thoburn, quoted in Drinnon, *Facing West*,
318; "God has not. . . . night," Albert Beveridge quoted in Ernest Tuveson,
Redeemer Nation: The Idea of America's Millennial Role (University of Chi-
cago Press: Chicago and London, 1968), vii; "just beyond . . . the world":
Albert Beveridge, "Our Philippine Policy," in Daniel Schirmer and Stephen
Rosskamm Shalom, eds., *The Philippines Reader: A History of Colonialism,
Neocolonialism, Dictatorship, and Resistance* (Harvard University Press: Cam-
bridge, Mass., 1987), 23.

215   "blessings of liberty and civilization": "Platform of the Republican Convention," *New York Times*, June 21, 1900, 5.

216   "any project . . . path": Mahan quoted in Walter LaFeber, "The 'Lion in the
Path': The U.S. Emergence as a World Power," *Political Science Quarterly*,
101 (1986), 705; "is never . . . burglarized": James Jeffrey Roche, quoted in
Jacobson, *Barbarian Virtues*, 257.

216 "we insist . . . happiness": American Anti-Imperialist League, quoted in Louise W. Knight, *Citizen: Jane Addams and the Struggle for Democracy* (University of Chicago Press: Chicago and London, 2005), 395.

216 "the fruits . . . us eat": Bryan quoted in Kazin, *Godly Hero*, 80; "wars of conquest": Bryan quoted in ibid., 103; "they have . . . willing to die": Carnegie quoted in Nasaw, *Carnegie*, 559.

217 "believe in it? . . . done": Mark Twain quoted in Tom Quirk, *Mark Twain and Human Nature* (University of Missouri Press: Columbia and London, 2007), 1.

218 "shall we go on. . . . proceeds?" Mark Twain, "To the Person Sitting in Darkness" [1901] in his *Tales, Speeches, Essays, and Sketches*, Tom Quirk, ed. (Penguin: New York, 2005), 268–69.

218 "our traditions. . . . Civilization": ibid., 274.

219 "an ever-merciful. . . . and thirst": Mark Twain, "War Prayer" [1903], reprinted in *Lapham's Quarterly*, 1 (2007), 170–72.

219 "God damn . . . Islands": William James to F. C. S. Schiller, August 6, 1902, quoted in Robert Beisner, *Twelve Against Empire* (McGraw-Hill: New York, 1968), 44; "puked up . . . squeamishness": James to Francois Pillon, June 15, 1898, in *Letters of William James*, Henry James, ed., 2 vols. (Atlantic Monthly Press: Boston, 1920), 2, 74; "We had supposed . . . before them": James to Pillon, same letter.

220 "in every national soul. . . . the truth about ourselves": James quoted in Robert D. Richardson, *William James: In the Maelstrom of American Modernism* (Houghton Mifflin: Boston and New York, 2006), 443.

220 " 'Will you . . . asked' ": William James, *The Principles of Psychology*, 2 vols. [1890] (Dover: New York, 1950), 2, 579.

221 "a real fight": William James, "Is Life Worth Living?" in his *The Will to Believe and Other Essays* (Longmans, Green: New York, 1897), 55.

CHAPTER SIX: LIBERATION AND LIMITATION

222 "the dynamos. . . . Americans adored": Henry Adams, *The Education of Henry Adams* [1907] (Modern Library: New York, 1931), 342–45.

224 "the period. . . . and what not": Henry Adams to John Hay, November 7, 1900, in Worthington C. Ford, ed., *Letters of Henry Adams*, 2 vols. (Riverside Press: Boston and New York, 1938), 2, 301.

224 "the dynamo. . . . infinite force": Adams, *Education*, 380.

225 "occult . . . divine substance": Adams, ibid., 383.

227 "best and strongest . . . out of anything": *Kansas City Post*, September 8, 1915, 2, quoted in John F. Kasson, *Houdini, Tarzan, and the Perfect Man: The White Male Body and the Challenge of Modernity in America* (Hill and Wang: New York, 2001), 136; "Chinese Water Torture Cell": ibid., 131.

229 "Ehrich, the Prince of the Air": Kenneth Silverman, *Houdini!!! The Career of Ehrich Weiss* (HarperCollins: New York, 1996), 6; "the founder of modern magic": ibid., 9.

230 "maniac cuff and belt": ibid., 16.

230 "I practice . . . piano": ibid., 25.

231 "Do others or they will do you": Houdini, answer to a questionnaire, quoted in ibid., 1.

233 "the drama . . . to dinner": Frank Norris, "A Plea for Romantic Fiction" in his *The Responsibilities of the Novelist and Other Essays* (Doubleday, Page: New York, 1902), 215; "the men . . . tissue-paper": Friedrich Nietzsche quoted in Miles Orvell, *The Real Thing: Imitation and Authenticity in American Culture, 1880–1940* (University of North Carolina Press: Chapel Hill and London, 1989), 69; "as ephemeral . . . animal spirits": [Charles Dudley Warner,] "Editor's Study," *Harper's Monthly*, 89 (1894), 798.

233 "to establish . . . passions of life": George Santayana, "The Academic Environment," *Character and Opinion in the United States* (Charles Scribner's Sons: New York, 1920), 44; "a sort of velvet jacket affair . . . women and aesthetes": Frank Norris, "Novelists of the Future" in *Responsibilities*, 208.

234 "thousands . . . a necessity": John Muir, *Our National Parks* (Houghton Mifflin: Boston, 1901), 1; "a white man's . . . playground": Theodore Roosevelt, *African Game Trails* (Syndicate Publishing: New York, 1910), 173.

235 "deep, brooding silence": John Muir, *The Mountains of California* [1894], in William Cronon, ed., *Muir: Nature Writings* (Library of America: New York, 1997), 358; "Nature's workshop": John Muir quoted in Michael Smith, *Pacific Visions: California Scientists and the Environment, 1850–1915* (University of California Press: Berkeley and London, 1987), 39.

235–236 "goes to the Alps. . . . a Duke's estate": ibid., 95; "the dark . . . all things": ibid., 57; "when we try . . . the universe": ibid., 92; "every rock . . . with life": ibid., 96; "one of the most bracing. . . . high festival": ibid., 98; "whatever is done . . . utility": George Santayana, *The Sense of Beauty* (Charles Scribner's Sons: New York, 1896), 28.

236–237 "Nature. . . . possible life": Santayana, "The Genteel Tradition in American Philosophy" [1911] in *Selected Critical Writings of George Santayana*, Norman Henfey, ed., 2 vols. (Cambridge University Press: Cambridge, England, 1968), 2, 95, 105–06; "hands . . . permanency": John Dewey, "The Influence of Darwinism Upon Philosophy," in R. Jackson Wilson, ed., *Darwinism and the American Intellectual* [1967], 2nd ed. (Dorsey Press: Chicago, 1989), 159.

237 "the life . . . experience": Oliver Wendell Holmes Jr., *The Common Law* [1881] (Lawbook Exchange: Clark, N.J., 2004), 1; "not learning . . . this living": T. J. McCormack, "The School and Society," *Open Court*, 16 (1902), 566.

238 "Religion . . . Future": Lucien Arrat, "The Religion of the Future," *Open Court*, 12 (1898), 97–100; "The truth is . . . the soul?": William Salter, "What Is Life? A Sunday Address," *Open Court*, 15 (1901), 596–607.

238–239 "discarnate spirits": James Hyslop, "Nature of Life After Death," *Harper's Monthly*, 102 (1901), 632–39; "a world of pure experience": William James, *Essays in Radical Empiricism* [1912] (Peter Smith: Gloucester, Mass., 1967), 39; "blooming buzzing confusion": William James, *Principles of Psychology*, 2 vols. [1890] (Dover: New York, 1950) 1, 488; "unclassified residuum":

William James, "What Psychical Research Has Accomplished," in his *The Will to Believe and Other Essays in Popular Philosophy* (Longmans, Green: New York, 1897), 299.

239 "beyond . . . conditions": William James, "The Powers of Men," *American Magazine*, 65 (1907), 57, 59.

239 "angelic. . . . cried": Charlotte Perkins Gilman, *The Living of Charlotte Perkins Gilman: An Autobiography* (D. Appleton-Century: New York and London, 1935), 89.

240 "a Prince . . . dream world": ibid., 23; "This was. . . . Just thirteen": ibid., 23–24.

240–241 "Am going . . . other people": ibid., 44; "became . . . stoic": ibid., 51; "traveling rings . . . a circus": ibid., 67; "get a nice . . . and cry": Charlotte Perkins Gilman diary, May 9, 1884, Arthur and Elizabeth Schlesinger Library, Cambridge, Mass., quoted in Ann J. Lane, *To Herland and Beyond: The Life and Work of Charlotte Perkins Gilman* (Pantheon: New York, 1990), 96; "Am sad . . . arrowpudding": Gilman diary, June 15, 1884, quoted in ibid., 96; "Get miserable . . . affection": Gilman diary, June 25, 1884, quoted in ibid., 98.

241–242 "the not well-ness . . . oftener": Gilman, *Living*, 87; "effects of nerve bankruptcy": ibid., 97.

242 "the duty . . . to grow": Charlotte Perkins Gilman, *Women and Economics* [1898] (Harper and Row: New York, 1966), 207; "It is time . . . changing": ibid., 137; "fulfillment . . . costs": Gilman, *Living*, 42.

242 "discovery of the unconscious": Henri Ellenberger, *The Discovery of the Unconscious* (Basic Books: New York, 1970), 1.

243–244 "forgotten truth. . . . first knot": Charles Tuckey, "How Suggestion Works: A Chapter from the Experience of a Famous London Physician," *Good Housekeeping*, 48 (1909), 641–42; "Fear . . . from within": ibid., 641.

244 "the most intense . . . feeling": Annie Payson Call, *Power Through Repose* (Boston, 1891), 64; "the work . . . made strong": "Not Poverty but Strength," *Outlook*, 72 (1902), 112; "increasing. . . . this direction": "An Evening at Emmanuel Church," *Good Housekeeping*, 46 (1908), 200.

245 "the subconscious. . . . consciousness": Elwood Worcester, Samuel McComb, and Isador Coriat, *Religion and Medicine* (Moffat, Yard: Boston, 1908), 74.

245 "back from . . . intenser life": Michael Williams, "Fletcherizing with Fletcher," *Good Housekeeping*, 46 (1908), 503; "In brief. . . . within him": Frances Bjorkman, "The Philosophy of Fletcherism": *Good Housekeeping*, 48 (1909), 506; "to become . . . thought": Hereward Carrington, "To Become Beautiful by Thought," *Good Housekeeping*, 49 (1909), 221–23.

245 "the vast majority. . . . but work": Richard Cabot, "The Dangers of Rest," *Good Housekeeping*, 48 (1909), 731.

245–246 "soul. . . . by God": Cabot, "The Work Cure, I: The Healing Power of Work," *Good Housekeeping*, 49 (1909), 298; "the root cause . . . miserliness": "Motives of Misers," *Current Literature*, 32 (1902), 428.

246 "stagnation. . . . investment": Woods Hutchinson, "The Joy of Eating," *Good Housekeeping*, 56 (1913), 672.

247 "It was Empire. . . . desires": Frank Norris, *The Pit: A Story of Chicago* (Dou-
     bleday, Page: New York, 1903), 62–63.

247 "The Secretary. . . . civilization": Simon Nelson Patten, *The New Basis of
     Civilization* [1907] (Harvard University Press: Cambridge, Mass., 1968), 15;
     "If. . . . progress": Edward Atkinson, "Mental Energy," *Popular Science
     Monthly*, 57 (1900), 634, 636.

248 "a sound . . . forget": Theodore Roosevelt Jr., quoted in Joseph Corn, *The
     Winged Gospel: America's Romance with Aviation, 1900–1950* (Oxford Uni-
     versity Press: New York, 1983), 4; "Thirty thousand . . . miracle": Charles K.
     Field quoted in ibid., 4; "Never . . . in their lives": "Grapho" [J. A. Adams]
     quoted in ibid., 4.

249 "Stay As Long As You Like": Rosenzweig, *Eight Hours for What We Will*,
     221.

250 "dance madness . . . bodies touch": quoted in Kathy Peiss, *Cheap Amuse-
     ments: Working Women and Leisure in Turn-of-the-Century New York* (Temple
     University Press: Philadelphia, 1986), 88, 102.

251 "serpentine undulations. . . . spiral. . . . Hebrew blood": Susan Glenn, *Female
     Spectacle: The Theatrical Roots of Modern Feminism* (Cambridge, Mass., and
     London, 2000), 19, 31; "whole-body comedy" . . . "I Don't Care": ibid., 61, 65.

252 "black voice": ibid., 51.

253 "a very dark place. . . . put on plenty of style": Sadie Frowne, "The Story of a
     Sweatshop Girl," *Independent*, 54 (1902), 2279–82.

255 "insect laden . . . ship": Saverio Rizzo, in Salvatore La Gumina, ed., *The Im-
     migrants Speak: Italian-Americans Tell Their Own Story* (Center for Migration
     Studies: New York, 1979), 6.

255 "an unskilled. . . . a girl mustn't be odd": Rose Fortune, "The Story of Rose
     Fortune: A New York Working Girl," *Frank Leslie's Popular Monthly*, 57
     (1903), 127–28, 134–35.

257 "I thought. . . . hell itself": "By a Georgia Negro Peon," "The New Slavery in
     the South—An Autobiography," *Independent*, 56 (1904), 410–14.

257 "threading . . . needle": *Toledo Union Leader*, March 13, 1914, quoted in
     David Montgomery, *The Fall of the House of Labor: The Workplace, the State,
     and American Labor Activism, 1865–1925* (Cambridge University Press: New
     York, 1987), 114.

257 "Lots of us. . . . most likely!": Gertrude Barnum, "The Story of a Fall River
     Mill Girl," *Independent*, 58 (1905), 242.

260 "the one best way": Robert Kanigel, *The One Best Way: Frederick Winslow
     Taylor and the Enigma of Efficiency* (Viking: New York, 1997), 7.

260 "so stupid . . . other type": Frederick Winslow Taylor, *The Principles of Scien-
     tific Management* [1911] (Norton: New York, 1967), 59.

261 ".00083 hours": Kanigel, *One Best Way*, 512; "high-priced man": Taylor, *Prin-
     ciples*, 44 ff.

261 "ROADS COULD . . . DO IT": *New York Times*, quoted in Kanigel, *One Best
     Way*, 433; "The problem . . . efficiency?": James, "Powers of Men," 57, quoted
     in advertisement for forthcoming Frederick Winslow Taylor, "The Gospel of

Efficiency: The Principles of Scientific Management," *American Magazine*, 71 (1911), 480; "under . . . not driven": Louis Brandeis quoted in Kanigel, *One Best Way*, 442.

262 "The whole scheme . . . scrap heap": James O'Connell quoted in ibid., 448–49.

263 "nothing to unlearn . . . bell time": Horace L. Arnold and Fay L. Faurote, *Ford Methods and the Ford Shops* [1915] (Arno Press: New York, 1972), 41–42.

263 "If these men . . . holidays": Ford official quoted in Montgomery, *House of Labor*, 236; "The men . . . as they should": *Elwood* (Indiana) *Call Leader*, May 14, 1913, quoted in ibid., 238.

263 "If . . . somebody . . . were heard": Aetna clerk quoted in Angel Kwolek-Folland, *Engendering Business: Men and Women in the Corporate Office, 1870–1930* (Johns Hopkins University Press: Baltimore and London, 1994), 106.

264 "I Love My Wife But OH! You Kid": postcard caption, c. 1909, quoted in ibid., 64; "efficiency and happiness": Marie Louise Wright, "City Cruel Only to Girls Who Are Not Efficient, Says Guardian of 2000," *Evening Mail*, May 8, 1913, n.p., quoted in ibid., 137.

265–266 "We are . . . sculptors": Mary Pickford quoted in Michael McGerr, *A Fierce Discontent: The Rise and Fall of the Progressive Movement in America, 1870–1920* (Oxford University Press: New York, 2003), 260; "reserve powers": Harrington Emerson, quoted in Montgomery, *House of Labor*, 251.

266 "in the course . . . coming holiday": Patten, *New Basis*, 141.

267 "On the 6th of June . . . if I should": Carry A. Nation, *The Use and Need of the Life of Carry A. Nation, Written by Herself* (F. M. Steves: Topeka, 1905), 69–70.

268 "It wasn't . . . factory": Boyd Fisher quoted in David Noble, *America by Design: Science, Technology, and the Rise of Corporate Capitalism* (Knopf: New York, 1977), 294.

269 "BOUNCE! . . . breakfast": Shredded Wheat Advertisement (1902), book 68, N. W. Ayer Collection, National Museum of American History, Smithsonian Institution, Washington, DC; "The Foe. . . . don't": Quaker Oats Advertisement, *Good Housekeeping*, 62 (1916), 109.

270 "adroitly. . . . products": Kasson, *Perfect Man*, 75.

270–271 "the chorus king": Glenn, *Female Spectacle*, 174; "It is system . . . straight lines": Ned Wayburn quoted in Kasson, *Perfect Body*, 172; "They burn. . . . trivialities": [Max Eastman,] "Margins," *The Masses* (January 1916), 11, quoted in Christine Stansell, *American Moderns: Bohemian New York and the Creation of a New Century* (Metropolitan Books: New York, 2000), 165.

271 "extra girls": Hilary Hallett, " 'In Motion Picture Land,' a Cultural History About the Creation of Early Hollywood," unpublished PhD dissertation, City University of New York, 2005, 1.

272 "unprecedented . . . life": William James, *The Varieties of Religious Experience* [1902] (Modern Library: New York, 1929), 113; "the religion of healthy-mindedness": lectures IV and V in ibid.; "the twice-born sick soul": lectures V and VI in ibid.

272–273 "There was . . . left him": John Jay Chapman, "William James," in Linda
        Simon, ed., *William James Remembered* (University of Nebraska Press: Lin-
        coln, 1996), 56; "hot place . . . *energy*": James, *Varieties*, 193; "the streaming
        moonlight . . . the inner life": James quoted in Robert D. Richardson, *William
        James: In the Maelstrom of American Modernism* (Houghton Mifflin: Boston
        and New York, 2006), 374–75.

273–274 "probably . . . reach": Adams, *Education*, 424; "the child of . . . nature":
        Adams, ibid., 496; "the mystery of Maternity": Henry Adams, "Prayer to the
        Virgin of Chartres" [1901] in his *Letters to a Niece and Prayer to the Virgin of
        Chartres* (Riverside Press: Boston and New York, 1920), 133.

274   "Crossing. . . . Son": ibid., 127; "Waiting . . . you!": ibid., 131; "the greatest . . .
        energies": Adams, *Education*, 384; "All . . . Chartres": ibid., 388.

                CHAPTER SEVEN: EMPIRE AS A WAY OF LIFE

276   "the bogus antique": Louis H. Sullivan, *The Autobiography of an Idea* (Press
        of the American Institute of Architects: New York, 1924), 324.

277   "By the time . . . living things": ibid., 325; "Business . . . Man": quoted in
        Steve Fraser, *Every Man a Speculator: A History of Wall Street in American Life*
        (HarperCollins: New York, 2005), 249.

279   "played . . . system": Walter LaFeber, *The American Search for Opportunity,
        1865–1913* (Cambridge University Press: New York, 1994), 185.

280   "I do not think . . . civilization": TR to Hay, August 19, 1903, quoted in Ste-
        phen Randall, *Colombia and the United States: Hegemony and Interdependence*
        (University of Georgia Press: Athens, 1992), 85–86.

280   "do what . . . towards us": TR to Joseph Bucklin Bishop, February 23, 1904, in
        Morison, ed., *Letters*, 4, 734.

281   "the usual . . . responsibility for it": Count von Bernstorff quoted in Friedrich
        Katz, *The Secret War in Mexico: Europe, the United States, and the Mexican
        Revolution* (University of Chicago Press: Chicago, 1981), 113.

282   "The Japs. . . . mankind": TR to Hay, 1904, in Morison, ed., *Letters*, 4, 865.

282–283 "Rapid distribution . . . freight carriage"; Patten, *The New Basis of Civiliza-
        tion* [1907] (Harvard University Press: Cambridge, Mass., 1968), 22; "Tropic
        riches . . . fund of goods": ibid., 22–23.

283   "sugar. . . . hemisphere": ibid., 19.

284   "annex . . . to conquer": J. Walter Thompson Company advertising circular
        [1904] quoted in Victoria DeGrazia, *Irresistible Empire: America's Advance
        Through Twentieth-Century Europe* (Harvard University Press: Cambridge,
        Mass., and London, 2005), 235.

284   "In the domestic life. . . . New York": William T. Stead, *The Americanization
        of the World* [1902] (Garland: London and New York, 1972), 138.

285   "misgoverned and misruled . . . as one man"; TR, *Letters*, 3, 675, quoted in
        LaFeber, *Opportunity*, 1914.

285   "stable, orderly . . . police power": Theodore Roosevelt, "Fourth Annual Mes-
        sage" [1904], in James D. Richardson, *A Compilation of the Messages and*

Papers of the Presidents, 10 vols. (Bureau of National Literature and Art: New York, 1895–1907), 10, 830.

286 "America . . . the world": David McCullough quoted in Jacobson, *Barbarian Virtues*, 264.

286–287 "To perpetuate. . . . as art": John Elfreth Watkins, "What Uncle Sam Is Doing: Perpetuating the Beauty of the Indian," *Ladies' Home Journal*, 24 (1907), 26; "the inconceivable alien": Henry James, *The American Scene* [1907] (Indiana University Press: Bloomington and London, 1968), 85, quoted in Alan Trachtenberg, *Shades of Hiawatha: Staging Indians, Making Americans 1880–1930* (Hill and Wang: New York, 2004), 101, 114.

287 "the color line . . . Patagonia": W. E. B. DuBois, "The Color Line Belts the World," *Collier's*, 28 (October 20, 1906), 30.

288 "civilization . . . savage men": World's Fair guide [1904] quoted in Drinnon, *Facing West*, 343; "Jingoism . . . spectator": J. A. Hobson, *Imperialism: A Study* [1902] (Cosimo Classics: New York, 2005), 215; "comic-opera. . . . seriously": Richard Harding Davis, *The Congo and Coasts of Africa* (T. Fisher Unwin: London, 1908), 211–12.

288 "out of the way . . . worth living": Roosevelt quoted in H. W. Brands, *TR: The Last Romantic* (Basic Books: New York, 1997), 649.

289 "Until within . . . this idea": United Fruit Company, *A Short History of the Banana and a Few Recipes for Its Use* (Boston Cooking School: Boston, 1906), 11, in Warshaw Collection, Foods, Box 45.

290 "a reproach . . . manhood": Robert Peary quoted in Michael Robinson, *The Coldest Crucible: Arctic Exploration and American Culture* (University of Chicago Press: Chicago, 2006), 122.

290 "The country is Salome mad": quoted in Susan Glenn, *Female Spectacle: The Theatrical Roots of Modern Feminism* (Harvard University Press: Cambridge, Mass., and London, 2000), 96ff.

290 "over the perils. . . . fellow-beings": Hobson, *Imperialism*, 215.

292 "Pierpont Morgan calls . . . he says": Finley Peter Dunne [Mr. Dooley] quoted in Strouse, *Morgan*, 405.

292 "unwarranted profit": Philander C. Knox, "The Northern Securities Case," unpublished memorandum in Philander Knox papers, Library of Congress, quoted in George Mowry, *The Era of Theodore Roosevelt, 1900–1912* (Harper and Row: New York, 1958), 131.

292–293 "the Wall Street. . . . none": TR quoted in Joseph B. Bishop, *Theodore Roosevelt and His Time Shown in His Own Letters*, 2 vols. (Charles Scribner's Sons: New York, 1920), 1, 185; "rule of reason": in Henry Steel Commager, ed., *Documents of American History*, 7th ed., 2 vols. (Appleton-Century-Crofts: New York, 1963), 2, 55–57.

293–294 "ignoble ease": Theodore Roosevelt, *The Strenuous Life* (Century: New York, 1900), 1; "regulate . . . by levees": TR quoted in *New York Times*, July 5, 1902, 2; "of all the forms . . . a plutocracy": Roosevelt, *Autobiography* [1913] (Library of America: New York, 2004), 685.

295   "the moral . . . class": Christopher Lasch, "The Moral and Intellectual Reha-
      bilitation of the Ruling Class," in his *The World of Nations* (Knopf: New York,
      1973), 80–91; "malefactors . . . wealth": TR quoted in George Mowry, *The Era
      of Theodore Roosevelt, 1900–1917* (Harper and Row: New York, 1958), 220;
      "and I have . . . cords of them": Rockefeller quoted in Ron Chernow, *Titan:
      The Life of John D. Rockefeller* (Random House: New York, 1998), 543.

295–296 "There goes. . . . the Big Chief!": Jean Strouse, *Morgan: American Finan-
      cier* (Random House: New York, 1999), 579; "From . . . to $1200": "L.L.E.,"
      "From $3500 a Year to $1200," *Ladies' Home Journal,* 46 (1908), 336–37;
      "I surrendered . . . at Newport": Finley Peter Dunne, "Mr. Dooley on Hard
      Times," *American Magazine,* 65 (1908), 341, 344.

297   "the incorporation of America": Alan Trachtenberg, *The Incorporation of
      America* (Hill and Wang: New York, 1982).

297   "the young men . . . America's elect": Kim Townsend, *Manhood at Harvard: William
      James and Others* (Harvard University Press: Cambridge, Mass., and London,
      1996), 121; "the democracy . . . foreign sources": Eliot quoted in ibid., 91.

298   "the present . . . Assisi": Robert Benchley quoted in Chernow, *Titan*, 585.

298–299 "there was money . . . taste"; Henry James, *The American Scene* [1907] (In-
      diana University Press: Bloomington and London, 1968), 192; "pawnbroker's
      shop for Croesuses": Berenson quoted in Strouse, *Morgan*, 504.

302   "on the tramp": Nick Salvatore, *Eugene V. Debs: Citizen and Socialist* (Univer-
      sity of Illinois Press: Urbana and Chicago, 1982), 18; "Benevolence Sobriety
      and Industry": ibid., 20; "that sacred little spot": ibid., 21; "the best people":
      ibid., 21.

303   "create all . . . to their detriment": Debs quoted in ibid., 59–60; "It is only . . .
      employers": Debs quoted in ibid., 61.

303   "is modern. . . . citizen": Debs in ibid., 80.

303–304 "The crime. . . . oppressed": Debs in ibid., 137; "Cain . . . denial": Debs
      quoting Herron in ibid., 151; "the revolutionary . . . enough": [Julius Way-
      land,] editorials, *Appeal to Reason*, April 26, 1902, August 3, 1901, quoted in
      ibid., 191.

304   "Socialism makes . . . was born": Debs quoted in Salvatore, *Debs*, 191; "real
      and ransomed individualism": George Herron, *The Day of Judgment* (Charles
      H. Kerr: Chicago, 1904), 24.

305   "the teachings . . . affairs": letter of mill worker to Bryan quoted in Michael
      Kazin, *A Godly Hero: The Life of William Jennings Bryan* (Knopf: New York,
      2006), 111; "facts and theories . . . no use": James, "The Will to Believe"
      [1896] in his *The Will to Believe and Other Essays* (Harvard University Press:
      Cambridge, Mass., 1979), 19.

305   "doing . . . humanity": Kazin, *Godly Hero*, 123.

306   "This giant race. . . . *corporate sinning*": Edward Alsworth Ross, "Sinning by
      Syndicate," *Atlantic Monthly*, 100 (1907), 531, 532, 534.

307   "to reduce . . . poor": Taft quoted in Donald E. Anderson, *William Howard
      Taft: A Conservative's Conception of the Presidency* (Cornell University Press:
      Ithaca, N.Y., 1973), 54.

308 "sheaves . . . promoters": James J. Hill quoted in Thomas C. Cochran and William Miller, *The Age of Enterprise* [1942] (Harper: New York, 1961), 189.

309 "industrial unionism . . . republic": Debs quoted in Salvatore, *Debs*, 247.

309 "in a tent. . . . the people": Tom Johnson, *My Story* (B. W. Huebsch: New York, 1913), quoted in Kevin Mattson, *Creating a Democratic Public: The Struggle for Urban Participatory Democracy During the Progressive Era* (Pennsylvania State University Press: University Park, 1998), 37.

310 "the topic . . . professor": Harriet Childs in ibid., 59.

310–311 "the corporate . . . state": James Weinstein, *The Corporate Ideal in the Liberal State, 1900–1918* (Beacon Press: Boston, 1972); "Men should be . . . always": letter, Mrs. John F. Park to Bryan, *The Commoner*, April 2, 1909, cited in Kazin, *Godly Hero*, 176.

312 "young men. . . . myself": Woodrow Wilson, address in Waterbury, Conn., December 14, 1899, *The Papers of Woodrow Wilson*, Arthur Link, ed., 69 vols. (Princeton, 1966–92), 11, 299, cited in John Milton Cooper, *The Warrior and the Priest: Woodrow Wilson and Theodore Roosevelt* (Harvard University Press: Cambridge, Mass., 1983), 58–59.

312–313 "We cannot . . . them": Wilson, address at New Rochelle, N.Y., February 27, 1905, *Papers* 16, 14; "Since . . . in the process": Wilson quoted in Frederick Pike, *Revolutionary Mexico: The Coming and Process of the Mexican Revolution* (University of California Press: Berkeley, 1987), 276; "imperialism of the spirit": William Appleman Williams, *The Tragedy of American Diplomacy* (Dell: New York, 1962), 63; "Because you steer. . . . North Star": Wilson, speech at Chicago, February 12, 1909, *Papers*, 19, 39; "The only thing . . . growth": Wilson, speech at Jersey City, September 28, 1910, *Papers*, 21, 191; "to release . . . time": Wilson, speech at Philadelphia, February 21, 1911, *Papers*, 22, 449–50.

313 "are you seeing . . . novel fields?": Wilson, speech at Atlantic City, May 6, 1910, *Papers*, 20, 467; "a principle . . . rests": John Reed quoted in Cooper, *Warrior and Priest*, 238; "some great orator . . . self-sacrifice": Wilson quoted in John Morton Blum, *Woodrow Wilson and the Politics of Morality* (Little, Brown: Boston, 1956), 40.

314 "I regard . . . Democratic Party": Wilson quoted in ibid., 45.

314 "champion of the common people": Wilson quoted in ibid., 49; "the foundation . . . is economics": Wilson, speech at New York, May 23, 1912, *Papers*, 24, 415; "The fine . . . rigidity": Ellen Maury Slayden, *Washington Wife: The Journal of Ellen Maury Slayden, 1897–1919* (Harper and Row: New York, 1963), 179.

314 "the men on the make . . . already made": Wilson, speech at Indianapolis, April 13, 1911, *Papers*, 21, 559; "a college professor . . . patriotism": TR to F. S. Oliver, in his *Letters*, 5, 352.

315–316 "The truth is. . . . berserkers": Taft to Otto Bannard, September 10, 1911, in Henry F. Pringle, *The Life and Times of William Howard Taft*, 2 vols. (Farrar and Rinehart: New York, 1939), 2, 748, quoted by Cooper, *Warrior and Priest*, 154; "Christian warrior . . . evangelist": Herbert Croly, *The Promise of American Life* (Macmillan: New York, 1909), 255; "heroic struggle": TR, speech at Osawatomie, Kansas, August 31, 1910, in *Theodore Roosevelt: Letters and Speeches*, Louis Auchincloss, ed. (Library of America: New York, 2004), 800.

316 "would be . . . il gran rifiuto": TR quoted in Cooper, *Warrior and Priest*, 156; "We stand . . . the Lord": TR, speech at Progressive Party Convention, *New York Times*, August 7, 1912, 9; "Ours. . . . experts": Wilson, speech at Buffalo, September 2, 1912, *Papers*, 25, 75, 77–78.

317 "we . . . class": Bill Haywood quoted in Salvatore, *Debs*, 56.

317 "to cleanse . . . the right": Wilson, an inaugural address, March 4, 1913, *Papers*, 27, 149.

319 "No one doubts. . . . principles": "The Financial Situation," *Commercial and Financial Chronicle*, 97 (December 13, 1913), 1685.

320 "the labor . . . commerce": "The Labor Provisions of the Clayton Act," *Harvard Law Review* 30 (1917), 632; "pandering . . . corporations": *New York Times*, quoted in Elizabeth Sanders, *Roots of Reform: Farmers, Workers, and the American State, 1877–1917* (University of Chicago Press: Chicago, 1999), 290; "The dogs . . . life": Martin Madden quoted in ibid., 290.

321 "the rise. . . . emporium": DeGrazia, *Irresistible Empire*, 3.

321 "The great barrier . . . of America": Wilson, Detroit address, July 10, 1916, *Papers*, 37, 383.

322 "the very highest medium. . . . purposes": Wilson quoted in DeGrazia, *Irresistable Empire*, 298–99; "one day. . . . new world": Philippe Soupault, quoted in ibid., 293.

322 "to teach . . . good men": Wilson quoted in Alan Dawley, *Changing the World: American Progressives in War and Revolution* (Princeton University Press: Princeton, 2003), 30.

323 "the supreme . . . perfect day": William Jennings Bryan, "Imperialism" [1900] in *Speeches of William Jennings Bryan, Revised and Arranged by Himself*, 2 vols. (Funk and Wagnalls: New York, 1913), 2, 49.

324 "will never . . . by conquest": Wilson, speech at Mobile, Alabama, October 27, 1913, in *Papers*, 28, 451.

324–325 "very solemnly . . . ours": Wilson quoted in Judis, *Folly of Empire*, 92; "the Americans . . . the country": Charles Moravia, quoted in Alan McPherson, "Americanism Against American Empire," *Americanism: New Perspectives on the History of an Ideal*, Michael Kazin and Joseph McCartin, eds. (University of North Carolina Press: Chapel Hill, 2006), 180; "for moral effect": Kazin, *Godly Hero*, 229.

326 "irony of fate": Wilson to E. G. Conklin, quoted in Ray Stannard Baker, *Woodrow Wilson: Life and Letters*, 7 vols. (Doubleday, Page: Garden City, N.Y., 1931), 4, 55.

CONCLUSION: DYING IN VAIN

328 "Peace Without Victory": Wilson, speech to U.S. Senate, January 22, 1917, in *The Papers of Woodrow Wilson*, Arthur Link, ed., 69 vols. (Princeton University Press: Princeton, 1966–92), 40, 533–39. Quoted phrase at 536.

329–330 "militarism . . . contemptible": William James, "The Moral Equivalent of War" [1910] in John J. McDermott, ed., *The Writings of William James* (Random House: New York, 1967), 664; "my second . . . self": Wilson quoted in John Morton Blum, *Woodrow Wilson and the Politics of Morality* (Little, Brown: Boston, 1956), 68; "as an economic . . . in battle": House diary, February 14, 1913, quoted in John Milton Cooper, *The Warrior and the Priest: Woodrow Wilson and Theodore Roosevelt* (Harvard University Press: Cambridge, Mass., 1983), 268.

330 "I am. . . . civilization": [E.M. House] *Philip Dru, Administrator* [1912] (Gregg Press: Upper Saddle River, N.J., 1969), 5; "And from . . . army": ibid., 8, 31.

331 "in that hell storm. . . . they sprang": ibid., 134.

331 "the plunge. . . . for words": Henry James quoted in Paul Fussell, *The Great War and Modern Memory* (Oxford University Press: New York, 1975), 8; "a great wave . . . overwhelmed us": Thomas Mann quoted in Alan Dawley, *Changing the World: American Progressives in War and Revolution* (Princeton University Press: Princeton and London, 2003), 36; "one beautiful . . . hearts": journalist quoted in ibid., 37.

332 "Among . . . progress": Romain Rolland in ibid., 36.

332 "grief . . . possible": Robert Bridges quoted in Fussell, *Great War*, 11.

333–334 "We have . . . her": Theodore Roosevelt, "The World War: Its Tragedies and Its Lessons," *Outlook*, 108 (September 23, 1914), 173; "treaties will . . . blood": "Timid Neutrality," *New Republic*, 1 (November 14, 1914), 7–8; "Wilson is . . . physically": TR to Cecil Spring-Rice, November 11, 1914, in *Letters*, 8, 841; "comes of . . . Civil War": TR to Kipling, November 4, 1914, ibid., 829–30.

334 "that vague pacifism. . . . unconquered France": Robert Herrick, "Recantation of a Pacifist," *New Republic*, 4 (October 30, 1915), 328–29.

334 "piracy" . . . "murder": TR quoted in Blum, *Morality*, 101; "There is such a thing . . . that it is right": Wilson, speech at Philadelphia, May 11, 1915, *Papers*, 33, 149; "the demagogue . . . soul": TR to Owen Wister, February 5, 1916, quoted in Wister, *Roosevelt: The Story of a Friendship* (Macmillan: New York, 1930), 355.

335 "the force of moral principle": Wilson quoted in Blum, *Morality*, 109; "We believe . . . integrity": Wilson, speech to League to Enforce Peace, May 27, 1916, *Papers*, 37, 115.

335 "No, no . . . He kept us out of war": Arthur Link, *Woodrow Wilson and the Progressive Era, 1910–1917* (Harper and Row: New York, 1954), 234.

336 "Deprived of glory . . . defend Verdun?" Wilson quoted in Cooper, *Warrior and Priest*, 310; "the things. . . . in vain": Ernest Hemingway, *A Farewell to Arms* (Charles Scribner's Sons: New York, 1929), 196.

336 "the silent . . . everywhere": Wilson, speech to U.S. Senate, January 22, 1917, *Papers*, 40, 538.

336–337 "the single supreme plan . . . cease to hate. . . .": Wilson, remarks to Southern Methodist Conference, *New York Times*, March 25, 1917, 1; "No peace . . . property": speech to U.S. Senate, January 22, 1917, *Papers*, 40, 537; "there is coming . . . the rights of sovereignty": Wilson, an address in Chicago to Non-Partisan Women, October 19, 1916, *Papers*, 38, 484.

337 "President Wilson . . . the mighty": TR citing Judges 5:23, quoted in *New York Times*, February 1, 1917, 3; "Without any delay. . . . in motion": "Postscript, Thursday morning, February 1st, 1917," supplement to *New Republic*, 10 (February 3, 1917).

337–338 "He is. . . . lofty sentence": TR to Hiram Johnson, February 17, 1917, *Letters*, 8, 1153–54; "there would thus. . . . recourse to arms": Wilson quoted in Thomas Knock, " 'Playing for Hundred Years Hence': Woodrow Wilson's Internationalism and His Would-be Heirs," unpublished paper delivered at the conference on "American Empire" at Tokyo University, March 8, 2005, 10.

339 "A little group . . . contemptible": Wilson quoted in David P. Thelen, *Robert M. LaFollette and the Insurgent Spirit* (Little, Brown: Boston, 1976), 134.

339 "The poor . . . will be heard": LaFollette quoted in ibid.; "the world. . . . liberty": Wilson, speech to U.S. Congress, April 2, 1917, in *Papers*, 41, 525; "My message . . . to applaud that": Wilson quoted in William E. Leuchtenberg, *The Perils of Prosperity, 1914–1932* (University of Chicago Press: Chicago, 1958), 30; " 'Once lead . . . he exclaimed": Frank Cobb quoted in Link, *Wilson*, 277.

340 "cheer leaders of the nation": L. B. Jones, "Advertising Men as the 'Cheer Leaders' of the Nation," *Printers Ink*, 102 (February 7, 1918), 62–65; "In the estimation . . . a convict": Champ Clark quoted in John Whiteclay Chambers II, *To Raise an Army: The Draft Comes to Modern America* (Free Press: New York, 1987), 165.

340–341 "you might . . . as he does": Butler quoted in Leuchtenberg, *Perils*, 45; "disloyal . . . abusive": Blum, *Morality*, 143; "slacker raids": Chambers, *To Raise an Army*, 213.

342 "unutterable. . . . overspending!": Ray Stannard Baker, quoted in Michael McGerr, *A Fierce Discontent: The Rise and Fall of the Progressive Movement in America, 1870–1920* (Free Press: New York, 2003), 282.

342 "millionaires' unit" . . . "Silk Stocking Regiment": Fraser, *Speculator*, 352–53.

342 "We can no longer . . . . world": Harvey W. Wiley, "Booze *or Bread?*" *Good Housekeeping*, 65 (July 1917, 59); "high and holy mission": Baker quoted in Leuchtenberg, *Peril*, 46.

342 "that there is. . . . under normal conditions": Lt. W. R. Gayner, "Doing More Than You Ever Dreamed You Could Do," *American Magazine*, 86 (1918), 44–45, 74–82.

344 Randolph Bourne, "Trans-National America" [1914] reprinted in his *War and the Intellectuals*, Carl Resek, ed. (Harper and Row: New York, 1964), 107–23.

344 "If your ideal. . . . you never transcend anything": Randolph Bourne, "Twilight of Idols" [1917], in ibid., 61.

344 "the academic mind. . . . suspense?": Randolph Bourne, "War and the Intellectuals" [1917] in ibid., 4, 3, 12.

345 "War is the health of the state": Randolph Bourne, "The State," ibid., 71; "playing for a hundred years hence": Wilson quoted in Knock, "Playing," 1.

345 "open covenants. . . . small states alike": address to the U.S. Congress, January 8, 1918, in *Papers*, 45, 552.

346 "How shall we . . . to the weak?" Wilson, statement to the American people, July 26, 1918, quoted in Erez Manela, *The Wilsonian Moment: Self-Determination and the Origins of Anticolonial Nationalism* (Oxford University Press: New York, 2007), 33; "think . . . men": Wilson, address to the U.S. Senate, September 30, 1918, quoted in ibid., 33.

346 "The Black Day of the German Army": Ludendorff quoted in Fussell, *Great War*, 18; "limited liability": TR quoted in Cooper, *Warrior and Priest*, 28; "let us . . . typewriters": TR to Henry Cabot Lodge, October 24, 1918, in *Letters*, 8, 1380.

347 "weaklings . . . nationalism": TR, *Metropolitan*, July 1918, in *The Works of Theodore Roosevelt*, Hermann Hagedorn, ed. (Charles Scribner's Sons: New York, 1926), 19, 324–325.

347 "For a brief interval. . . . a Messiah": H. G. Wells, *The Shape of Things to Come* (Macmillan: New York, 1933), 82.

348 "to respect . . . the League": Article X of the Covenant of the League of Nations, Part I of the Treaty of Versailles, www.yale.edu/lawweb/avalon/imt/menu.htm

348–349 "We are depending. . . . the condemnation of the world": Wilson quoted in Blum, *Morality*, 169; "the League . . . the treaty": "Peace at Any Price," *New Republic*, 19 (May 24, 1919), 100–02; "the most drastic . . . of Germany": Walter Lippmann quoted in Christopher Lasch, *The New Radicalism in America, 1889–1963: The Intellectual as a Social Type* (Vintage Books: New York, 1965), 217.

349 "would willingly . . . for the good of the world": Wilson quoted in Knock, "Playing," 13.

350 "The only way . . . to do": Wilson, address in Billings, Montana, September 11, 1919, *Papers*, 55, 268–76.

351 "The world . . . principle": address in Princess Theater, Cheyenne, Wyoming, September 24, 1919, *Papers*, 63, 468; "the infinite . . . the world": ibid., 469; "the taproot . . . family": Wilson, address in Salt Lake City, September 23, 1919, *Papers*, 63, 459; "Shall the great sacrifice . . . it not?": Wilson, speech at Helena, Montana, September 11, 1919, *Papers*, 63, 181; "There is . . . before": Wilson, speech at Pueblo, Colorado, September 25, 1919, *Papers*, 63, 513.

353–354 "those big . . . unhappy": James Joyce, *Ulysses* [1922], Vintage Books ed. (New York, 1961), 31; "an unanalyzable . . . to be": Randolph Bourne, "A War Diary" [1918] in *War and the Intellectuals*, 39.

354 "Mons, Loos. . . . Shotvarfet": Pat Barker, *The Ghost Road* (Viking: New York, 1995), 257, 263–64, 274.

BIBLIOGRAPHICAL NOTE

It is hard to say when research on this book started, since I have been reading, thinking, and writing about the emergence of modern America for nearly four decades. Like my other books, this one is based on a variety of sources: on mass-market as well as up-market magazines (from *Frank Leslie's Illustrated Weekly* to the *Atlantic Monthly*), on letters and memoirs (from Theodore Roosevelt's *Autobiography* to *The Diary of a Hard-Worked Woman* in frontier Colorado), on fictions, sermons, and speeches as well as systematic thought, on advertisements and entertainments. These primary sources are cited throughout my end notes. But—as the end notes also reveal—because this is a synthetic reinterpretation of the period, it is even more dependent on other scholars' work than my previous books have been. I will try, however inadequately, to discharge those debts here. The scholarly literature is voluminous, and any bibliographic note will inevitably be selective and partial.

INTRODUCTION: DREAMING OF REBIRTH

When I started out in graduate school in the 1970s, two names dominated discussion of the period called the Gilded Age and Progressive Era: Richard Hofstadter and Robert Wiebe. They had opened up the field to discovery and debate; they were guides but also targets. Hofstadter's elegant style and probing insights in books like *The American Political Tradition* (Knopf: New York, 1948) and *Anti-Intellectualism in American Life* (Knopf: New York, 1963) made him an inspiring figure. But in *The Age of Reform: From Bryan to F.D.R.* (Knopf: New York, 1955), Hofstadter displayed less of his characteristic sensitivity; he fell into an easy dismissal of the Populists and to a lesser extent of the Progressives as well. For him, the New Deal's pragmatic liberalism fulfilled the promise of the Age of Reform, and anything that did not tend in that direction could be explained as an anxious response to declining status. Though not as impressive as Hofstadter's other works, *The Age of Reform* has preserved a longer-lasting influence than any of the rest, perhaps because its anti-rural prejudices reflect those of the journalists who like to quote it. Wiebe's *The Search for Order, 1877–1920* (Hill and Wang: New York, 1967) offered a more nuanced treatment of Progressive reform, recognizing the importance of managerial ideology and its capacity to coexist, sometimes uneasily, with Progressive moralism. But ultimately Wiebe, like Hofstadter, seemed too interested in writing the history of winners. In both accounts, there was too little attention paid to the persistent cultural tensions provoked by modernity, and to the ways that social transformations served certain interests at the expense of others.

Christopher Lasch's seminal essay "The Moral and Intellectual Rehabilitation of the Ruling Class," in his *The World of Nations* (Viking: New York, 1971), suggested a framework for a more capacious interpretation, one that explored the ways elites maintained power rather than assuming (falsely) that they lost it. Alan Trachtenberg's *The Incorporation of America: Politics and Culture in the Gilded Age* (Hill and Wang: New York, 1982) advanced this interpretation by moving the corporation to center stage, recognizing its role in shaping new imperial hierarchies at home and abroad. My *No Place of Grace: Antimodernism and the Transformation of American Culture, 1880–1920* (Pantheon: New York, 1981) took another approach to the persistence of elite power, exploring the paradoxical part played by antimodern tendencies in creating a modern therapeutic culture well-suited to a corporate system.

Synthesis was out of fashion in the 1980s and 1990s, and the emergence of social and cultural history as the dominant U.S. fields apparently discouraged historians from attempting old-style interpretations that brought politics into the picture. Only recently has the vogue of transnational history begun to produce some new attempts at synthesis, notably Eric Rauchway's *Blessed Among Nations: How the World Made America* (Hill and Wang: New York, 2006), an ingenious effort to show that the exceptionally privileged status of the twentieth-century United States emerged from the fortunate global economic circumstances the nation encountered in the late nineteenth century, rather than from any peculiarly American skills and virtues. My approach is different. Rather than debunk romantic nationalism (which surely is in need of debunking), *Rebirth of a Nation* reconsiders the romantic nationalist creed from the inside out, to see how it served the needs of the changing Protestant mind and soul. It also departs from existing scholarship in its effort to sort out the long-term emotional impact of the Civil War—a topic almost no one interpreting the period has seen fit to address at length.

CHAPTER ONE: THE LONG SHADOW OF APPOMATTOX

In the wake of 9/11, historians have rediscovered the centrality of war in American history. Fred Anderson and Andrew Cayton's *The Dominion of War: Empire and Liberty in North America, 1500–2000* (Viking: New York, 2005) is a sober and searching example of the genre, exploring the imperial ambitions that consistently coexisted with the rhetoric of liberty. Robert Kaplan's *Dangerous Nation* (Knopf: New York, 2006) is a neoconservative tract masquerading as history, ignoring the anti-imperial strain in republican thought and celebrating heedless interventionism as a vital imperial tradition. Wolfgang Schivelbusch's *The Culture of Defeat: On National Trauma, Mourning, and Recovery* (Metropolitan Books: New York, 2003) is an imaginative effort to put the U.S. Civil War in the context of a broad "rebarbarization" of war between Shiloh and the Somme.

The Civil War has come in for new kinds of scrutiny by historians, who have been reminded by phrases like "collateral damage" that bland language can neutralize horror. The fearful human cost of the war, and the cultural strategies that sufferers used to justify their pain, have animated several extraordinary studies: Charles Royster's *The Destructive War: William Tecumseh Sherman, Stonewall Jackson, and the Americans* (Knopf: New York, 1991), Harry Stout's *Upon the Altar of the Nation: A Moral History of the Civil War* (Viking: New York, 2006), and Drew Faust's *This Republic of Suffering: Death and the American Civil War* (Knopf: New York, 2008). Among older studies, George Frederickson's *The Inner Civil War: Northern Intellectuals and the Crisis of the Union* (Harper and Row: New York, 1967) remains useful. On the postwar construction of public memories of the war, David Blight's *Race and Reunion: The Civil War and American Memory* (Harvard University Press: Cambridge, Mass., and London, 2000) is probing and essential. I have relied heavily on it. The racial politics of the post-Reconstruction era are powerfully recounted in C. Vann Woodward's *Origins of the New South, 1877–1913* (Louisiana State University Press: Baton Rouge, 1951), a classic in a class by itself. Steven Hahn's *A Nation Under Our Feet: Black Political Struggles in the Rural South from Slavery to the Great Migration* (Harvard University Press: Cambridge, Mass., and London, 2003) is a recent and important study that has proven invaluable to me. Woodward's *The Burden of Southern History* (Louisiana State University Press: Baton Rouge, 1960) raises profound questions about the impact of the war on Southern (and national) public life.

The relation between the frontier and the history of American violence has been creatively explored by legions of historians since Frederick Jackson Turner's classic essay "The Significance of the Frontier in American History" in 1893. Among the most persuasive is Richard Slotkin. In a magisterial trilogy—*Regeneration Through Violence: The Mythology of the American Frontier, 1600–1860* (Wesleyan University Press: Middletown, Conn., 1973), *The Fatal Environment: The Myth of the Frontier in the Age of Industrialization* (Atheneum: New York, 1985), and *Gunfighter Nation: The Myth of the Frontier in Twentieth-Century America* (Atheneum: New York, 1992)—Slotkin illuminates the myriad ways that frontier fantasies interacted with Indian-white relations, class and race conflict, and imperial foreign policy. This work has informed my own. Essential social, political, and economic background is in Richard White's *"It's Your Misfortune and None of My Own": A New History of the American West* (University of Oklahoma Press: Norman and London, 1991). On the packaging of frontier experience, I have also found useful Richard Drinnon's *Facing West: The Metaphysics of Indian-Hating and Empire-Building* (University of Minnesota Press: Minneapolis, 1980); Joy Kasson's *Buffalo Bill's Wild West: Celebrity, Memory, and Popular History* (Hill and Wang: New York, 2000); Rob Kroes and Robert W. Rydell's *Buffalo Bill in Bologna: The Americanization of the World, 1969–1922* (Oxford University Press: New York, 2005); Louise K. Barnett's *Touched by Fire: The Life, Death, and Mythic Afterlife of George Armstrong Custer* (Henry Holt: New York, 1996); and especially Evan S. Connell's *Son of the Morning Star: Custer and the Little Big Horn* (North Point Press: San Francisco, 1984).

On the connection between Indian wars and later imperial adventures, the literature is vast but the references are often fleeting. John Judis's *The Folly of Empire: What George W. Bush Could Learn from Theodore Roosevelt and Woodrow Wilson* (Scribner: New York, 2004) is a journalistic account, useful but far too concerned with exonerating Roosevelt and Wilson from the taint of imperialism. Walter LaFeber's *The American Search for Opportunity, 1865–1913* (Cambridge University Press: New York, 1994) is superb on tracing the circuitous path to empire through the tangled domestic politics of the Gilded Age. Stuart Creighton Miller's *"Benevolent Assimilation": The American Conquest of the Philippines, 1899–1903* (Yale University Press: New Haven and London, 1982) is indispensable for establishing links between wars for internal and external empire.

The ties between racial politics and overseas empire are carefully delineated in Paul A. Kramer's "Empires, Exceptions, and Anglo-Saxons: Race and Rule Between the British and United States Empires, 1880–1910," *Journal of American History* (March 2002), 1315–53, and Matthew Frye Jacobson's *Barbarian Virtues: The United States Encounters Foreign Peoples at Home and Abroad, 1876–1917* (Hill and Wang: New York, 2000). Jacobson is also excellent on the revitalization of white manhood through self-testing, as is Michael Robinson, in *The Coldest Crucible: Arctic Exploration and American Culture* (University of Chicago Press: Chicago and London, 2006). Two imaginative and helpful literary studies are David Spurr's *The Rhetoric of Empire: Colonial Discourse in Journalism, Travel Writing, and Imperial Administration* (Duke University Press: Durham, N.C., 1993) and Amy Kaplan's *The Anarchy of Empire in the Making of U.S. Culture* (Harvard University Press: Cambridge, Mass., and London, 2002).

Throughout this study, biographies have proven a critical resource for fleshing out interpretation in individual lives. The most useful for this chapter were Louis Menand's *The Metaphysical Club* (Farrar, Straus, and Giroux: New York, 2001), which contains (along with other fine intellectual biographies) the best available account of Oliver Wendell Holmes Jr.'s war experience and its consequences; R. W. B. Lewis's *The Jameses: A Family Narrative* (Farrar, Straus, and Giroux: New York, 1991), on Wilky James; T. J. Stiles's *Jesse James: Last Rebel of the Civil War* (Knopf: New York, 2002); William S. McFeely's *Frederick Douglass* (Norton: New York, 1991); Louise Knight's *Citizen: Jane Addams and the Struggle for Democracy* (University of Chicago Press: Chicago and London, 2005); Robert Richardson's *William James: In the Maelstrom of Modernity* (Houghton Mifflin: New York, 2007); Justin Kaplan's *Mr. Clemens and Mark Twain* (Simon & Schuster: New York, 1966); and William H. Harbaugh's *The Life and Times of Theodore Roosevelt*, rev. ed. (Collier Books: New York, 1963).

CHAPTER TWO: THE MYSTERIOUS POWER OF MONEY

My thinking on market culture has long been shaped by Weberian, Freudian, and Marxist tradition. Max Weber's *The Protestant Ethic and the Spirit of Capitalism* [1904] (English translation, Scribner: New York, 1958) placed the process of rationalization—the drive for outer control of the environment and inner control of the self— at the heart of modernity. One of Weber's best critics is Colin Campbell, whose *The Romantic Ethic and the Spirit of Modern Consumerism* (Oxford University Press: Oxford and New York, 1987) emphasizes the "Other Protestant Ethic" of endless, sanctioned longing as the key sentiment animating consumption. The pairing of control and desire suggests the continuing relevance of Freudian ideas of ambivalence and the return of the repressed, which I began exploring in *No Place of Grace.* I have also been influenced by the culturalist Marxism of E. P. Thompson, Raymond Williams, and Antonio Gramsci, especially Gramsci's concept of cultural hegemony, introduced in his *Prison Notebooks* (translated by Joseph Buttigieg and Antonio Callari, Columbia University Press: New York, 1992) and elaborated in my "The Concept of Cultural Hegemony: Problems and Possibilities," *American Historical Review,* 90 (June 1985), 567–93.

On American settings for market culture, my best guides have been Jean-Christophe Agnew, *Worlds Apart: The Market and Theater in Anglo-American Thought, 1550–1750* (Cambridge University Press: New York, 1986); Karen Halttunen, *Confidence Men and Painted Women: A Study of Middle-Class Culture in America, 1830–1870* (Yale University Press: New Haven and London, 1982); Ann Fabian, *Card Sharps, Dream Books, and Bucket Shops: Gambling in Nineteenth-Century America* (Cornell University Press: Ithaca, N.Y., and London, 1990); and James Cook, *The Arts of Deception: Playing with Fraud in the Age of Barnum* (Harvard University Press: Cambridge, Mass., and London, 2001). All these works creatively explore the confidence games at the core of market exchange, the subtle dialectics of belief and doubt that animated dreams of social transparency and self-made manhood, and that revealed the irrational dimensions of capitalism, over against the Weberian model. I have tried to follow this lead in my own work on advertising and luck, which also informs this chapter as well as parts of chapters 6 and 7: see especially "From Salvation to Self-realization: Advertising and the Therapeutic Roots of the Consumer Culture, 1880–1930," in Richard Fox and T. J. Jackson Lears, eds., *The Culture of Consumption: Critical Essays in American History, 1880–1980* (Pantheon: New York, 1983); *Fables of Abundance: A Cultural History of Advertising in America* (Basic Books: New York, 1994); and *Something for Nothing: Luck in America* (Viking Penguin: New York, 2003).

An indispensable source for the history of money in America is Steve Fraser's *Every Man a Speculator: A Cultural History of Wall Street in America* (HarperCollins: New York, 2005), which deftly reconstructs the strategies of the wildcat speculators and white-shoe investment bankers as well as the arguments of their critics. Also valuable is Lendol Calder's *Financing the American Dream: A Cultural History of Consumer Credit* (Princeton University Press: Princeton and London, 1999), which debunks any assumptions about a golden age of thrift by documenting the pervasiveness of debt and default in nineteenth-century America.

On the bourgeois psychology of scarcity and the pervasiveness of neurasthenia, my *No Place of Grace* provides the beginnings of a comprehensive interpretation, with reference to religious change as well as contradictory gender expectations. Also worthwhile and idiosyncratic is Tom Lutz's *American Nervousness, 1903: An Anecdotal History* (Cornell University Press: Ithaca, N.Y., and London, 1991). For the religious and therapeutic response to neurasthenia, the crucial introduction is still the groundbreaking Donald Meyer's *The Positive Thinkers: Religion as Pop Psychology from Mary Baker Eddy to Norman Vincent Peale,* 2nd ed. (Pantheon: New York,

1980). Gender dimensions are usefully emphasized in Beryl Satter's *Each Mind a Kingdom: American Women, Sexual Purity, and the New Thought Movement, 1875–1920* (University of California Press: Berkeley and London, 1999).

Apart from newspaper and magazine accounts, my main guides to working-class life and politics have been David Montgomery, *The Fall of the House of Labor: The Workplace, the State, and American Labor Activism, 1865–1925* (Cambridge University Press: New York, 1987), which is rich in detail and supple in interpretation; Roy Rosenzweig, *Eight Hours for What We Will: Workers and Leisure in an Industrial City, 1870–1920* (Cambridge University Press: Cambridge, England, and New York, 1983), which contains critical background on the eight-hour movement; Leon Fink, *Workingmen's Democracy: The Knights of Labor and American Politics* (University of Illinois Press: Urbana, 1983); David Brody, *Steelworkers in America: The Nonunion Era* (Harvard University Press: Cambridge, Mass., 1960); and James Green, *Death in the Haymarket: A Study of Chicago, the First Labor Movement, and the Bombing that Divided Gilded Age America* (Pantheon: New York, 2006), which provides a compelling narrative account of that event.

The lives of Carnegie and Rockefeller can best be reconstructed from their own writings and from two recent and superb biographies: David Nasaw, *Andrew Carnegie* (Penguin: New York, 2006), and Ron Chernow, *Titan: The Life of John D. Rockefeller, Sr.* (Random House: New York, 1998). The first stirrings of Progressive reform are ably chronicled in Daniel Rodgers, *Atlantic Crossings: Social Politics in a Progressive Age* (Harvard University Press: Cambridge, Mass., and London, 1998).

CHAPTER THREE: THE RISING SIGNIFICANCE OF RACE

Crucial background to the rise of Jim Crow in the South and the persistence of comparative fluidity in race relations can be found in Edward Ayers, *The Promise of the New South: Life After Reconstruction* (Oxford University Press: New York, 1992), a probing and capacious synthesis; also in Hahn, *A Nation Under Our Feet* and Woodward, *Origins of the New South*. On the rise of post–Civil War racism, useful sources include Thomas F. Gossett, *Race: The History of an Idea in America*, new ed. (Oxford University Press: New York, 1997); Joel Williamson, *The Crucible of Race: Black-White Relations in the American South Since Emancipation* (Oxford University Press: New York, 1984); and Grace E. Hale, *Making Whiteness: The Culture of Segregation in the South, 1890–1940* (Pantheon: New York, 1998).

On the precariousness of white manhood, see Kim Townsend, *Manhood at Harvard: William James and Others* (Harvard University Press: Cambridge, Mass., and London, 1996); Clifford Putney, *Muscular Christianity: Manhood and Sports in Protestant America, 1880–1920* (Harvard University Press: Cambridge, Mass., and London, 2001); Gail Bederman, *Manliness and Civilization: A Cultural History of Gender and Race in the United States, 1880–1917* (University of Chicago Press: Chicago and London, 1995). The connections between racism and the gold standard are inventively examined by Michael O'Malley, "Specie and Species: Race and the Money Question in Nineteenth Century America," *American Historical Review*, 99 (April 1994), 369–95.

The best general history of immigration in the late nineteenth and early twentieth centuries is John Bodnar's *The Transplanted: A History of Immigrants in Urban America* (Indiana University Press: Bloomington, 1985). Werner Sollors, *Beyond Ethnicity: Consent and Descent in American Culture* (Oxford University Press: New York, 1986), poses important interpretive challenges. The essays collected in Virginia Yans, ed., *Immigration Reconsidered* (Oxford University Press: New York, 1991) are also illuminating, as is Matthew Frye Jacobson's *Whiteness of a Different Color: European Immigrants and the Alchemy of Race* (Harvard University Press: Cambridge, Mass., and London, 1998). The best source on the Chinese in the West is Alexander Saxton, *The Indispensable Enemy: Labor and the Anti-Chinese Movement in California* (University of California Press: Berkeley, 1971). His more conceptually ambitious *The Rise and Fall of the White Republic: Class Politics and Mass Culture in Nineteenth-Century America* (Verso: London and New York, 1990) is also worth consulting. The classic text on the relation between white racism and the labor movement is David Roediger's *The Wages of Whiteness: Race and the American Working Class*, rev. and expanded ed. (Verso: London, 2007). A pathbreaking exploration of black racial attitudes is Mia Bay's *The White Image in the Black Mind: African-American Ideas About White People, 1830–1925* (Oxford University Press: New York, 2000).

On the fate of Indian people in the white cultural imagination, see Philip Deloria, *Playing Indian* (Yale University Press: New Haven and London, 1998), and Alan Trachtenberg, *Shades of Hiawatha: Staging Indians, Making Americans, 1880–1930* (Hill and Wang: New York, 2004). Trachtenberg perceptively connects the rhetorical elevation of the "first Americans" with the rising suspicion of the most recent, immigrant Americans. For an exceptionally sensitive and philosophically acute account of the Crow people's fate in particular, see Jonathan Lear, *Radical Hope: Ethics in the Face of Cultural Devastation* (Harvard University Press: Cambridge, Mass., and London, 2007).

Women's increasing visibility in public life, and male resistance to it, is capably explored in Rebecca Edwards, *Angels in the Machinery: Gender in American Party Politics from the Civil War to the Progressive Era* (Oxford University Press: New York, 1997); Kathryn Sklar, *Florence Kelley and the Nation's Work*, 2 vols. (Yale University Press: New Haven and London, 1995); and Peggy Pascoe, *Relations of Rescue: The Search for Female Moral Authority in the American West, 1874–1939* (Oxford University Press: New York, 1990). William Leach, *Land of Desire: Merchants, Power, and the Rise of a New American Culture* (Pantheon: New York, 1994), interprets department stores as part of a new commercial public sphere, increasingly available to women—as well as an expression of the consolidating power of a merchant class. A sensitive account of Prohibition, particularly its roots in antimarket sentiments and women's concerns, is Norman Clark's *Deliver Us From Evil: An Interpretation of American Prohibition* (Norton: New York, 1976).

Essential biographies include Louis R. Harlan's *Booker T. Washington: The Making of a Black Leader, 1856–1901* (Oxford University Press: New York, 1975); Ruth Bordin's *Frances Willard: A Biography* (University of North Carolina Press: Chapel Hill and London, 1986); and Paula Giddings's *Ida, a Sword Among Lions: Ida B.*

Wells and the Campaign Against Lynching (Amistad: New York, 2008). The auto-biographies of all three of these figures are equally essential, as is the symptomatic fiction of Frank Norris, Jack London, and John Hay.

CHAPTER FOUR: THE COUNTRY AND THE CITY

My title comes from Raymond Williams's great book of the same name (Oxford University Press: Oxford and New York, 1973), which forcefully argues that the contrast between country and city in pastoral literary tradition concealed power relations both within and between the two realms. This is something of what I want to argue here—that rural and urban life were economically interdependent, and that neither was as utopian nor as hellish as their advocates and detractors suggested. Other works that address technological modernization and its consequences imaginatively are Leo Marx, *The Machine in the Garden: Technology and the Pastoral Ideal in America* (Oxford University Press: New York, 1964); John Kasson, *Civilizing the Machine: Technology and Republican Values in America, 1776–1900* (Grossman: New York, 1976); and David Nye, *American Technological Sublime* (MIT Press: Cambridge, Mass., 1994).

On the relation between Chicago and its hinterland, William Cronon's *Nature's Metropolis: Chicago and the Great West* (Norton: New York, 1992) is indispensable with respect to the details of economic production and distribution. Timothy Spears's *Chicago Dreaming: Midwesterners and the City, 1871–1919* (University of Chicago Press: Chicago and London, 2005) captures the imaginative dimensions of the urban-rural relationship. The novels and memoirs of Theodore Dreiser, Sherwood Anderson, Hamlin Garland, Willa Cather, and other Midwesterners remain an essential source as well.

The rural South is brought to life in Woodward, *Origins of the New South,* and Ayers, *Promise of the New South.* Woodward's *Tom Watson: Agrarian Rebel* [1938] (Oxford University Press: New York, 1969) is more than a sympathetic biography of that misunderstood man; it also discusses the Populists and their opponents at length—notably Henry Grady, whose vision of a New South is in shreds by the end of the book. Paul Gaston's *The New South Creed* (Knopf: New York, 1970) is an extended and perceptive discussion of the modernizers' worldview. Also helpful is Jonathan M. Wiener's *Social Origins of the New South: Alabama, 1860–1885* (Louisiana State University Press: Baton Rouge and London, 1978). Ferald Bryan's *Henry Grady or Tom Watson? The Rhetorical Struggle for the New South, 1880–1890* (Mercer University Press: Macon, Ga., 1994) lays out the choices before the region with exceptional clarity. Pete Daniel's *Breaking the Land: The Transformation of Cotton, Tobacco, and Rice Cultures Since 1880* (University of Illinois Press: Urbana, 1985) is a classic work in the neglected field of agricultural history. Alfred Chandler, *The Visible Hand: The Managerial Revolution in American Business* (Belknap Press: Cambridge, Mass., 1977) puts James B. Duke and the tobacco industry in the largest possible context.

The historiography of Populism has been a battlefield. Ever since Hofstadter debunked the Populists by juxtaposing "the agrarian myth" with "commercial realities," historians have quarreled over the movement's significance. Most have tried to redeem the Populists, usually with some success, from Hofstadter's exaggerated and mostly unwarranted charges of anti-Semitism and sentimental nostalgia. By far the most successful account of Populism as a social movement is Lawrence Goodwyn's *Democratic Promise: The Populist Moment in America* (Oxford University Press: New York, 1976), which effectively captures the Populists' humane attempts to restore democracy to American public life—particularly in the realm of monetary policy. Bruce Palmer, in *"Man Over Money": The Southern Populist Critique of American Capitalism* (University of North Carolina Press: Chapel Hill and London, 1980), makes a similar and equally convincing claim for the Populists' political seriousness. Michael McGerr's *The Decline of Popular Politics: The American North, 1865–1928* (Oxford University Press: New York, 1986) is useful on the relationship between late Gilded Age partisanship and the proliferation of third parties. While Goodwyn stresses the breach between Populists and Democrats, more recent studies— notably Michael Kazin's *A Godly Hero: The Life of William Jennings Bryan* (Knopf: New York, 2006) and Charles Postel's *The Populist Vision* (Oxford University Press: New York, 2007)—have persuasively emphasized continuity between Populist ideas and Progressive tendencies in the Democratic Party. My own interpretation melds Goodwyn and these later views.

CHAPTER FIVE: CRISIS AND REGENERATION

Hofstadter opened the whole subject of the nineties as a watershed with his idea that imperialism was rooted in the "psychic crisis of the nineties." He advanced this claim in "Cuba, Manifest Destiny, and the Philippines," in Daniel Aaron, ed. *America in Crisis: Fourteen Crucial Episodes in American History* [1952] (Archon Books: Hamden, Conn., 1971). Lasch provided a social framework for this argument in his "Rehabilitation of the Ruling Class" essay, and I tried to broaden our cultural understanding of the crisis in *No Place of Grace.* In *Rebirth of a Nation,* I aimed to reconnect culture and politics.

Much ink has been spilled over the significance of the White City. Among the most cogent accounts are Robert Rydell's *All the World's a Fair: Visions of Empire at American International Expositions, 1876–1916* (University of Chicago Press: Chicago, 1984); Neil Harris's "Great American Fairs and American Cities: The Role of Chicago's Columbian Exposition," in his *Cultural Excursions: Marketing Appetites and Popular Tastes in Modern America* (University of Chicago Press: Chicago and London, 1990); and Trachtenberg, *Incorporation of America,* chapter 7.

The crash of 1893 and its aftermath are well-documented in the *New York Times,* in such national periodicals as *Scribner's* and the *Atlantic,* and in the private comments of observers like Henry Adams, volume 4 of whose *Letters* (6 vols., Harvard University Press: Cambridge, Mass., and London, 1982–88) offers portraits in acid of patrician panic. My accounts of Bryan and Morgan depend on two recent and valuable biographies: Kazin's *Godly Hero* and Jean Strouse's *Morgan: American Financier* (Random House: New York, 1999), both of which re-create compelling characters. The Protestant clergy's response to the economic crisis is thoroughly reconstructed in Henry May's *Protestant Churches and Industrial America*, 2nd ed. (Harper and Row: New York, 1967). Jane Addams's probing essay "A Modern Lear" is in Christopher Lasch, ed., *The Social Thought of Jane Addams* (Bobbs-Merrill: Indianapolis, 1965). George Tindall, ed., *A Populist Reader: Selections from the Works of American Populist Leaders* (Harper and Row: New York, 1966), is a fair sampling of agrarian radical thought. The key event in the white Southern counterrevolution receives exhaustive treatment in Timothy B. Tyson and David S. Cecelski, eds., *Democracy Betrayed: The Wilmington Race Riot of 1898 and Its Legacy* (University of North Carolina Press: Chapel Hill and London, 1998). Rodgers, *Atlantic Crossings*, is a surefooted guide to the transatlantic origins of Progressive thought; Michael McGerr, *A Fierce Discontent: The Rise and Fall of the Progressive Movement in America, 1870–1920* (Oxford University Press: New York, 2003), is perceptive on the American roots of reform, especially Protestant visions of moral regeneration. Kevin Mattson, *Creating a Democratic Public: The Struggle for Urban Participatory Democracy During the Progressive Era* (Pennsylvania State University Press: University Park, 1998), provides a useful, well-grounded perspective.

My views on the imperialist turn of the 1890s—like those of many other historians—have been influenced by the work of William Appleman Williams, particularly *The Tragedy of American Diplomacy* [1959], 2nd rev. and enlarged ed. (Dell Books: New York, 1972), and *The Contours of American History* [1961] (Quadrangle Books: New York, 1966). Lloyd C. Gardner, *Imperial America: American Foreign Policy Since 1898* (Harcourt Brace Jovanovich: New York, 1976), is a useful overview. LaFeber, *The American Search for Opportunity, 1865–1913*, casts strong light on key events and policy decisions, as does Miller, *"Benevolent Assimilation."* Jacobsen, *Barbarian Virtues*, focuses on connections between domestic cultural anxieties and foreign military adventures, as I do in *No Place of Grace*. So also, in varying ways, do Drinnon, *Facing West* and Robinson, *Coldest Crucible*. Kristin Hoganson makes the gender argument explicit in her *Fighting for American Manhood: How Gender Politics Provoked the Spanish-American and Philippine-American Wars* (Yale University Press: New Haven and London, 1998). On technology and American empire, the key source is Michael Adas, *Dominance by Design: Technological Imperatives and America's Civilizing Mission* (Harvard University Press: Cambridge, Mass., and London, 2006). For the critique of empire, Robert Beisner, *Twelve Against Empire: The Anti-imperialists, 1898–1900* [1968] (McGraw-Hill: New York, 1985) is reliable but helpfully supplemented by Miller, *"Benevolent Assimilation,"* and the biographies of leading figures such as James, Carnegie, and Bryan.

CHAPTER SIX: LIBERATION AND LIMITATION

This chapter addresses many themes that are present in my earlier work on antimodern dissent, advertising, and luck. It begins with Henry Adams, whose *Education* remains one of the most extraordinary efforts to understand the transformations of the era in all their complexity. Among other, more recent attempts to understand the revolt against positivism historically (and beyond the boundaries of the United States), I have space to mention only a few classics: H. Stuart Hughes, *Consciousness and Society: The Reorientation of European Social Thought, 1880–1930* (Knopf: New York, 1958); Stephen Kern, *The Culture of Time and Space, 1880–1918* (Harvard University Press: Cambridge, Mass., 1982); and Carl Schorske, *Fin de siècle Vienna: Politics and Culture* (Vintage Books: New York, 1981). A pioneering comparative effort to link antipositivism and political thought is James Kloppenberg's *Uncertain Victory: Social Democracy and Progressivism in European and American Thought, 1870–1920* (Oxford University Press: New York, 1986). David Hollinger, *In the American Province: Studies in the History and Historiography of Ideas* [1985] (Johns Hopkins University Press: Baltimore and London, 1989), probes key philosophical issues with clarity and perception.

On the mass marketing of fun, see among many other possibilities: John Kasson, *Amusing the Million: Coney Island at the Turn of the Century* (Hill and Wang: New York, 1978); Rosenzweig, *Eight Hours for What We Will*; Kathy Peiss, *Cheap Amusements: Working Women and Leisure in Turn-of-the-Century New York* (Temple University Press: Philadelphia, 1986); Nan Enstad, *Ladies of Labor, Girls of Adventure: Working Women, Popular Culture, and Labor Politics at the Turn of the Twentieth Century* (Columbia University Press: New York, 1999); and Miriam Hansen, *Babel and Babylon: Spectatorship and American Silent Film* (Harvard University Press: Cambridge, Mass., and London, 1991). Hansen makes a strong argument that the movies (along with department stores) constituted part of an emerging commercial public sphere, one that welcomed women as well as men. Susan Glenn extends this interpretation fruitfully in *Female Spectacle: The Theatrical Roots of Modern Feminism* (Harvard University Press: Cambridge, Mass., and London, 2000). The dreams of liberation associated with air power are explored in Joseph Corn's *The Winged Gospel: America's Romance with Aviation, 1900–1950* (Oxford University Press: New York, 1983).

On the rise of a managerial ethos, the best sources are Olivier Zunz, *Making America Corporate, 1870–1920* (University of Chicago Press: Chicago and London, 1990); Angel Kwolek-Folland, *Engendering Business: Men and Women in the Corporate Office, 1870–1930* (Johns Hopkins University Press: Baltimore and London, 1994); David Noble, *America by Design: Science, Technology, and the Rise of Corporate Capitalism* (Knopf: New York, 1979); Harry Braverman, *Labor and Monopoly Capital: The Degradation of Work in the Twentieth Century* (Monthly Review Press: New York, 1975); Chandler, *Visible Hand*; and Montgomery, *Fall of the House of Labor*. On Taylor the most complete account is Robert Kanigel, *The One Best Way: Frederick Winslow Taylor and the Enigma of Efficiency* (Viking: New York, 1997), but see also the challenging interpretation, informed by Eriksonian psychoanalysis, of Sudhir Kakar, *Frederick Taylor: A Study in Personality and Innovation* (MIT Press: Cambridge, Mass., 1970).

Houdini's life has been chronicled most recently (and thoroughly) by Kenneth Silverman, *Houdini!!! The Career of Ehrich Weiss* (HarperCollins: New York, 1996). John Kasson illuminates Houdini's broader cultural significance in *Houdini, Tarzan, and the Perfect Man: The White Male Body and the Challenge of Modernity in America* (Hill and Wang: New York, 2001). The diffuse fascination with "real life" is a major leitmotif in my *No Place of Grace* and receives fresh treatment

in Miles Orvell, *The Real Thing: Imitation and Authenticity in American Culture,
1880–1940* (University of North Carolina Press: Chapel Hill and London, 1989).
Valuable accounts of later quests for authentic experience can be found in Chris-
tine Stansell's *American Moderns: Bohemian New York and the Creation of a New
Century* (Metropolitan Books: New York, 2000), and Casey Nelson Blake's *Beloved
Community: The Cultural Criticism of Randolph Bourne, Van Wyck Brooks, Waldo
Frank, and Lewis Mumford* (University of North Carolina Press: Chapel Hill and
London, 1990). There is of course no substitute for the writings of the seekers them-
selves: the essays collected in Claire Sprague, ed., *Van Wyck Brooks: The Early Years*,
rev. ed. (Northeastern University Press: Boston, 1993), or Santayana's *The Sense of
Beauty* (Scribner: New York, 1896), as well as Norman Henfrey, ed., *Selected Criti-
cal Writings of George Santayana*, 2 vols. (Cambridge University Press: Cambridge,
England, 1968). For samples of the most remarkable search, see William James, *The
Will to Believe and Other Essays in Popular Philosophy* [1897] (Harvard University
Press: Cambridge, Mass., and London, 1979) and *Essays in Radical Empiricism; and
a Pluralistic Universe* [1912] (Peter Smith: Gloucester, Mass., 1967).

Two classic and still valuable accounts of the turn-of-the-century fascination
with nature are Roderick Nash, *Wilderness and the American Mind* [1967], 4th ed.
(Yale University Press: New Haven and London, 2001), and Peter Schmitt, *Back
to Nature: The Arcadian Myth in Urban America* [1969], 2nd ed. (Johns Hopkins
University Press; Baltimore and London, 1990). Michael Smith, *Pacific Visions: California Scientists and the Environment, 1850–1915* (University of California Press:
Berkeley and London, 1987) is an ingenious account of how, for a while, California's
physical environment shaped a different sort of "Pacific science." My account of
Muir depends on Smith's work. William Cronon, ed., *Uncommon Ground: Toward
Reinventing Nature* (Norton: New York, 1995), is a collection of challenging essays
emphasizing the ways that human conceptions of nature are constructed in accordance with changing historical and cultural circumstances. Donald Worster, *A Passion for Nature: The Life of John Muir* (Oxford University Press: New York, 2008),
brings together many themes that have animated Worster's distinguished career.
Annette Kolodny, *The Land Before Her: Fantasy and Experience of the American
Frontiers, 1630–1860* (University of North Carolina Press: Chapel Hill and London,
1984), provides crucial alternative readings of nature from a female perspective,
less concerned with mastery than understanding—a perspective that also character-
izes the writing of Sarah Orne Jewett and Gene Stratton-Porter, especially Stratton-
Porter's *Girl of the Limberlost* (Grosset and Dunlap: New York, 1909) in the period
I am studying.

The influence of Darwinian evolution on social thought preoccupied intellectual historians during the mid-twentieth-century decades, but the best studies
recognized that evolution was part of a broader rejection of static categories and
formulas—an "antiformalist" tendency, as the philosopher Morton White called it
in his influential *Social Thought in America: The Revolt Against Formalism* [1949]
(Oxford University Press: New York and London, 1976). Thomas Haskell followed
White's lead creatively in *The Emergence of Professional Social Science: The American Social Science Association and the Nineteenth-Century Crisis of Authority* [1977]

(Johns Hopkins University Press: Baltimore and London, 2000), arguing that the recognition of social interdependence marked the key departure from nineteenth-century liberal thought. Richardson, *William James*, Menand, *Metaphysical Club*, and Robert Westbrook, *John Dewey and American Democracy* (Cornell University Press: Ithaca, N.Y., and London, 1987) all demonstrate how much turn-of-the-century social thought was rooted in particular historical and biographical circumstances, rather than simply a series of "responses to Darwinism."

My account of Charlotte Perkins Gilman is based on her *The Living of Charlotte Perkins Gilman: An Autobiography* (D. Appleton-Century: New York and London, 1935) as well as on Ann Lane's sensitive biography, *To Herland and Beyond: The Life and Work of Charlotte Perkins Gilman* (Pantheon: New York, 1990). Classic works on the transformation of psychology and the emergence of a therapeutic worldview are Philip Rieff, *The Triumph of the Therapeutic: Uses of Faith After Freud* (Harper and Row: New York, 1966); Henri Ellenberger, *The Discovery of the Unconscious: The History and Evolution of Dynamic Psychiatry* (Basic Books: New York, 1970); Meyer, *Positive Thinkers*; Elizabeth Lunbeck, *The Psychiatric Persuasion: Knowledge, Gender, and Power in Modern America* (Princeton University Press: Princeton and London, 1994); and Rochelle Gurstein, *The Repeal of Reticence: A History of America's Cultural and Legal Struggles over Free Speech, Obscenity, Sexual Liberation, and Modern Art* (Hill and Wang: New York, 1996), which traces the broader impact of the therapeutic obsession with "openness." I have also been influenced by the argument of Michel Foucault in his *The History of Sexuality: An Introduction* (translated by Robert Hurley, Pantheon: New York, 1980), which notes how the rhetoric of sexual freedom could conceal new forms of coercion.

David Nasaw, *Going Out: The Rise and Fall of Public Amusements* (Basic Books: New York, 1993), charts the racial limits of the new mass culture, and Calder, *Financing the American Dream*, the economic limits. Charles Ponce de Leon, *Self-Exposure: Human Interest Journalism and the Emergence of Celebrity in America, 1890–1940* (University of North Carolina Press: Chapel Hill and London, 2002), illuminates the new commercial ways of constructing public personae. Steven Watts, *The People's Tycoon: Henry Ford and the American Century* (Knopf: New York, 2005), is the best new biography of the enigmatic man whose career epitomized both liberation and limitation.

CHAPTER SEVEN: EMPIRE AS A WAY OF LIFE

My title is from William Appleman Williams's book-length essay of the same name (New York, 1980). It is not the best thing he ever wrote, but it does capture in a phrase the interdependence between consumer culture and American interventions abroad—an argument later made more crudely by Thomas Friedman in *The Lexus and the Olive Tree* (Farrar, Straus, and Giroux: New York, 1999): "If we want to have McDonald's, we've got to have McDonnell-Douglas." This is the key point overlooked by the legions of apologists who have claimed that the United States' lack of interest in acquiring territory abroad means that there is no such thing as an American empire. Recent years have brought more overt talk about the need for "the world's only superpower" to adopt an imperial perspective, notably Niall Ferguson's Kiplingesque screed *Empire: The Rise and Demise of the British World Order and the Lessons for Global Power* (Basic Books: New York, 2003), which urges the United States to pick up the white man's burden so unceremoniously dropped by the British. Andrew Bacevich has cut through this cant of conquest in *American Empire: The Realities and Consequences of American Diplomacy* (Harvard University Press; Cambridge, Mass., and London, 2002) and in *The New American Militarism: How Americans Are Seduced by War* (Oxford University Press: New York, 2005). His work brings clarity to issues too often enveloped in clouds of moralism.

Louis Sullivan's ideas are best available in his *The Autobiography of an Idea* (Press of the American Institute of Architects: New York, 1924), and the context of his work is explored in Daniel Bluestone, *Constructing Chicago* (Yale University Press: New Haven and London, 1991). The consumerist dimensions of empire are delineated in Victoria DeGrazia, *Irresistible Empire: America's Advance Through Twentieth-Century Europe* (Harvard University Press: Cambridge, Mass., and London, 2005); Kristin Hoganson, *Consumers' Imperium: The Global Production of American Domesticity, 1865–1920* (University of North Carolina Press: Chapel Hill and London, 2007); and Kroes and Rydell, *Buffalo Bill in Bologna*. Kaplan, *Anarchy of Empire*; Kasson, *Houdini, Tarzan, and the Perfect Man*; Glenn, *Female Spectacle*; and my *Fables of Abundance* are among many sources that document the imperial primitivism of early-twentieth-century U.S. culture and the connections between racism at home and empire abroad. Glenn is good on the exoticist fantasies surrounding Salome. DuBois's recognition of the global color line is amply documented in Kaplan, *Anarchy of Empire*, and in David Levering Lewis's magisterial *W. E. B. DuBois: Biography of a Race, 1868–1919* (Henry Holt: New York, 1993). Blight, *Race and Reunion*, re-creates DuBois's response to the fiftieth anniversary of Emancipation and documents the whites-only commemoration at Gettysburg.

On imperial politics, LaFeber, *The American Search for Opportunity*, and Kazin, *Godly Hero*, are indispensable, while Harbaugh, *Roosevelt*, George Mowry, *The Era of Theodore Roosevelt, 1900–1912* (Harper and Row: New York, 1958), Richard H. Collin, *Theodore Roosevelt's Caribbean* (Louisiana State University Press: Baton Rouge, 1990), and David Healy, *Drive to Hegemony: The United States in the Caribbean, 1898–1907* (University of Wisconsin Press: Madison, 1988), remain helpful. Also useful are Friedrich Katz, *The Secret War in Mexico: Europe, the United States, and the Mexican Revolution* (University of Chicago Press: Chicago and London, 1981), and Frederick Pike, *The Coming and Process of the Mexican Revolution* (University of California Press: Berkeley, 1987).

On Progressive politics, along with Rodgers, *Atlantic Crossings*, McGerr, *Fierce Discontent*, and Mattson, *Creating a Democratic Public*, there are a host of other valuable studies emerging in recent years. The drift of their interpretations is summarized in Robert Johnston's "Re-Democratizing the Progressive Era: The Politics of Progressive Era Political Historiography," *Journal of the Gilded Age and Progressive Era*, 1 (January 2002), 68–92. Among the most important of the works "re-democratizing" progressivism—some of which appeared after Johnston's article—are Johnston's own *The Radical Middle Class: Populist Democracy and the Question of Capitalism in Progressive Era Portland, Oregon* (Princeton University Press: Princeton and London, 2003); Glenda Gilmore, *Gender and Jim Crow: Gender and the Politics of White Supremacy in North Carolina, 1896–1920* (University of North Carolina Press: Chapel Hill and London, 1996); Maureen A. Flanagan, *Seeing With Their Hearts: Chicago Women and the Vision of the Good City, 1871–1933* (Princeton University Press: Princeton and Oxford, 2002) and her *America Reformed: Progressives and Progressivisms, 1890s–1920s* (Oxford University Press: New York, 2007); and Elizabeth Sanders, *Roots of Reform: Farmers, Workers, and the American State, 1877–1917* (University of Chicago Press: Chicago and London, 1999). Sanders's work has been especially helpful to me, in its emphasis on the persistence of agrarian populism in the Democratic Party (long after the death of the Populist Party) and its clarifying distinction between statutory and discretionary regulation.

On the rehabilitation of the ruling class, besides the Lasch essay, Fraser, *Every Man a Speculator*, illuminates the fitful rapprochement between Wall Street and Washington, along with its culmination in the Jekyll Island "duck hunting expedition" and the Federal Reserve Act of 1913. James Livingston, *Origins of the Federal Reserve System: Money Class, and Corporate Capitalism, 1890–1913* (Cornell University Press: Ithaca, N.Y., and London, 1986), offers a convincing class analysis, only partially revised by Sanders's emphasis on inter-class negotiation. The role of philanthropy in legitimating established elites comes across forcefully in Nasaw, *Carnegie*, Strouse, *Morgan*, and Chernow, *Titan*, as well as Kathleen McCarthy, *Women's Culture: American Philanthropy and Art, 1830–1930* (University of Chicago Press: Chicago and London, 1991).

Kazin skillfully charts the uneasy collaboration between Bryan and Wilson in *Godly Hero*. Other biographies that have proven essential for understanding important political figures are Nick Salvatore, *Eugene Debs: Citizen and Socialist* (University of Illinois Press: Urbana and Chicago, 1982); David P. Thelen, *Robert LaFollette and the Insurgent Spirit* (Little, Brown: Boston, 1976); John Morton Blum, *Woodrow Wilson and the Politics of Morality* (Little, Brown: Boston, 1956); Arthur Link, *Woodrow Wilson and the Progressive Era, 1910–1917* (Harper and Row: New York, 1954) as well as his *Wilson: Campaigns for Progressivism and Peace* (Princeton University Press: Princeton, 1965) and *Wilson: The New Freedom* (Princeton University Press: Princeton, 1967). The contrast between the two Progressive presidents is sharply etched in John Milton Cooper, *The Warrior and the Priest: Theodore Roosevelt and Woodrow Wilson* (Harvard University Press: Cambridge, Mass., 1983); this probing character study has proven enormously helpful to me. Also indispensable for this chapter and the conclusion is the monumental editorial project conducted by Arthur Link et al., *The Papers of Woodrow Wilson*, 69 vols. (Princeton University Press: Princeton, 1966–92).

CONCLUSION: DYING IN VAIN

Besides the works on Wilson already mentioned, other important perspectives on the long-term significance of his wartime and postwar policies are provided in Thomas J. Knock, *To End All Wars: Woodrow Wilson and the Quest for a New World*

Order (Oxford University Press: New York, 1992); David S. Foglesong, *America's Secret War Against Bolshevism: U.S. Intervention in the Russian Civil War, 1917–1920* (University of North Carolina Press: Chapel Hill and London, 1995), Lloyd C. Gardner, *Safe for Democracy: Anglo-American Response to Revolution, 1913–1923* (Oxford University Press: New York, 1984); and the essays in John Milton Cooper and Charles E. Neu, eds., *The Wilson Era: Essays in Honor of Arthur S. Link* (Harlan Davidson: Arlington Heights, Ill., 1991). Erez Manela, *The Wilsonian Moment: Self-Determination and the Origins of Anticolonial Nationalism* (Oxford University Press: New York, 2007), marks a bold departure in its interpretation of the radical (if largely unintended) consequences of Wilson's ideas.

On the links between Progressivism and American foreign policy, Alan Dawley, *Changing the World: American Progressives in War and Revolution* (Princeton University Press: Princeton and London, 2003), is recent and useful. Christopher Lasch, *The New Radicalism in America: The Intellectual as a Social Type, 1889–1963* (Vintage Books: New York, 1965), continues to cast revealing light on Progressives' motivation, especially their obsession with (vicarious) immersion in the "real life" of righteous combat. Lasch also provides an exceptionally clear sense of alternatives to intervention. On that issue, Randolph Bourne's writings are an important source as well: they are collected in his *War and the Intellectuals: Collected Essays, 1915–1919*, Carl Resek, ed., (Harper and Row: New York, 1964). Robert Westbrook, "Bourne over Baghdad," *Raritan*, 27 (Summer 2007), 104–17, is a persuasive argument for the relevance of Bourne to contemporary debate. On the home front, David M. Kennedy, *Over Here: The First World War and American Society* (Oxford University Press: New York, 1980), is comprehensive. Christopher C. Gibbs, *The Great Silent Majority: Missouri's Resistance to World War I* (University of Missouri Press: Columbia, 1988), is focused and convincing with respect to the depth of popular antiwar sentiment. John Whiteclay Chambers II, *To Raise an Army: The Draft Comes to Modern America* (Free Press: New York, 1987), demonstrates the strength of resistance to conscription in major cities as well as in the countryside.

On the language of war, Paul Fussell, *The Great War and Modern Memory* (Oxford University Press: New York, 1975), is extraordinarily insightful. James Dawes, *The Language of War: Literature and Culture in the United States from the Civil War through World War II* (Harvard University Press: Cambridge, Mass., and London, 2002), argues persuasively for the continuing value of the Geneva Conventions. John Morton Blum, *V Was for Victory: Politics and American Culture During World War II* (Harcourt Brace Jovanovich: New York, 1976), documents the resistance to heroic grandiosity among both soldiers and civilians. Pat Barker's trilogy—*Regeneration* (Viking: New York, 1991); *The Eye in the Door* (Viking: New York, 1994); and *The Ghost Road* (Viking: New York, 1995)—is unsurpassed, both in its repudiation of grand illusions and its re-creation of the realities of war.

INDEX